Performance Analysis of Local Computer Networks

*P*erformance Analysis
of Local
Computer Networks

Joseph L. Hammond
Clemson University

Peter J.P. O'Reilly
GTE Laboratories, Inc.

▲▼▼ **Addison-Wesley Publishing Company**

READING, MASSACHUSETTS   MENLO PARK, CALIFORNIA   DON MILLS, ONTARIO
WOKINGHAM, ENGLAND   AMSTERDAM   SYDNEY   SINGAPORE   TOKYO   MADRID
BOGOTÁ   SANTIAGO   SAN JUAN

Library of Congress Cataloging-in-Publication Data

Hammond, Joseph L.
  Performance analysis of local computer networks.

  1. Local area networks (Computer networks)
I. O'Reilly, Peter J. P. II. Title.
TK5105.7.H36 1986 004.6'8 85-13526
ISBN 0-201-11530-1

ABCDEFGHIJ-MA-89876

To Edith and Carmel

*P*reface

This text covers the field of local computer networks with emphasis on performance analysis. In this preface we make a few comments on the evolution and final selection of topics, their relation to the general area of computer networks, and the intended uses of the book.

Computer Networks

Computer networks, or computer–communication networks, is an area that focuses on the study of communication structures—interfaces, connecting media, access and routing algorithms, flow and error control, and related topics. These structures make it possible for physically separated data processing devices to exchange data. The data processing devices include such items as mainframe computers, personal computers, terminals, mass storage units and displays. As the field has developed, it has become apparent that design issues for computer networks are determined to a large extent by the physical size of the area covered by the network. Thus "wide area" networks, which in the extreme span the globe, require different communication structures from "local" networks, which are restricted in extent to one building or the area of a college campus. This text is concerned with the study of local networks.

As with any significant topic, there are many aspects to the design of local computer networks. The more important of these are: communication hardware, protocols, hardware and software for interfacing equipment, access algorithms, and network performance. The major emphasis in this text is on the analysis of network performance. The development, however, is such that significant attention is also given to the other important issues in the design process.

Evolution of Text Material

The material for the text was put together while the authors were with the Georgia Institute of Technology. The evolution of the material to a major extent coincided with the maturing of local area networks as a distinct area.

The idea, first for a course and then for a textbook, originated in the late seventies while one of the authors (JLH) routinely taught a course covering wide area networks. It seemed possible to us to treat in a unified fashion most of the mathematical performance models that were being proposed for local area networks. We also felt that the topic of local networks would not only provide a study area of manageable size, but one of increasing general interest.

The level and emphasis of first the course and then the text were based on the following considerations. Local networks are extended forms of communication systems and thus logically fit with communication courses in an electrical engineering curriculum. Electrical engineering students, especially those in communications, are accustomed to a quantitative approach and to computing system performance. Thus an emphasis on performance analysis of local networks seemed logical, with details of hardware and software provided as essential introductory material. It can be noted parenthetically that, even though the text has evolved in an electrical engineering context, it is not tied to an electrical engineering background or prerequisites. Thus the book should be useful for computer scientists and will complement alternative approaches such as the layered approach emphasizing network architecture and protocols.

Since mathematical models for performance of local networks are at best approximate, it did not seem reasonable to us to develop the models with excessive mathematical rigor. Thus we decided that an undergraduate course in probability was all that was needed as a mathematical prerequisite.

The evolving material was taught in a senior electrical engineering course over several years, first as a special topic course and then as an approved senior elective. The book was developed as an extension of the notes used for these courses.

Organization

The book has eleven chapters, the contents of which are reviewed in Chapter 1. The material can be organized for different courses of varying length: parts of Chapter 2 as a review, Chapters 3 and 5–9 comprise a basic package on performance analysis with essential background. This selection of material can be covered in one quarter and is the basis of the Georgia Tech senior elective.

For a one semester course, the material on PBX local networks in Chapter 4 and/or the material on protocols in Chapter 10 can be added. The bus networks discussed in Chapter 11 can be included with either of the above selections as time permits.

As still another alternative, the material in Chapter 2 can be covered in depth, with some elaboration, to provide an introductory course on data communication. If this route is taken, most of the remaining chapters of the book can be covered in a single quarter or semester.

Objectives of the Text and Required Prerequisites

The book is intended for practicing engineers and for students in electrical engineering and computer science at colleges and universities. The level of the presentation is appropriate for seniors or first year graduate students. Mastery of this material should prepare the reader to carry out design studies through performance analysis and to understand the technical literature in the area.

The text is meant to be quantitative but not rigorous. Every effort has been made to use as little mathematical detail as possible consistent with the study of performance analysis. Emphasis is placed on interpreting and using performance equations rather than on proofs.

The mathematical background required is an undergraduate course in probability. It is preferred that students take a prior course in data/digital communications; however, basic material from this area is given in the first part of the book. A course on general computer networks is not required but clearly would add to the student's perspective in the area. No specific computer languages, information on digital circuit design, or knowledge of operating systems is required.

Most of the chapters of the book contain problems for solution, which may be used as part of a formal course or for self-study.

Acknowledgments

As noted above, the contents of this book have evolved over a number of years through contacts with students and with the developing technical literature. The influence of the latter in defining and structuring the technical content and of the former in shaping the material, into what we hope is an understandable form are gratefully acknowledged.

The text material was reviewed by several persons whose comments contributed to its development. We are especially indebted to John Spragins for a careful review of the complete manuscript and many helpful suggestions. Thanks are also due to Suzie Roe for her encouragement and excellent typing.

Acknowledgment is made of support from a National Science Foundation Local Course Improvement grant (SER–8160975) under which some of the course development took place.

JLH
POR

*C*ontents

CHAPTER *1*

*I*ntroduction

1.1   A Perspective on Computer Communication Networks

In the early days of computing, intelligent resources were localized in a single main frame. A few peripherals, such as printers, card readers, or terminals, might be connected to the main frame facilities, but these devices were close by and operated as secondary slave facilities.

As the computing discipline matured and equipment evolved, facilities spread out. More terminals and other peripherals were connected at increasingly greater distances from the main frame. Intelligent devices were moved from the main frame to remote locations, and the concept of computer communication networks came into being.

The term *computer network* is somewhat ambiguous in current usage when it is used synonymously with *distributed system*. There seems to be agreement that a computer network is an interconnection of autonomous computers that are capable of exchanging information. When the independent computers act together to form a distributed system, however, several competing definitions come into play. The focus of this text is not on distributed computing. Thus Tanenbaum's view that "a distributed system is a special case of a network" [1] seems reasonable, and allows the focus to be placed on what occurs in the communication medium that couples the computers and its interfaces, i.e., the network itself. This text focuses on the latter aspect of computer communication networks in the special context of local networks. *Computer communication network* is used in the section heading to emphasize that this text focuses on issues that concern the network as it provides for communication between its attached devices. This term is awkward, however, and the more usual term *computer network* is used throughout this text.

For purposes of this text, a computer network can be viewed as a facility that makes possible communication between computers and other devices. Major components of the network include the connecting links, the interface between devices and the network, and protocols, which are rules for managing the network resources.

Computer networks can be classified in a variety of ways that include their geographical extent. On this basis there are wide area, or long-haul, networks and local, or local area, networks. Long-haul networks extend over wide geographical areas, which in some cases are literally global in extent. Local networks, on the other hand, cover only short distances, usually not exceeding a few miles.

The differences in geographical extent account for significant differences in the design of long-haul and local networks because of the different requirements for the node-to-node links. For local networks it is possible for a single organization to purchase and install high-speed, low-noise links. On the other hand, long-haul networks require the use of shared links for which large bit rates are expensive. Furthermore, links for long networks can be noisy.

For a number of reasons, which include the need to make optimum use of expensive communication links, long-haul networks are structured with irregular placement of the nodes. Modern long-haul networks make use of store-and-forward packet switching, which means that packets of data proceed through the network much like automobiles move over a freeway system. At each node, addresses carried with each packet must be read, and the packets must be routed toward their ultimate destination.

The manner of operation just described causes long-haul networks to operate at relatively low bit rates. Thousands to tens of thousands of bits per second are typical, although satellite links can operate in the megabit range. The long distances usual for the links make propagation time over the links a significant factor.

Representative design issues for long-haul networks include:

• Bit rate capacity assignments for the connecting links;
• Choice of network geometry;
• Design of routing algorithms;
• Congestion control; and
• Design of network architectures, including protocol hierarchies.

Because local computer networks can be designed around a high-speed, low-noise connecting link, these networks operate quite differently from long-haul networks. Local computer networks are usually designed so that all nodes are connected by a single high-speed shared channel that typically supports data rates in the range of 500 kilobits per second (kbps) to 50 megabits per second (Mbps).

Data is packetized, as in long-haul networks, but for local networks the packets all traverse the same channel, and normally the path of a given packet carries it past all nodes on the network. Thus, although addressing information is still required, routing is unnecessary. Several geometries can be used for the shared channel, but choice of the geometry is not a design issue per se. Congestion control and design of network architectures and protocols are issues for local networks as well as for their long-haul cousins.

The design of either type of computer network could be approached on a top-down basis by starting with the network architecture and the protocol hierarchy. Tanenbaum [1], for example, structures his book on computer networks to parallel the seven layers that have been identified for the protocol hierarchy (see Chapter 10 for a discussion of these layers).

1.2   Local Computer Networks

The previous subsection notes that local networks extend over a limited geographical area and are structured around a high-speed channel. Networks of this type have been developed in response to several clear-cut needs.

As hardware costs for intelligent devices have decreased, these devices have been installed in more locations within a single facility, such as an office building or a university campus. It is still expensive, however, to duplicate line printers, disk storage, and other such devices, and, even if it were not, such devices are not fully utilized when they are installed with the intelligent devices at each workstation. Local networks are used as one way to share these expensive resources.

A second motivation for local networks is the need to share data resources. Central data files are costly to duplicate and expensive to maintain. It is often expedient to maintain central files or data banks that are shared by devices at workstations throughout a local computer network.

In addition to the two primary justifications for local networks, there are a number of secondary influences. The distributed resources of a local network provide redundancy for many devices and thus backup in the event of failures. Many local networks provide speed and code conversion, which enables equipment from different manufacturers to be connected easily without expensive special purpose interfaces. Another point is that some networks also provide for local editing of code.

Computer networks were introduced as the coupling of computers. From the preceding discussion, it should be clear that local computer networks are used to couple many types of devices, not limited to computers. Examples of equipment that can be coupled to local computer networks are:

- Computers;
- Word processors;
- Terminals;
- Graphics terminals;

- Local storage;
- Line printers;
- Telephones; and
- Data files.

As in any new area, terminology and definitions are somewhat fluid, and the exact boundaries of what is and what is not a local network are not always clear. Stallings [2], in a recent text on local networks, makes a contribution to this terminology by identifying, in addition to long-haul networks, the following four categories: multiprocessor systems, high-speed local networks, computerized branch exchanges, and local area networks. Multiprocessors, according to Stallings, are more tightly coupled than are local area networks, and have completely integrated communications and usually some central control. High-speed local networks are usually used in a computer room to provide high throughputs between such devices as mainframe computers. Computerized branch exchanges (CBXs) are digitized telephone networks that can switch data circuits at reasonably rapid rates. Finally, according to Stalling's definitions, *local area networks* have the properties previously attributed to *local networks*.

The majority of this text is devoted to local area networks in Stallings' terminology, although in what follows, the terms *local network* and *local computer network* are often used interchangeably with local area network. Computerized branch exchanges are treated in Chapter 4. Multiprocessor systems and high-speed local networks are not covered.

One further point of terminology needs to be made. Because of the distances involved, some definitions of local networks would seem to exclude broadband networks that operate over a CATV-type system. Such networks are included in local networks for purposes of this text. Along these same lines, it is convenient in discussing random access protocols in Chapter 9 to initiate the discussion by describing protocols normally used on multiaccess radio and satellite links. It would seem that little is lost by including such networks in the category of local networks.

The following list cites several application areas for local networks:

- *Campus computing facilities:* Typical uses include data processing, data interchange, and data storage;
- *Office automation:* Intelligent workstations in this application provide such services as word processing, electronic mail, and electronic copying;
- *Factory automation:* Typical uses include intelligent workstations for engineers, computer aided design, computer aided manufacturing, and inventory control;
- *Library systems:* Typical uses include book inventory and check-out, document retrieval, and electronic copying; and
- *Legal systems:* Typical uses include case retrieval, billing, and word processing.

1.3   Local Network Design and Performance

Physically a local network consists of a communication channel to which a number of intelligent nodes is coupled. The intelligent nodes have several functions: they must transmit and receive signals on the channel; they must control access to the channel; and they must interface the devices coupled to the network at the node. Three types of design problems arise:

1. Design of the network architecture and protocols;
2. Design of the nodal hardware; and
3. Design of the nodal software.

A top-down design begins with step 1. Standards are being developed for a layered architectural structure with three layers for covering the communication aspects of the network. These layers are identified as the *physical layer,* the *media access layer,* and the *logical link control layer.* Briefly, the physical layer deals with generating and transmitting over the channel the physical signals that represent bits. The media access layer manages access to the channel, determining which node can transmit at any given time. The logical link layer operates with bits grouped into packets and manages those functions associated with activities such as error control. More detail on these layers is given in Chapter 10.

Physical layer functions are largely carried out by hardware with some support from software, which usually runs on microprocessor equipment at the nodes. The media access functions tend to use software, again running on microprocessor equipment at the node, with a little support from hardware. The logical link control functions are mostly carried out by software. A complete local network design is a relatively complicated systems problem with subsystems of both hardware and software.

This text is concerned with performance analysis of local computer networks. Performance analysis in this sense has come to mean the development and study of mathematical models that predict the performance of networks in some well-defined sense. As carried out in this text, performance analysis is performed after the fact. That is to say that various common local network designs are taken as given and then analyzed to determine their performance.

As it relates to the design process, performance analysis is carried out in conjunction with the design of network architecture, step 1 in the list of design problems. Usually several designs and their performance are considered and compared. The particular media access technique chosen tends to dictate several different implementations that may have different performance models and thus have different performance.

This book is structured to emphasize performance analysis, which in turn results in detailed studies of media access. An attempt is made, however, to balance this approach in several ways. Chapter 2 is included to cover most of the issues that occur in the designing of the physical layer of local networks. Chapter 10 has a section on logical link control protocols. To carry out performance analysis of the various types of networks, a more or less complete description of each type of network is given.

Thus, although the thrust of the book is performance analysis, some insight into most local network issues is provided.

1.4   Outline of Book Contents

This section describes the contents of each chapter of this book.

Chapter 2 reviews the various aspects of data communication in sufficient depth to make later uses of the material understandable.

Chapter 3 provides the necessary background for modeling the flow of data packets in a network. The chapter covers such material as Little's Law and an introduction to queuing theory.

Chapter 4 is a self-contained treatment of circuit-switched local networks. This chapter presents a quantitative treatment of the problem of PBX sizing.

Chapter 5 is a detailed introduction to local networks. It also discusses assumptions and definitions used in the following chapters and includes brief comments on several practical networks.

Chapter 6 introduces three extreme access protocols that are tractable to analysis and together illustrate the full range of performance.

Chapters 7 through 9 provide detailed discussions of polling, ring, and random access networks. Each chapter begins with a detailed discussion of the design of networks in the class and develops a performance model for networks of the type treated.

Chapter 10 discusses various protocol issues, including the ISO seven-layer model and the IEEE 802 draft standards for local networks.

Chapter 11, the final chapter, contains a case study of random access and token bus networks.

1.5   Summary

This chapter gives a perspective on computer communication networks, discusses the various types, and comments on some of the design problems. Local networks are defined, their characteristics are enumerated, and several application areas are noted.

Design and performance issues for local networks are discussed briefly and the point is made that the text is structured to emphasize performance analysis. Secondary aspects of the book, however, balance this approach with other types of information on local networks. A final section of the chapter outlines the topics covered by the book.

Chapter 1 is followed by a discussion of the first of several topics required as background for a study of local networks. This material, in Chapter 2, reviews several useful data communication topics.

References

[1] A. S. Tanenbaum. *Computer Networks*. Englewood Cliffs, NJ: Prentice–Hall, Inc., 1981.

[2] W. Stallings. *Local Networks: An Introduction*. New York: Macmillan Publishing Company, 1984.

CHAPTER *2*

*D*ata Communication

2.1 Introduction

It is logical to initiate a study of local computer networks, which implement communication between many data processing devices, with a review of the problems involved in carrying out data communication between only two devices. This simpler problem shows that understanding data communication between two devices involves some knowledge of a number of other more specific topics that pertain first to digital communication and then to data communication.

Digital communication involves the following topics:

- Construction of digital signals to convey information;
- Characterization of digital signals in time and frequency;
- Transmission and reception of digital signals; and
- Trade-offs between bandwidth and data rate.

Data communication requires additional structure over and above that required for digital communication. Thus it is necessary to discuss the various ways in which digital data is organized into characters, packets, and so forth, and then to examine the ways in which these blocks of data are transmitted and received. Organizing data into blocks requires synchronization and rules or conventions called protocols, which make communication between two devices possible.

Physical media and devices do not operate without error. On the other hand, digital operation requires precision in the meaning of each segment of data, with serious consequences if segments are in error. Thus some form of error control is always necessary. Error control is typically carried out in data transmission systems by introducing redundancy into the data stream in such a way that errors distort prescribed patterns. Patterns with errors can be detected so that blocks of data in error can be identified and retransmitted.

All the topics just listed are discussed in this chapter. In addition to these topics, which are essential to understanding data communication, common methods of sharing costly transmission facilities between several communicating pairs of devices are also discussed under the heading of multiplexing and switching.

In digital communication discussions, it is assumed that the data to be transmitted consists of a sequence of binary numbers, which is termed a *binary information sequence*. Data inherently in some other form can always be converted to such a sequence. For example, a binary information sequence that represents an analog time function can be obtained by sampling and quantizing the analog signal. Output from a digital computer is already in the desired form.

2.2   Digital Communication

2.2.1   Signals for Digital Transmission

A signal is typically a time-varying quantity used to convey information or to represent a physical quantity. There are many different types of signals and, indeed, a number of different ways to classify signals. Even the term *digital signal* does not have a unique connotation.

This present study is restricted to data communication and in this application the message to be transmitted consists of a sequence of binary numbers. To transmit a sequence of binary numbers, the transmitted signal is typically constructed as a sequence of basic signals, each existing on a short time interval and each conveying one increment of data, either one bit from the message sequence or sometimes several bits from this sequence. The duration of each basic signal is termed a *signaling interval,* with length denoted as T seconds. The collection of possible basic signals is called a *signal set.*

Consider, as an example, the message sequence shown in Fig. 2.1(a) and the binary signal set shown in Fig. 2.1(b), which consists of two signals, both constant over the signaling interval, with $s_1(t) = V$ representing a "1" and $s_2(t) = 0$ representing a "0."

Each basic signal conveys one bit of information. Thus the encoded message sequence is a time signal for transmission that consists of one basic signal from the signal set to represent each bit of the message sequence, as shown in Fig. 2.1(c). Since the message sequence for the example is twelve bits long, the time signal, using the binary signal set, is twelve signaling intervals in length.

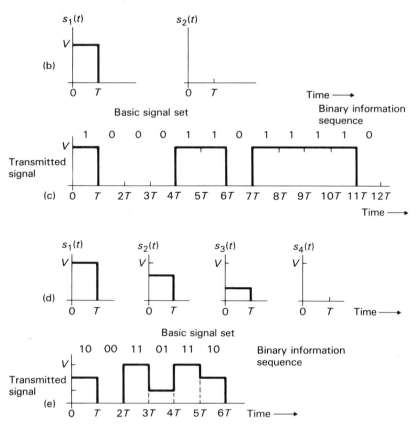

Figure 2.1   **Digital Signals for Transmitting Binary Data**

(a) Information sequence
(b) Binary signal set
(c) Transmitted signal for binary signal set
(d) Quaternary signal set
(e) Transmitted signal for quaternary signal set

It is not necessary to restrict the basic signal set to only two signals. The information contained in one signal from a set of M is defined as $\log_2 M$ in bits. For example, if the signal set is enlarged to contain four signals, then each basic signal conveys $\log_2 4 = 2$ bits of information.

A signal set with four basic signals is shown in Fig. 2.1(d), along with the complete signal to represent the information sequence in Fig. 2.1(e). Note that when two bits of information can be transmitted on each signaling interval, only six signaling intervals are required in the time signal to transmit the twelve bits of the message sequence.

One important consideration in the design of digital transmission systems is the ability of the system to transmit signals, $s_i(t)$, from the basic signal set. The signal sets considered so far consist of rectangular pulses, constant over the signaling intervals and of varying amplitude. As is discussed in detail in the next section, the major design parameter of the basic signals is bandwidth, a parameter which measures the ease with which signals can be transmitted without appreciable distortion.

In practice, only a relatively few variations on the rectangular pulse are used for the basic signal sets. Two of the more important types are discussed and analyzed in the next subsection.

2.2.2   Bandwidth of Signals and Systems

The parameter of most significance in designing a transmission system for undistorted transmission of basic signals is *bandwidth*. Bandwidth for an ideal transmission system is defined as the range of frequencies passed by the system in an undistorted manner. Similarly, the bandwidth of a signal is defined as the range of (positive) frequencies contained in the signal. A proper match between signal and transmission system results if the passband of the system extends over the complete range of frequencies contained in the signal.

The frequency spectrum of an idealized signal that contains, for example, frequencies from 0 to W_1 Hz and none outside of this range is shown in Fig. 2.2. A transmission system gain characteristic, with constant gain, A, from 0 to W_2 Hz is also shown in the figure. If W_1 is less than W_2, undistorted transmission of the signal, whose spectrum is shown, results.

To quantify these general remarks on bandwidth and its effect on transmission of basic signals, it is necessary to use Fourier transforms. The Fourier transform of a time function $s(t)$ is $S(f)$ given by

$$S(f) = F\{s(t)\} = \int_{-\infty}^{\infty} s(t) \, e^{-j2\pi ft} dt \tag{2.1}$$

The inverse transformation gives $s(t)$ from $S(f)$ as

$$s(t) = F^{-1}\{S(f)\} = \int_{-\infty}^{\infty} S(f) \, e^{j2\pi ft} df \tag{2.2}$$

A study of linear transmission systems shows that the Fourier transforms of the system output, $S_2(f)$, and input, $S_1(f)$, are related by

$$S_2(f) = S_1(f) \, H(f) \tag{2.3}$$

where $H(f)$ is the system function of the transmission system.

All three quantities $S_2(f)$, $S_1(f)$, and $H(f)$ are in general complex functions of the frequency f. Complex variable theory, however, shows that equation (2.3) can be equivalently written as these two equations:

$$|S_2(f)| = |S_1(f)| \, |H(f)| \tag{2.4}$$

$$\text{angle } S_2(f) = \text{angle } S_1(f) + \text{angle } H(f) \tag{2.5}$$

where equation (2.4) relates the magnitude functions of the quantities and (2.5) relates the angle functions. In most cases of interest here the angle

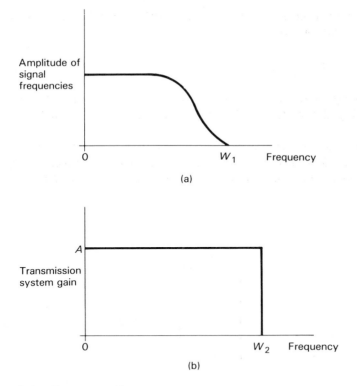

Figure 2.2 Frequency Spectra
    (a) Idealized signal spectrum
    (b) Transmission system gain function

functions of the output spectrum determine what delay, if any, the output time signal will experience. If all basic signals experience the same time delay, the information content of a transmitted signal usually is not affected, and so the angle function can be ignored.

Assuming that the angle function can be ignored, (2.4) is the only equation of interest, and the magnitude of the output signal spectrum is obtained as the product of the magnitude of the input signal spectrum and the magnitude of the system function. The magnitude of the system function can be interpreted physically as the gain characteristic of the transmission system. It can be measured by determining the system gain for sinusoidal excitations at different frequencies.

As previously noted, one common signal shape for basic signals is a rectangular pulse that extends over the signaling interval and is defined as

$$
s(t) = \begin{cases} A, & -\dfrac{T}{2} \le t \le T/2 \\ 0, & \text{otherwise} \end{cases} \tag{2.6}
$$

The Fourier transform of $s(t)$ can be obtained from tables or by equation (2.1). The result for $|S(f)|$ is

$$|S(f)| = AT \left| \frac{\sin \pi fT}{\pi fT} \right| \tag{2.7}$$

The signal $s(t)$ and the magnitude of its Fourier transform, $|S(f)|$, are plotted in Fig. 2.3. Note that the signal spectrum is not restricted to a finite range.

Another class of basic signals often used has a raised cosine type of spectrum that goes to zero outside of a limited range. The spectrum of such signals is always real and positive so that both the Fourier spectrum and its

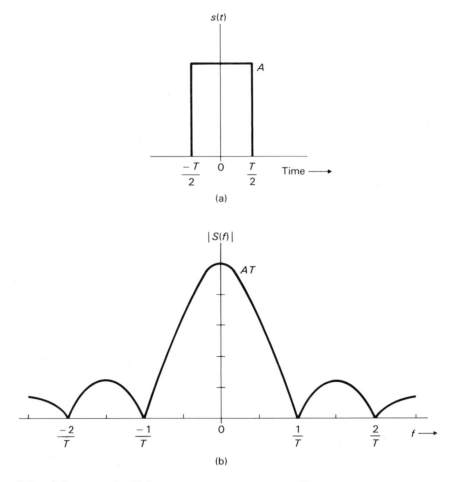

Figure 2.3   A Rectangular Pulse
(a) Time pulse
(b) Magnitude of its Fourier transform

magnitude are given by

$$S(f) = |S(f)| = \begin{cases} A , & |f| \leq \dfrac{1}{T} - \alpha \\[2mm] A\cos^2 \dfrac{\pi}{4\alpha}(|f| - \dfrac{1}{T} + \alpha), & \dfrac{1}{T} - \alpha < |f| \leq \dfrac{1}{T} + \alpha \\[2mm] 0 , & |f| > \dfrac{1}{T} + \alpha \end{cases} \qquad (2.8)$$

where the roll-off factor α has a value between 0 and $1/T$. The corresponding shape of the basic signal in time is obtained as the inverse Fourier transform of $s(t)$ and is given by

$$s(t) = \frac{(2A)}{T} \frac{\cos 2\pi\alpha t}{1 - (4\alpha t)^2} \frac{\sin(2\pi t/T)}{2\pi t/T} \qquad (2.9)$$

Several signals from the raised cosine spectrum class and their corresponding spectra are given in Fig. 2.4. Note that this type of signal has a spectrum that is zero for the magnitude of f greater than $1/T + \alpha$. In this case, however, the basic time pulse $s(t)$ is not limited to the signaling interval $-T/2 \leq t \leq T/2$, but extends outside of this range.

To design transmission systems for any type of basic signal, including those just discussed, it is necessary to determine the basic signal bandwidth. The definition above, defining bandwidth as the range of positive frequencies present in a signal, is adequate for the class of raised cosine pulses. Applying this definition gives the bandwidth, B, for such pulses as

$$B = \frac{1}{T} + \alpha \qquad (2.10)$$

The effect on the time signal of changing the bandwidth by varying α can be noted in Fig. 2.4. The fact that the time signal extends outside of the signaling interval should also be noted; this point is discussed later.

If the given definition of bandwidth is applied to the rectangular pulse of Fig. 2.3, it must be concluded that the bandwidth of this pulse is infinite since the range of frequencies in its Fourier spectrum is unbounded.

To investigate pulse transmission further, it is instructive to determine the effect of the bandwidth of an ideal transmission system in transmitting a rectangular pulse of the type shown in Fig. 2.3. Using equation (2.4), the magnitude of the spectrum of the output of the transmission system is given by the product of $|S_1(f)|$ and $|H(f)|$.

An ideal low-pass transmission system has a system function magnitude given by

$$|H(f)| = \begin{cases} 1 , & |f| \leq W \\ 0 , & \text{otherwise} \end{cases} \qquad (2.11)$$

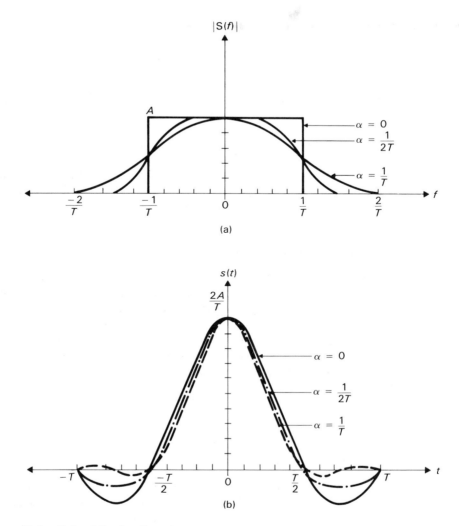

Figure 2.4   Raised Cosine Spectra
  (a) Frequency spectra
  (b) Corresponding time pulses

The spectrum of the output of such a transmission system for a rectangular input pulse with a time width equal to that of the signaling interval, T, is given by

$$|S_2(f)| = \begin{cases} AT \left| \dfrac{\sin \pi fT}{\pi fT} \right|, & -W \leq f \leq W \\ 0, & \text{otherwise} \end{cases} \tag{2.12}$$

The output pulse, which is given by the inverse transform of $|S_2(f)|$, is sketched in Fig. 2.5 for several values of the system bandwidth. Note that the

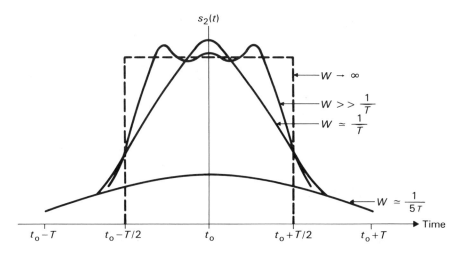

$s_2(t)$

$W \to \infty$

$W \gg \dfrac{1}{T}$

$W \approx \dfrac{1}{T}$

$W \approx \dfrac{1}{5T}$

Time

$t_0 - T \qquad t_0 - T/2 \qquad t_0 \qquad t_0 + T/2 \qquad t_0 + T$

Figure 2.5   Idealized System Output Pulses for Several Choices of Bandwidth

two parameters of importance are the transmission system bandwidth, W, and the length, T, of the signaling interval.

Examination of the output pulse shape for several values of W shows that a bandwidth much wider than $1/T$ is required to transmit the pulse without appreciable distortion. In fact, as previously noted, to make the output pulse a precise replica of the input pulse, an infinite bandwidth is required to pass all the signal frequencies. Values of bandwidth on the order of $1/T$ produce a discernible output pulse, but considerable distortion is present.

To convey digital information with basic signals it is not necessary to preserve the precise signal shape. Thus, intuitively, it would seem necessary to preserve only the "important" frequency content in a signal. For signals such as the rectangular pulse whose spectrum extends over an unlimited frequency range, and for transmission systems whose gain does not drop exactly to zero for any finite frequency, it is useful to define bandwidth in such a way that only frequencies at which the system has a reasonable gain or at which the signal component has a reasonable amplitude are included. Such revised definitions of bandwidth are not unique and several are in common use. Perhaps the best known is "half-power bandwidth," defined as the frequency range between points at which the magnitude of the spectrum, or the system gain, is equal to $1/\sqrt{2}$ times its maximum value. Since power is proportional to signal amplitude squared, this is equivalent to the range of frequencies between points at which signal components have one-half of the maximum power.

For the rectangular pulse, the half-power bandwidth, B_{HP}, (again over positive frequencies) is obtained by solving for f in the equation

$$\left[\frac{AT \sin(\pi f_{HP} T)}{\pi f_{HP} T} \right] = \frac{1}{\sqrt{2}} AT \tag{2.13}$$

The result gives

$$B_{HP} = .44/T \tag{2.14}$$

From Fig. 2.5 it can be inferred that if the ideal transmission system bandwidth is set equal to the half-power bandwidth of the input pulse, the output pulse is distorted but discernible.

The raised cosine pulse has a restricted, finite bandwidth, and thus its bandwidth is typically taken to include all frequency components, as opposed to the half-power definition. An ideal transmission system with bandwidth equal to or exceeding the bandwidth of the raised cosine pulse, $1/T + \alpha$, transmits the pulse without distortion.

As a final comment on bandwidth, note that practical transmission systems often have a passband that is nonideal. For example, a single resistance–capacitance (R–C) combination is often the predominant factor in determining bandwidth, and for such a case $| H(f) |$ is given by

$$|H(f)| = \sqrt{\frac{\beta^2}{\beta^2 + (2\pi f)^2}} \tag{2.15}$$

where $\beta = 1/RC$.

As shown in the plot of Fig. 2.6, $| H(f) |$ does not go to zero at any finite frequency, and thus the half-power definition of bandwidth is used for this type of system. From equation (2.15) it can be determined that $| H(f) | = 1/\sqrt{2}$ for $f = \beta/2\pi$, and thus B_{HP} is given by

$$B_{HP} = \beta/2\pi \tag{2.16}$$

Figure 2.7 gives the time responses of an R–C system to a rectangular pulse of width T for several choices of β in relation to T.

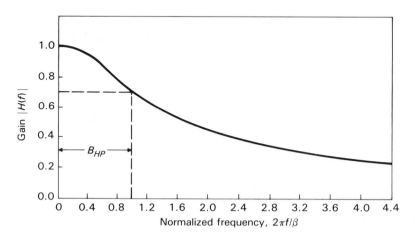

Figure 2.6 The Magnitude of the Gain Characteristic, $| H(f) |$, versus Normalized Frequency, $2\pi f/\beta$, for an R–C Transmission System

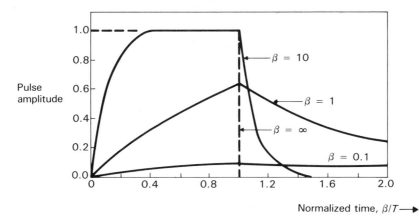

Figure 2.7 The Response of an R–C Transmission System to a Rectangular Input Pulse for Several Values of β

2.2.3 Modulation

The pulses and transmission system passbands considered so far have a low-pass characteristic in that the frequency content of the signals and the passband of the transmission systems extend from zero to some maximum value. Basic signals are typically generated to have just such characteristics and are referred to as *baseband* signals.

Transmission systems must use some available channel to convey signals from one point to another. For several reasons, channels have a preferred range of frequencies to use for signal transmission. For example, low-bit rate telephone circuits that use copper wire lines have a transmission characteristic similar to that shown in Fig. 2.8. Examination of this transmission character-istic shows that a desirable flat transmission range extends from approxi-mately 1100 to 2500 Hz, a range that does not include zero Hertz.

In the design of linear transmission systems, an operation, termed *modula-tion,* can be used to shift the frequency content of a signal from one region of the spectrum to another. In its simplest form, modulation, or more precisely, *amplitude modulation,* involves multiplying a signal, such as one of the basic pulses, by another sinusoidal signal, called a carrier. If a basic signal $s(t)$ is multiplied by $\cos 2\pi f_o t$, the resulting modulated signal, $s_m(t)$, is given by

$$s_m(t) = s(t) \cos 2\pi f_o t \tag{2.17}$$

A basic Fourier transform theorem, appropriately called the *modulation theorem,* states that if a time function, $s(t)$, with transform $S(f)$, is multiplied by $\cos 2\pi f_o t$, then the spectrum $S_m(f)$ of $s_m(t)$ is given by

$$S_m(f) = \frac{1}{2} [S(f - f_o) + S(f + f_o)] \tag{2.18}$$

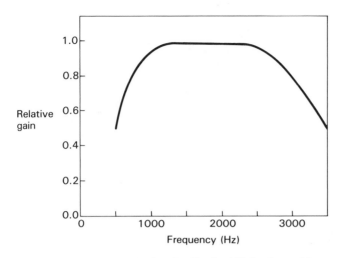

Figure 2.8   Gain Characteristic of a Typical Telephone Line and Local Loop Plant Equipment

Modulating a rectangular pulse, using $\cos 2\pi f_o t$ as the carrier, results in the modulated pulse and modulated spectrum shown in Fig. 2.9. Basic signal sets that consist of several different pulse amplitudes of either the rectangular or raised cosine type modulate into basic signal sets that consist of several modulated pulses with different amplitudes. One feature of the modulated signal spectrum worth noting is that the bandwidth of the amplitude modulated pulse is twice that of the baseband pulse.

If the baseband signal set consists of $s_1(t) = V$ and $s_2(t) = 0$, in both cases over a signaling interval T, then the modulated waveform is termed a binary ASK (amplitude shift keying) signal. Other examples of signal sets for digital transmission are given in Section 2.2.6.

For linear transmission systems, the operation of modulation shifts the frequency content of a signal from a baseband frequency range to a region about the carrier frequency and doubles the occupied bandwidth in the process. Another operation, called *demodulation,* is used for shifting the received modulated signal frequencies back to baseband.

Demodulation in its simplest form can be accomplished by multiplying the received modulated signal by a signal equal to the modulating carrier. Thus if a modulated signal is given by

$$s_m(t) = s(t) \cos 2\pi f_o t \tag{2.19}$$

multiplication[†] by $\cos 2\pi f_o t$ yields a signal, $s_d(t)$, given by

$$s_d(t) = s_m(t) \cos 2\pi f_o t = s(t) \cos^2 2\pi f_o t \tag{2.20}$$

[†]To multiply by $\cos 2\pi f_o t$ at the receiver, the receiver must be in carrier synchronization with the transmitter. This is a point of importance in detailed receiver design.

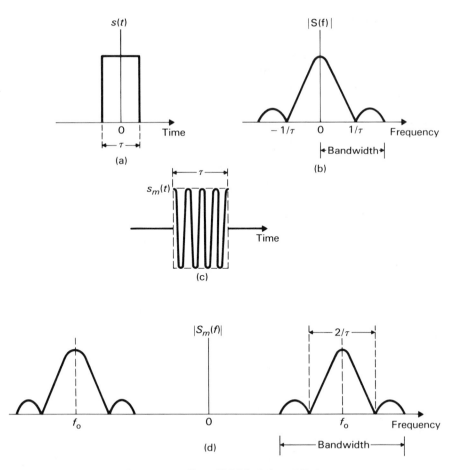

Figure 2.9   Baseband and Corresponding AM Modulated Pulses
    (a) Baseband time pulse
    (b) Frequency spectrum of baseband pulse
    (c) Modulated time pulse
    (d) Frequency spectrum of modulated pulse

Use of a trig identity reduces (2.20) to

$$s_d(t) = \frac{s(t)}{2} + \frac{1}{2} s(t) \cos 4\pi f_o t \qquad (2.21)$$

Equation (2.21) shows that $s_d(t)$ consists of two components: the original baseband signal, $s(t)$, multiplied by a gain factor of one-half, and the signal $s(t)$ modulated by a carrier of $\cos 4\pi f_o t$. The spectrum of frequencies in the modulated signal component is centered at $2 f_o$. This is usually a range much higher than the baseband signal component, and it can be removed by an appropriate filter. Thus the demodulated signal that remains after the filter is just the baseband signal within a constant gain factor.

Section 2.2   **Digital Communication**

The type of modulation previously discussed is amplitude modulation. Other types of modulation, such as phase and frequency modulation, are possible and, in fact, are more commonly used for data transmission. Phase modulation, as used with phase shift keying (PSK), can be analyzed in essentially the same way as amplitude modulation, but frequency modulation is more difficult to analyze. Several types of signals used for data transmission, including phase and frequency modulated signals, are discussed in Section 2.2.6.

For purposes of understanding the rudiments of modulation, it is sufficient to regard modulation and demodulation as a package. Modulation shifts the frequency content of signals from one band to another more suitable for transmission over some specified channel, and demodulation, applied after transmission over the specified channel, shifts the frequency content back to the original band. Unless interest is focused on the design of that part of the transmission system that involves the modulated signal, the modulator–demodulator package can be regarded merely as a component that enables the communication system to use a particular channel. In further discussion of data transmission, this point of view is adopted.

2.2.4 Transmission of Digital Information

The next step after the discussion of the relation of bandwidth to the transmission of basic signal pulses is to consider the complete transmission system that receives an input message sequence of "0"s and "1"s, such as discussed in Section 2.2.1, and produces the same sequence at its output. The transmission system consists of a transmitter, which is basically a modulator, a channel, and a receiver. The latter is basically a demodulator, as shown in Fig. 2.10. The terms modulation and demodulation are used here generically: in this context a modulator is a device that transforms a message bit sequence into a signal suitable for transmission over the channel by changing its frequency spectrum. The demodulator converts the received signal back to a bit sequence.

At the transmitter, each bit in the message sequence is encoded into one choice from a binary signal set, or alternatively, several bits are encoded into one member of a larger signal set. The basic signals on each signaling interval are transmitted over the channel to the receiver that converts each basic signal back into the bit, or group of bits, that were encoded into the particular basic signal at the transmitter. For a properly operating transmission system, the input and output message sequences are identical.

As an example, Fig. 2.10 shows a particular message sequence, the baseband signal, the transmitted modulated and received signals under ideal conditions, and the output message sequences. The signals are shown for the case of $M = 2$, i.e., two basic signals, and for amplitude shift keying (ASK).

Transmission systems must be designed to cope with two sources of error, namely:

1. Noise and other extraneous signals that make it difficult to distinguish one basic signal from another in the same signal set; and

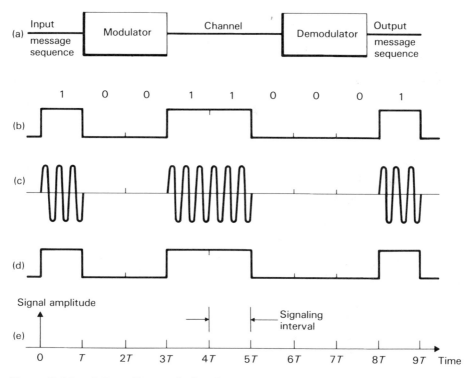

Figure 2.10   A Data Transmission System and Associated Noise-free Signals

(a) Transmission system
(b) Input message sequence and baseband input signal
(c) Transmitted (ASK) modulated signal
(d) Demodulated baseband signal
(e) Timing scale for all signals

2. Distortion of the basic signals, which causes a basic signal on one signaling interval to "spill over" into an adjacent signaling interval and thus produces intersymbol interference.

Noise type errors limit the number of basic signals that can be used in a signal set to a relatively small number, such as eight for relatively noisy channels or possibly 16 or 32 if the channel is extremely quiet. Binary systems require the least attention (and associated expense) to reducing the effects of noise, with system sophistication and expense increasing with the number of basic signals in the signal set.

Before intersymbol interference is discussed, note that synchronization is required between receiver and transmitter to distinguish the beginning and ending of the signaling intervals. The content of every signaling interval is a single basic signal that is converted from a time-varying signal to one, or at most several, bits. Thus, it is usually sufficient to sample the received baseband basic signal at some appropriate point in the signaling interval. For example, in the idealized ASK system illustrated in Fig. 2.10, a single sample on each signaling interval is clearly sufficient to distinguish the two levels.

When rectangular pulses are transmitted through limited bandwidth systems, each basic pulse is distorted, as shown for the rectangular pulse, for example, in Fig. 2.5. Thus a "101" sequence might produce the distorted received baseband signal shown in Fig. 2.11. Such a distorted signal can be correctly decoded if it can be sampled at the appropriate instants. The key to such sampling, of course, is accurate synchronization. The distortion of the basic signal on one signaling interval due to spill over of signals from earlier intervals is, of course, intersymbol interference. It is minimized for rectangular pulses by using sufficient system bandwidth to keep pulse distortion within acceptable bounds. For rectangular pulses of duration T seconds, this is accomplished by using system bandwidths of several times $1/T$ Hz, as can be seen qualitatively from Fig. 2.5.

The raised cosine pulse previously discussed provides a different method for dealing with intersymbol interference. Since this type of pulse requires only a limited bandwidth, the received pulse is not distorted. However, the undistorted pulse is not limited to a single signaling interval, but extends over many such intervals. The key to controlling intersymbol interference with raised cosine pulses is to adjust the timing of samples so that the major lobe of each basic pulse conveys the information for the sampling interval in which it occurs, while nulls in the time pattern of the basic pulses occur at the sampling instances of all other sampling intervals. A sequence of basic pulses used in this manner is shown in Fig. 2.12.

One advantage of using raised cosine pulses is that the system bandwidth to transmit these pulses in an undistorted manner is precisely known. This required bandwidth for baseband signals is given in (2.10) as $B = \alpha + 1/T$.

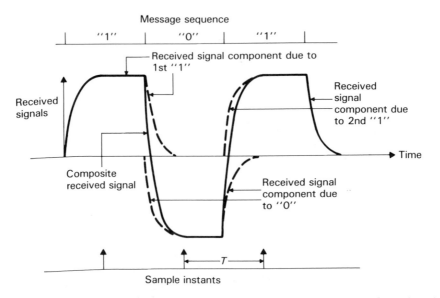

Figure 2.11 The Received Signals for the Message Sequence 1 0 1, Showing the Effect of Intersymbol Interference with Rectangular Pulses (The effect of signals outside the sequence 1 0 1 is not shown)

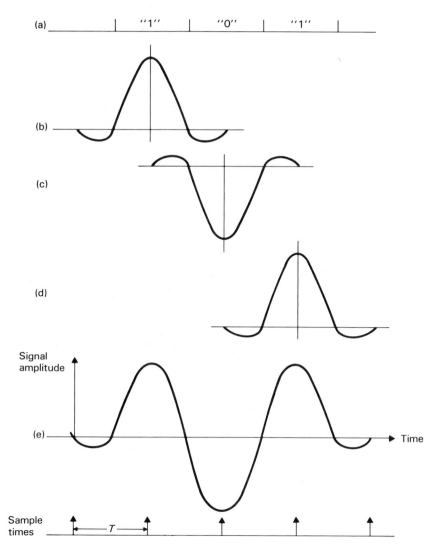

Figure 2.12   The Received Signal and Signal Components for the Message Sequence 1 0 1, Using Raised Cosine Pulses (The effect of signals outside the sequence 1 0 1 is not shown)

(a) Message sequence
(b) Signal component for first "1"
(c) Signal component for "0"
(d) Signal component for second "1"
(e) Composite received signal

This subsection on transmission of digital information concludes with several comments on terminology. Note that transmitters and receivers are unidirectional devices. Thus a transmission circuit that contains one transmitter and one receiver works in one direction only and is termed a *simplex* connection. Two simplex circuits that operate in different directions make up what is referred to as a *full duplex* connection. The modulator and demodulator needed at each end of a full duplex connection are often housed in the same cabinet, and the combination is called a *modem,* which is a contraction of modulator/demodulator.

There are applications for which only a single line or channel is used to connect two devices. Such a channel can transmit in either direction, given appropriate transmitters and receivers, but cannot transmit in both directions at once. A connection of this sort is called a *half duplex* connection. In dealing with a half duplex connection it is often necessary to account for the time required to "turn the line around," i.e., to switch out one device (a transmitter or receiver) and switch in the other at each end of the line.

2.2.5   Data Rates—Bandwidth/Data Rate Trade-offs

An overall measure of effectiveness for data transmission is the rate at which data is transferred, or the data rate, R, in bits per second. Data rate is closely related to the length, T, of the signaling interval. If a binary signal set is used, one bit is transferred on each signaling interval and the data rate is given by

$$R = 1/T \text{ bits/second} \tag{2.22}$$

If a larger signal set, with $M > 2$, is used, one basic signal or symbol is still transferred on each signaling interval. In this case, however, $\log_2 M$ bits are communicated with each basic signal and the data rate is given by

$$R = \frac{1}{T} \log_2 M \text{ bits/second} \tag{2.23}$$

The term *baud* is sometimes used to denote one basic signal or symbol per second. Thus, in the present notation, the signaling rate is $1/T$ symbols per second or baud. For a binary system, the number of baud and the bit rate are identical. For systems using signal sets with $M > 2$, the signaling rate is still $1/T$ baud, while the bit rate, as given by (2.23), is $\log_2 M$ times as large. For example, an ASK system that uses four different voltage amplitudes as basic signals might operate at a symbol rate of 2400 baud and convey information at 4800 bits/second.

An issue of primary importance in data communication is how fast data can be communicated over a channel with a specified bandwidth. The issue, stated concisely, is the number of bits per second per Hertz of bandwidth that can be achieved with a given transmission system.

The bandwidth occupancy of basic signals is discussed in Section 2.2.2, using the Fourier transform of the signal amplitude. The bandwidth required to transmit a composite signal that represents a complete message sequence is a slightly different problem since the composite signal is a random time variable made up of a sequence of basic signals that change in accordance with the random occurrence of "0"s and "1"s in the message sequence. A random signal does not have a deterministic amplitude function that can be Fourier transformed to obtain a frequency spectrum. Instead, the variation of signal power with frequency is determined and expressed as a *power spectral density* of the random signal.

Fortunately, the random signal that represents a long message sequence has a power spectral density closely approximated by the power spectral density of a single basic signal. Furthermore, the power spectral density of a basic signal is given by the magnitude squared of the Fourier transform of the signal amplitude. Total bandwidth occupancy and half-power bandwidth are thus useful measures of bandwidth from the point of view of either the amplitude spectrum or the power spectrum of the signal.

Equations (2.22) and (2.23), given previously, relate data rate to the reciprocal of the signaling interval. Baseband signal bandwidth, as discussed in Section 2.2.2, has been determined for two types of basic pulses along with the system bandwidth required for transmitting the pulses with tolerable intersymbol interference. These results, for bandwidth, are in terms of pulse width, which is also determined by the length of the signaling interval. Thus, since both data rate and bandwidth are ultimately determined by the signaling interval, a relation between data rate and bandwidth can be found.

Raised-cosine pulses are the more common choice for state-of-the-art encoders, and for such pulses the occupied bandwidth is given precisely by equation (2.10). Thus use of (2.10) with (2.22) or (2.23), yields, after eliminating T,

$$R = B - \alpha \tag{2.24}$$

and

$$R = (B - \alpha) \log_2 M \tag{2.25}$$

as the relations between data rate in bits/second and baseband bandwidth in Hertz for binary and M-ary transmission respectively. Recall that α, which is between 0 and $1/T$, is the roll-off factor for the raised cosine pulse, and thus controls its bandwidth. Extreme values of α yield $R = B \log_2 M$ and $R = B/2 \log_2 M$ for the general relation. Note that the bandwidth occupancy of a signal produced by a type of linear modulation is twice that of the baseband signal. Thus, for a modulated signal, B in equations (2.24) and (2.25) must be replaced by half the bandwidth of the modulated signal.

The bandwidth occupancy of rectangular pulses is less well defined than for raised-cosine pulses. Nonetheless, similar, though less precise, relations between bit rate and bandwidth can be found.

Good general references for most of the topics in Section 2.2 up to this point are the texts by Stremler [1] and by Ziemer and Tranter [2]. The next subsection gives examples of signals used in practical local area networks.

2.2.6 Signaling Schemes for Local Area Networks

This subsection catalogs some of the signal sets and waveforms that are used with local networks. The properties of the signals chosen can be explained with the basic concepts developed in the early parts of this chapter.

In a commonly used terminology, local networks are classified, in terms of the type of signals used, as *baseband* and *broadband* local area networks. A baseband local network uses signals whose frequency spectrum extends from zero Hertz and, of course, connecting links that pass the frequency spectrum of such signals. A single-channel broadband local area network, on the other hand, uses one of several modulation schemes to locate the frequency spectrum of the signals in a desired region of the spectrum, which normally does not extend down to zero Hertz.

A number of different signal structures appropriate to both classes of networks are in a list that follows. For any one of these basic signal structures, the baseband pulses, which are shown as rectangular, can be shaped into members of the raised cosine class to restrict the bandwidth. This is normally done by replacing each rectangular component of the signal by a raised cosine pulse of the same time width.

In what follows, the signal structures are defined, and the spectrum of a typical steady state transmission is given for each particular signal structure, assuming random and equally likely "0" and "1" message bits.

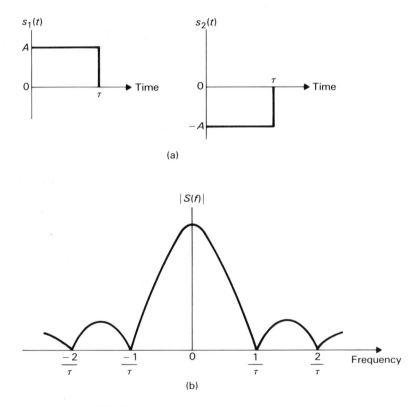

(a)

(b)

Figure 2.13   Polar NRZ Signals
(a) Basic signal set
(b) Associated frequency spectrum

Typical signal structures used in practical baseband networks include:

Polar non-return to zero (NRZ),
Manchester,
Differential Manchester,
Alternating mark inversion (AMI),
Duobinary.

The signal structures and their spectra are given in Figs. 2.13–2.16. Several summary comments on each type are given in the following paragraphs.

POLAR NRZ: Polar NRZ signals are termed *non-return to zero* since a message sequence of all "1"s is encoded into a long constant signal. The

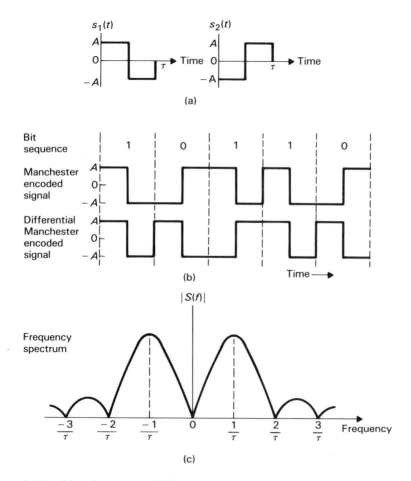

(a)

(b)

(c)

Figure 2.14   Manchester and Differential Manchester Encoded Signals
    (a) Basic signal set
    (b) Encoded sequences
    (c) Frequency spectrum for both cases

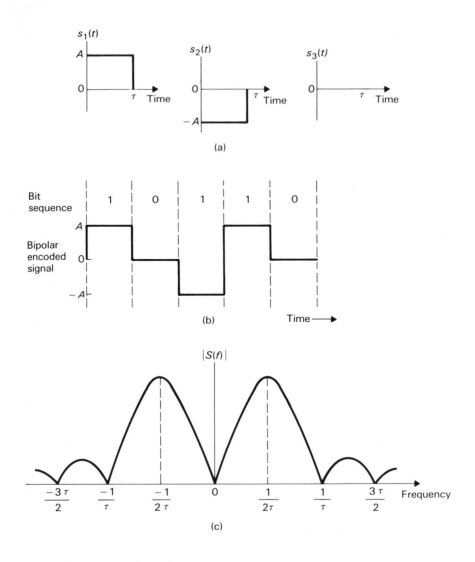

Figure 2.15 Bipolar AMI Signals
(a) Basic signal set
(b) Typical encoded sequence
(c) Frequency spectrum

absence of frequent transitions in voltage level is a disadvantage of this type of signal since it results in a large low-frequency component of the spectrum, as shown in Fig. 2.13.

MANCHESTER AND DIFFERENTIAL MANCHESTER: Manchester encoding uses the basic signal $s_1(t)$ to represent a "1" and $s_2(t)$ to represent a "0." The differential version chooses $s_1(t)$ or $s_2(t)$ so that the signal that represents a "1" is chosen to have no initial transition from the voltage level at the end of

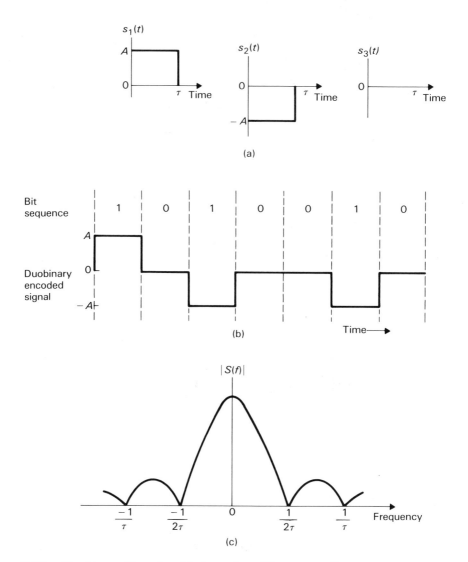

Figure 2.16 Duobinary Signals with Associated Frequency Spectrum
  (a) Basic signal set
  (b) Typical encoded sequence
  (c) Frequency spectrum

the previous signaling interval, while the signal that represents a "0" has an initial transition. Note that Manchester encoded signals require twice the bandwidth of polar NRZ signals.

ALTERNATING MARK INVERSION: As shown in Fig. 2.15, there are three basic AMI signals. A message bit "0" is encoded as $s_3(t)$, while "1"s are alternately coded as $s_1(t)$ and $s_2(t)$. The bandwidth of AMI signals is the same as for polar NRZ, but the spectrum is shifted away from dc (0 Hertz).

DUOBINARY: There are three basic duobinary signals, as shown in Fig. 2.16. A "0" message bit is transmitted as $s_3(t)$. A "1" message bit is encoded into either $s_1(t)$ or $s_2(t)$ according to the following algorithm:

(a) A "1" is encoded into the same basic signal as was used for the last "1" if the number of "0"s between the two "1"s is even;

(b) The second "1" is encoded with the opposite basic signal ($s_1(t)$ or $s_2(t)$) if the number of "0"s separating the two "1"s is odd.

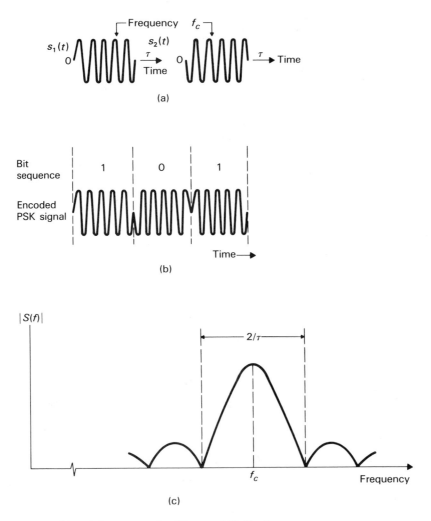

Figure 2.17   Signal Structure for Phase-shift Keying

(a) Basic signal set
(b) Typical encoded sequence
(c) Frequency spectrum

Signal structures used in single-channel broadband local area networks include:

Amplitude shift keying (ASK)
Phase shift keying (PSK)
Frequency shift keying (FSK)
Minimum shift keying (MSK).

Amplitude shift keying is discussed previously, and the signal set is shown in Figs. 2.9 and 2.10. Phase and frequency shift keying are defined in Figs. 2.17 and 2.18. Minimum shift keying is defined and summary comments on each type of signal set are given in the following paragraphs.

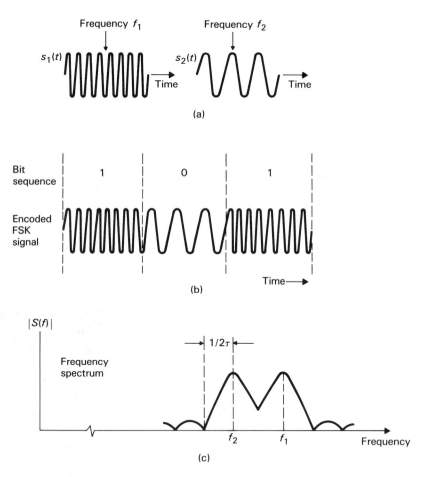

Figure 2.18   Signal Structure for Frequency-shift Keying
(a) Basic signal set
(b) Typical encoded sequence
(c) Frequency spectrum

PHASE SHIFT KEYING: Note that $s_2(t)$ and $s_1(t)$ are phase shifted by $\pm 180°$. Note also that the process of modulation has shifted the center of the frequency band to f_c, the carrier frequency, and that the required bandwidth is twice that of the baseband signal.

FREQUENCY SHIFT KEYING: The basic signals have two different frequencies for FSK, and the frequency spectrum for the signal set depends on the relative values of these frequencies. For the basic signals shown, $s_1(t)$ and $s_2(t)$ are equal at $t = 0$. This particular form of FSK is called *phase coherent FSK*.

MINIMUM SHIFT KEYING: Minimum shift keying is a special case of FSK for which

$$|f_1 - f_2| = 2/T$$

The bandwidth between the first zero-crossings of the frequency spectrum for this signal set is $1.5/T$. This is the smallest possible bandwidth for FSK signals.

2.2.7 Data Transmission

The emphasis so far in this section has been on transmitting isolated bits over a communication link. For communicating data, however, bits are typically organized into blocks of varying numbers of bits. One reason for this is the use of blocks in control procedures, which is discussed in the following subsection. Another reason is that blocks of more than one bit are more efficiently handled by both hardware and software.

Typical blocks of increasing size are called characters (or bytes), packets, and messages. *Characters* are usually the basic block dealt with as a unit by hardware. The number of bits in a character is fixed for a particular communication control procedure. Characters can be any integer length from five to 10 bits.

A *packet* is a larger group of bits arranged in a fixed format that typically includes data and overhead. Computer networks usually deal with packets as a unit. The overhead bits contain such information as addresses and perform functions such as error control. Packet lengths vary from a dozen to many thousands of bits, with the maximum fixed for any particular system.

A *message* is a group of bits of unrestricted length conveniently identified for a particular application. For transmission over a network, a message is typically broken up into an ordered set of shorter packets. In addition to the character, packet, and message structure for networks, the term *word* is sometimes used to identify an ordered set of characters that is the normal unit for operations, such as storage, within a computer.

A basic entity, such as a character, can be transferred over a channel in one of two ways: serial or parallel. A *serial character* consists of an ordered time sequence of bits one after the other. For example, an eight-bit serial character consists of eight bits transmitted one after the other in time sequence. A serial transfer requires only one channel and a time interval long enough to transfer the number of bits contained in the character. A binary system, for example, requires eight signaling intervals to transfer an eight-bit character.

A *parallel character,* in contrast, consists of some fixed number of bits on different channels at the same time. For example, on a binary system, an eight-bit parallel character requires eight channels and exists for only one signaling interval.

Typical serial and parallel eight-bit characters for a binary system are shown in Fig. 2.19.

Many devices, such as a buffer or random access memory (RAM), can be read into in either a serial or parallel manner. Parallel transfers are faster, but require a number of lines or channels. Serial transfers are slower, but require only one line. Since only short connections are needed, transfers within a device are frequently done in parallel to minimize the time required. On the other hand, transfers across a network are almost always serial because of the cost of multiple connections over any reasonable distance.

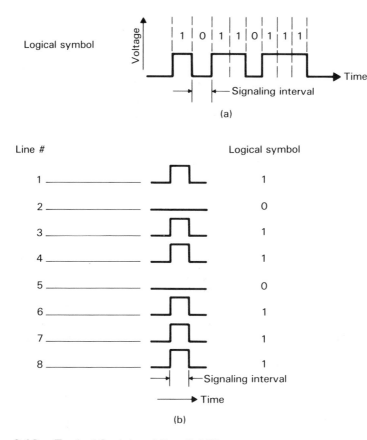

Figure 2.19   Typical Serial and Parallel Characters
(a) Serial character
(b) Parallel character

Now consider the problem of transmitting characters from one device to another over a dedicated line or channel. This type of transmission is a central part of data transfer. Another aspect of data transfer, setting up and controlling a data circuit, is discussed under the heading Communication Control Procedures in the next subsection.

Transmission of packets and messages amounts to proper grouping of characters. This problem is typically treated as a network problem rather than an issue pertinent to an isolated point-to-point link.

Transmission of characters and packets takes place either synchronously or asynchronously, and the two choices lead to distinct transmission modes.

Asynchronous Data Transmission

Asynchronous transmission is carried out without continuous character synchronization between the transmitting and receiving devices. In this mode each character or "chunk" of data has to be identified separately, and hence the beginning and the end of each character must be marked. Figure 2.20 shows a typical asynchronous data character format. The start bit can be identified as a transition from the idle state of the transmitting line or channel to its complementary state. The stop bit is sometimes given a minimum duration of 1.5 to 2 times other bits to make it distinctive. The maximum duration is unrestricted since the stop bit becomes the idle state of the line.

An asynchronous serial data transmitter is shown in Fig. 2.21. Its operation is explained as follows: When actuated by a load command, a character is shifted into the shift register in parallel from the source transmitting data, which is usually a computer. The load command also activates a shift clock that causes the bits in the character to be shifted out over a line one bit at a time through the flip-flop. When the stop bit has been shifted into the flip-flop, this device, and the line over which data is being transmitted, shifts to the stop bit state and remains in this state until another character is transmitted.

The zero detector senses the state of each element of the shift register, and when all states are zero (which indicates that the character has been shifted out), a flag is sent to the computer to indicate that another character can be processed.

Figure 2.22(a) shows an Asynchronous Serial Data Receiver. This device identifies the start bit with a start bit detector and uses this information to start a sampling clock, which in turn causes a bit sampler to sample once every bit period. The outputs of the bit sampler are fed in series into a shift register.

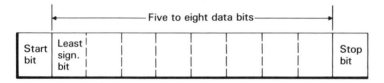

Figure 2.20   Asynchronous Data Character Format

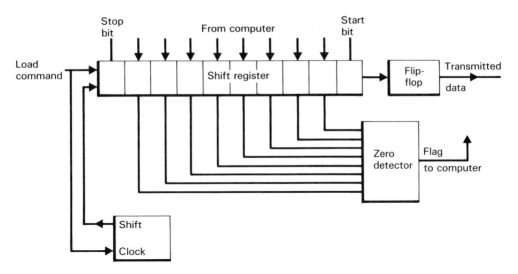

Figure 2.21   Asynchronous Serial Data Transmitter

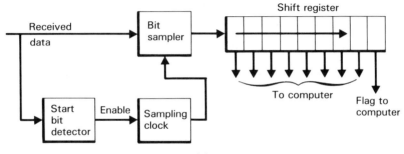

(a)

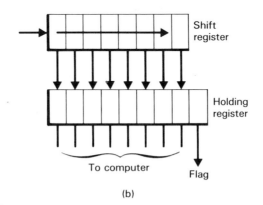

(b)

Figure 2.22   An Asynchronous Serial Data Receiver
(a) Block diagram
(b) Registers for double buffering

When all the bits in a character have been received, a flag is generated and sent to the computer to indicate that a complete character is present and ready for parallel transfer into a computer register.

As previously noted, each bit of a serial character exists on the communication line for only the duration of a bit period. Thus the output of the bit sampler must be coupled immediately into a storage element so it is not lost. A loss can occur if the shift register still contains a previous character because the computer has been too busy to receive it.

Figure 2.22(b) shows a double buffering arrangement that can afford some flexibility in receiving data. With the extra holding register, the contents of the shift register can be shifted into the holding register to allow for receiving an incoming character. The computer then has an interval, equal to the time required for receiving the incoming character into the shift register, to transfer out the contents of the holding register.

Synchronous Data Transmission

Synchronous data transmission differs from asynchronous data transmission in that the transmitting and receiving devices can have character synchronization for a significant period of time. During the time that the devices are synchronized, it is possible to transfer data without marking the extremes of each character. This makes it possible to omit stop and start bits and increase transmission efficiency and speed.

For synchronous operation, synchronization is achieved through use of one or more special characters that precede the data, as shown in the synchronous data format of Fig. 2.23(a). The synchronization character is chosen to have a distinctive pattern that is unlikely to occur in a sequence of data bits.

When a sync character is received, the receiver initiates a bit-by-bit search for a match between the received sync character and that character stored in the sync code register. If a match is found, "in sync" is declared and data is shifted out of the receive shift register into the receive data register and on to the data bus. If the received special character does not match the one stored in the sync code register, transfer out of the receive shift register is inhibited and the search for sync continues.

There is always some chance that data or data plus noise will produce the sync pattern. This probability is relatively large if the signal is out of sync since parts of two characters are observed. As a result, two sync characters are sometimes used to reduce the risk of false synchronization. If two sync characters are used, both must be correctly matched to achieve an "in sync" condition.

Once synchronization is achieved, the circuitry assumes that it is in sync for the duration of a block of data. Operation of the transmitter and receiver, shown in Fig. 2.23(b), in the "in sync" condition is such that the transmitter clocks bits out of the transmit shift register over the line in a continuous fashion. As a character is clocked out in serial fashion, during the last half of its last bit, another character is loaded in parallel without interruption of the data flow. If a character is not available in the transmit register, a dummy

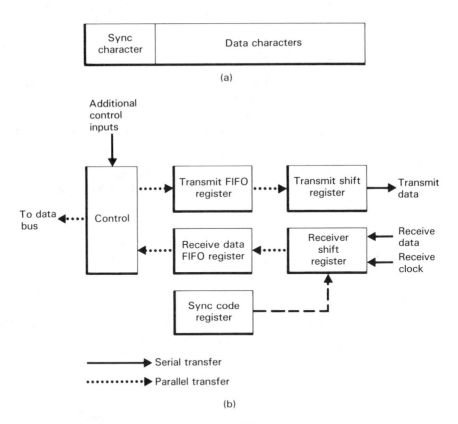

Figure 2.23   A Synchronous Transmitter and Receiver
(a) Synchronous data format
(b) Simplified block diagram

character is inserted to maintain character synchronization. For this condition an underflow signal is sent to the register. The receiver reads bits into the receive shift register and through the receive data register to the data bus as long as synchronization is maintained.

2.2.8   Communication Control Procedures

Up to this point in the discussion, the existence and proper functioning of a communication link between source and destination have been assumed. In this subsection some attention is given to how the communication link is established and terminated and to the process of maintaining data transfer—all part of communication control procedures.

To be more explicit, communication control procedures establish the rules for exchanging data between devices over a communication link. In general terms, there are several phases in the process of exchanging data:

1. Establish a connection,
2. Identify the sender and receiver,

3. Transfer the message,
4. Terminate the message transfer, and
5. Terminate the connection.

Communication control procedures implement these phases of communication. The flow of characters, discussed in the last subsection, takes place during the message transfer phase.

As control procedures have evolved, control of data transmission has fallen into two distinct parts:

1. Control of the establishment of a physical connection between communicating devices, ensuring the transfer of bits without regard to their organization, and
2. Control of data interchange, including such aspects as error control and recovery from abnormal conditions.

Separate standards have been developed for these two aspects of data link control.

This chapter is limited to the transfer of data between devices over a single point-to-point connection. In a more general context, transfer of data is a subset of a larger problem related to user-to-user communication over a link or network. This larger problem is addressed to a limited extent in Chapter 10.

A full duplex point-to-point connection of the type being considered is diagrammed in Fig. 2.24. The device at either end of the connection is referred to generically as *data terminal equipment* (DTE), while the modem is one form of *data circuit-terminating equipment* (DCE).

The first part of the control procedure for data transmission is establishing and maintaining the connections between the DTEs and the DCEs, and releasing the connections when the data transfer is completed. To accomplish this type of control, a number of connections in addition to the transmit and receive lines are required in the interface between the DTE and the DCE, as shown in Fig. 2.24.

Standards, such as the Electrical Industry Association's RS-232-C, which apply to the physical connection for DTE/DCE interfaces, deal with four aspects of the connection: the mechanical, the electrical, the functional, and the procedural. The procedural specifications, which are of primary interest here, deal with procedures that need to be performed to enable the transmis-

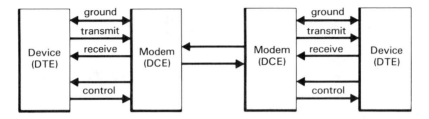

Figure 2.24   A Full Duplex Point-to-point Connection

Chapter 2   Data Communication

sion of bits over the point-to-point connection. The mechanical aspect specifies the connectors for the cables, giving such details as the number of pins and pin connections. The electrical aspect prescribes voltage and impedance levels, and the functional aspect identifies interchange circuit functions in the categories of data, control, timing, and grounds.

There are a number of different standards and procedures for carrying out communication control for a data link. Each procedure has its own specific sequence of steps and exchanges of control information between the sending and receiving stations. A description of the more common of these specific procedures can be found in Green [3] or McNamara [4]. This subsection concludes with a brief discussion of the more important generic steps in any communication control procedure.

First, to establish a link and begin to transfer bits or characters, control wires are used to convey the following signals:

"Request to send," which turns the modem on (and off) for half duplex applications;
"Clear to send," which indicates that the modem is ready to transmit data;
"Data set ready," which indicates that the modem is powered and not in a nondata mode; and
"Received line signal detection," which indicates reception of signals from the modem at the other end of the connection.

After a sequence of signals, such as that just described, is sent, bits or characters can be transmitted over a transmit line and received on a receive line at the other end of the connection.

Once a flow of bits or characters between the DTEs at either end of the connection is established, it is possible to begin an interchange of information. To transfer information over a bit stream without errors in an error-prone environment, it is usually necessary to organize bits into some structure that consists of well-defined blocks that aid in providing certain control features. These blocks, used for communication control over a point-to-point link, may or may not coincide with packets or messages as identified by a network that contains the link. Even though precise details vary with particular procedures, several features must be present. The more important of these for point-to-point links are methods for:

1. Distinguishing information bits from control bits;
2. Checking for errors and initiating action to correct errors;
3. Acquiring and maintaining block synchronization;
4. Link management; and
5. Abnormal recovery.

Items 1 and 2 are self-explanatory. Acquiring and maintaining frame synchronization refers to being able to identify the beginning and end of a block of data. Link management, usually assigned to one master station, pertains to controlling transmission direction and identifying which station is going to send and which is going to receive. Abnormal error recovery is required to supervise action taken to recover from such occurrences as an illegal sequence or other violation of defined conditions.

The features just listed, such as error checking, can be provided through the use of special or dedicated bits added as overhead to the data bits. A detailed discussion of the use of overhead bits for error detection is given in the next subsection.

2.3 Error Control

2.3.1 Introduction

In considering any type of channel for transmitting information, it is necessary to account for the effects of unavoidable noise. The effects of noise cannot be ignored in practical systems and their net effect is to produce bit errors in signals transmitted over links in a network. Such noise is introduced in a variety of ways. Perhaps two of the most basic sources are thermal noise, which is present in every type of channel and is ultimately due to random motion of electrons in dissipative elements, and shot noise in active electronic circuits.

Noise is also injected into transmission systems from outside effects such as lightning, and man-made sources such as discharges from electric ignition systems, motors, and so forth. This type of noise tends to be "bursty" in the sense that it appears for a short length of time and then disappears.

As noted in Section 2.2.3, the major effect of noise on data communication systems is to make it difficult to distinguish one basic signal from another at the receiving end of a transmission system. Each incorrect identification of a basic signal results in one bit error in a binary system or one or more bit errors in a more general M-ary system.

As also noted in Section 2.2.3, intersymbol interference can have the same effect as noise in obscuring one basic signal from another in the same set. System bandwidth is the primary factor affecting intersymbol interference, and this parameter, determined at the time the transmission system is designed, is not subject to variation in most systems. However, the times at which the received pulses are sampled also have a bearing on the intersymbol interference and such times are subject to variations due to noise. Thus noise can also cause errors indirectly by causing intersymbol interference.

The effect of noise of various types on digital systems and mathematical models for such noise have been the subjects of study for a number of years. A good reference is the text by Cooper and McGillem [5].

Another direction taken is to bypass models for noise and concentrate on measuring bit errors in digital transmissions directly. Statistical models, which give the probability of bit errors, have been matched to this empirical data, and such models describe the statistics of bit errors directly (see, for example, Kanal [6]).

Statistical models that give the probability of bit errors directly are the most useful of the two methods for designing error control strategies. The simplest model of this type represents bit errors as occurrences that are independent from one bit interval to another. Only one parameter, the probability, p, of a bit error is required and the probability of more than one error is easily determined with the multiplicative probability rule for independent events.

Other somewhat more realistic statistical models inject a correlation between bit errors to account for burstiness. Such models are often structured as Markov processes.

In the following discussions the simple, independent bit error model is used to illustrate approaches. Practical error control strategies, however, have been designed using the more complicated models.

Whereas errors due to noise and other phenomena cannot be ignored, it is also necessary to note that careful design of equipment can keep the bit error rate small—error rates on the order of one error in ten million bits or less (probabilities of error less than 10^{-7}) are typical. The difficulty is that bit rates can also be high. Thus an error probability of 10^{-7} results in an error once every second on the average for a 10 Mbps link, or once every ten seconds if the error probability is reduced to 10^{-8}. Such errors, uncorrected, are unacceptably high for some computer communication applications.

To deal with practical error rates, some sort of error control is normally necessary, and this requires a mechanism for detecting and ultimately correcting errors. In this connection it is useful to note that if every sequence of symbols is a proper message, it is impossible to detect errors. Thus error detection is accomplished by adding redundant bits to a data stream and allowing only restricted sequences of received bits to be proper messages.

A method for error control, which is almost universally used, involves segmenting the bit stream into blocks and adding redundant bits in a well-defined pattern to each block. Errors in the bit stream destroy the well-defined patterns, so error detection is possible. Once errors are detected, it is possible to retransmit the flawed blocks. This type of error control is called *error detection with automatic-repeat-request* (ARQ).

A structure for operating with this type of error control must provide for storage of a block of data at the transmitting node until it can be successfully transmitted. It is also necessary for the receiving node to return acknowledgements (either positive or negative) to the transmitting node to instruct the latter either to destroy the stored block, if successfully transmitted, or to retransmit it when an error is detected.

A diagram showing error control operations for a point-to-point link is given in Fig. 2.25. A point worth emphasizing is that the transmission link, which is subject to noise, transmits bits with no regard for their significance. Error control, or more specifically error detection, is accomplished by encoding a block of data bits into a related, but different, block of bits to be transmitted using an encoding rule that makes detection of errors possible. Considerable flexibility in choice of this encoding rule is possible; this is discussed in the next two subsections.

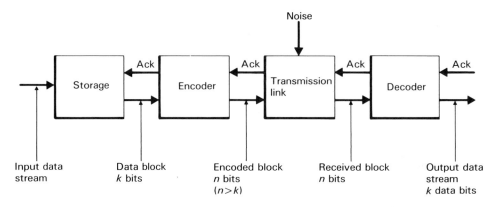

Figure 2.25 **A Block Diagram Showing Error Control Operations for a Point-to-point Link**

As a final introductory idea, consider the obvious encoding strategy of duplicating the block of k data bits to form an encoded block of $n = 2k$ bits. If the transmitted block is constructed as two parts, each containing the k data bits in their original sequence, then the decoder can check for errors by comparing the two parts. If an error or errors occurs in either part of the transmitted block, the two parts do not match and the presence of an error or errors is revealed. (Errors in the same position in both halves of the transmitted block are not detected, but such an occurrence is unlikely.) This obvious strategy is effective because almost any error pattern is detected. It is costly, however, because k redundant bits are necessary.

Redundancy is defined as the ratio of the transmitted block length to the data block length. In the case of the strategy just discussed, the ratio is 2.0, which is poor. Another closely related measure is *excess redundancy,* or the ratio of the number of redundant bits to the number of data bits. Excess redundancy is 1.0 for k redundant bits in a block of $n = 2k$ and is equivalent to a redundancy of 2.

In the design of error-detecting codes, either of these measures of redundancy is a useful criterion for a good code, although excess redundancy will be used as a matter of preference. To this measure of cost must be added a measure of quality. One such measure used in the following discussion is the probability of undetected errors for a particular code.

2.3.2 Parity Checks

In its simplest form a parity check applied to a binary bit stream of zeros and ones adds one redundant bit to a sequence of $n - 1$ bits to form a block of n bits. The parity bit is chosen at the transmitter so that the whole block has an even (or odd) number of ones, or even (or odd) parity.

A bit error changes a zero into a one or a one into a zero. Thus an odd number of errors in transmitting the block results in an odd number of ones at the receiver. In other words, even parity is destroyed. The receiver can thus detect any odd number of errors by checking parity, i.e., by determining whether the number of ones is even or odd.

Excess redundancy for a single parity check is $1/(n - 1)$. Note that the measures of cost depend on the block size. For example, excess redundancy takes on the values 0.11, 0.01, and 0.001 respectively for $n = 10$, 100, and 1000.

The "quality" of a single parity check can be measured in terms of the probability of undetected errors. This probability can be determined for the simple error probability model of independent bit errors occurring with probability, p, as follows. The probability of m errors in a block is $p^m(1 - p)^{n-m}$ if the errors are in specified locations. If errors can be in any possible location, as is typically the case, the result becomes

$$\frac{n!}{(n - k)!m!} p^m (1 - p)^{n-m}.$$

Table 2.1 below gives the probability expressions for 1, 2, 3, and 4 errors and approximate numerical values for $n = 100$ and 1000 and $p = 10^{-3}$ and 10^{-6}.

The table shows that for the values used the probability of undetected errors is approximately the probability of two errors (the smallest even number), since the probability of larger even numbers of errors is negligible in comparison.

The probabilities can be given physical significance in terms of a bit stream being transmitted over a 10 Mbps channel that transmits, for example, one hundred bit blocks in 10^{-5} seconds/block. The probability, 9×10^{-2}, of a bit error in a block of 100 bits, resulting for a bit error probability of $p = 10^{-3}$, can be interpreted as approximately nine errors on the average during the transmission of 100 blocks. Since 100 blocks are transmitted in 1 msec, this is nine errors per millisecond, or approximately 0.11 msec between errors. Similar calculations are shown in Table 2.2, which gives the time between errors and between undetected errors for the two choices of p and block lengths of 100 and 1000.

Although the numbers in Table 2.2 are calculated with the simple error model, they give an idea of results for a simple parity check. Clearly the average time between undetected errors that can be achieved is too short for steady-state practical operation. As a result, more complicated error detection procedures have been developed.

Table 2.1   Probabilities for Bit Errors in a Block of n Bits

Number of Errors	Probability expression	Approximate value $n = 100$		Approximate value $n = 1000$	
		$p = 10^{-3}$	$p = 10^{-6}$	$p = 10^{-3}$	$p = 10^{-6}$
1	$np(1 - p)^{n-1}$	9×10^{-2}	10^{-5}	.37	10^{-3}
2	$[n(n - 1)/2]p^2(1 - p)^{n-2}$	4.5×10^{-3}	5×10^{-9}	.18	5×10^{-7}
3	$[n(n - 1)(n - 2)/3!]p^3(1 - p)^{n-3}$	1.5×10^{-4}	1.6×10^{-13}	6.1×10^{-2}	1.7×10^{-10}
4	$[n(n - 1)(n - 2)(n - 3)/4!]p^4(1 - p)^{n-4}$	3.6×10^{-6}	4×10^{-18}	1.5×10^{-2}	4×10^{-14}

Table 2.2   Time Between Errors Using a Simple Parity Check (10 Mbps Channel)

	n = 100		n = 1000	
	AVG. TIME BETWEEN ERRORS	AVG. TIME BETWEEN UNDETECTED ERRORS	AVG. TIME BETWEEN ERRORS	AVG. TIME BETWEEN UNDETECTED ERRORS
$p = 10^{-3}$	0.11 msec.	2 msec.	.3 msec.	.6 msec.
$p = 10^{-6}$	1 sec.	0.5 hours	10^{-1} sec.	3.3 min.

A straightforward extension of simple parity checks is structured with characters. One parity check bit is added to each character and an additional "check character" is added after some number of characters, such as five. The check character bits are chosen to produce even (or odd) parity for columns if the five characters are listed, one above the other, as shown in Fig. 2.26(a). In this scheme the character parity is referred to as *vertical redundancy check* (VRC) and the column parity is called *longitudinal redundancy check* (LRC).

The VRC/LRC scheme is an improvement over a simple parity check as is now demonstrated. Assume that two errors occur in, say, character 2 complementing two bit values as shown underlined in Fig. 2.26(b). Even parity for character 2 is still present, so the parity check for this character does not reveal the errors. However, it can be noted that columns 2 and 7 now have an odd number of ones, and this information can be used to detect the errors.

The improved scheme not only can detect double errors, it can detect any

```
        Data bits              ┌── Parity check
     ───────────────              ↓
   1  0  0  1  1  0  0  0    1    Character 1
   0  1  1  1  0  1  0  1    1    Character 2
   1  1  0  0  1  1  0  0    0    Character 3
   1  0  0  0  1  0  0  0    0    Character 4
   0  1  0  0  1  1  1  0    0    Character 5
   1  1  1  0  0  1  1  1    0    Check character

            (a)

   1  0  0  1  1  0  0  0    1
   0  0  1  1  0  1  1  1    1
   1  1  0  0  1  1  0  0    0
   1  0  0  0  1  0  0  0    0
   0  1  0  0  1  1  1  0    0
   1  1  1  0  0  1  1  1    0

            (b)
```

Figure 2.26   Typical Transmissions with VRC and LRC
   (a) Transmitted sequence
   (b) Received sequence with errors in one character (underlined)

combinations of even errors in characters (all odd error patterns are, of course, detected) that do not result in an even number of errors in a column. For example, errors in columns 2 and 5 in both characters 1 and 5 could not be detected, while errors in columns 2 and 5 in character 1 and errors in columns 1, 3, 4, and 7 in character 5 could be detected.

For the VRC/LRC scheme, the undetected error probability is less than the probability of four errors in a block, since some, but not all, quadruple errors are undetected. An idea of the improvement this produces can be seen by comparing the probabilities of two and four errors in Table 2.1, which of course assumes the simple independent bit error model.

Excess redundancy for the specific VRC/LRC scheme depicted in Fig. 2.26 is given by 14/54 or 0.26.

Even though the VRC/LRC scheme is a substantial improvement over simple parity checks, it is still not adequate in some applications. Thus the results of further research on codes, specifically extensions of the general idea of parity checks, have been applied to error control. Cyclic codes, which are in some sense a generalization of parity checking, are the type most commonly used for error detecting in computer networks. These codes have produced cyclic redundancy checks (CRC) that are in widespread use; these are discussed in the next subsection.

2.3.3 Cyclic Redundancy Checks

Simple parity checks, such as those discussed in Section 2.3.2, are limited in terms of performance and in terms of flexibility to be tailored to specific applications. Codes used for what are termed cyclic redundancy checks are more complicated than simple parity checks and depend on a specialized body of coding theory for their development.

The purpose of this section is to present sufficient background to enable the reader to be aware of general approaches and use the results of coding theory. A systematic development that uses standard approaches is not intended. Readers interested in an introduction to systematic developments can consult such references as Hamming [7] and Lin and Costello [8].

The approach to be taken is to treat advanced codes[†] as an extension of parity checks. Parity checks have been used previously in three different implementations: to check parity over a complete block of n bits, to check parity of characters (VRC), and to check parity of columns formed by several characters (LRC). The basic idea of parity checks can be extended to check the parity of any number of almost arbitrarily chosen groups of bits in a block.

Some of the results of coding theory and insight into the use of codes can be provided as an extension of parity checking. A first step in the development requires systematic ways to represent and manipulate parity checks for complete blocks and groups of bits in a block.

---

†The codes to be considered are linear, cyclic codes.

Systematic Representations of Codes

A general transmission system that uses error control coding is shown earlier in Fig. 2.25. A sequence of k data or message bits is assumed to arrive from a message source to the encoder. The encoder observes the sequence of message bits and adds $(n - k)$ check bits to form a transmitted block of n bits.

At the receiver, the n bit received block is observed by the decoder, which uses the check bits to determine if errors are present. If not, the k message bits are further processed through the system. If errors are detected, the block of bits must be retransmitted.

To design sophisticated codes, it is necessary to introduce a mathematical framework. A sequence of bits, such as an n-bit block, is represented by a mathematical model that allows well-defined operations on the sequence of bits. Two slightly different representations are used. In one representation, a sequence of j bits is modeled as a vector, where each zero or one in the sequence is a component of the vector. In another representation, each bit in a sequence of j bits is used as one binary coefficient in a polynomial of degree $j - 1$.

As an example, consider the sequence of bits, 1 0 0 1 1 1 0 1 0 1, in which the leftmost bit is assumed to arrive first in a time sequence. For the vector representation, the symbol $\underline{v}$ is used and

$$\underline{v} = [1 \quad 0 \quad 0 \quad 1 \quad 1 \quad 1 \quad 0 \quad 1 \quad 0 \quad 1] \tag{2.26}$$

For the polynomial representation, $V(X)$ is used as the symbol and

$$V(X) = 1 + X^3 + X^4 + X^5 + X^7 + X^9. \tag{2.27}$$

Note in $V(X)$ that the powers of X with zero coefficients are not included and that the polynomial has degree 9 (or less) to conform with the sequence that contains 10 bits.

Either of the representations provides a mathematical framework for manipulating groups of bits. For both cases, modulo-2 arithmetic that satisfies the following rules is used:

Addition rules	Multiplication rules
$0 + 0 = 0$	$0 \cdot 1 = 0$
$0 + 1 = 1$	$1 \cdot 0 = 0$
$1 + 0 = 1$	$1 \cdot 1 = 1$
$1 + 1 = 0$	$0 \cdot 0 = 0$

Note that the multiplication rules are the same as standard multiplication, and that modulo-2 addition is the same as using standard addition, then dividing the result by 2, and using the remainder as the answer.

As examples of addition using the two approaches, consider the bit sequence above along with the sequence 0 1 1 0 1 0 1 1 1 0. The two sequences are represented as

$$\underline{v} = [1 \quad 0 \quad 0 \quad 1 \quad 1 \quad 1 \quad 0 \quad 1 \quad 0 \quad 1];$$
$$\underline{w} = [0 \quad 1 \quad 1 \quad 0 \quad 1 \quad 0 \quad 1 \quad 1 \quad 1 \quad 0]$$

$$V(X) = 1 + X^3 + X^4 + X^5 + X^7 + X^9$$

$$W(X) = X^1 + X^2 + X^4 + X^6 + X^7 + X^8$$

Addition using the two approaches results in

$$\underline{v} + \underline{w} = [1 \quad 1 \quad 1 \quad 1 \quad 0 \quad 1 \quad 1 \quad 0 \quad 1 \quad 1 \quad]$$
$$V(X) + W(X) = 1 + X^1 + X^2 + X^3 + X^5 + X^6 + X^8 + X^9$$

Multiplication is not normally used with the vector representation. For the polynomial representation, multiplication is illustrated for the sequences $V_1(X) = 1 + X + X^3$, $V_2(X) = X + X^3$ as $V_1(X) \cdot V_2(X) = X + X^2 + X^3 + X^6$.

Division of polynomials can be carried out using the long division rule of algebra. In general a quotient and a remainder result. For example, division of $V_1(X) = 1 + X + X^3$ by $V_2(X) = 1 + X$ results in

$$
\begin{array}{r}
X^2 + X \\
X + 1 \overline{\smash{\big)}\ X^3 + X + 1} \\
\underline{X^3 + X^2 } \\
X^2 + X + 1 \\
\underline{X^2 + X } \\
1 = \text{remainder}
\end{array}
$$

The result can be stated as

$$V_1(X) = (X^2 + X)V_2(X) + 1$$

As further notation, $\underline{c}$ is used to denote a transmitted block of n bits regarded as a row vector and also termed a *code vector*. The symbols $\underline{r}$ and $\underline{e}$ are used respectively for the received code vector and the error vector. The latter is defined as

$$\underline{e} = \underline{c} + \underline{r} \tag{2.28}$$

Note that $\underline{e}$ has "zero" components for any positions in which the transmitted and received vector components are the same, and "one" components where they are not the same.

A corresponding notation $C(X)$, $R(X)$ and $E(X)$ is used with the polynomial representation.

A *parity check matrix, M,* can now be defined to organize work with parity check bits. To begin, consider the simple parity check over $n - 1$ bits. As just noted, an nth parity check bit is added to the $n - 1$ message bits to form a block of n bits, including the check bit.

For this case the parity check matrix, M, is defined as one row, a $(1 \times n)$

matrix,

$$M = [1 \quad 1 \ldots 1] \tag{2.29}$$

and the parity check operation can then be stated as

$$\underline{c} \, M^t = \sum_{i=1}^{n} c_i \tag{2.30}$$

where M^t indicates the transpose of a matrix. The c_i are the elements of the code vector, $\underline{c}$, which take on the values zero or one to correspond to the bits in the block. Using modulo-2 arithmetic, the sum of the c_i is zero for an even number of ones and one for an odd number of ones. This is, of course, exactly what the parity check operation is set up to produce.

The result of the parity check operation is typically termed a *syndrome, s*, which is in general a row vector and, in the case of a simple parity check, is a single element. Stated as an equation, $\underline{s}$ is given by

$$\underline{s} = \underline{c} \, M^t \tag{2.31}$$

For the simple parity check, $\underline{s} = 0$ if (even) parity is preserved, and $\underline{s} = 1$ if the parity check fails.

When the parity check is used for error control on a point-to-point link, the transmitted code vector is chosen so that

$$\underline{c} \, M^t = 0 \tag{2.32}$$

The syndrome of the received vector, given by

$$\underline{s} = \underline{r} \, M^t \tag{2.33}$$

is used to test for errors.

A parity check matrix can be formulated for carrying out any combination of parity checks over portions of a transmitted block of bits. Each row of M defines a separate parity check. Through the operation $\underline{c} \, M^t$, the elements of $\underline{c}$, at the locations where ones appear in the rows of M, are added together to produce one element of the row vector $\underline{s}$. The syndrome, $\underline{s}$, is then a row vector with the results of each parity check as its elements.

As an example, consider the parity check matrix defined for a 7-bit block as

$$M = \begin{bmatrix} 0 & 1 & 0 & 1 & 1 & 0 & 0 \\ 1 & 0 & 0 & 0 & 1 & 1 & 1 \\ 0 & 0 & 1 & 0 & 0 & 0 & 1 \end{bmatrix} \tag{2.34}$$

The syndrome associated with this parity check matrix is given by

$$\underline{c}M^{t} = [c_1 c_2 c_3 c_4 c_5 c_6 c_7] \begin{bmatrix} 0 & 1 & 0 \\ 1 & 0 & 0 \\ 0 & 0 & 1 \\ 1 & 0 & 0 \\ 1 & 1 & 0 \\ 0 & 1 & 0 \\ 0 & 1 & 1 \end{bmatrix}$$

$$= [c_2 + c_4 + c_5, c_1 + c_5 + c_6 + c_7, c_3 + c_7] = \underline{s} \qquad (2.35)$$

Note that the elements of $\underline{s}$ give the results of three parity checks over positions 2, 4 and 5; 1, 5, 6 and 7; and 3 and 7.

As another example, consider the VRC/LRC parity checks discussed in Subsection 2.3.2. Recall that this type of code checks parity for each of five 8-bit characters, adding the parity bit to make the extended character nine bits long. The parity of each of the nine columns formed by listing the extended characters one above the other is then checked.

A block for such a code is five extended characters plus the nine additional check bits, or 54 bits long. The parity check matrix, M, for this code has 15 rows, one for each parity check, and 54 columns, one for each bit in the block. The first row of M has ones in the first nine columns and zeros elsewhere. Thus the first element of $\underline{s}$ is the modulo-2 sum over the first character. Similarly, rows two–six have nine ones in positions such that elements two–six in $\underline{s}$ provide the modulo-2 sums respectively over characters two–five and over the final group of nine check bits. The seventh row begins the column parity checks and has ones in columns 1, 10, 19, 28, 37, and 46. Rows 8–15 continue the column parity checks, having six ones each, in positions to check columns two–nine, one at a time. Elements 7–15 in $\underline{s}$ contain the results of the parity checks over columns.

Now consider the generation of code vectors given a specified parity check matrix. The sequence of message bits can be assumed to arrive at the transmitter k bits at a time for transmission. Thus, in principle, collections of bits to be covered by parity checks can be observed in the arriving sequence and parity bits computed. These can then be combined with the message bits to form the transmitted block.

Encoding in the manner just discussed can be cumbersome, and a code generator matrix, G, is typically used to aid in code generation. The code generator matrix has a minimal set of linearly independent code vectors as its rows. It is a basic property of linear codes that all code vectors can be determined as linear combinations of a minimal set of vectors such as used for the generator matrix. Thus, if $\underline{u}$ is a message vector, a code vector can be generated by the operation

$$\underline{c} = \underline{u}\, G \tag{2.36}$$

The code generator matrix is related to the parity check matrix and can be determined from it. Recall from equation (2.32) that for any code vector $\underline{c}\, M^t = 0$. Thus $\underline{u}\, G\, M^t = 0$ and, since $\underline{u}$ is not identically zero,

$$G\, M^t = 0 \tag{2.37}$$

Equation (2.37) can be used to construct G from M by choosing rows of G that are orthogonal† to columns of M^t (or rows of M), and are linearly independent. Note, however, that the choice of G is not unique, although the complete sets of code words generated with any possible G are the same. The procedure just described can be used in principle to determine G. A less cumbersome method based on more sophisticated theory is, however, used in actual practice.

The development presented is complete in the sense that both encoding and decoding operations are completely specified, given the desired parity checks. Later sections discuss implementation and the issue of determining parity checks (or equivalent operations) to produce good codes.

In summary, the following structure has been developed.

Notation:

M = Parity check matrix $((n - k) \times n)$

G = Code generator matrix $(k \times n)$

u = Message vector $(1 \times k)$

c = Transmitted code vector $(1 \times n)$

r = Received code vector $(1 \times n)$

Equations:

$\underline{c}\, M^t = 0$	Constraint satisfied by code words
$G\, M^t = 0$	Rule for determining G from M
$\underline{c} = \underline{u}G$	Encoding rule
$\underline{s} = \underline{r}\, M^t$	Syndrome calculation for detecting errors

Unfortunately, most current implementations of CRC generating and error-detecting hardware are based on the polynomial representation of codes rather than on the vector–matrix representation. It is also common practice to define a code by its generator polynomial rather than by some other method. It

---

†Two vectors $\underline{a}$ and $\underline{b}$ are said to be orthogonal if $\underline{a}\underline{b}^t = 0$.

is thus desirable to obtain a structure, comparable to that just summarized, but that uses a polynomial representation.†

Since a rigorous development is not the purpose of the present study, the polynomial structure that corresponds to the one just developed using vectors and matrices is simply presented, followed by an example in which the two approaches are shown to be equivalent.

Notation:

$M(X)$ = Parity check polynomial of degree k

$G(X)$ = Code generator polynomial of degree $(n - k)$

$U(X)$ = Message polynomial of degree $(k - 1)$

$C(X)$ = Transmitted code polynomial of degree $(n - 1)$

$R(X)$ = Received code polynomial of degree $(n - 1)$.

Equations: Remainder after dividing $M(X)C(X)$ by $X^n + 1$ is zero (2.38)

$$G(X) M(X) = X^n + 1 \tag{2.39}$$
$$C(X) = U(X) G(X) \tag{2.40}$$

Remainder after dividing $R(X)$ by $G(X)$ is $S(X)$, (2.41)

As used previously, n is the length of the transmitted block.

These equations correspond in some general sense to those listed for the vector representation.

The following example is used in the remainder of this subsection to illustrate some of the properties of codes. Consider a code seven bits long, with three check bits and four message bits. The parity checks are specified to cover bit positions 1, 4, 6, 7; 2, 4, 5, 6; and 3, 5, 6, 7. The parity check matrix is (3 × 7) and is constructed with ones in the specified check positions for each row to obtain

$$M = \begin{bmatrix} 1 & 0 & 0 & 1 & 0 & 1 & 1 \\ 0 & 1 & 0 & 1 & 1 & 1 & 0 \\ 0 & 0 & 1 & 0 & 1 & 1 & 1 \end{bmatrix}$$

The matrix G is constructed, in principle, from $G M^t = 0$, so that the vector product of each row of G with a column of M^t gives 0. Such products are not unique and the rows of G are chosen to be linearly independent in the sense that no linear combination of rows adds to zero. One possible result for G is

---

†Polynomial representations apply to a restricted class of codes called *cyclic codes.*

$$G = \begin{bmatrix} 1 & 1 & 0 & 1 & 0 & 0 & 0 \\ 0 & 1 & 1 & 0 & 1 & 0 & 0 \\ 0 & 0 & 1 & 1 & 0 & 1 & 0 \\ 0 & 0 & 0 & 1 & 1 & 0 & 1 \end{bmatrix}$$

It is easy to check that $G\,M^t = 0$ and to check specific combinations of rows of G to see that they are linearly independent. It is tedious, however, to construct G using the method described.

Given G, the 16 possible code vectors can be constructed from $u\,G$ using all possible four bit sequences for u. For example if $u = [0\ 1\ \overline{1}\ 0]$, $u\,G$ is constructed as follows

$$[0\ \ 1\ \ 1\ \ 0] \begin{bmatrix} 1 & 1 & 0 & 1 & 0 & 0 & 0 \\ 0 & 1 & 1 & 0 & 1 & 0 & 0 \\ 0 & 0 & 1 & 1 & 0 & 1 & 0 \\ 0 & 0 & 0 & 1 & 1 & 0 & 1 \end{bmatrix} = [0\ \ 1\ \ 0\ \ 1\ \ 1\ \ 1\ \ 0]$$

The first three elements of the result are obtained as

$$[0 \cdot 1 + 1 \cdot 0 + 1 \cdot 0 + 0 \cdot 0,$$
$$0 \cdot 1 + 1 \cdot 1 + 1 \cdot 0 + 0 \cdot 0, \ \ 0 \cdot 0 + 1 \cdot 1 + 1 \cdot 1 + 0 \cdot 0, \dots]$$

A listing of all of the code vectors follows:

Message, u	Code vector, c
[0 0 0 0]	[0 0 0 0 0 0 0]
[1 0 0 0]	[1 1 0 1 0 0 0]
[0 1 0 0]	[0 1 1 0 1 0 0]
[1 1 0 0]	[1 0 1 1 1 0 0]
[0 0 1 0]	[0 0 1 1 0 1 0]
[1 0 1 0]	[1 1 1 0 0 1 0]
[0 1 1 0]	[0 1 0 1 1 1 0]
[1 1 1 0]	[1 0 0 0 1 1 0]
[0 0 0 1]	[0 0 0 1 1 0 1]
[1 0 0 1]	[1 1 0 0 1 0 1]
[0 1 0 1]	[0 1 1 1 0 0 1]
[1 1 0 1]	[1 0 1 0 0 0 1]
[0 0 1 1]	[0 0 1 0 1 1 1]
[1 0 1 1]	[1 1 1 1 1 1 1]
[0 1 1 1]	[0 1 0 0 0 1 1]
[1 1 1 1]	[1 0 0 1 0 1 1]

The syndrome is obtained for any received vector r as $s = r\,M^t$. If an error vector

$$e = [0\ \ 0\ \ 1\ \ 0\ \ 0\ \ 0\ \ 0]$$

is added to the second of the code vectors tabulated above, a possible received vector

$$\underline{r} = [1 \quad 1 \quad 1 \quad 1 \quad 0 \quad 0 \quad 0]$$

is obtained. The syndrome for this received vector is given by

$$\underline{s} = [1 \quad 1 \quad 1 \quad 1 \quad 0 \quad 0 \quad 0] \begin{bmatrix} 1 & 0 & 0 \\ 0 & 1 & 0 \\ 0 & 0 & 1 \\ 1 & 1 & 0 \\ 0 & 1 & 1 \\ 1 & 1 & 1 \\ 1 & 0 & 1 \end{bmatrix} = [0 \quad 0 \quad 1]$$

Note that since the error is in position 3 in the $\underline{e}$ vector, the parity check over positions 3, 5, 6, 7 fails and produces a one in the third element of $\underline{s}$.

Having worked this example with the vector representation, it is now instructive to use the polynomial representation to make some of the same calculations. To begin, note that G is given in the standard form

$$G = \begin{bmatrix} g_0 & g_1 & g_2 & g_3 & 0 & 0 & 0 \\ 0 & g_0 & g_1 & g_2 & g_3 & 0 & 0 \\ 0 & 0 & g_0 & g_1 & g_2 & g_3 & 0 \\ 0 & 0 & 0 & g_0 & g_1 & g_2 & g_3 \end{bmatrix}$$

with $g_0 = 1$, $g_1 = 1$, $g_2 = 0$, and $g_3 = 1$. (Other forms of G can be manipulated to this form by replacing rows with linear combinations of rows.) The g_i are the coefficients of the generator polynomial, which for this case is

$$G(X) = 1 + X + X^3$$

The basic operations of code construction and calculation of the syndrome are illustrated here using the same calculations previously made with vectors.

Code construction:

$$C(X) = U(X)\,G(X)$$
$$U(X) = X + X^2; \; G(X) = 1 + X + X^3$$
$$U(X)\,G(X) = (X + X^2)\,(1 + X + X^3)$$
$$= X + (X^2 + X^2) + X^3 + X^4 + X^5$$
$$= X + X^3 + X^4 + X^5$$
$$= C(X)$$

Syndrome determination:

$$R(X) = 1 + X + X^2 + X^3$$

(equivalent to $\underline{r} = [1 \quad 1 \quad 1 \quad 1 \quad 0 \quad 0 \quad 0])$

$$\begin{array}{r} 1 \\ X^3 + X + 1 \overline{\smash{\big)}\ X^3 + X^2 + X^1 + 1} \\ \underline{X^3 \qquad\quad + X\ + 1} \\ X^2 \qquad\qquad\quad = S(X), \text{syndrome.} \end{array}$$

(2.43)

Note that $C(X)$ and $S(X)$ as computed with polynomials are equivalent to $\underline{c}$ and $\underline{s}$ respectively as computed with vectors.

Equations (2.39) and (2.38) are now verified for the example. Equation (2.39) can be expressed as

$$M(X) = \frac{X^n + 1}{G(X)}$$

which states, in effect, that $X^n + 1$ is evenly divisible by $G(X)$. This is demonstrated by long division:

$$\begin{array}{r} X^4 + X^2 + X + 1 \\ X^3 + X + 1 \overline{\smash{\big)}\ X^7 + 1} \\ \underline{X^7 + X^5 + X^4} \\ X^5 + X^4 + 1 \\ \underline{X^5 + X^3 + X^2} \\ X^4 + X^3 + X^2 + 1 \\ \underline{X^4 + \qquad\quad X^2 + X} \\ X^3 + X + 1 \\ \underline{X^3 + X + 1} \\ 0 \quad\ 0 \quad\ 0 \end{array}$$

The requirement of (2.38) can also be demonstrated by long division as follows:

$$\begin{aligned} C(X)\,M(X) &= (X + X^3 + X^4 + X^5)\,(X^4 + X^2 + X + 1) \\ &= X + X^2 + X^8 + X^9 \end{aligned}$$

$$\begin{array}{r} X^2 + X \\ X^7 + 1 \overline{\smash{\big)}\ X^9 + X^8 + X^2 + X} \\ \underline{X^9 \qquad\qquad X^2} \\ X^8 \qquad\qquad + X \\ \underline{X^8 \qquad\qquad + X} \\ 0 \qquad\qquad 0 \end{array}$$

It is often convenient to produce code words in *systematic* form such that, for example, the first k bits are message digits and the last $n - k$ bits of the transmitted block are parity check digits. This can be done by using the polynomial representations as follows. Multiply the $(k - 1)^{th}$ degree polynomial $U(X)$ by X^{n-k}. This gives an $(n - 1)^{th}$ degree polynomial, $X^{n-k}U(X)$. The division of this polynomial by $G(X)$ produces a quotient $Q(X)$ and a remainder $B(X)$ so that

$$X^{n-k}U(X) = Q(X)\,G(X) + B(X) \tag{2.44}$$

The polynomial $Q(X)\,G(X)$ is a multiple of a code generator polynomial and is thus a code polynomial. Solving for this code polynomial gives

$$Q(X)\,G(X) = X^{n-k}\,U(X) + B(X) \tag{2.45}$$

which is equivalent to a code word in the desired form

$$[u_0, u_1, \ldots u_{k-1}, b_0, b_1, \ldots b_{n-k-1}]$$

Implementation of Encoders and Decoders

A typical encoder implements the logic of equation (2.45), i.e., it produces a code word in systematic form. Reference to this equation shows that three operations are required in the mathematical model:

1. Multiply the message sequence by X^{n-k};
2. Divide the resulting sequence by the generator polynomial, $G(X)$; and
3. Add the remainder polynomial, $B(X)$, that results from step 2 to $X^{n-k}\,U(X)$ to obtain the polynomial representation of the code word.

Before the hardware implementation of these mathematical operations is discussed, the reader should have in mind the corresponding operations for the decoder.

The decoder for an error detecting code, described with polynomials, must produce the syndrome polynomial, $S(X)$, and the output message polynomial $U(X)$. This is accomplished with the logic of equation (2.41), which gives $S(X)$ as the remainder after the received polynomial $R(X)$ is divided by the generator polynomial $G(X)$. Since the code vector is constructed in systematic form, $R(X)$ is in systematic form, with $(n - k)$ check bits following the k message bits. Thus producing $U(X)$ merely requires selecting the first k bits of the received word.

A review of both the encoder and decoder operations shows that hardware implementations must be obtained for operations modeled as:

1. Multiplying by X^{n-k};
2. Dividing either $X^{n-k}\,U(X)$ or $R(X)$ by $G(X)$; and
3. Adding $B(X)$ to $X^{n-k}\,U(X)$.

In summary, the operations of polynomial multiplication, division, and addition must be implemented.

A brief description is now given of the hardware devices available to implement the mathematical operations required. Figure 2.27 shows the three devices: n-stage shift registers, binary scalar multipliers, and modulo-2 adders.

A shift register is a coupled string of storage devices, or stages, each of which stores one bit. The shift register is operated by clock pulses that cause bits stored in one stage of the register to move to the next stage. For example, consider a 4-stage register, initially empty, to which is applied the digital

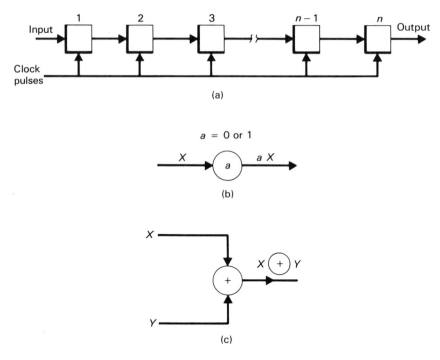

Figure 2.27   Hardware Devices for Implementing Error Control Coding

(a) n-stage shift register
(b) Binary scalar multiplier
(c) Modulo-2 adder

sequence 1 0 0 1 0 1. (Recall that the leftmost bit is assumed to occur first, and it exists for one clock cycle.) Assume that on the first clock cycle of observation the digital sequence is initially applied. Thus on this cycle the arriving "1" is shifted into the first stage of the register, and the other three stages remain empty, as shown in Figure. 2.28. On the next three clock cycles, 0 0 1 is shifted into the register so that at the end of four cycles the stored pattern is 1 0 0 1, and so on. If the process is continued with only the inputs shown being applied, the bits move through the register until, at the end of the 10th clock cycle, it is empty again, as traced in Fig. 2.28.

Operation of the scalar multiplier and modulo-2 adder is straightforward. The scalar multiplier multiplies its input by a binary number, set as a parameter, to produce an output aX from an input X. Note that since a is a binary number, the scalar multiplier amounts to a direct connection when $a = 1$ and no connection when $a = 0$. The modulo-2 sum adder simply provides the modulo-2 sum of its inputs.

The steps involved in both encoding and decoding require division by the generator polynomial. The division operation can be carried out by the feedback shift register circuit shown in Fig. 2.29(a). This circuit is set up to

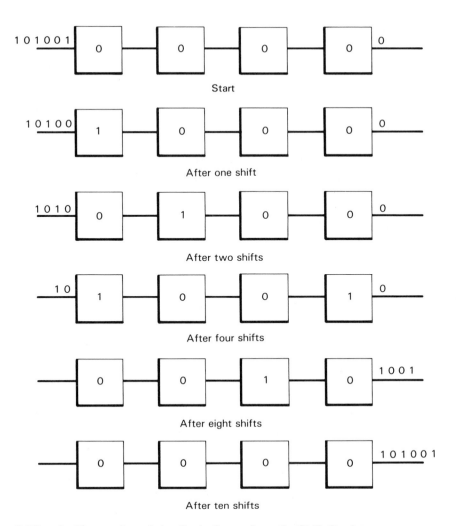

Figure 2.28   An Illustration of the Basic Operation of a Shift Register

handle the general case of $D(X)/G(X) = Q(X) + B(X)/G(X)$ where

$$Q(X) = q_{k-1} X^{k-1} + q_{k-2} X^{k-2} + \cdots + q_0$$

$$D(X) = d_{n-1} X^{n-1} + d_{n-2} X^{n-2} + \cdots + d_0$$

$$G(X) = g_{n-k} X^{n-k} + g_{n-k-1} X^{n-k-1} + \cdots + g_0$$

$$B(X) = b_{n-k-1} X^{n-k-1} + b_{n-k-2} X^{n-k-2} + \cdots + b_0$$

The coefficients of $G(X)$ are set as parameters of the scalar multipliers using the fact that the leading coefficient, g_{n-k} is always 1. The coefficients of $D(X)$ are shifted into the shift register one at a time on the input line. If the elements of the shift register are initially empty, actual calculation does not begin until the shift after the leading coefficient d_{n-1} is shifted into stage number $n - k - 1$. On the following shift, when d_{n-1} is shifted into stage $n - k - 1$, $q_{k-1} = d_{n-1}$ is shifted out on the output line and fed back to affect earlier operations (q_{k-1} is multiplied by each of the q_i). After shifting q_{k-1} out, the shift registers hold the first in a sequence of remainders. The process of shifting in the d_i and shifting out the q_i continues through k shifts until the coefficients of $Q(X)$ have all been produced, and the coefficients of $B(X)$ are left as the last remainder in the stages of the shift register.

The division operation is examined in more detail with the following example: Consider the particular $D(X)$ and $G(X)$ given and the division process carried out with long division.

$$G(X) = X^2 + g_1 X + g_0$$

$$D(X) = d_3 X^3 + d_2 X^2 + d_1 X + d_0$$

$$
\begin{array}{r}
d_3 X + (d_2 + g_1 d_3) \qquad (Q) \\
X^2 + g_1 X + g_0 \overline{\smash{\big)}\ d_3 X^3 + d_2 X^2 + d_1 X + d_0} \\
\underline{d_3 X^3 + g_1 d_3 X^2 + g_0 d_3 X} \\
(d_2 + g_1 d_3) X^2 + (d_1 + g_0 d_3) X + d_0 \qquad (B_1) \\
\underline{(d_2 + g_1 d_3) X^2 + g_1 (d_2 + g_1 d_3) X + g_0 (d_2 + g_1 d_3)} \\
[(d_1 + g_0 d_3) + g_1 (d_2 + g_1 d_3)] X + d_0 + g_0 (d_2 + g_1 d_3) \qquad (B)
\end{array}
$$

Q denotes the quotient and B_1 and B the first and final remainders. The circuit to implement the division operation is given in Fig. 2.29(b).

Consider the first shift after that in which d_3 is stored in stage 1 and d_2 in stage 0. On this shift, d_3 is shifted out of stage 1 to become q_1, and it is also fed back. The signals shifted into stages 1 and 0 respectively are $d_2 + g_1 d_3$ and $d_1 + g_0 d_3$, which can be verified from the diagram. Thus at the end of the first shift, stage 1 holds $(d_2 + g_1 d_3)$, stage 0 holds $(d_1 + g_0 d_3)$, and d_0 is the next input. Compare the shift register result to the long division operation, and note that after the first shift the correct $q_1 = d_3$ is shifted out, and the proper finite remainder (B_1) is stored in the registers that are extended to include the next input.

On the second shift, $(d_2 + g_1 d_3)$ is shifted out of stage 1 to become q_0 and is fed back to replace d_3. The signals shifted into stages 1 and 0 on the second shift are, respectively, $(d_1 + g_0 d_3) + g_1 (d_2 + g_1 d_3)$ and $d_0 + g_0 (d_2 + g_1 d_3)$. These signals, of course, become the content of the two registers. Reference to the results of the long division operation shows that q_0 and B are also correct.

In light of the discussion on the hardware implementations of the necessary operations, consider the three steps of the complete encoding operation. This is done with an example based on the generator polynomial $G(X) = X^3 + X + 1$. The encoding circuit is shown in Fig. 2.30. The first step of multiplying the message sequence by X^{n-k} amounts to shifting this sequence by $n - k = 3$ shifts. This is accomplished by feeding the message in through three stages of the shift register, as shown in the figure. The implementation of the second step employs the shift register with appropriate feedback connections to divide by $G(X)$. The message sequence is shifted out over the output line

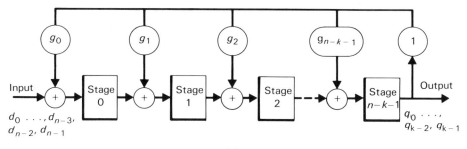

(a)

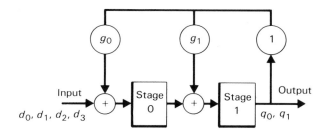

(b)

Figure 2.29   Division with a Shift Register
(a) General case
(b) Specific case

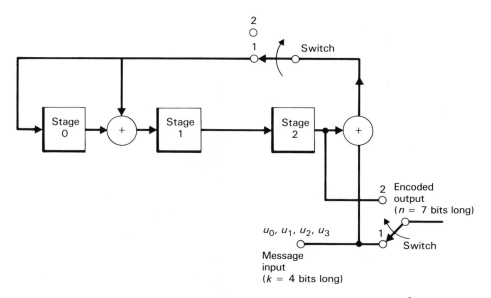

Figure 2.30   Encoding Circuit for a Generator Polynomial $G(X) = X^3 + X + 1$

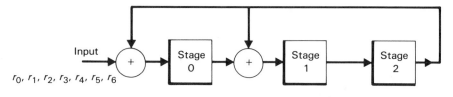

The syndrome is the content of the register stages after
all seven received bits are shifted in.

Figure 2.31 **Syndrome Circuit for a Code with Code Polynomial** $G(X) = X^3 + X + 1$

and at the same time is shifted through the shift register circuit. When the last
bit of the message sequence has been shifted into stage 0 of the shift register,
the collection of registers holds a remainder that is the sequence of check bits
for the particular message. At this point, the switch is moved to position 2, and
the contents of the shift register are moved onto the line that follows the
message bits, which accomplishes step 3 and completes the encoded block.
(Note that the feedback circuit is broken while the contents of the shift
registers are shifted out.)

As just noted, decoding, or more specifically error detection, is accomplished by determining the syndrome, $S(X)$, which is the remainder after the
received polynomial $R(X)$ is divided by $G(X)$. This division, which produces
the desired remainder, can be carried out in a straightforward manner with
the shift register circuit previously discussed. A syndrome circuit for the code
of Fig. 2.30 is given in Fig. 2.31.

Properties of Error Detecting Codes
The construction and use of error detecting codes just discussed assume a
given parity check matrix or its equivalent, that is, a code generator matrix or
polynomial. In this subsection the quality of codes, as determined by their
error detecting ability, is discussed and related to properties of the parity
check matrix.

To begin the discussion, recall that a transmitted code word consists of n
bits: k information bits and $n - k$ parity or check bits. Each such code word, c,
(represented as a vector) is constructed so that $c \, M^t = 0$. Hence not all
arbitrary sequences of n bits qualify as a proper code word, and this fact is the
basis for error detection. (Recall the statement made earlier that errors cannot
be detected if all sequences of symbols are proper messages.)

The number of proper code words can be determined easily. There are 2^k
different sets of message bits that can be properly encoded. This is usually
reduced to $2^k - 1$ since the all-zero message is not used. A unique set of parity
bits is computed for each set of message bits, and thus the total number of
proper code words is the same as the number of messages, $2^k - 1$. For
reference, there are 2^n different combinations of n bits in an encoded block.

Error detection is based on the ability to determine when a received code word is corrupted so that it is no longer in the class of $2^k - 1$ proper code words. Error detection is carried out by computing the syndrome of the received vector (given by $\underline{r} = \underline{c} + \underline{e}$), and noting whether or not it is zero, as it would be for a proper code word. Mathematically the syndrome is given by

$$\underline{s} = \underline{r}\,M^t = \underline{c}\,M^t + \underline{e}\,M^t = \underline{e}\,M^t \qquad (2.46)$$

The last part of this equation follows from the facts that $\underline{r} = \underline{c} + \underline{e}$ and $\underline{c}M^t = 0$. This equation indicates that the syndrome is only a function of the error pattern and not the transmitted code word.

Error detection relies on the assumption that the syndrome will have nonzero components if errors are present. Unfortunately this is not always the case, as there are error patterns for which $\underline{e}M^t = 0$. Such undetectable error patterns occur if the pattern of errors is identical to the pattern of a proper code word so that $\underline{e} = \underline{c}$, where $\underline{c}$ indicates some proper code word. Since there are $2^k - 1$ proper code words, there are $2^k - 1$ undetectable error patterns.

For linear codes, the modulo-2 sum of two code words is another code word. Thus if $\underline{e} = \underline{c}$ and $\underline{c} = \underline{c}_1 + \underline{c}_2$, where $\underline{c}_1$ and $\underline{c}_2$ are code words other than $\underline{c}$, then

$$\underline{e} = \underline{c}_1 + \underline{c}_2 \text{ or } \underline{c}_1 = \underline{e} + \underline{c}_2 \qquad (2.47)$$

Equation (2.47) shows that an undetectable error pattern can also be thought of as an error pattern that changes one code word into another code word.

Using the point of view just described, a good code can be seen to be one for which proper code vectors differ in a large number of components so that it takes a large number of errors to change one into another. This idea has been quantified by defining *Hamming distance* for a code as the minimum difference between any two possible code vectors. Using modulo-2 arithmetic, Hamming distance can be defined mathematically as

$$\text{Hamming distance} = \min\,[\underline{c}_i + \underline{c}_j] \qquad (2.48)$$

for any two distinct code vectors i and j. It can be shown that the Hamming distance of a code is equal to the smallest number of columns in the parity check matrix that sum to zero. Since $\underline{c}_i + \underline{c}_j$ is another code word, the Hamming distance equals the minimum *weight* of the nonzero code words. (The weight of a code word is the number of "1"s that appear in it.)

To have an undetectable error, there must be at least as many errors as the Hamming distance of the code. Stated another way, the code can detect any random combination of errors with a number of errors less than the Hamming distance of the code.

In addition to the detection of random combinations of errors in a transmitted block, some statements can be made concerning the burst error detecting abilities of linear cyclic codes. An error burst is defined as a group of errors confined to a limited number of positions in the transmitted block of bits. The desired results follow from the manner in which the code words are constructed, and they can best be obtained with the polynomial representations.

Consider a code of block length n with k message bits and $(n - k)$ parity check bits. The following discussion shows that such a code is capable of detecting any error burst of length $(n - k)$ or less.

The argument involves the polynomial representations of the error pattern and the code word. An error burst of length $n - k$ starting at position i is represented by a polynomial $X^i K(X)$, where $K(X)$ is a polynomial of degree $n - k - 1$, as shown in Fig. 2.32. Note that the burst must start with an error and terminate $(n - k - 1)$ bit positions later with another error. Written as an equation, the error polynomial is given by

$$E(X) = X^i K(X) \tag{2.49}$$

where $0 \le i \le n - 1$ and $K(X)$ is a polynomial of degree $n - k - 1$.

Recall that each code polynomial is constructed with the code generator polynomial from the product $U(X) G(X)$, where $U(X)$ is a message polynomial. To have undetectable errors, the error pattern must be a code word pattern, i.e., $E(X) = U(X) G(X)$ for some $U(X)$.

Stated in another way, $E(X)$ must be divisible by $G(X)$ to have undetectable errors. Since $K(X)$ is of degree $n - k - 1$, less than that of $G(X)$, which is of degree $(n - k)$, $K(X)$ is not divisible by $G(X)$. It can be shown that $X^i K(X)$ is also not divisible by $G(X)$. The conclusion, then, is that all error bursts of length $(n - k)$ or less can be detected.

Using arguments very similar to the one just given, it can be shown that for error bursts longer than $(n - k)$ bits the fraction $2^{-(n-k-1)}$, of bursts of length $n - k + 1$, are detectable and that the fraction $2^{-(n-k)}$, of bursts of any length greater than $n - k + 1$, are undetectable. This assumes that all bit patterns are equally likely.

Most codes used for error detection can detect all single and double errors and all errors resulting in odd parity, in addition to the burst error properties previously described. The "natural" block length of typical codes generated by a polynomial of degree $n - k$ is $2^{n-k} - 1$. For generator polynomials of degree 16 and higher, the natural block length is very long and is usually truncated on

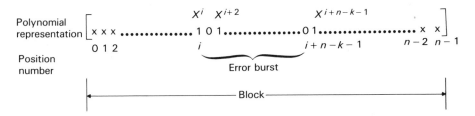

Figure 2.32 A Typical Error Burst

the order of 2,000 bits without affecting the error detecting properties of the code.

Current practice seems to favor CRC polynomials of degree 16, although standards for such polynomials of degree 32 have been prepared, and some are being used. The standard choices detect all single and double errors and all errors that result in odd parity in blocks of any practical length. For 16 check bits, all error bursts of 16 bits or less are detected, along with approximately $(1 - 2^{-15}) \times 100\%$ or 99.997% of bursts of length 17 bits and $(1 - 2^{-16}) \times 100\%$ or 99.998% of bursts longer than 17 bits. The corresponding figures for 32 check bits are all bursts of 32 bits or less, 99.99999995% of bursts of length 33, and 99.99999998% of bursts longer than 33. Code generator polynomials specified in several standards are:

CRC-16 $\qquad 1 + X^2 + X^{15} + X^{16}$

CRC-CCITT $\quad 1 + X^5 + X^{12} + X^{16}$

CRC-32 $\qquad 1 + X + X^2 + X^4 + X^5 + X^7 + X^8 + X^{10} + X^{11} + X^{12}$

$\qquad\qquad\quad + X^{16} + X^{22} + X^{23} + X^{26} + X^{32}$

As a final comment on CRC codes, note that undetected error probabilities depend on the error patterns characteristic of the channel used. Good codes, of the type cited above, have very low undetected error rates and hence require enormous amounts of data for empirical estimates of error. Brayer [9], in working with measured data on the Autovon channel, has found no undetected errors in 157,000 blocks of 2048 bits in length using the 32-bit code previously cited (20,264 error bursts greater than 32 bits occurred). Hammond [10] has estimated the probability of undetected error, under essentially the conditions used by Brayer, at 3×10^{-14}. Comparable data for other codes do not seem to be available.

2.3.4 ARQ Schemes

An integral part of the error-detection with retransmission, or ARQ, approach to error control is the retransmission strategy. For ARQ to function, the receiving station must be able to inform the transmitting station whether or not a transmisson is received correctly, without errors. To accomplish this, a reverse channel, from receiver to transmitter, must always exist. Over this reverse channel the receiver can send back positive and negative acknowledgements (ACK and NAK), or only positive acknowledgements. If only ACKs are used, the existence of a bad transmission is discovered through the absence of an ACK in some specified "timeout" period. The latter approach is often used with full duplex channels, and the ACK is frequently piggybacked onto the next outgoing transmission over the reverse channel.

There are two principal ARQ variations—stop-and-wait ARQ and continuous ARQ. What precise scheme is best to use depends on a number of factors: the channel propagation delay, packet size, the bit error rate on the channel, and perhaps the trade-off between channel utilization and nodal storage. For both types of ARQ, a copy of the transmitted packet is retained at the transmitting node until there is confirmation that it has been received without error.

In *stop-and-wait* ARQ, the sending node sends one block of data and waits for an acknowledgement before the next block is sent. If an ACK is received, the copy of the transmitted block stored at the node is discarded, and the next block is transmitted. If a NAK is received, either as an explicit transmission or through a time-out, the block is retransmitted. Stop-and-wait ARQ is most effective when the block transmission time is much greater than the sum of the propagation delays and the decoding time at the receiving node.

An alternative to this strategy is to transmit blocks continuously without waiting for acknowledgements, although some ceiling is usually put on the number of unacknowledged messages that are outstanding. This approach is called a *sliding window* scheme, where the size of the window is the maximum number of unacknowledged messages permitted. As a matter of fact, stop-and-wait can be regarded as a special case of a sliding window protocol where the window size is one. A disadvantage of the sliding window method is that for a sending window of size n, the transmitting node must have n buffers to store copies of the n messages in transit that may require retransmission.

There are two basic approaches to the handling of errors with the sliding window scheme. In *go-back-N* ARQ, the transmitting station must retransmit the block that was detected in error as well as all succeeding blocks. After the receiving station detects an error in a block, it does not store it or any succeeding blocks until the arrival of the retransmitted block that corrects the error. This ensures that the blocks at the receiving node are in the correct sequence with a minimum of processing and without much storage. A disadvantage is that the procedure is inefficient with respect to channel utilization, especially if the error rate is high.

In the *selective repeat* strategy, which is the alternative approach, only the block detected in error is retransmitted. This is much more efficient with respect to channel utilization, but more buffer space and more complex processing are required at the receiving node to store all the blocks received correctly and then reassemble them into the correct sequence after the block originally in error is properly retransmitted. A further drawback to selective repeat is that multiple errors in different blocks can lead to very complex recovery sequences.

2.4 Switching and Multiplexing

2.4.1 Introduction

Discussion so far in this chapter has centered on certain design considerations for transmitting data over dedicated point-to-point connections. Such issues as basic waveforms for transmitting bits in a bit stream, the effect of channel bandwidth, effects of noise, and error control, have been discussed.

Communication networks, both local and global, are designed to provide data communication paths between any pairs of users connected to the network. A connection between users must be available when needed, but demand for specific connections is highly variable—a connection is often needed for short periods of time and then is not required for even longer periods. Given this type of demand, it is typically not economical to provide a dedicated connection between every pair of users connected to the network. Thus networks and parts of networks are designed to share circuits and to share point-to-point links. Both types of facility sharing are discussed in this subsection under the headings of switching and multiplexing. The latter refers to the sharing of circuits and the former to sharing of links or channels.

2.4.2 Switching

Switching enables a network to operate with less than the facilities that would be required to provide dedicated connections between every pair of users. With switching, two users are not permanently connected. However, a link between the users can be set up on demand when it is needed.

A dedicated link between every pair of users obviously provides the highest grade of service. Cost is the (significant) drawback for such operation. Cost is significantly reduced when a connection on demand is provided with switching. The attendant difficulties include: availability—can a circuit be provided when needed? connection and release time—the delay in making the user-to-user connection and in releasing it when the need is over; and required overhead, if all transmitted data cannot be used for messages.

Switching is normally done in one of two general ways: circuit switching or store-and-forward switching. Circuit switching sets up on demand a dedicated connection between users. The connection may extend across a complete network, through a number of intermediate nodes, and consists of a sequence of physical links connected as required. The connection is initially set up with some sort of control signals, and when the message transmission is complete, the connection is released. Store-and-forward switching, in contrast to circuit switching, does not set up links dedicated to the required connection. For typical store-and-forward type operation, messages to be transmitted are partitioned into packets, and the packets are then sent independently through the network in much the same way as automobiles proceed through a freeway system.

Circuit switching is the older of the two methods and has been in use for many years in the telephone system. Its characteristics are rather straightforward. When demand for a connection arises, some time is required to set up the physical sequence of links required for the connection. This is the time consumed in dialing in a telephone system. Although not of concern to a single user, some amount of time is required to break an established connection and free the links for other users. This break time is also a part of network overhead.

In addition to the time to make and break a connection, there are two other major features of circuit switching:

1. Once a connection is made, control overhead is low, since routing and so forth are not problems, and
2. Once a connection is made, it remains in force for the duration of data exchange whether or not the data flow is uniform.

The former is an advantage, while the latter can be a disadvantage when the data flow ceases for substantial parts of a data exchange interval; other users could be using the channel during this idle time.

This discussion assumes that links are available to make end-to-end connections when they are required. A final point for circuit switching is that sufficient facilities must be provided to meet peak needs. Such "busy hour" demands can normally be provided on a statistical basis so that most customers are satisfied most of the time.

Store-and-forward operation using packet switching[†] is less straightforward than circuit switching. For this type of operation, messages are partitioned into packets, with appropriate addresses, CRC and other overhead, and the packets are transferred through the network, moving from node-to-node. At each node, packets are stored temporarily to read overhead information, such as packet destination, and to check for errors. Also, if adaptive routing is used, a route for the packet must be determined. As a part of error control, a copy of each packet is retained at each transit node until an acknowledgment is received to indicate that the packet was received correctly at the succeeding node.

There are two modes in which to operate a store-and-forward network: to provide virtual circuits or to deliver datagrams. For datagram service, the network delivers packets as isolated units. Packets are checked for errors as they are transferred from node to node, but they are not guaranteed to be delivered in order or even be delivered at all. Each packet must contain its own destination address.

Virtual circuits, on the other hand, have some of the properties of switched circuits. An end-to-end set-up procedure that requires that initial packets have a destination address is initiated first. This is followed by a data transfer phase during which packets follow an established route and do not need their own addresses. Packets are delivered in order, and packets with errors are retransmitted. An end-to-end shut-down phase is required when data transfer is over.

There are several advantages and some disadvantages to store-and-forward operation. Although there are differences between the two modes of operation,

---

†Message, as opposed to packet, switching is also possible but not discussed here.

Chapter 2 **Data Communication**

the major advantage shared by both is the increased utilization of network facilities. Packets from several connections can share a channel and follow one another with little or no lost time in between. This should be contrasted to circuit switching for which channels and other facilities can be idle for significant periods during a connection phase if the transmitter is active only in bursts.

Store-and-forward operation, which naturally subdivides the data stream into blocks, makes error control of the type discussed in the last subsection easy to apply. It also makes possible speed conversion (i.e., operation of a connection with different input and output rates).

To mention several of the disadvantages, delay for both types of store-and-forward operation can be greater than for a switched circuit. Once a circuit switch makes a connection through physical links, the only delay suffered by a data stream is that due to propagation. A flow of packets in store-and-forward operation, on the other hand, is from node to node, with delays experienced at each node. Creating packets and reassembling them is another source of delay. The need for overhead in some or all of the packets makes store-and-forward operation less efficient than circuit switched operation if traffic requires continuous, uniform data flows.

2.4.3 Multiplexing

Multiplexing is the term for using a single channel to carry several different data streams concurrently. The need for this type of link sharing can be shown by an examination of characteristics of transmission media.

A typical voice communication channel can support data rates of up to 9600 bps, while microwave radio and coax cables can support rates up to hundreds of megabits per second. The cost of such transmission media is not directly proportional to bandwidth or data rate. On the contrary, available media tend to come with several quantized values of cost and with several quantized values of bandwidth and possible data rates.

Data processing devices also produce, or require, data rates that are relatively inflexible. Low speed devices, such as teletype machines, produce bit rates in hundreds of bits per second when they are active. CRT terminals operate in the 1 to 10 Kbps range, with smart terminals at the high end of the range. Computers, when they communicate from a disk or some other type of memory, can output data at rates that approach the clock rate of the computer. All types of digital data, of the sort being discussed, tend to be "bursty" in the sense that the idle time between bursts or segments of data is often much greater than the actual data transmission time.

Ideal utilization of a connecting link maintains traffic over the links at a value close to the capacity of the transmission medium. The characteristics of such media and data sources lead, however, to a mismatch in data rates between most single devices and most single choices of transmission medium for the device to communicate over. For example, a high-grade voice telephone channel can support a continuous data rate up to 9600 bps. A computer communicating data from a disk requires substantially more capacity than this, while a teletype machine, when active, requires only a fraction of the available capacity.

Such considerations have led to line sharing or multiplexing to produce a net data rate that uses line capacity effectively. In operation, a multiplexer combines signals at one end of the shared channel, and a demultiplexer sorts them out at the other end and routes each signal to the proper destination. By way of terminology, both multiplexers and demultiplexers are often termed MUX. Line sharing reduces the costs of connecting links, and the more uniform data rates that result also lead to economies in other parts of a network.

Three important types of line sharing or multiplexing are discussed: frequency division multiplex (FDM), synchronous time division multiplex (STDM), and asynchronous time division multiplexing (ASTDM) or concentration. Frequency division multiplex and synchronous time division multiplex both make a fixed deterministic subdivision of the available bandwidth independently of the instantaneous traffic profile of the data sources. Asynchronous time division multiplex, on the other hand, leads to more efficiencies by assigning channel bandwidth on a demand basis to those stations that currently need it. Each type of multiplex is now discussed in turn.

Frequency Division Multiplex

Of the three types of multiplex, frequency division multiplex (FDM) is the simplest to describe and understand. For this type of multiplexing, a number of different users share the same transmission medium through deterministic allocations of different segments of bandwidth to each user. The signal spectrum for each user's signal is shifted into the proper bandwidth slot through modulation.

Figure 2.33 shows a basic block diagram for a typical modulator and also shows the baseband spectrum for a single signal and the corresponding shifted spectrum after modulation. Figure 2.34(a) shows how a number of different signals can be fitted into a sequence of frequency slots spread out across the transmission band of the channel. This is of course accomplished by choosing the appropriate sequence of modulating frequencies. A complete FDM system, with N users sharing the line, is shown in Fig. 2.34(b).

As can be noted in Fig. 2.34(a), with normal filters it is difficult to achieve a rapid cutoff of the signal spectra and hence sharp separation between user signal bands. It is thus necessary to specify narrow *guard bands* between different allocations of bandwidth. Such guard bands result in wasted increments of the transmission band and hence reduced bandwidth efficiency.

Other properties of FDM worth noting are: the signals that correspond to the various different users do not have to be synchronized, and the cost of an FDM system is primarily in the modulators, demodulators, and filters that are

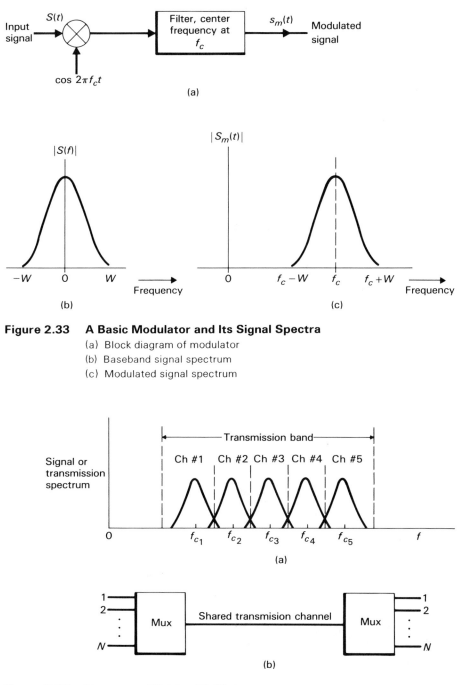

Figure 2.33   A Basic Modulator and Its Signal Spectra

(a) Block diagram of modulator
(b) Baseband signal spectrum
(c) Modulated signal spectrum

Figure 2.34   Frequency Division Multiplex

(a) Signal spectrum
(b) Block diagram for N shared users

required to subdivide the transmission band. If the channel transmission bandwidth is B Hertz, the approximate bandwidth allocated to each of N users is B/N. Because bit rate and bandwidth are proportional, each user can communicate at a bit rate of $1/N^{th}$ of that of the bit rate supported by the unshared channel.

Synchronous Time Division Multiplex

Synchronous time division multiplex (STDM) carries out the sharing of the transmission medium by making a deterministic, sequential allocation of time

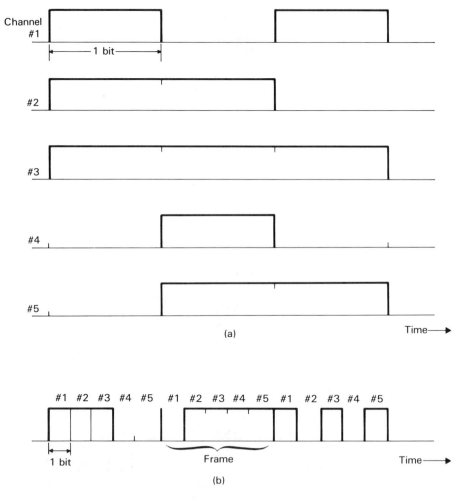

Figure 2.35 A Time Division Multiplex for Five Signals
(a) Signals on input channels
(b) Output multiplexed signal

intervals, or slots, to each user. The time slots, one for each user plus overhead, are typically organized into frames so that each active user is allocated a time slot in each frame. The multiplexer transmitter and receiver operate much like a pair of synchronized switches, which activate one user–user connection at a time.

As an example, a time division multiplex for five signals is shown in Fig. 2.35. In this simple example, overhead is not considered, so the time allocations to the five users, shown in the figure, add up to the full frame. Since this is the case, the shared line connecting the multiplexers must have a bit rate equal to five times that of each multiplexed signal, or, stated another way, the bit periods of each user signal are five times the bit periods on the shared channel. Representative, but idealized, signals for each of the multiplexed users and for the shared channel are shown in the figure.

In typical applications, multiplexing speed is set so that either one bit (as implied in Fig. 2.35), one byte, or even a fixed length packet, is transmitted each time a particular connection is made. During the time interval allocated to each user, the full bit rate of the medium can be used. Thus, if the bit rate of the shared channel is R bits/second, then, when there are N users being multiplexed, each can operate at a data rate of R bits/second one N^{th} of the time or at an equivalent continuous rate of R/N bits/seconds, neglecting overhead. In general, TDM systems need buffers to facilitate speed conversion between input and output data rates.

Unlike FDM, STDM requires that the multiplexed signals be synchronized. The need for synchronization in STDM is apparent since the multiplexed signals are interleaved in time and thus require fixed relative phases. In addition to synchronization of the input signals, STDM requires frame synchronization between the input MUX and the output MUX to route signals to the proper users.

Synchronization of incoming signals for STDM can be achieved in many cases by using a single clock to time all signals. If this is not possible, some means such as "pulse stuffing"† must be used to bring signals timed by different clocks into synchronization.

Frame synchronization is maintained by overhead bits in a special pattern to identify the beginning (and possibly also the ending) of each frame. Frame synchronization is initially acquired by a sequence of several special frames with dedicated bit patterns. These synchronization patterns are identified and "locked onto" by multiplex circuitry in a frame acquisition phase of operation during which no data is sent.

As a final comment, even though STDM requires synchronization and FDM does not, a properly operating STDM multiplexer achieves better utilization of the high-speed shared medium than does FDM.

---

†Pulse stuffing is a technique of periodically adding a redundant pulse to bring one bit stream into synchronization with another. The "stuffed" pulse must be tracked and removed before data is extracted from the bit stream.

Asynchronous Time Division Multiplexing

Asynchronous time division multiplexing (ASTDM), or concentrating, is a technique for combining a number of signals so a common channel is shared on a demand basis. Recall that for STDM and FDM, each user is allocated channel capacity on a fixed deterministic basis that does not vary with time. As a result of the fixed allocations, channel capacity is often wasted if user demands fluctuate in a random manner. Asynchronous time division multiplexing is tailored to accommodate input that fluctuates randomly; for such input, utilization of the shared channel can be significantly increased.

Figure 2.36 shows the essential parts of a concentrator or ASTDM. The line from each input is terminated in a short term buffer memory that stores packets as they arrive. These line buffers, for all the input, are polled by a scanner that immediately transfers bytes or packets from the line buffers into a central buffer where they join a queue for the shared channel. Since packets from all the user input are mixed on the shared channel, each packet must be identified with overhead data that gives its destination for use at the output of the concentrator pair. At the output, destination addresses for each packet must be read and the packets routed to the proper destination. Unlike STDM, the packets transmitted by different users do not necessarily have the same length.

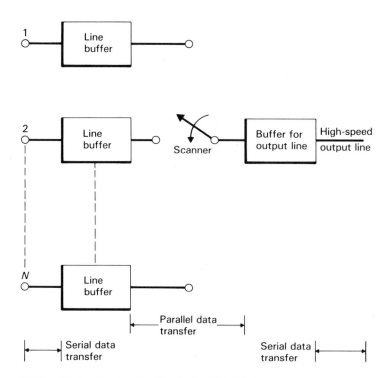

Figure 2.36   Major Parts of a Statistical Multiplexer

For the ASTDM type of operation, under light loads a packet from any user is picked up almost immediately by the input scanner, transferred to the central buffer, and processed out over the shared channel. Users with no packets to send contribute little overhead since their line buffers remain empty and hence require no attention other than that required to identify their condition as empty. With increasing loads, the channel-sharing technique still functions, but with more delay. The scanning operation is slowed down as more packets must be transferred to the central buffer, and a queue for the shared channel builds up. With this type of operation, it is possible for buffer overflow or blocking to occur for sufficiently high loads; in such a case, packets are lost.

The central design issue for concentrators is the tradeoff between time delay, number of user input lines, and output channel capacity. As mentioned previously, overhead in terms of addresses is also required, but this overhead is often necessary for other reasons apart from the multiplexing.

As a concluding comment, a properly designed concentrator pair can allow a number of users to make efficient use of a shared channel with tolerable time delays. The trade-offs favor a type of service for which user demand fluctuates randomly, as opposed to steady and deterministic demand. For this type of operation, the users gain ready access to the shared channel when they have data to transmit. As demands from some users lessen, other users take over without the rigidity imposed by a deterministic allocation of channel capacity.

2.4.4 Broadband Systems

In the terminology of local networks, a multichannel broadband system is one for which FDM is used to create a number of separate transmission bands on a single transmission system, such as a coaxial cable. The bands are created with modulated signals with different carrier frequencies spaced to provide the required bandwidths for each band. A significant feature of the modulated signals is that transmission and reception are unidirectional and depend on the location of the transmitter and the receiver. This is in contrast to baseband signals for which transmission and reception can be in either direction over the same channel.

Since a station on a network should be able to transmit to and receive from any other station, FDM broadband systems are designed so that a station transmits in a band with one carrier, for example, f_1, and receives in a different band with a different carrier, such as f_2. To make this system operable, frequency translation from one passband to another should take place somewhere in the system. This is done at the so-called *headend*—a term borrowed from the Community Antenna Television (CATV) industry. A station transmits to the headend at f_1 and receives from the headend at f_2 so that transmission for any band is in only one direction.

As indicated in Fig. 2.37, this type of transmission can be implemented in either of two ways. In the dual-cable mode, the stations transmit on one cable

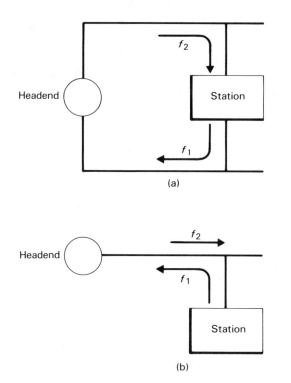

(a)

(b)

Figure 2.37   Transmission and Reception on Broadband Systems
        (a) Dual-cable mode
        (b) Single-cable mode

and receive on the other. In this case, the carrier frequencies can be either the same or different.

In the other mode, a single cable is used. Transmission "upstream," to the headend, takes place over one group of bands, often low frequency bands, and transmission "downstream," from the headend to the stations, takes place over a different group of bands, often high frequency bands.

2.5   Summary

This chapter reviews data communication as a background for topics covered later in the text. The material is discussed under three headings: Digital Communications, Error Control, and Switching and Multiplexing.

Digital communications deal with the problems of representing and transmitting digital signals on a bit-by-bit basis. Key concepts are those of bandwidth of both signals and systems, modulation, and signal sets.

Conveying of bits over a channel is carried out in time sequence, either one bit at a time (serial) or several bits at a time (parallel). Both modes of operation can be either synchronous or asynchronous. Each of these variations is discussed in the chapter in some detail.

The next topic is error control, which treats the issue of preserving the integrity of data in a noisy environment to meet the stringent requirements of computers. The method discussed is a strategy called automatic repeat request (ARQ), which is typically used in local networks. This type of error control requires two steps: detection of errors, using some type of redundancy, and retransmission of blocks in which errors are detected. Common types of error detecting codes are reviewed briefly in the chapter.

The final topics of Chapter 2 concern ways in which a number of users can share the same network and ways in which a number of signals can share the same channel. Network sharing includes a discussion of switching, which is contained in Section 2.4.2. Channel sharing leads to a discussion of multiplexing, which can be carried out as time division or frequency division multiplexing, or asynchronous time division multiplexing.

The next step is to develop the background required to discuss the flow of discrete entities, such as packets, when such flow is random in nature. Chapter 3 develops the required concepts for data flow in networks and queues.

References

[1] F. G. Stremler. *Introduction to Communication Systems.* 2nd Edition. Reading, MA: Addison-Wesley, 1982.

[2] R. E. Ziemer and W. H. Tranter. *Principles of Communication.* Boston: Houghton-Mifflin Company, 1976.

[3] P. E. Green. *Computer Network Architectures and Protocols.* New York: Plenum Press, 1982.

[4] J. E. McNamara. *Technical Aspects of Data Communication.* Maynard, MA: Digital Press, 1978.

[5] G. R. Cooper and C. D. McGillem. *Probabilistic Methods of Signal and System Analysis.* New York: Holt, Rinehart and Winston, Inc., 1971.

[6] L. N. Kanal and A. R. K. Sastry. "Models for Channels with Memory and Their Applications to Error Control." *Proceedings of the IEEE* 66 (July 1978): 724–744.

[7] R. W. Hamming. *Coding and Information Theory.* Englewood Cliffs, NJ: Prentice-Hall, Inc., 1980.

[8] S. Lin and D. J. Costello. *Error Control Coding: Fundamentals and Applications.* Englewood Cliffs, NJ: Prentice-Hall, Inc., 1983.

[9] K. Brayer and J. L. Hammond. "Evaluation of Error Detection Polynomial Performance on the Autovon Channel." Conference Record, National Telecommunications Conference, New Orleans, LA (1975): 8-21–8-25.

[10] J. L. Hammond, J. E. Brown, and S. S. Liu. "Development of a Transmission Error Model and an Error Control Model." Technical Report, Rome Air Development Center, RADC-TR-75-138, (May 1975).

Problems and Exercises

1. (a) One sometimes sees the bandwidth of a communication link given in bits/sec. Assume a binary system with sinusoidal roll-off pulses transmitted by modems. Relate data rate, R, to bandwidth in Hz and comment on the initial statement.

   (b) For a fixed data rate in bits/sec., give two ways that the required bandwidth can be reduced. State specifically how the bandwidth can be reduced to $\frac{1}{3}$ of its value in (a).

2. A square time pulse has a width of 5 μsec.

   (a) Sketch the magnitude of its Fourier Transform as a function of frequency.

   (b) Determine the bandwidth (between half-power points) required to transmit the pulse with acceptable distortion.

3. An 8-bit storage register is filled in parallel by a computer and is used to transmit data serially. The system clock rate is 1 Mbps; a character is eight bits, both for the computer and on the serial line. What time is required to fill the register, and what time is required to transmit a serial character?

4. (a) A communication line has a 4KHz bandwidth. Find the maximum data rate for binary-type signaling:

   (i) Using the rule of thumb, and

   (ii) Assuming that the transmitted signals have a raised cosine shape with a role-off factor equal to 1.

   (b) Modify the rule of (a) to apply if two overhead bits must be added to every eight bits. Line bandwidth should be related to *data* rate in bits/second.

5. The major components of an asynchronous data link are shown in the diagram below. The transmit holding register is supplied 8 data bits by a computer (not shown). Assume that start and stop bits are supplied instantaneously. The transmit shift register clocks out bits at the bit rate of the connecting line (4600 bps). At the instant the last bit of a 10-bit character is out of the transmit register, the register is refilled by transferring bits in parallel from the holding register over a 9600 bps line. The 10-bit asynchronous character on the serial link contains 8 data bits and start and stop bits.

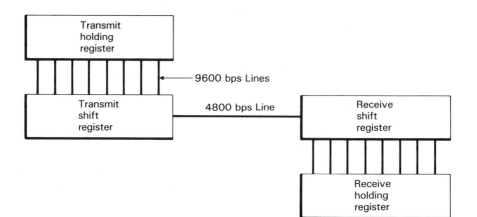

(a) Without restriction to the structure shown, what is the least possible time required to transmit a 10-bit character over the 4600 bps line?

(b) What time, T_1, is required to clock out a 10-bit character already stored in the transmit register?

(c) What time, T_2, is required to refill the transmit register with 8 data bits?

(d) What is the average bit rate on the line for steady-state operation as described?

(e) What is the average data bit rate on the line for steady-state operation as described?

6. The basic signal set for Manchester encoding is given in Fig. 2.14. Sketch the Manchester and differential Manchester encoded signals for the bit sequence 1 0 1 1 1 0 1.

7. (a) Using pulses with raised cosine frequency characteristics with $\alpha = 0.3, 0.5$, and 1, find the channel bandwidths required for modems of baud rates 1800, 9600, and 50K Baud respectively.

(b) If Manchester encoded pulses are used for such baseband transmissions (with $\alpha = 1$) find the required channel bandwidth for each of the modems.

8. Synchronous transmissions use at least one sync character or byte. Consider an 8-bit sync character such as the ASCII SYN (10010110).

(a) What is the probability that such a SYN character will be matched by data?

(b) If q is the bit error probability, what is the probability of any character, such as SYN, being in error?

(c) ASCII characters include a parity bit. What is the probability of such a character error being detected?

(d) It is often required that two consecutive SYN characters be decoded before synchronous transmission can develop. If p is the character error probability, what is the probability of the synchronous transmission not developing if

(i) two consecutive SYN characters are transmitted;

(ii) three consecutive SYN characters are transmitted;

(iii) four consecutive SYN characters are transmitted.

9. A code uses $g(X) = X^3 + X^2 + 1$ as the generator polynomial. Determine the code vectors that correspond to the message vectors 1001 and 1011.

10. A code uses $X^3 + X^2 + 1$ as the generator polynomial. The vector 1 0 0 1 0 0 1 is received. Use long division to determine the syndrome of the received vector, and hence whether or not errors are present.

11. A basic "group" for an A-type channel bank in the Bell system hierarchy contains 12 voice grade signals multiplexed using FDM. The bandwidth of each voice signal is 3 KHz plus a 1 KHz guard band which is required between adjacent signals. The frequency division multiplex is carried out using a form of amplitude modulation for which the lower sideband is removed leaving only the carrier and upper sideband. (This type of modulation is termed single sideband or SSB.)

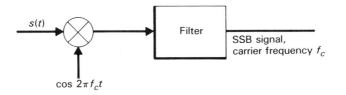

(a) Sketch the frequency spectrum of the multiplexed signal taking 60 KHz as the lower edge of the band.

(b) A basic modulator can be diagramed as shown above using a multiplier and an appropriate filter. Show a block diagram of the complete 12-signal multiplexer indicating all input signals.

12. The Bell system T1 carrier has 24 voice channels multiplexed using TDM. Each 4 KHz voice channel is sampled at an 8 KHz rate (referred to as Nyquist sampling). The resulting samples are quantized and converted to 7-bit digital "codewords" which are transmitted as pulse code modulation, i.e. using a positive pulse for each "1" bit and a space of equal length to the pulse width for each "0" bit. An extra sync bit is added to each codeword. Sampling is carried out by sampling one channel at a time in sequence until all 24 channels are sampled. All of the pulses for the codewords from the 24 channels are combined into a "frame." The frame has a single extra bit for frame sync.

(a) How many discrete quantizing levels are available with the 7-bit digital codeword?

(b) Sketch a frame of the T1 carrier.

(c) What is the overall data rate on the channel?

(d) Estimate the required channel bandwidth.

*D*ata Flow in Networks and Queues

3.1 Introduction

The data flow in computer communication networks is typically nonuniform or stochastic in nature. At any point in a network, the times of arrival of the basic data unit (character, packet, message) are random variables.

The time to process a message over a channel or through a device typically depends on the number of bits in the message, although the time to process one bit or one character is often constant. In many applications the message length is a random variable, and when this is the case, the processing time for a message also becomes a random variable.

Performance analysis of computer networks is concerned with the nature and characteristics of data flow. Efficiency, throughput, delay, and other parameters of interest are measures of how the network processes the messages it must transmit to fulfill its function. Thus, to carry out quantitative performance analysis, mathematical models that interrelate the important parameters of message flow must be employed. The mathematical framework of queueing theory provides one important type of model that is frequently used for this purpose.

Queueing systems deal with processes in which customers arrive or are generated, wait their turn for service, are serviced, and then depart. Many of the access protocols for local area networks involve such a sequence, with messages playing the role of customers in the processes. Thus, appropriate queueing models can be used to study local area networks to develop quantitative measures of performance, such as the average delay–throughput tradeoff characteristics.

Section 3.2 discusses properties of steady-state data flows of networks that do not depend on the statistical nature of the message lengths and their arrival times to the network. Section 3.3 then analyzes a general class of queueing models that involve a single buffer and channel. Two more specific models are developed in greater detail. Section 3.4 follows with an analysis of priority queues, in particular, the nonpreemptive type. The chapter concludes with a brief discussion of networks of queues.

3.2 Steady-state Data Flow

Several important properties of the steady-state (average) flow of discrete entities such as messages or packets can be developed independent of the precise statistical distributions of the parameters that define the flows. These properties are shared by systems with other variables, such as automobiles on a freeway or people in an amusement park.

Consider a closed boundary, such as that in Fig. 3.1, that contains a network with one or more input message ports and one or more output message ports that cross the boundary. Assume that the network conserves messages in the sense that messages are not created, destroyed, or modified by the network. Because messages are not created or destroyed, they can then either flow in or out of the network across the boundary or be stored in the network within the boundary.

If the average input rate across the boundary exceeds the average output rate, then the number of messages stored within the boundary constantly increases. On the other hand, if the average output rate exceeds the average input rate, the number of messages stored constantly decreases to zero, at which point the average output rate can no longer exceed the average input rate.

From these considerations it is concluded that for a stable network in the steady state (i.e., after a long time), the average input and output rates across the closed boundary must be equal.

The term *average* has been used without an explicit definition. Actually, the random flows of messages into and out of networks are modeled as random processes for which averages are defined in two ways: as time averages, or as statistical or ensemble averages. Fortunately, for stable networks that operate in the steady state, behavior at one time is statistically equivalent to behavior at another. Furthermore, stable networks in the steady state are typically modeled by random processes for which averages over time are equal to

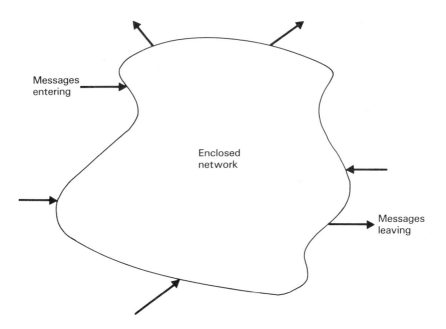

Figure 3.1　A Network within a Closed Boundary

statistical averages over many different samples. Equality of the two kinds of averages is assumed throughout the following analyses.

It is instructive to refer to Fig. 3.1 again and consider more quantitatively the behavior of several quantities that describe flow. Let $\alpha(t)$ denote the number of input messages and $\delta(t)$ the number of output messages for the network in some time interval $(0, t)$. The difference in these quantities, $N(t)$, is the increase in the number of messages stored in the network over the interval, that is,

$$N(t) = \alpha(t) - \delta(t) \tag{3.1}$$

Typical time histories of these variables over a short time interval are shown in Fig. 3.2 for the sequence of inputs and outputs shown. Since the input and output sequences are random, the time profiles of the variables would potentially be different for other intervals.

Tractable, deterministic measures of flow can be obtained by averaging variables such as those just defined. The average input rate over an interval of length t, λ_t, is a measure of this type defined as

$$\lambda_t = \frac{\alpha(t)}{t} \tag{3.2}$$

Another measure, $\gamma(t)$, is the total time all messages have spent in the network, (i.e., $\gamma(t)$ is the total area between the curves $\alpha(t)$ and $\delta(t)$. Thus,

$$\gamma(t) = \int_0^t N(x)\, dx \tag{3.3}$$

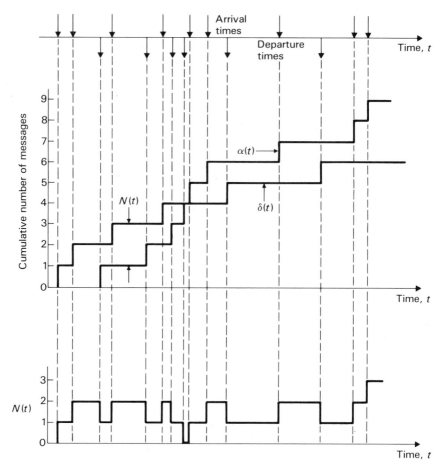

Figure 3.2   Typical Time Histories of Inputs, Outputs, and Number in the Network for Steady-state Flow

Proceeding one step further, the average number of messages, N_t, in the network over the interval $(0, t)$ is clearly given by

$$N_t = \frac{1}{t} \int_0^t N(x)\,dx = \frac{\gamma(t)}{t} \tag{3.4}$$

The time messages spend in the network, which is equal to the time interval between message arrival and departure, is a further variable of interest. Examination of the typical time history of Fig. 3.2 shows that time spent in the network is different for almost every message and that it is also a random variable. Its average, T, over all messages that arrive in a long time interval is used frequently in characterizing network behavior. Let T_t be the average time spent in the network during $(0, t)$ by all those messages that entered the network during the same period. Since $\gamma(t)$ is the total time spent by $\alpha(t)$ messages in the network, it follows that the average time spent in the network by any single message is given by

$$T_t = \frac{\gamma(t)}{\alpha(t)} \tag{3.5}$$

(This equation ignores the fact that some messages, entering on $(0,t)$ and thus included in $\alpha(t)$, may not have departed within the interval. However, as t grows, the effect of such messages becomes negligible.)

The three average variables λ_t, N_t, and T_t are clearly not independent, and the relationship between them follows from combining Eqs. (3.2), (3.4), and (3.5) to obtain

$$N_t = \lambda_t \, T_t \tag{3.6}$$

Assume that as t gets very large (i.e., $t \to \infty$), N_t, λ_t and T_t all remain finite so that

$$\lambda = \operatorname*{Lim}_{t \to \infty} \lambda_t$$

$$T = \operatorname*{Lim}_{t \to \infty} T_t$$

$$N = \operatorname*{Lim}_{t \to \infty} N_t \tag{3.7}$$

Thus, for large t, Eq. (3.6) becomes

$$N = \lambda T \tag{3.8}$$

which is a very important result for the average behavior of a network. This result, known as Little's Law, states that the average number of messages stored in a network is equal to the product of the average arrival rate of messages to the network and the average time these messages spend in the network. The result applies to any closed boundary that contains network elements, so that "closed boundary" could replace "network" in the preceding descriptions.

While the preceding argument offers a heuristic proof of Little's Law, more rigorous proofs have been made by a number of authors; unfortunately, all of these depend on stochastic process theory, which is beyond the scope of the present treatment. Stidham [1] gives one of the most thorough proofs, and his work can be consulted by those with sufficient background.

Little's Law is valid for any deterministic or stochastic input–output system in which discrete units enter the system, remain for a finite period of time, and then depart. A sort of continuity of flow is required in the sense that discrete units either are moving through the system or are stored while all available channels are busy.

Several additional relations between averaged quantities in the steady state can be obtained by considering a typical network, such as that shown in Fig. 3.3, which has a single output channel. A time history of variables, similar to that in Fig. 3.2, can be constructed for the single-output network subject to the

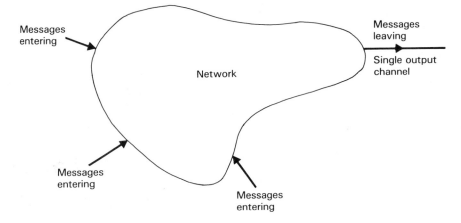

Figure 3.3   A Typical Network with One Output Channel

following additional restrictions. It is assumed that only one message can depart at a single instant of time and that the messages are processed and leave in the same order as they arrive. (Multiple arrivals at the same instant are not prohibited; the order of the departures of such messages must be decided by some suitable scheme.) This type of processing, or service, is known as *first-come, first-served* (FCFS).

Figure 3.4 shows a diagram for the time interval between the departures of the ith and $(i + 1)^{th}$ messages. In the figure, N_i and N_{i+1} denote the number of messages stored in the network immediately after the departure of the ith and $(i + 1)^{th}$ messages respectively at the times t_i and t_{i+1}. A difference equation will be constructed to relate N_i and N_{i+1}. Two cases are distinguished, namely: $N_i > 0$ and $N_i = 0$. Difference equations are written for the two cases separately and then they are combined by an appropriately defined variable.

For $N_i > 0$, there is at least one message in the network to be processed out over the channel, and hence processing on message $(i + 1)$ begins immediately after message i departs, as shown in Fig. 3.4(a). During the processing of message $(i + 1)$, new messages can arrive into the network. Thus the number of messages stored after message $(i + 1)$ departs is given by

$$N_{i+1} = N_i - 1 + A_{i+1}, \quad N_i > 0 \tag{3.9}$$

where A_{i+1} denotes the number of arrivals during the processing time of message $(i + 1)$.

In the second case, shown in Fig. 3.4(b), no message is present at t_i, and the network remains empty until an arrival occurs. Once an arrival does occur, the network immediately begins processing it as the $(i + 1)^{th}$ message. Upon departure of this message, i.e., at time t_{i+1}, the number of messages left in the network is just the number that arrived during that processing time, which begins immediately after the arrival of the $(i + 1)^{th}$ message and continues

Chapter 3   Data Flow in Networks and Queues

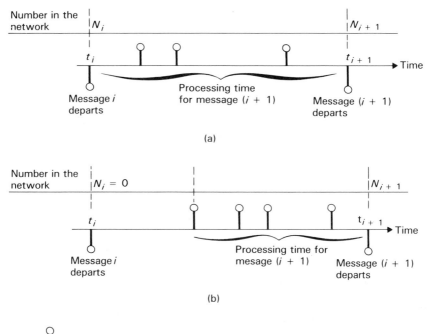

(a)

(b)

Message arrivals — Note that although several arivals are shown in the processing interval for message $(i + 1)$, only one or no arrivals can occur on the average for the system to be stable.

Figure 3.4   A Typical Processing Interval for a Network in the Steady State
(a) $N_i > 0$
(b) $N_i = 0$

until this message departs. Mathematically,

$$N_{i+1} = A_{i+1}, \quad N_i = 0 \tag{3.10}$$

where A_{i+1} is still defined as the number of arrivals in the processing time of the $(i + 1)^{\text{th}}$ message.

By defining $U(N_i)$ as

$$U(N_i) = \begin{cases} 1, & N_i > 0 \\ 0, & N_i = 0 \end{cases} \tag{3.11}$$

Eqs. (3.9) and (3.10) can be combined to obtain

$$N_{i+1} = N_i - U(N_i) + A_{i+1} \tag{3.12}$$

Further useful relationships result from averaging both sides of (3.12) to obtain

$$\overline{N}_{i+1} = \overline{N}_i - \overline{U(N_i)} + \overline{A}_{i+1} \tag{3.13}$$

Due to the steady-state assumption, the average number of messages in the network is not a function of time, so that

$$\overline{N}_{i+1} = \overline{N}_i \tag{3.14}$$

Using (3.14) in (3.13) gives

$$\overline{U}(N_i) = \overline{A}_{i+1} \tag{3.15}$$

which states in words that the average of $U(N_i)$ is equal to the average number of arrivals in the time to process the $(i + 1)^{th}$ message.

The variable $\overline{U}(N_i)$ can be used as a measure of average channel activity. Examination of (3.11), which defines $U(N_i)$, shows that this variable is an indicator of whether the channel is busy. This statement is justified by the fact that if the network is not empty ($N_i > 0$), then there must be a message in the channel being processed. For this condition, $U(N_i) = 1$. On the other hand, if the network is empty, so that $N_i = 0$, then there can be no message being processed. For this condition, $U(N_i) = 0$. The average of $U(N_i)$ over a large number of N_i thus gives the fraction of times, t_i, for which the channel is busy.

The average fraction of time the channel is busy (without restriction to specific t_i) is a significant parameter of network behavior that is typically denoted by ρ and called traffic intensity. Obviously, from its definition,

$$0 \le \rho \le 1 \tag{3.16}$$

If $\overline{U}(N(t))$ is used to denote the average of a quantity that satisfies (3.11), with $N(t)$ the number of messages in the network at any time t not restricted to departure instants, then

$$\overline{U}(N(t)) = \rho \tag{3.17}$$

This discussion of properties of networks, which are independent of the precise statistical distributions of the inputs and outputs, concludes with a very special network that consists of one storage facility or buffer and one output channel with bit rate C bits per second. Such a network, along with a schematic representation, is shown in Fig. 3.5(a). It is further assumed that the average input rate is λ messages per second and that the random length messages have an average length of $1/\mu$ bits per message.

In the model associated with the schematic representation of Fig. 3.5(a), the complete message is assumed to arrive in the network instantaneously. On the other hand, a message is considered to be still in the network until the last bit of the message had reached the destination. Thus the minimum delay a message can have in the network is the time to transmit the complete message over the channel. Since the average length of the message is $1/\mu$ bits, and the channel bit rate is C bps, the average transmission or processing time is $1/\mu C$ seconds.

In the steady state, the average input rate and the average output rate must be equal, and in this case equal to λ messages per second. When there are messages in the channel, however, as noted previously, they are processed out at an average rate of μC messages per second. The difference in λ and μC is

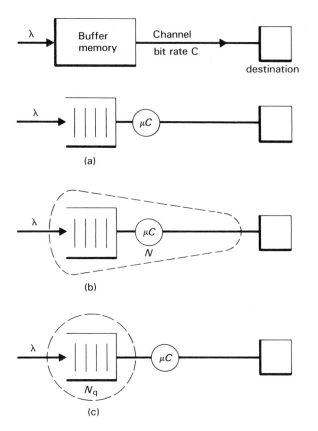

Figure 3.5   A Buffer Memory and Associated Channel
(a) Schematic representation
(b) A closed system that contains storage and channel
(c) A closed system that contains storage only

accounted for by the fact that the channel is not always busy and thus the average output rate of λ results from averaging over both busy periods, when the channel processes messages at a rate μC, and idle periods when the output rate is zero.

Since the average fraction of time the channel is busy is ρ, the relation between λ and μC can be expressed as

$$\lambda = \rho \mu C \tag{3.18}$$

or

$$\rho = \lambda / \mu C \tag{3.19}$$

The last relation indicates that the traffic intensity is equal to average arrival rate divided by average channel processing rate expressed in compatible units.

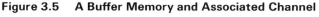

For messages not to accumulate on the average and thus lead to unstable steady-state behavior, the average arrival rate must be less than or equal to μC, the average processing rate of the channel. This of of course consistent with (3.19) and the fact that ρ is less than or equal to 1.

Little's Law can be used to relate N, the average number of messages stored in the complete network of buffer and channel, to N_q, defined as the average number of messages stored in the buffer. The analysis to be made also relates average time in the buffer, W, to average time in the system, T.

Little's Law can be applied to the two boundaries shown in Fig. 3.5(b) and (c). Using the boundary that encloses the whole network yields

$$N = \lambda T \tag{3.20}$$

which relates quantities for the whole network, whereas the boundary around only the buffer yields

$$N_q = \lambda W \tag{3.21}$$

The average delays T and W can be related by noting that the average delay for both buffer and channel is the sum of average delay in the buffer and the average time, $1/\mu C$, required to process a message over the channel once processing begins. Thus

$$T = W + 1/\mu C \tag{3.22}$$

Note that this result neglects the time for a signal to propagate over the channel, normally at a substantial fraction of the speed of light. Significant propagation delays do sometimes occur, however, and should be added to $1/\mu C$ in (3.22).

A relation between N and N_q results from multiplying both sides of (3.22) by λ and substituting from (3.20) and (3.21) to obtain

$$N = N_q + \rho \tag{3.23}$$

This equation shows that the average number of messages stored in the network is equal to the average number stored in the buffer plus ρ, which must represent the average number stored in the channel. This result is not unexpected since at any instant the channel is processing either 0 or 1 message, and the resulting average is a number, ρ, between 0 and 1. It may also be recalled from (3.17) that ρ equals $\overline{U(N(t))}$, where $U(N(t))$ indicates whether the channel is busy at arbitrary time t.

3.3 A Class of Queueing Models

In Section 3.2, properties of the average flow through networks are examined and developed as far as possible without explicit assumptions about the statistical properties of arriving and departing messages.

This section discusses simple networks that consist of a buffer memory and a single output channel, such as shown in Fig. 3.5. The input process is modeled specifically as a Poisson process. The assumptions make possible useful relations for the average number of messages stored in the network and the average time delay through the network in terms of the specific parameters of the Poisson arrival process and general properties of the service process. Two different characterizations of the service process are then made; these lead to specific relations between traffic intensity and average number of messages stored, and between traffic intensity and average time delay for the cases chosen.

Note that queueing theory specialists have developed a notation for indicating the assumptions on input process, service process, and number of output channels (or servers in classical queueing problems). This notation lists in order: a one-letter symbol for the specific input process, a slash, a one-letter symbol for the specific service process, another slash, and a number that indicates the number of output channels. For example, the case of a Poisson input process, no restriction on the service process, and one output channel is denoted M/G/1. *M* stands for a (Markovian) *memoryless* process that is equivalent to one with Poisson statistics. *G* stands for a *general* service process, and the 1 indicates one channel or server.

Results for the M/G/1 case are developed first in this section. The general service process is then replaced by one with Poisson statistics to give the M/M/1 case, and by another with a constant service time to give the M/D/1 case. With respect to the notation, *M* again stands for the Poisson process, while *D* stands for *deterministic,* a nonrandom type of process for which a constant is a special case.

3.3.1   M/G/1 Model

Consider again the network of Fig. 3.5. An M/G/1 model for the network assumes Poisson input statistics, a general service process, and one output channel. With respect to the service process, it is convenient to regard the message processing times as a sequence of statistically independent, identically distributed random variables with the same unspecified distribution function.

The message processing time, Y, is defined as the message length in bits divided by the channel bit rate. The channel bit rate is assumed to be a constant C bits per second, and the message length is random. Although the message length distribution is not specified, its mean, denoted $1/\mu$ bits/message, is assumed to be known. The average message processing rate that results for the channel is μC messages per second.

For the Poisson type of input process, the number of arrivals in any time interval is statistically independent from the number in any other nonoverlapping interval. The probability of k arrivals in an interval of length T is given by

$$P\{k \text{ arrivals in } T \text{ seconds}\} = \frac{(\lambda T)^k e^{-\lambda T}}{k!}, \, k = 0, 1, 2 \ldots \tag{3.24}$$

The average arrival rate, which is the average number of arrivals in an interval of $T = 1$ second, is λ messages per second.

It can be shown that for Poisson arrivals, the average number of messages in the network at a random time, t, is the same as the average number at an arbitrary service completion time. This justifies setting $\rho = \overline{U}[N(t)] = \overline{U}(N_i)$.

As a final qualification, it is implicit in the assumptions that both the number of arrivals in a fixed interval and the message processing time are statistically independent of the number of messages stored in either the network or the buffer.

To begin the analysis, the general difference equation (3.12), which relates the number of messages in the network at consecutive departure times to the number of arrivals in the intervening message processing time, applies to the M/G/1 queue as a special case, as does (3.15), which is derived from (3.12). Since the input process is Poisson, the number of arrivals in any message processing time is independent of the length of other processing times and the number of messages in the network. Thus the subscript on A_{i+1} in (3.15) can be dropped, since the number of arrivals depends only on the random processing time, Y, which is independent of the index $(i + 1)$. Equation (3.15), written without the subscript on A and using the properties of $U(N_i)$ previously discussed, becomes

$$\overline{U}(N_i) = \rho = \overline{A} \tag{3.25}$$

The results obtained by averaging both sides of (3.12) can be extended by averaging the square of both sides of this equation:

$$N_{i+1}^2 = N_i^2 + U^2(N_i) + A^2 - 2N_i U(N_i) - 2A\, U(N_i) + 2N_i\, A \tag{3.26}$$

and

$$\overline{N_{i+1}^2} = \overline{N_i^2} + \overline{U^2(N_i)} + \overline{A^2} - \overline{2N_i U(N_i)} - \overline{2A\, U(N_i)} + \overline{2N_i A} \tag{3.27}$$

Each of the averaged terms can now be considered separately. The first two terms $\overline{N_{i+1}^2}$ and $\overline{N_i^2}$ cancel since the mean square value of the number in the network does not change in the steady state from the departure of one message to the departure of another. Examination of Eq. (3.11), which defines $U(N_i)$, shows that $U^2(N_i) = U(N_i)$ so that

$$\overline{U^2(N_i)} = \overline{U(N_i)} = \rho \tag{3.28}$$

The same equation shows that $N_i\, U(N_i) = N_i$ so that

$$2\overline{N_i\, U(N_i)} = 2\overline{N_i} \tag{3.29}$$

The remaining two terms in Eq. (3.27) involve the average of products; both reduce to the product of averages of single random variables since the variables involved are all statistically independent. Thus

$$2\overline{A\, U(N_i)} = 2\overline{A}\, \overline{U}(N_i) = 2\rho^2 \tag{3.30}$$

and

$$2\overline{N_i A} = 2\overline{N_i}\rho \tag{3.31}$$

Using the results of (3.28) − (3.31), and the fact that $\overline{N_{i+1}^2}$ and $\overline{N_i^2}$ cancel, (3.27) becomes

$$0 = \rho + \overline{A^2} - 2\overline{N_i} - 2\rho^2 + 2\overline{N_i}\rho \tag{3.32}$$

For Poisson, input processes $\overline{N_i} = \overline{N}(t)$; furthermore, for steady-state operation, this average number of messages in the network is not a function of time. Thus $\overline{N_i}$ can be replaced by N, and (3.32) can then be solved for N to obtain

$$N = \frac{\rho + \overline{A^2} - 2\rho^2}{2(1 - \rho)} \tag{3.33}$$

To complete the derivation for the M/G/1 model, it is necessary to evaluate $\overline{A^2}$, which depends on both the nature of the arrival process and the first and second moments of the message processing time, as the following argument shows. The number of arrivals in a fixed interval of time is given by the assumed Poisson distribution for arrivals. Unfortunately, A is the number of arrivals in the message processing time, Y, which is random and thus not fixed or known.

To determine $\overline{A^2}$, it is first necessary to evaluate $E[A^2 \mid Y]$, the expected value of A^2 given a fixed Y. Since the variance of a random variable Z equals $E(Z^2) - (E(Z))^2$, it follows that

$$E[A^2 \mid Y] = \text{Var}\,(A \mid Y) + [E(A \mid Y)]^2 \tag{3.34}$$

where $E[A \mid Y]$ is the expected value of A given Y. With Y fixed and playing the role of T in (3.24), the moments of the Poisson distribution are: $E[A \mid Y] = \lambda Y$ and $\text{Var}\,(A \mid Y) = \lambda Y$. Thus (3.34) becomes

$$E[A^2 \mid Y] = \lambda Y + \lambda^2 Y^2 \tag{3.35}$$

To continue the analysis, use is made of an important result from probability theory (see, for example, Feller [3])

$$E[E(A^2 \mid Y)] = E(A^2) \tag{3.36}$$

which makes it possible to average both sides of (3.35) and obtain $\overline{A^2}$ as

$$\overline{A^2} = E(A^2) = E\,(\lambda Y + \lambda^2 Y^2) \tag{3.37}$$

Given that the mean of Y is $1/\mu C$, that $\rho = \lambda/\mu C$, and that σ_Y^2 is the variance of Y, (3.37) reduces to

$$\overline{A^2} = \rho + \rho^2 + \lambda^2\,\sigma_Y^2 \tag{3.38}$$

Substitution of (3.38) into (3.33) then gives

$$N = \frac{2\rho - \rho^2 + \lambda^2\sigma_Y^2}{2(1 - \rho)} = \rho + \frac{\rho^2 + \lambda^2\sigma_Y^2}{2(1 - \rho)} \tag{3.39}$$

Use of Little's Law, as expressed by (3.8), gives a companion expression to (3.39) for T, namely

$$T = \frac{1}{\mu C} + \frac{\rho + \lambda \mu C \sigma_Y^2}{2\mu C(1 - \rho)} = \frac{1}{\mu C} + \frac{\rho(1 + CV_Y^2)}{2\mu C(1 - \rho)} \tag{3.40}$$

where CV_Y is the coefficient of variation of Y equal to $\sigma_Y \mu C$.

These last two equations, which are simplified as much as possible for the assumptions of the M/G/1 model, are referred to as the Pollaczek–Khinchine mean-value formulas. They give the average number of messages stored in a network and average message delay in terms of traffic intensity, ρ, average input traffic rate, λ, and the first two moments of the message processing time. Thus, to determine N and T for an M/G/1 system, the mean and variance of the message processing time must be known, although knowledge of the actual distribution of message processing times is not necessary.

Observe from the Pollaczek–Khinchine formulas that both N and T increase linearly with the variance of the message processing time if all other variables remain constant. Note also that the mean number in the system and the mean delay are both minimized if the variance of message processing time is zero. (It cannot be negative.) This occurs if the message processing time is constant.

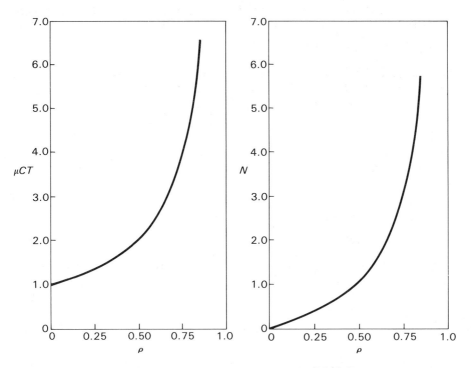

Figure 3.6   Curves of μCT and N versus ρ for an M/M/1 Queue

Chapter 3   Data Flow in Networks and Queues

3.3.2   M/M/1 Model

The M/M/1 model is a special case of the M/G/1 model that results from specifying message processing time as a Poisson process or, equivalently, one with an exponential distribution. It can be shown that for an exponential distribution the coefficient of variation is 1 so that

$$\sigma_Y^2 = (1/\mu C)^2 \tag{3.41}$$

After an algebraic step, the substitution of (3.41) into (3.39) yields

$$N = \frac{\rho}{1 - \rho} \tag{3.42}$$

The same result can be obtained directly by setting up a Markov chain model and solving steady-state difference equations specifically for the M/M/1 model. This approach is used in Chapter 4 and yields an expression for the distribution function of the number of messages stored.

To continue the development, the average time delay for a message in traversing the buffer-channel of an M/M/1 queue is related to N by Little's formula, (3.8). Thus

$$\lambda T = N = \frac{\rho}{1 - \rho}$$

and

$$T = \frac{1}{\lambda}\left(\frac{\rho}{1 - \rho}\right) = \frac{1}{\mu C(1 - \rho)} \tag{3.43}$$

Curves of μCT and N versus ρ are given in Fig. 3.6.

Expressions for N_q, the average number of messages stored in the buffer, and W, the average time in the buffer, can be obtained from (3.23) and (3.22) respectively as

$$N_q = N - \rho \tag{3.44}$$

and

$$W = T - 1/\mu C \tag{3.45}$$

Using (3.42) for N and (3.43) for T, N_q and W can be expressed in terms of ρ and μC as

$$N_q = \frac{\rho^2}{1 - \rho} \tag{3.46}$$

$$W = \frac{\rho}{\mu C(1 - \rho)} \tag{3.47}$$

Plots of N_q and μCW are given in Fig. 3.7.

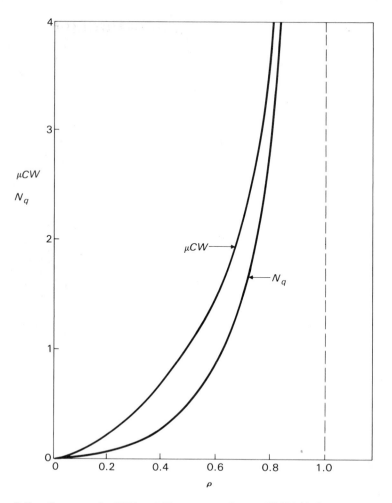

Figure 3.7   Curves of μCW and N_q versus ρ for an M/M/1 Queue

3.3.3   M/D/1 Model

The M/D/1 model is also a special case of the M/G/1 model, with the message processing time in this case specified as constant and denoted as $1/\mu C$. The variance of a constant is 0, and thus (3.39) and (3.40) reduce respectively to

$$N = \rho + \frac{\rho^2}{2(1-\rho)} = \frac{\rho(2-\rho)}{2(1-\rho)} \tag{3.48}$$

and

$$T = \frac{1}{\mu C} + \frac{\rho}{2\mu C(1-\rho)} = \frac{2-\rho}{2\mu C(1-\rho)} \tag{3.49}$$

Note that for this case, CV_Y is also 0. Plots of N and μCT versus ρ are shown in Fig. 3.8 for the M/D/1 queue as compared to similar plots for the M/M/1 queue.

The results that correspond to (3.48) and (3.49) for N_q, the average number stored in the buffer, and W, the average time spent by a message in the buffer, are then given respectively by

$$N_q = \frac{\rho^2}{2(1 - \rho)} \tag{3.50}$$

and

$$W = \frac{\rho}{2\mu C(1 - \rho)} \tag{3.51}$$

Equations (3.51) and (3.47) show that the average buffer delay for an M/D/1 system is one-half that for an M/M/1 system.

3.3.4 General Comments

Examination of the curves of N and μCT versus ρ for the M/M/1 and M/D/1 queues in Fig. 3.8 shows several general properties of these variables. As traffic intensity, ρ, approaches unity, N and μCT for both cases increase

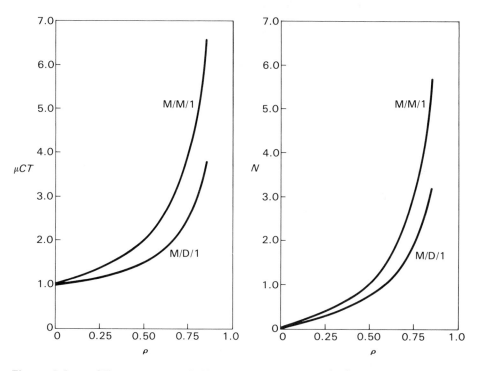

Figure 3.8 μCT versus ρ and N versus ρ for an M/D/1 Queue Compared to Similar Results for an M/M/1 Queue

without bound. This occurs as the average input rate, λ, approaches the average channel processing capacity (or clock rate), μC. As previously noted, an average input rate greater than μC causes the buffer-channel to block. For a practical network with limited buffer capacity, blocking would be evidenced by buffer overflow and lost messages. Thus, for steady-state conditions to exist, λ must be strictly less than μC (i.e., ρ must be less than 1).

For values of ρ less than 1, there is a nonlinear relation between N and ρ and between T and ρ, as shown in the figures. The average number of messages stored becomes 0 when ρ is equal to 0 for both types of queues.

The curves for average message delay, T, have been plotted to show a normalized quantity μCT versus ρ. Since $1/\mu C$ is the average message transmission time, T divided by $1/\mu C$, which is μCT, is the average delay normalized to units of the average transmission time. Note that $1/\mu C$ is also the minimum average delay, which would be experienced by messages that enter the channel immediately, without waiting in the buffer.

The curves for normalized average delay, μCT, for both types of queues have a minimum of unity for traffic intensity equal to 0. The curves then show a nonlinear increase of normalized average delay with traffic intensity between 0 and 1. As ρ approaches unity, μCT approaches infinity.

Note that for small values of traffic intensity, messages seldom accumulate in the buffer but enter the channel directly; this explains the shape of the curves. The messages are then processed by the channel in an average time of $1/\mu C$, which is, of course, equivalent to a value of unity for normalized delay. As traffic intensity increases, the number of messages stored in the buffer increases, as does the waiting time of a typical message for access to the channel. This is shown directly by the curves of μCW and N_q versus ρ for the M/M/1 queue in Fig. 3.7. The quantity μCT increases with μCW since T is the sum of average waiting time and average message processing time by the channel, $1/\mu C$. Finally, as traffic intensity increases to approach unity, the buffer stores more and more messages, and the waiting time increases without limit.

The curves for the M/M/1 and M/D/1 queues for both N and T have a similar shape. Figure 3.8 clearly shows that the M/D/1 queue has smaller values for average number of messages stored and average message delay for any value of traffic intensity. In fact, the M/D/1 queue gives lower values of N and T than any other distribution of processing time, since, as previously mentioned, the Pollaczek–Khinchine formulas are linear in the variance of the processing time (which is, of course, zero for the constant distribution of the M/D/1 model). This property of the M/D/1 queueing system is used in later chapters to provide a lower bound reference for performance for different types of local area networks.

3.4 Priority Queues

In the discussion of queues up to this point, it has been tacitly assumed that messages are served on a first-come-first-served (FCFS) basis. This clearly is not the only form that the service discipline can take. Some alternatives are: last-come-first-served (LCFS), random order of service, and priority queueing. For priority queueing, messages are classified into different groups, each with a priority index. The notation to be used here assigns a larger index number to a higher priority (i.e., messages of priority $(p + 1)$ are served before messages of priority p or less).

Within each priority group for priority queueing, there are also different service disciplines. The most common is head-of-the-line (HOL) service, which implies that messages are served in the same order as they arrive—the same as FCFS for a complete system without any priority structure.

There are two other refinements possible in priority situations: preemptive and nonpreemptive. For preemptive systems, a message with higher priority is allowed to disrupt the service of a message with lower priority. Such a disruption leads to a further classification about whether the disrupted service is to be continued from the point of interruption at a later time or be restarted from the beginning. For nonpreemptive systems, there is no interruption because the higher priority message must wait until the service in progress is completed.

In this section, the discussion of priority queueing systems is confined to HOL nonpreemptive priority systems, with attention focused on the case of only two priority groups. Such restricted systems arise in at least one type of local computer network.

The class of priority systems of interest is now analyzed to determine an expression for the average waiting delay, W_p, encountered by a typical tagged

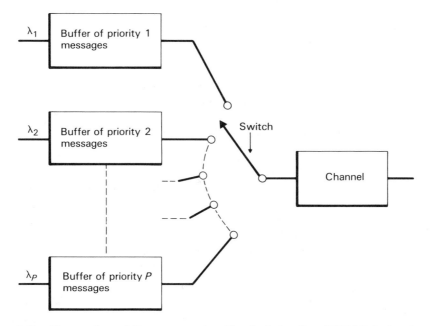

Figure 3.9   Illustration of Nonpreemptive Head-of-the-line (HOL) Priority Queueing Systems

message from priority group p. The integer p is selected from the set $\{1, 2, \ldots P\}$ of priority groups, in which primary interest is in the case $P = 2$. The symbol W_i is used to denote the average waiting delay for a message from priority group i.

Figure 3.9 illustrates the type of nonpreemptive queueing system under consideration. Each of the buffers operates on a first-come-first-served basis while being serviced by the channel. After a transmission is completed, the switch moves to the buffer with the highest priority of those with messages queued and ready to transmit.

Messages arrive at each priority buffer from independent Poisson processes with mean arrival rates denoted λ_i, $i = 1, 2, \ldots P$. Let $\overline{Y}_i$, $i = 1, 2, \ldots P$, denote the average channel processing time for a message of priority i. All messages are transmitted out over the same channel so that each $\overline{Y}_i$ depends not only on the common channel bit rate, but also on the potentially different mean message lengths for each priority class.

Let ρ_i be the fraction of time that the channel is occupied with messages of priority i. This quantity is, of course, the traffic intensity for priority i traffic, and hence it is given by

$$\rho_i = \lambda_i \, \overline{Y}_i \tag{3.52}$$

since only one priority of traffic is transmitted at a given time. If ρ denotes the total network traffic, it follows that under steady-state, stable conditions

$$\rho = \sum_{i=1}^{P} \rho_i < 1 \tag{3.53}$$

The queueing (or waiting) delay encountered by a tagged message has three component parts:

1. The delay, if any, due to a message already in service (i.e., already being transmitted over the channel);
2. The delay due to messages that arrive *before* the tagged message and that are served before this message; and
3. The delay due to messages that arrive *after* the tagged message and that, nonetheless, receive their service before the tagged message.

Expressions for the mean values of each of these three components of delay are now developed.

Let W_0 be the mean delay to the tagged message due to a message already in service (i.e., delay component 1 in the preceding list). What is required is an expression for the remaining, or residual, service time of a message, if any, already in service at the random time of arrival of the tagged message. A diagram that shows a possible relation between the several variables involved is shown in Fig. 3.10. The random variable Y_i is the total service time of a message with priority i assumed to be found in service at the arrival time of the tagged message. The average value of the remaining service time, $\overline{Z}_i$, is the desired quantity.

If the service times Y_i are exponentially distributed, as would be the case for

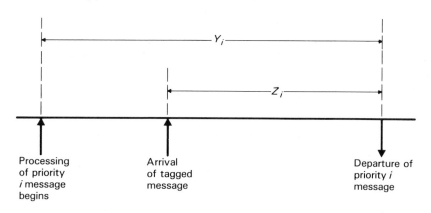

Processing
of priority
i message
begins

Arrival
of tagged
message

Departure of
priority *i*
message

Figure 3.10   Illustration of Residual Service Time

M/M/1 queues, then the "memoryless" property of the exponential distribution can be used. The memoryless property states that the expectation of the remaining service time is always $\overline{Y}_i$ for a tagged message arriving from a Poisson process.

If the Y_i are not exponentially distributed, the problem of determining $\overline{Z}_i$ is generally more difficult. Texts, such as Feller [3] or Kleinrock [2], deal with this more general case and show that $\overline{Z}_i$ is given by

$$\overline{Z}_i = \overline{Y_i^2}/2\overline{Y}_i \tag{3.54}$$

(Of course, when Y_i has an exponential distribution, $\overline{Y_i^2} = 2(\overline{Y}_i)^2$ and thus $\overline{Z}_i = \overline{Y}_i$.)

To complete the determination of an expression for the mean delay, W_0, note that ρ_i is the probability that a message from priority group *i* is in service when the tagged message arrives. Thus the mean delay due to a group *i* message already in service is $\overline{Y_i^2}/2\overline{Y}_i$ with probability ρ_i, and 0 with probability $(1 - \rho_i)$. The mean delay, W_0, due to any priority group message found in service, is thus given by

$$W_0 = \sum_{i-1}^{P} \rho_i \frac{\overline{Y_i^2}}{2\overline{Y}_i} \tag{3.55}$$

where the sum accounts for all priority groups with their corresponding probabilities. Using Eq. (3.52), (3.55) becomes

$$W_0 = \sum_{i-1}^{P} \lambda_i \overline{Y_i^2}/2 \tag{3.56}$$

Now consider the second component of mean delay, to be denoted by W_A, which is the delay due to messages that are already in the system before the arrival of the tagged message and that receive service before the tagged message of priority *p*. Define N_{ip} as the number of such messages from group *i*.

Each of the N_{ip} messages requires a service time of average value $\overline{Y}_i$, giving a total mean service time of $\overline{N_{ip}}\, Y_i$ for each group with priority i. All message groups with priority p and above already in the system before the arrival of the tagged message are serviced before it. Thus the total mean delay, W_A, from this source is given by

$$W_A = \sum_{i=p}^{P} \overline{N_{ip}}\, Y_i \tag{3.57}$$

Since N_{ip} represents the number of messages of priority i in the network at an arbitrary time (the time the tagged message arrives), Little's Law can be applied to the priority i messages to obtain

$$\overline{N_{ip}} = \lambda_i W_i, \quad i = p, \ldots . P \tag{3.58}$$

where W_i is the average delay suffered by priority i messages. Substituting (3.58) into (3.57) and using (3.52) gives

$$W_A = \sum_{i=p}^{P} \lambda_i W_i \overline{Y_i} = \sum_{i=1}^{P} \rho_i\, W_i \tag{3.59}$$

As a final step, consider the third component of delay caused by messages that arrive after the tagged message but that receive service before the tagged message. Let the mean value of this delay be W_B. Denote the number of such messages with priority i as M_{ip} and the average number of such messages as $\overline{M_{ip}}$. By an argument similar to that used to obtain W_A, it follows that

$$W_B = \sum_{i=p+1}^{P} \overline{M_{ip}}\, Y_i \tag{3.60}$$

since $\overline{M_{ip}}$ includes only messages with priority higher than that of the tagged message.

All the messages included in M_{ip} arrive during the waiting delay of the tagged message since they arrive after the tagged message. To contribute to the delay of the tagged message, they must arrive before service for the tagged message begins. Little's Law can be applied to relate $\overline{M_{ip}}$ and W_p. The result is

$$\overline{M_{ip}} = \lambda_i W_p, \quad i = p + 1, \ldots , P \tag{3.61}$$

Substituting (3.61) into (3.60) and using (3.52) then gives

$$W_B = \sum_{i=p+1}^{P} \rho_i W_p \tag{3.62}$$

Since W_p is the sum of W_0, W_A, and W_B, (3.59) and (3.62) combine to give

$$
\begin{aligned}
W_p &= W_0 + \sum_{i=p}^{P} \rho_i W_i + \sum_{i=p+1}^{P} \rho_i W_p \\
&= W_0 + \sum_{i=p+1}^{P} \rho_i W_i + \sum_{i=p}^{P} \rho_i W_p
\end{aligned}
\tag{3.63}
$$

Solving (3.63) for W_p gives

$$W_p = \frac{W_0 + \sum\limits_{i=p+1}^{P} \rho_i W_i}{1 - \sum\limits_{i=p}^{P} \rho_i} \tag{3.64}$$

where W_0 is given by (3.56). Equation (3.64) holds for all values of p since the priority of the tagged message is arbitrary. Using $p = 1, 2, \ldots P$ then gives a set of P equations that can then be solved for the P unknowns, namely, $W_1, W_2, \ldots W_P$.

Of particular interest in this text is when P equals 2. For $p = 1$ and $p = 2$, (3.64) gives respectively

$$W_1 = \frac{W_0 + \rho_2 W_2}{1 - \rho_1 - \rho_2} \tag{3.65}$$

and

$$W_2 = \frac{W_0}{1 - \rho_2} \tag{3.66}$$

Substituting (3.66) into (3.65) then gives

$$W_1 = \frac{W_0}{(1 - \rho_1 - \rho_2)(1 - \rho_2)} \tag{3.67}$$

For this special case of just two priority groups, (3.56) reduces to a simpler expression for W_0, namely,

$$W_0 = (\lambda_1 \overline{Y_1^2} + \lambda_2 \overline{Y_2^2})/2 \tag{3.68}$$

Note that when there is only one priority group (in other words, no priority at all), the priority queueing system becomes simply an M/G/1 queue. In this case, with $\rho = \rho_1$ and $W = W_1$, (3.64) reduces to

$$W = \frac{W_0}{1 - \rho} \tag{3.69}$$

With the subscript on λ_1 and Y_1 also dropped, the expression for W_0 becomes simply

$$W_0 = \lambda \overline{Y^2}/2 \tag{3.70}$$

so that

$$W = \frac{\lambda \overline{Y^2}}{2(1 - \rho)} \tag{3.71}$$

Since the average message processing or transmission time is simply $\overline{Y}$, the total average delay encountered by a message is

$$T = \overline{Y} + \frac{\lambda \overline{Y^2}}{2(1 - \rho)} \tag{3.72}$$

It is easy to show that this result is identical to (3.40) in which $1/\mu C$ replaces $\overline{Y}$, and σ_y^2 is the variance of the message transmission time, Y.

3.5 Networks of Queues

In Section 3.3, a single-stage queueing system that contains one storage device and its associated input and output channels is considered, and analytic expressions are derived for the mean delay and average number of messages stored in the buffer. Such a queueing system is adequate for modeling many local computer networks.

There are cases, however, in which a single-stage queueing system is not an adequate model since the path for message or packet flow in the network contains several storage devices connected by appropriate channels. In such cases, a multistage queueing system is required to model the network. Analytic expressions for mean delay and average number of messages stored in the buffers for such multistage queueing systems must be obtained to study network performance.

Multistage queueing networks can be divided into three classes: open, closed, and mixed queueing systems. Each of these classes is illustrated in Fig. 3.11 with two-stage queueing networks. In the case of the open system, all the arrivals progress to the second queue after receiving service in the first queue. Open multistage queueing systems are characterized by the fact that the number of messages in the system is not constrained and external arrivals and departures are permitted.

Closed systems of the type in Fig. 3.11(b), on the other hand, have a fixed number of messages that circulate in the system, and no external arrivals or departures from the system are allowed. Mixed systems, as shown in Fig. 3.11(c), combine the characteristics of open and closed systems. Some messages circulate, as indicated by the feedback path for the second queue, but external arrivals and departures from the system are allowed.

All three classes of multistage queueing networks have been studied, and a number of general results have been obtained (see, for example, Jackson [4] and Baskett et al. [5]). However, the open queueing system model is the type most often used for modeling multiaccess networks, and thus attention is restricted to this type.

To commence the discussion of such networks, consider a single M/M/1 queueing system. Let the input Poisson process have mean arrival rate λ. Then, as is shown in Kleinrock [6] and Burke [7], the output process is also Poisson with the same rate λ. This property of an M/M/1 system leads to *Kleinrock's independence assumption* for open queueing models of computer networks. When this assumption is feasible, a tractable analysis is possible.

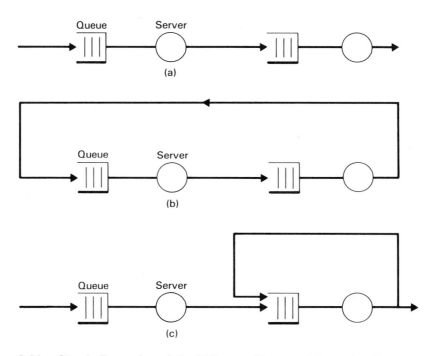

Figure 3.11   Simple Examples of the Different Classes of Queueing Systems

(a) Open system
(b) Closed system
(c) Mixed system

To continue the discussion, consider the computer network represented by the three-stage open queueing model shown in Fig. 3.12. All external arrival processes are assumed to be Poisson, and it is also assumed that message lengths can be approximated by an exponential distribution.

By Burke's Theorem, the output of the first queue is Poisson. However, the length of a particular message, after it is chosen from an exponential distribution, is fixed. This means that the service times at the three nodes are not independent, so the three-stage network cannot be modeled exactly as

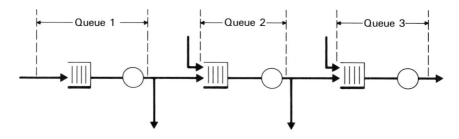

Figure 3.12   An Open Queueing Model with Three Queues in Tandem

three separate M/M/1 queues. However, if it is assumed that a new choice of message length is made at each node, then the average delay for a message passing through the system is the sum of the average delays given by the three independent M/M/1 submodels.

For the independence assumption to be strictly valid, the message lengths at the input to the second and third queues must be selected from independent exponential distributions. This, of course, is not exactly the case. Referring again to Fig. 3.12, under the assumption that the length of a message entering queue 1 is chosen from an exponential distribution, the first queue is M/M/1 since its arrivals are from a Poisson process, its message lengths are exponentially distributed, and arrivals and message lengths are independent random variables.

As the message proceeds to queue 2, however, there is clearly a correlation between arrival time and message length since large messages take longer to be processed out of the first queue. Thus, strictly speaking, message lengths and arrival times cannot be independent, so the second and subsequent queues cannot be M/M/1.

Kleinrock has shown that the independence assumption gives quite accurate results if the traffic intensity is small or if there is sufficient mixing at each node in the sense that messages join the queue from several input lines.

The breakdown of complicated multistage queueing models into a collection of independent M/M/1 or M/G/1 submodels makes the analysis of many computer networks relatively straightforward. When this is not possible, the problem is very intractable, and simulation or some other nonanalytical technique must be used.

3.6 Summary

The chapter provides background material for determining the parameters associated with the average flow of packets or messages through network structures under steady-state conditions. The flows are typically random in nature, and many of the required techniques are taken from queueing theory.

The chapter begins by discussing properties that are independent of specific distributions of the variables. Little's Law, a key equation from queueing theory, relates average input rate, average time delay, and average number of messages stored within any closed boundary.

The second major topic develops equations for average time delay and average number of messages stored in a network segment, consisting of storage and an output channel, for specific assumptions about the distributions of the variables. In the notation of queueing theory, M/G/1 and M/M/1 models are developed. Equations and normalized curves are obtained for relating average time delay and average number stored to traffic intensity for the M/M/1 and M/D/1 cases.

Priority queues and networks of queues are also discussed in the chapter.

Chapter 4 begins the discussion of local networks with a description and analysis of private branch exchanges or PBX networks.

References

[1] S. Stidham. "A Last Word on L = λW." *Operations Research* 22 (1974): 417–421.
[2] L. Kleinrock. *Queueing Systems*. Vol. 1, *Theory*. New York: Wiley–Interscience, 1975.
[3] W. Feller. *An Introduction to Probability Theory and its Applications*. Vol. 2. New York: John Wiley & Sons, 1968.
[4] J. R. Jackson. "Jobshop-like Queueing Systems." *Management Science* 10 (1963): 131–142.
[5] F. Baskett, K. M. Chandy, R. R. Muntz, and F. C. Palacios. "Open, Closed, and Mixed Networks of Queues with Different Classes of Customers." *Journal Assn. Computing Machinery* 22, no. 2 (April 1975): 248–260.
[6] L. Kleinrock. *Queueing Systems*. Vol. 2, *Computer Applications*. New York: Wiley–Interscience, 1976.
[7] P. J. Burke. "The Output of a Queueing System." *Operations Research* 4 (1966): 699–706.

Problems and Exercises

1. In the following stable network, Little's formula applies and the channel must be busy if messages are present at its input. The average inputs, λ, in messages/second, the average storage at the nodes, $\overline{N}$, in messages, and the ρ are given on the figure. What is the average time delay for messages through the complete network and output channel?

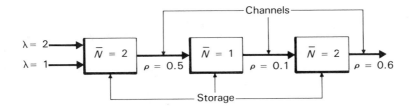

2. The following questions concern an $M/M/1$ queue for which ρ is fixed at 0.6.
   (a) What is the average number of messages stored?
   (b) Can a 1-second average time delay per message be achieved? How? (Specify λ and μC.)
   (c) What is the average number of messages in service?
   (d) Is there a single time at which this average number of messages is in service?

3. Students arrive at a cash-dispensing machine in a random pattern with an average interarrival time of 3 minutes. The length of transactions at the terminal is exponentially distributed, with an average of 2 minutes.

   (a) What is the probability that a student arriving at the terminal will have to wait?

   (b) What is the average length of the waiting lines that form from time to time?

   (c) The bank plans to install a second terminal when they become convinced that an arriving customer would expect to wait at least 5 minutes before using the cash-dispensing machine. At what average interarrival time will this occur? For this arrival rate, find the average transaction delay and the average number of people queueing.

   (d) At what average interarrival time will the queues grow interminably long?

4. A concentrator can be modeled as an $M/M/1$ queue. The output line capacity is 1200 bps and there are 100 bits/message. Each of N inputs to the concentrator has an average of 0.1 messages/second.

   (a) If the total average concentrator delay (i.e., waiting + channel time) is to be less than or equal to 1 second, how many inputs can the concentrator use?

   With the number of inputs to the concentrator equal to 60:

   (b) What is the average number of messages stored in the buffer?

   (c) What is the average queueing delay (i.e., delay through the buffer)?

   (d) What is the traffic intensity?

   Note: The N Poisson inputs to the concentrator combine into a single Poisson input of 0.1 N mess/sec.

5. Several 300-bps terminals are connected to a concentrator, which is then connected to a computer over a 1200-baud synchronous line. All messages from the terminals are exactly 28 bytes long, whereas output messages from the concentrator are 30 bytes long (the data plus 2 bytes that give the terminal number). Each terminal produces messages randomly, with an average of three per minute.

   (a) What is the maximum number of terminals that may be connected to the concentrator?

   (b) Use an $M/D/1$ queueing model to find a relationship between the number of terminals and the mean amount of buffer storage needed in the concentrator (including space for the messages being transmitted). Sketch this relationship.

6. Assume that a complete computer can be modeled as a single $M/M/1$ queue with a buffer holding jobs (messages) while they wait to be served by the CPU, with a processing speed of C bits/sec. Let each job be $1/\mu$ bits in length. Make the assumption (not necessarily valid) that the cost of a computer is proportional to processing speed, so that one large computer costs the same as 10 smaller computers, each with 1/10th the processing speed. Given a fixed job rate of λ jobs/sec, compare one large computer operating on all incoming jobs (i.e., λ jobs/sec) with a processing rate C bits/sec to 10 small computers, each operating on 1/10th of the inputs (i.e., $\lambda/10$), with processing rates of $C/10$ bits/sec. Specifically, determine the average fraction of time the computers are busy and the average system delay times for the two cases. For this simple model, which is the best choice?

7. A buffer is filled over a single input channel and emptied by a channel with capacity $C = 10^4$ bps. Measurements are made in the steady state for this system

with the following results:

Average number of packets stored in the system = 0.1 packet;
Average wait in buffer/packet = 0.02 sec; and
Average packet length = 100 bits.

Find the average input rate λ in packets/sec.

8. The channel associated with a given network is monitored, and the following data is obtained:

Bit rate = 10^6 bits/sec;
Average packet length = 100 bits/packet;
Steady-state input = 10^3 packets/sec; and
Average number of packets stored in a section of network = 10 packets.

(a) What is the traffic intensity, ρ?
(b) What is the average time delay, T, in the section of the network?

9. A node in a computer network can be modeled as an M/M/1 queue. The capacity of the line out of the node is 1400 bps, and there are 10 bits per message. Under certain conditions it is known that an average of 50 messages are stored in the system (storage buffer and output line).

(a) Under these same conditions, what is the input rate?
(b) What is the total average time delay through the system?
(c) What is the average number of messages stored in the buffer?
(d) What is the average queueing delay?
(e) What is the traffic intensity?

10. The output of a device is 10 bits/sec at a uniform rate when the device is active, and 0 bits/sec when it is inactive. Ten such devices, each active at random intervals amounting to 50% of the time, on the average, are to be multiplexed.

(a) What output line capacity is required for a time-division multiplexer?
(b) What output line capacity is required for a statistical multiplexer with a system delay less than 0.1 sec? Assume that the message length is 1 bit.

11. Carry out the details of solving Eq. (3.63) to obtain (3.64) for W_P.

12. Show that the result of Eq. (3.73) for T reduces to the same expression as that given by (3.40). This serves to confirm the result for priority queues since the case of a single priority is shown to reduce to that obtained earlier.

13. In the text, expressions for W_1 and W_2 are derived in terms of W_0 and priority group utilizations for the special case of $P = 2$. Derive expressions for W_P, W_{P-1}, and W_{P-2} in the general case. Hence, deduce an expression for W_K with K arbitrary.

14. For an exponential distribution of parameter λ, show that the mean and variance are given respectively by $1/\lambda$ and $(1/\lambda)^2$.

15. For a Poisson distribution of parameter λ, show that the mean and variance both equal λ.

16. Use the state transition-rate approach to derive an expression for the average number of messages in an M/M/1/K queueing system, in which K denotes the maximum number of messages in the system at any time.

17. Use the state transition-rate diagram to derive an expression for the probability of k messages in a system under the following assumptions:

• The number of sources generating messages is C, a finite number;

Problems and Exercises

- Each source can generate only one message at a time so that a new message is generated only when the previous one has left the queueing system;
- The interarrival times for a source generating messages are exponentially distributed with parameter τ; and
- All service times are exponentially distributed with parameter μ.

  Consider two cases:

  (a) A single server; and

  (b) Enough servers so that there is never any queueing.

  In each case calculate the average number of messages in the system.

*C*ircuit-Switched Local Networks

4.1 Introduction

As discussed in the introductory chapter, digital private branch exchanges (PBXs) differ from local area networks in the switching technique used and in the transmission bit rates. PBXs use circuit switching, have a maximum transmission rate of 64 kbps, and use a star topology with a digital switch located at the center of the star.

Circuit switching involves setting up a specific end-to-end path through the network for each desired call or connection. As a result, the most important phase of a circuit-switched connection is the call setup, or call establishment, phase, in which control signals move through the network to establish connections that remain in place for the duration of the call. Since the PBX is structured with a star topology, there are no routing problems and the only point in the network at which congestion can occur is at the central switch itself.

An important characteristic of any star network is its blocking characteristic. Blocking is a phenomenon that occurs in a switch when there is no available path through the switch to connect an input port to an output port. Blocking, of course, occurs only during the call setup phase of a circuit-switched connection. At the sacrifice of other features, a nonblocking switch can be designed so that all stations can always be connected at the same time with no possibility of any end-to-end path being blocked, assuming that the destination station is available.

Performance measures for circuit-switched networks are quite different from measures for networks that transmit information in independent packets. Typical performance measures for PBX systems are the switch, or PBX, capacity (i.e., the maximum number of simultaneous calls the system can handle), the call setup time, and the probability of blocking, if the system can be blocked. In many cases propagation and switching delays are negligible. Of the performance criteria listed, probability of blocking is often the most important.

This chapter traces the development of digital PBXs from manual systems to the all-digital private exchanges. This is followed by an in-depth look at the heart of the PBX, the digital switch; time- and space-division switching are treated separately first and then together in multiple-stage switches. Since many PBXs are blocking, the chapter concludes with a blocking analysis of loss and delay systems and a section on sizing PBX systems.

The recent text by Stallings [1] contains a good discussion of the digital PBX in the context of local networks. The following treatment covers some of the same topics as Stallings, but delves more deeply into performance aspects such as blocking probabilities and average queueing delays.

4.2   Digital PBXs

Digital PBXs have evolved from private telephone switching systems owned or leased by large organizations. These private systems, also called PBXs, were originally manually operated with one or more operators at the switchboard to provide the switching function. The switchboard was of course directly connected to the outside world (i.e., the public telephone network). These manual exchanges were subsequently replaced by electromechanical (relay) switching systems and dial telephones, and this combination became known as the private automatic branch exchange (PABX). In these first-generation systems, modems were needed to transmit data over the system designed for voice.

The second-generation systems, introduced in the mid 1970s, use electronic rather than electromechanical switching. Such a system, which uses stored program control (SPC), is sometimes referred to as a computerized branch exchange (CBX). Although the internal switching in these CBXs is purely digital, and most of the signals within the switch are digital, the CBXs were nonetheless designed for an analog environment. The equipment is very much voice-oriented, with modems again needed to connect data services to the system.

Third-generation systems are designed for an integrated voice-date environment, with all transmission and switching in digital form so that modems are unnecessary. Emphasis in this text is on this generation of PBXs because this class offers the same range of services to the user as a local area network.

There are many third-generation PBX systems available to the user. A recent survey [2] lists 17 vendors who supply integrated voice-data switching systems. Even though these third-generation systems are all digital, there are a number of significantly different implementations. Differences can be noted in the architecture of the switch, the amount of decentralization, multiplexing schemes, voice-data integration, etc. A general discussion of these current PBX designs is given by Junker and Noller [3]. Because of the many differences in specific PBX systems, a generic approach is taken here, and no particular implementation is emphasized.

A typical PBX has a star topology, such as shown in Fig. 4.1. The PBX can provide interfaces for: analog trunks, analog voice, local area networks, data terminals, digitized voice, and intelligent workstations (both voice and data). While digital devices connect directly to the switch, analog devices are connected to the switch through appropriate interfaces; for example, an analog telephone connects through a codec (which converts analog signals to synchronous TDM), while an analog trunk using FDM must connect through a trans-multiplexer, which converts FDM to TDM.

The type of line used to connect devices to a digital switch is most often a twisted-pair wire line. For full duplex operation within the same frequency band, two such pairs are needed for data devices such as terminals and computers, one for each direction of transmission. On the other hand, there are several schemes for transmitting digitized voice. The most obvious also requires two twisted pairs, one for each direction, and no additional equipment. Two other schemes use only one twisted pair. One approach requires an

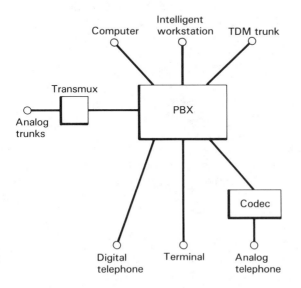

Figure 4.1   Structure of a Digital PBX

echo-canceling circuit at each handset to eliminate the feedback signal from the listener's previous transmission. Another approach, which capitalizes on the fact that voice signals do not require simultaneous transmission in both directions, uses time-compression multiplexing (TCM), sometimes called "ping-pong," in which short talkspurts are transmitted alternately in each direction. This method requires that the actual transmission rate be at least twice the information rate to ensure that the talkspurts in the two directions do not interfere.

The central switch, at the heart of the digital PBX, must interface with all the different types of input signals listed for the PBX itself. It must also provide processing capabilities for voice storage, protocol conversion, and electronic mail.

Third-generation PBXs often have many of the following characteristics:

• Distributed architecture;
• Integrated voice and data capability;
• Essentially nonblocking behavior;
• Protocol support; and
• Local area network interfaces.

Distributed architecture implies that much of the processing of the central switch is located in network interface units that can be located at some distance from the central switch, as indicated in Fig. 4.2. As is discussed in the next section, one of the first functions of a switch is to multiplex different digital lines into a single TDM stream. This multiplexing is often accompanied by concentration, which thereby introduces the possibility of blocking. As shown in Fig. 4.2, the multiplexing component of the switch can be located remotely, often up to 6000 feet from the central switch. The connecting link, which carries the synchronous TDM bit stream to the central switch from the multiplexer, is often a fiber-optic or coaxial cable.

Remote units can also have processing capability so that they operate as miniature local switches and thus decentralize this feature also.

Integrated voice and data on a PBX simply means that voice and data can be transmitted and switched in the same way. Since user data rates are often much less than 64 kbps, several of these signals are often submultiplexed or concentrated onto one channel. In so-called integrated workstations, simultaneous voice and data transmissions are accomplished by multiplexing 64 kbps of voice with, for example, 56 kbps of data and 8 kbps of signaling. The data part of this 128 kbps signal can, of course, be obtained by multiplexing several lower data-rate signals. Normally, integrated workstations require two twisted pairs.

Protocol conversion, which provides the ability for different systems to communicate, is another feature supplied by a digital PBX. Interfaces with the public telephone network through a T1 interface and with public packet-switched networks are also features supplied by most digital PBXs. Since a local area network and a PBX may coexist in the same location, interfacing between these two kinds of local networks is also desirable.

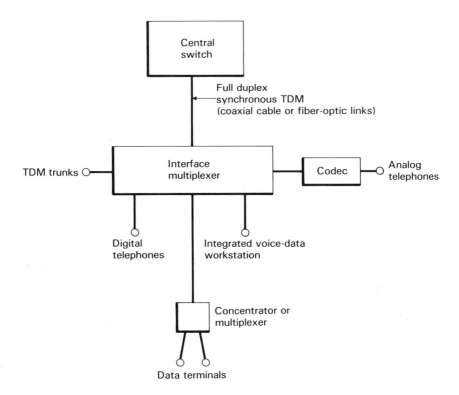

Figure 4.2   A Distributed PBX Architecture

In many ways PBXs and local area networks provide similar services; in fact, there has been considerable discussion (see Pfister and O'Brien [4]) on the comparative advantages and disadvantages of integrated PBXs and local area networks. It is clear from such a discussion that a major limitation of the PBX is its transmission speed. Thus PBXs are limited to voice and low data-rate applications, whereas local area networks can be used for high-speed data and video applications as well. It seems likely that since both systems have unique features, there may be a need for both types of local networks within the same user environment.

4.3   Digital Switches

The function of any switch is to set up and release connections between a pair of users as such connections are requested. The use of the term *digital* in digital switching implies that the signals that represent messages move through the switch in digital form. For efficient transmission through the switch, digital bit streams are time multiplexed so that the switching system serves a number of TDM lines.

A comprehensive account of the development of digital switching is given by Joel [5]. In what follows, the central ideas of the two principal types of digital switches are presented and discussed from the point of view of their use in digital PBXs.

To begin the discussion, consider basic TDM notation and operation as it applies to digital switches. Each multiplexed user is commonly called a *channel*, so a multiplex with 12 users is called a 12-channel multiplex. The time interval for transmitting signals from a particular channel is called a *time slot*. Typically, a time slot is filled with a single sample from the channel, although the sample could consist of a number of individual pulses in a time sequence. A sequence of time slots that covers all channels is called a *frame*.

The basic operation of a digital switch is illustrated in Fig. 4.3. The switch interconnects *N* input and output TDM links. For example, channel 2 of TDM link 1 could be connected to channel 12 of TDM link 6, and channel 8 of TDM link 10 could be connected to channel 3 of TDM link 1. If the latter connection is part of a voice conversation link, then a return connection is required, namely, channel 3 of TDM link 1 to channel 8 of TDM link 10.

As can be seen from Fig. 4.3, each one-way connection requires two translations: one in space (link-to-link), and one in time (slot-to-slot). Thus, a digital switch inherently requires at least one space-division switching stage and at least one time-division switching stage. As discussed later, large switches use multiple stages of both types. However, space- and time-division switches need to be considered separately first.

4.3.1 Space-division Switching

Space-division switches for TDM transmission lines are used to interconnect the input and output TDM links for a single time-slot period. This is very

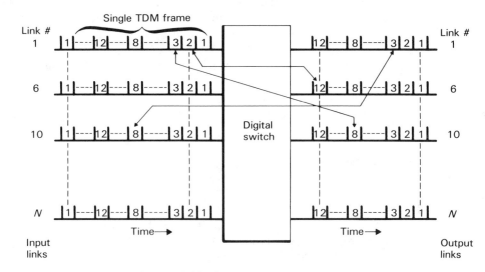

Figure 4.3 Operation of a Digital TDM Switch

different from space-division switching for analog signals where the connection is maintained for the duration of the complete message. Space-division switching in the present time-division context is more correctly known as time-multiplex switching (TMS). In considering the basic operation of space-division switches, however, it is unnecessary to consider the nature of the signals being switched. Thus a single-stage space-division switch is first described in a general context.

As the term space-division implies, the connecting paths between the input and output links are separated in space, and thus the kernel of the switch is the electronic crosspoint or semiconductor gate that can be opened or closed by a control unit. Figure 4.4(a) shows a simple rectangular crossbar matrix with n inputs and m outputs for a total of mn crosspoints. In a switch with such a matrix, referred to simply as a crossbar switch, there is a distinction between input and output links; this is not so in the triangular, or folded, matrix and associated switch, shown in Fig. 4.4(b), which has $n(n-1)/2$ crosspoints. A crossbar switch is potentially blocking if $n > m$, whereas a single-stage folded switch is strictly nonblocking.

A disadvantage of crossbar switches is the number of crosspoints required (proportional to n^2 for a square matrix); this is costly for large n and produces a large amount of capacitive loading on the message paths. Other disadvan-

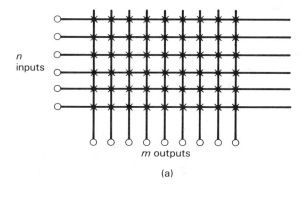

n inputs

m outputs

(a)

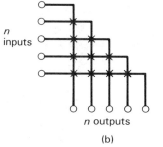

n inputs

n outputs

(b)

Figure 4.4   Single-stage Space-division Switches
(a) Rectangular (crossbar) matrix
(b) Triangular (folded) matrix

tages are the absence of any alternate paths in the case of crosspoint failure and the inefficient utilization of each crosspoint.

All these problems are circumvented by multiple-stage switching. Figure 4.5 shows a typical three-stage space-division switch. The first stage of this symmetric switch consists of a number N/n of $(n \times k)$ crossbar matrices, each of which has n input lines and k output lines. Usually each of these units is of the expansion type, with $k > n$ and therefore strictly nonblocking. The second set of arrays in the three-stage switch is square, and the third set is of the concentrator type, with more input than output lines. Since alternate paths are provided through the three-stage matrix, the use of concentrators in the output stage does not imply that the overall switch is blocking.

To investigate this further, note that the complete switch is nonblocking if each source–destination pair has an available path at all times. In Fig. 4.5, consider a source A, which has one input to one of the arrays in the first stage, and a destination B, which is reached through one output from one of the arrays in the last stage. In the intermediate stage, the path from A to B must go through one of the k arrays that comprise the intermediate stage. Under the worst possible conditions, $(n - 1)$ of the inputs to the array used by A in the first stage could be occupied by other inputs. Similarly, $(n - 1)$ other inputs could be applied to the output array used to reach B. All told, a minimum of $2(n - 1) + 1$ paths must be available through the intermediate stage, or k must be at least $2(n - 1) + 1 = 2n - 1$ for the switch to be nonblocking.

The total number of crosspoints, N_x, in the three-stage switch can be determined from the number of crosspoints in each array of each stage. In the first and last stages, there are nk crosspoints in each of N/n arrays, or $2nk(N/n) = 2kN$ total crosspoints. Similarly, there are $(N/n)^2$ crosspoints in

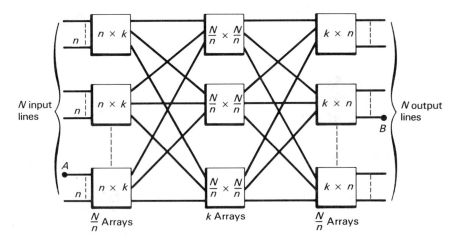

Figure 4.5   A Symmetric Three-stage Space-division Switch

each of k arrays in the intermediate stage, giving

$$N_x = 2Nk + k(N/n)^2 \qquad (4.1)$$

Substituting the minimum value of k for nonblocking into (4.1) yields

$$N_x = 2N(2n - 1) + (2n - 1)(N/n)^2 \qquad (4.2)$$

The optimum value of n to minimize the number of crosspoints for this switch is obtained by putting dN_x/dn equal to 0 and solving this equation. This gives a cubic equation in n; for large values of N, the solution can be approximated by $(N/2)^{1/2}$. With this value of n, the minimum number of crosspoints for large N is

$$\min N_x = 4N(\sqrt{2N} - 1) \qquad (4.3)$$

It should be noted that this number of crosspoints, required to make a three-stage switch nonblocking, is less than that for a corresponding single-stage switch only when N is 24 or greater. As an example of the crosspoint savings for large N, the number of crosspoints needed for $N = 512$ is about 63,500 for a symmetric three-stage switch, whereas a single-stage switch needs approximately 261,600 crosspoints.

When a space-division switch is not designed to be strictly nonblocking, the actual amount of blocking that takes place is very much dependent on the loads on the incoming lines (i.e., the fraction of time that these lines are busy). A switch is usually designed to have a very low blocking probability (approximately 0.002), using some prior knowledge of the expected utilization of the incoming links in the calculation.

The discussion up to this point applies to any type of space-division switch. A time-multiplexed switching unit has the special requirement that connections be made for only a single time slot of a frame. A switch adapted to satisfy this requirement is shown in Fig. 4.6. A control store, often implemented as a

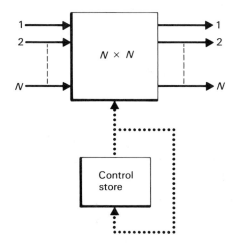

Figure 4.6 A Time-multiplexed Switch

random access memory, provides the necessary information about the required connections for each time slot.

4.3.2 Time-division Switching

Any type of switch has the task of connecting one of the channels served by the switch to another such channel; for example, channel i could be connected to channel j. Once the switch connection is made, data from channel i flows into channel j and, if the connection is full duplex, data from channel j flows into channel i.

Time-division switches interconnect channels from a single set of channels that share a TDM frame. In such a frame, samples of data from the multiplexed channels are transmitted in sequence. Thus to accomplish switching, at least for the duration of a frame, the data from the slot allocated to channel i must be moved to the slot allocated to channel j and vice versa for full duplex operation. The basic component of most time-division switches performs just this time-slot interchange operation and is called a *time-slot interchange* (TSI) unit. Figure 4.7 illustrates a TSI unit interchanging the contents of the slot for channel i with the contents of the slot for channel j in a full duplex manner.

A common approach to interchanging the data in two slots of a TDM frame is to store the contents of every slot on one frame cycle and then read out the stored data in the desired sequence on the next frame cycle. This approach, of course, introduces a delay proportional to the separation of the input and output time slots in the TDM frame.

A circuit for implementing a TSI unit is shown in Fig. 4.8. The central feature of the TSI circuit is a random access memory that uses words with the same number of bits as a time slot of the TDM signal and one word of storage for each of the C channels in the TDM frame. Data is read into the memory in a slot-by-slot sequence over a complete frame. The same data is then read out on the next frame cycle in an order controlled by an address store that positions a pointer at the proper address for reading out each stored word. (A stored word corresponds to the contents of some time slot, which in turn is the data from one of the channels that makes up the frame.)

Thus the address store maps the input sequence of channel slots into the

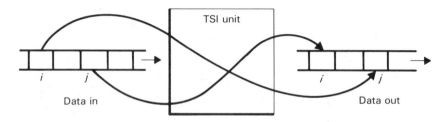

Figure 4.7   Time Slot Interchange Operation

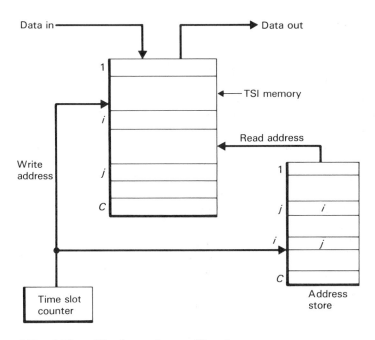

Figure 4.8   A Time Slot Interchange Circuit

desired output sequence. For example, to interchange slots i and j, the output frame is constructed by positioning the read pointer at the contents of slot i when slot j is read out in the output frame cycle. The contents of the address store reflect the existing connections and remain unchanged for the duration of a circuit-switched call.

The mode of operation just described is strictly nonblocking; however, a TSI unit can support only a limited number of connections since both a read and a write operation is necessary for each channel in the frame. (Recall that the contents of each slot are read as a word into the random access memory and then read out in the proper position in the new frame.) The read and write operations must take place in real time to keep up with the incoming data. Thus the memory access speed determines how rapidly the data in one slot can arrive and, indirectly, how many channels can be served.

As an example, consider a unit with a 0.5 μs memory access time on a per-word basis, or 1.0 μs to both read and write. This unit could then keep up with data arriving as rapidly as 1.0 μs per slot. If a TDM signal, such as a T1 frame, has a frame length of 125 μs, then 125 slots or channels (i.e., 62 full duplex connections) could be supported.

This characteristic of a single TSI unit is undesirable, and multiple time stages can be used to obtain more favorable tradeoffs. Multiple time stages must be used in conjunction with space-division stages, however, to connect different TDM streams. The next subsection looks at some basic multistage switches of this composite type.

4.3.3 Multiple-stage Switches

In most PBXs, a number of time- and space-division stages are concatenated. Kasson [6] gives a good survey of digital PBX designs, pointing out that the architecture of most digital PBXs provides multiplexing, concentration, and coding/decoding (for analog signals) using both space and time stages. If T is used to denote a time-division stage and S a corresponding space-division stage, two of the most common combinations used in switch designs are STS and TST. Note that the multiple-stage switches tend to use the S and T stages in a symmetrical manner from input to output.

The operation of a STS switch, such as shown in Fig. 4.9, is functionally the same as a three-stage space switch with the switch strictly nonblocking for $k = 2N - 1$. If there are C slots in each TDM frame, this switch effectively connects each of CN input channels to any one of CN output channels.

The operation of a TST switch, such as that shown in Fig. 4.10, is somewhat different from that of the STS switch. First, whereas there are k paths between any specific source and destination in the STS switch, there is only one such path in the TST switch, assuming that the space-division stage is, in fact, a single-stage switch. Furthermore, blocking is possible for the TST switch unless the number of slots in a frame at the input to the space stage is greater than the number in the original switch-input TDM bit stream. If there are C slots in the switch-input bit stream, there must be l slots in a frame at the space-stage input, and l must be at least $2C$-1 for the TST switch to be strictly nonblocking. This result follows by direct analogy to three-stage space switches.

The tradeoff between space and time stages is essentially a tradeoff between number of crosspoints and memory requirements. Time expansion in a TST switch is less costly than space expansion in an STS switch, and for switches with low but nonzero blocking probabilities, TST switches become

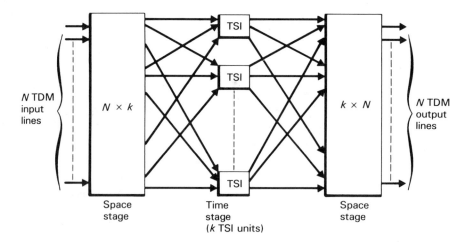

Figure 4.9   A Space–time–space (STS) Switching Structure

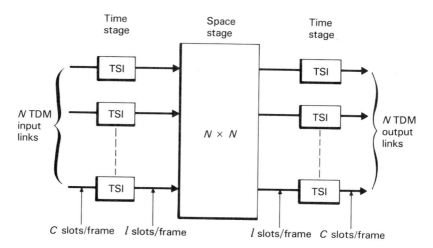

Figure 4.10   A Time–space–time (TST) Switching Structure

more cost-effective than corresponding STS switches for high channel utilizations.

A digital switch generally provides such additional features as multiplexing and demultiplexing and, when a digital switch is connected to an essentially analog world, coding and decoding. To provide these features, a typical switch architecture has the structure MTSTM, where M denotes multiplexing/demultiplexing, with the symmetric structure preserved. Multiplexing generally converts space-divided digital signals to a TDM stream, and in many cases, including PBXs, the multiplexer also provides concentration, which results in fewer time slots than input lines. Many switches are designed so that blocking occurs at the concentration stage rather than in the TDM part of the switch, which is often nonblocking.

4.4   Blocking Analysis

In a circuit-switched system, blocking does not occur if there is always a circuit available when needed. The luxury of a completely nonblocking system may be too costly and inefficient, however, especially for the type of randomly varying demands typically encountered. A totally nonblocking system must have the capacity to meet peak demands. Thus, if demand during some rare busy periods is 20 or 30 percent greater than average, a nonblocking system would have to be designed so that 20 or 30 percent of its capacity is rarely used. Thus, for the sake of cost and efficient utilization of equipment, many PBX systems are designed for busy hour, rather than peak, loading, and thus calls are blocked under certain peak loading conditions.

A circuit-switched system is blocked to a call (either a voice or data message) if an end-to-end connection is not available. Under such conditions the call is either refused entry to the PBX and lost, or the call is stored and delayed until a connection is available. As previously discussed, switches and parts of switches can be designed in a variety of ways—in particular, with and without concentration. Without concentration, the number of input and output channels are equal, whereas with concentration, the number of output channels from the concentrator is less than the number of input channels. In general, blocking at the switch itself, if at all possible, is much less likely than blocking due to concentration. Blocking analysis in this section is thus confined to blocking caused by concentration, which can be either remote or in the first stage of the switch.

The first subsection develops the mathematical framework for the evaluation of blocking probabilities and average delays due to blocking. State transition-rate diagrams are used to derive an expression for the probability of having a specified number of messages in the system.

In the second and third subsections, consideration is given to traffic analysis as used for performance evaluation of blocking PBXs. Such PBXs can be designed as either *loss* or *delay* systems. In a loss system, overload traffic is rejected without being served, whereas in a delay system, overload traffic is stored until a circuit becomes available.

With regard to assumptions made in developing mathematical models, it is assumed that the total arrival process from all sources is Poisson. Such an arrival process is a reasonable first approximation to most practical situations, and it has desirable mathematical properties.

Although the number of input channels is clearly always finite, for mathematical tractability it is assumed that the number of sources is infinite. The infinite source models that are developed tend to be most accurate when the ratio of the number of input channels to the number of output channels is reasonably large, for example, 5 to 10. For the same amount of total offered traffic, the infinite source model always gives greater blocking probabilities than corresponding finite source models. Thus infinite source models used to size PBXs give conservative results.

Infinite source models are subsequently developed and analyzed for both loss- and delay-type systems. In each case, the blocking probability is evaluated, and, in the case of delay systems, the average queueing delay is also determined in terms of the system parameters. A birth–death model, in conjunction with state transition-rate diagrams, is used in the analysis. Basic concepts of this model are developed in the next subsection.

4.4.1 Transition-rate Diagrams

The analytic framework developed in this subsection is closely related to that developed for the $M/M/1$ queue in Chapter 3. The material to be presented here could have been used to develop the $M/M/1$ queueing expressions of Subsection 3.3.2, but is directed toward a more general result than the average number stored in a queue, as found in Chapter 3. The present objective requires an expression for the probability of the number stored in a queue under less stringent restrictions than those used in the previous chapter.

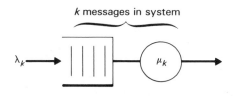

k messages in system

$\lambda_k \longrightarrow$ | | | | $\longrightarrow$ μ_k $\longrightarrow$

Figure 4.11   A Queueing System

A rigorous approach to the present subject would be based on a rich branch of the theory of stochastic processes called Markov Chain Theory. Markov chains, both in discrete and continuous form, are used extensively as a modeling tool in the analysis of computer networks. Kleinrock [7], for example, presents a very complete and readable exposition of the theory. However, for present purposes, it is possible to take a simplified view that avoids much of the rigorous theory.

Consider a single-server queueing system, such as shown in Fig. 4.11, and assume that both the arrival rate of messages to the system and the departure rate of messages from the system depend on the current number in the system, including messages in service. Note that this approach is more general than that used in Chapter 3, where interest is restricted to average behavior. To continue, with reference to Fig. 4.11, let the arrival and service rates in messages/second be denoted respectively as λ_k and μ_k, where the subscript indicates the dependence of arrival and service rates on the number of messages in the system. Only a single arrival or a single departure is permitted at any instant of time in the system considered. Such a system is in the general category of *birth–death processes*. For such a process, the state is the number, k, in the system, and this number can change to $(k - 1)$ through a death (departure) or to $(k + 1)$ through a birth (arrival).

A transition-rate diagram, such as that shown in Fig. 4.12, is a convenient way to represent a birth–death process. In such a diagram, the number in the circle is the system state, and the transition arrows, labeled λ_k and μ_k, represent the rates at which arrivals and departures to and from a given state can occur. It is assumed that transitions between states can occur at any point in time, so that time between transitions is completely independent of how

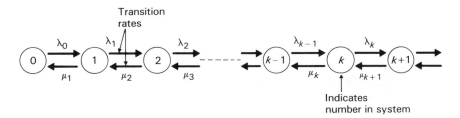

Transition rates

Indicates number in system

Figure 4.12   State Transition-rate Diagram

long the system has been in the current state. For this to be true, the system must have no memory with respect to sojourn time in each state.

For continuous probability distributions, this memoryless property holds only for exponential distributions. Thus the sojourn time in each state (i.e., the time between state transitions), must be exponentially distributed. This characterization of the sojourn time, in turn, implies that arrivals to the system in a given state form a Poisson process, and that the service times for this state are exponentially distributed. Note that in the fairly general formulation so far, parameters of all of the distributions can still depend on the system state, k. Without memory, the system is completely described by its current state, independent of history. This property is called the Markov property.

A difference equation is now developed for the steady-state probability that the system is in state k. As a first step, let $p_k(t)$ be the probability that the system is in state k at time t. Now consider a small time increment Δt, so small that only one of three possible events, an arrival, a departure, or no arrival or departure, has any nonnegligible probability of occurring. In the time Δt as described, the system state can then only change as follows: from state k to state $(k + 1)$ if an arrival occurs, from state k to state $(k - 1)$ if a departure occurs, or from state k to state k (no change) if neither an arrival nor a departure takes place. Using the transition rates as defined, the probabilities of these transitions can be expressed respectively as $\lambda_k \Delta t$, $\mu_k \Delta t$, and $(1 - (\lambda_k + \mu_k)\,\Delta t)$.

An expression is now determined for the probability, $p_k\,(t + \Delta t)$, that the system is in state k at time $t + \Delta t$. For small Δt, the event that the system is in state k at time $t + \Delta t$ is equal to the union of three events:

Event 1: System in state k at time t with no arrival or departure in Δt;
Event 2: System in state $(k + 1)$ at time t with no arrival and one departure in Δt; and
Event 3: System in state $(k - 1)$ at time t with one arrival and no departure in Δt.

The three events are disjoint and furthermore each is the intersection of three other events that are assumed to be statistically independent. Thus, using the relationships from probability for disjoint events and for the intersection of statistically independent events, $p_k(t + \Delta t)$ can be expressed as

$$p_k\,(t + \Delta t) = p_k(t)[1 - (\lambda_k + \mu_k)\Delta t] +$$

$$p_{k+1}(t)\,\mu_{k+1}\,\Delta t + p_{k-1}(t)\,\lambda_{k-1}\,\Delta t \qquad (4.4)$$

The system can be assumed to be *ergodic* in the steady state, meaning that its state at any one time is very much like the state at any other time. This means that dependence on t can be dropped so that

$$p_k(t) = p_k(t + \Delta t) = p_k \qquad (4.5)$$

Under these conditions (4.4) can be written as

$$(\lambda_k + \mu_k)\, p_k = \lambda_{k-1}\, p_{k-1} + \mu_{k+1}\, p_{k+1} \tag{4.6}$$

since the Δt's can be cancelled from both sides of the equation.

Equation (4.6) can be derived in another, more heuristic, fashion with an analogy between flow of probability and the flow of a fluid. From examination of Fig. 4.12, the rate at which probability flows into state k is given by

$$\text{flow into } k = \lambda_{k-1}\, p_{k-1} + \mu_{k+1}\, p_k \tag{4.7}$$

whereas

$$\text{flow out of } k = (\lambda_k + \mu_k)\, p_k \tag{4.8}$$

Under equilibrium conditions, flow is conserved; input flow to any state must equal the output flow from that state. Equation (4.6) then follows from equating the right-hand sides of (4.7) and (4.8).

Equation (4.6) holds for all values of $k \geq 1$. For the boundary state $k = 0$, examination of Fig. 4.12 leads to the special equation

$$\lambda_0\, p_0 = \mu_1\, p_1 \tag{4.9}$$

It is now possible to carry out an iterative solution for p_k in terms of p_0, beginning with (4.9), which yields

$$p_1 = \frac{\lambda_0}{\mu_1}\, p_0 \tag{4.10}$$

Equation (4.6), using $k = 1$, then gives

$$(\lambda_1 + \mu_1)\, p_1 = \lambda_0\, p_0 + \mu_2\, p_2 \tag{4.11}$$

which through use of (4.10) reduces to

$$p_2 = \frac{\lambda_0 \lambda_1}{\mu_1 \mu_2}\, p_0 \tag{4.12}$$

Continuing the process using $k = 2$ in (4.6) gives

$$\mu_3\, p_3 = (\lambda_2 + \mu_2)\, p_2 - \lambda_1\, p_1 \tag{4.13}$$

or, after use of (4.10) and (4.12),

$$p_3 = \frac{\lambda_0 \lambda_1 \lambda_2}{\mu_1 \mu_2 \mu_3}\, p_0 \tag{4.14}$$

The process can clearly be continued to express p_k as

$$p_k = \frac{\lambda_0 \lambda_1 \cdots \lambda_{k-1}}{\mu_1 \mu_2 \cdots \mu_k}\, p_0 = p_0 \prod_{i=0}^{k-1} \frac{\lambda_i}{\mu_{i+1}}, \quad k \geq 1 \tag{4.15}$$

The system must be in some state k, $k = 0, 1, 2 \ldots$ so that

$$\sum_{k=0}^{\infty} p_k = 1 \tag{4.16}$$

Using (4.16), it is possible to find p_0. Substituting (4.15) into (4.16) yields, after simplification,

$$p_0 = \left[1 + \sum_{k=1}^{\infty} \prod_{i=0}^{k-1} \frac{\lambda_i}{\mu_{i+1}} \right]^{-1} \tag{4.17}$$

The results of (4.15) and (4.17) are general and can be used for any queueing system that satisfies the assumptions underlying the birth–death model. Loss and delay systems, which are to be discussed, fit this framework, as do a number of other common queueing systems.

The M/M/1 system, discussed in Chapter 3, is a special case that results when the transition rates do not depend on the state k. For this special case, (4.15) reduces to

$$p_k = p_0 \, (\lambda/\mu)^k$$

and, after some simplification, (4.17) becomes

$$p_0 = (1 - \lambda/\mu)$$

The average number stored in the queue in the steady state can be obtained from the probability function, using the expression for average value as

$$N = \sum_{k=0}^{\infty} k \, (1 - \lambda/\mu) \, (\lambda/\mu)^k$$

The infinite sum can be evaluated to obtain

$$N = \frac{\rho}{1 - \rho}$$

which is identical to Eq. (3.42). Note that here $\rho = \lambda/\mu$, whereas in the notation of Chapter 3, $\rho = \lambda/\mu C$.

4.4.2 Loss Systems

In this subsection, PBXs designed to be loss systems are considered. For such systems, a fixed number, m, of input messages can be served without overflowing some critical system component, considered in this case to be a concentrator. When m messages are in service, further arriving messages are rejected and lost.

The arrival process accounting for all sources is assumed to be Poisson, with an average arrival rate λ. Message lengths are assumed to be exponentially distributed so that the average message requires $1/\mu$ sec for transmission. The part of the PBX that can cause blocking is modeled as a unit with one input channel on which λ messages/second arrive, and m output channels, each with a rate of μ messages/second, as indicated in Fig. 4.13.

Since the original work with loss systems was done in the early days of telephony, it is interesting, and useful when using the literature, to give the terminology used in this application. Messages are termed *calls*, and the time

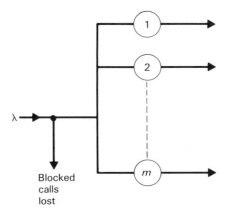

Figure 4.13   A Model for a Lost Calls Cleared (LCC) System

to transmit a message is called the *holding time*. A system for which blocked calls are lost is referred to as a *lost calls cleared*, or LCC, system.

The blocking unit can also be viewed as an M/M/m/m queue, where M/M denotes Poisson arrivals and exponential message lengths, and the final m/m denotes respectively m servers and a maximum of m messages in the system. With the number of servers equal to or greater than the number of messages in the system, there is, of course, never any queueing.

The birth–death model discussed in the previous subsection is general enough to include blocking units of the type being considered. Consider the state transition-rate diagram of Fig. 4.12 for general birth–death systems. For the general case, the state transition rates, λ_k and μ_k, are state-dependent, and the number of states is unlimited.

A loss system can be identified as a special case of this general birth–death system. First, the maximum number of messages that the loss system can handle is m, which becomes the largest state. Also, the arrival rate is a constant, λ, as long as the number in the system is less than m; stated mathematically,

$$\lambda_k = \begin{cases} \lambda, & k < m \\ 0, & k \geq m \end{cases} \tag{4.18}$$

The departure rate is μ on each output channel, and one channel is used for each message. Thus the total rate μ_k at which messages are being served is given by

$$\mu_k = \begin{cases} k\mu, & k = 1, 2, \ldots m \\ 0, & k > m \end{cases} \tag{4.19}$$

The transition-rate diagram for the loss system is given in Fig. 4.14.

The results of the birth–death model can now be used to evaluate the

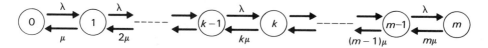

Figure 4.14   Transition-rate Diagram for a Lost Calls Cleared (LCC) System

probability of blocking for the loss system. First, (4.18) and (4.19) are substituted in (4.17) to give the probability, p_0, of the system being empty. The result is

$$p_0 = \left[1 + \sum_{k-1}^{m} \prod_{i-0}^{k-1} \frac{\lambda}{(i + 1)\mu} \right]^{-1} = \left[1 + \sum_{k-1}^{m} \left(\frac{\lambda}{\mu} \right)^k \frac{1}{k!} \right]^{-1}$$

$$p_0 = \left[\sum_{k-0}^{m} \left(\frac{\lambda}{\mu} \right)^k \frac{1}{k!} \right]^{-1} \tag{4.20}$$

In carrying out the last step, recall that $0! = 1$.

Equation (4.15) now gives the probability, p_k, of k messages in the system as

$$p_k = \begin{cases} p_0 \displaystyle\prod_{i-0}^{k-1} \frac{\lambda}{(i + 1)\mu}, & k \leq m \\ 0, & k > m \end{cases}$$

or

$$p_k = \begin{cases} \left(\dfrac{\lambda}{\mu} \right)^k \dfrac{1}{k!} \left[\displaystyle\sum_{j-0}^{m} \left(\dfrac{\lambda}{\mu} \right)^j \dfrac{1}{j!} \right]^{-1}, & k \leq m \\ 0, & k > m \end{cases} \tag{4.21}$$

The blocking probability, or probability of message loss, P_L, is the probability of exactly m messages in the system, namely

$$P_L = p_m = \frac{(\lambda/\mu)^m}{m! \displaystyle\sum_{j-0}^{m} (\lambda/\mu)^j \frac{1}{j!}} \tag{4.22}$$

The result of (4.22) is known as Erlang's loss formula, or the Erlang B formula, as it was first derived by A. K. Erlang in 1917. Values obtained from (4.22) have been tabulated extensively (see, for example, Bellamy [8] or Briley [9]). A representative group of curves is given in Fig. 4.15, which shows the loss probability, P_L, as a function of offered traffic per channel, λ/μ. Note that λ/μ is the total traffic intensity that has a value between 0 and m for this m-server system. In telephony terms, λ/μ, which is the product of the total average arrival rate and the mean holding time, is given in units of Erlangs.

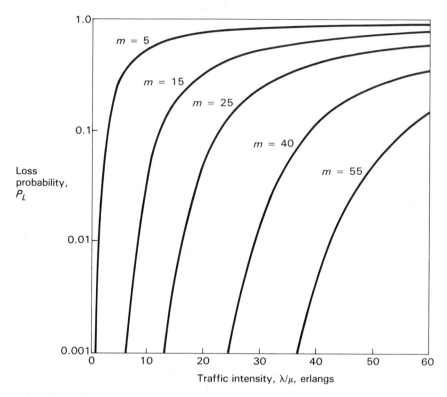

Figure 4.15   Loss Probability versus Offered Traffic for the LCC Model

4.4.3   Delay Systems

An earlier subsection classified blocking PBXs of the type being considered as either loss systems or delay systems. The latter are the subject of this subsection.

The delay systems to be considered are similar in many respects to the loss systems discussed in Subsection 4.4.2. The same assumptions and parameters are used for the mathematical model, with the only difference being the presence of a buffer, of assumed infinite capacity, for queueing blocked messages. The delay system model, which is traditionally termed a *lost calls delayed* (LCD) system, is shown in Fig. 4.16.

From the point of view of a queueing model, the delay system is an $M/M/m$ queue, in which three symbols have the same significance as for the loss system, and the absence of a fourth symbol indicates an infinite buffer capacity. As with the loss system, the delay system can be represented as a special case of the birth–death process shown in Fig. 4.12. The parameters are determined as follows. The arrival process is independent of the number of messages in the system, and hence the arrival rate is given by

$$\lambda_k = \lambda, \quad k = 0, 1, 2 \ldots \tag{4.23}$$

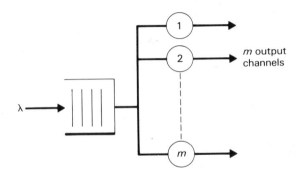

Figure 4.16   A Model for a Lost Calls Delayed (LCD) System

The actual service or departure rate depends on the number of channels in use. There is a maximum of m channels, and hence the departure rate is given by

$$\mu_k = \begin{cases} k\mu & 0 \le k < m \\ m\mu & k \ge m \end{cases} \tag{4.24}$$

where $1/\mu$ is the average time to service one message. The transition-rate diagram for the delay system is given in Fig. 4.17.

The general result of (4.15) for birth–death systems can be applied in this case to carry out a blocking analysis. Thus, substituting for λ_k and μ_k in (4.15) yields for the two cases $k < m$ and $k \ge m$,

$$p_k = p_0 \prod_{i=0}^{k-1} \frac{\lambda}{(i+1)\mu} = p_0 \left(\frac{\lambda}{\mu}\right)^k \frac{1}{k!}, \quad k < m \tag{4.25}$$

and

$$p_k = p_0 \prod_{i=0}^{m-1} \frac{\lambda}{(i+1)\mu} \prod_{i=m}^{k-1} \frac{\lambda}{m\mu} = p_0 \left(\frac{\lambda}{\mu}\right)^k \frac{1}{m! \, m^{k-m}}, \quad k \ge m \tag{4.26}$$

Unlike the loss system, the delay system may not be ergodic, and if this basic assumption is violated, the preceding results are not valid. The condition for ergodicity and for finite queue lengths is that the total arrival rate be less than the maximum service rate, or

$$\lambda/m\mu < 1 \tag{4.27}$$

If this condition is satisfied, (4.25) and (4.26) are valid.

The next step in the analysis is to evaluate p_0 by substituting for λ_k and μ_k in

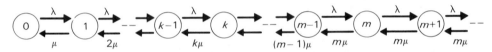

Figure 4.17   Transition-rate Diagram for a Lost Calls Delayed (LCD) System

(4.17). This yields

$$p_0 = \left[1 + \sum_{k=1}^{m-1} \frac{(\lambda/\mu)^k}{k!} + \sum_{k=m}^{\infty} \left(\frac{\lambda}{m\mu} \right)^k \frac{m^m}{m!} \right]^{-1}$$

or, after reduction with the sum of a geometric series,

$$p_0 = \left[\sum_{k=0}^{m-1} \frac{(\lambda/\mu)^k}{k!} + \frac{(\lambda/\mu)^m}{m!} \frac{1}{1 - \lambda/m\mu} \right]^{-1} \tag{4.28}$$

Note that $\lambda/m\mu$ must be less than 1 for the geometric series to converge. This condition is just that of (4.27), which ensures that the system is ergodic.

It is now possible to determine the probability of delay, denoted P_D, for delay systems. An incoming message is delayed if there are m or more messages already in the system. Thus, using (4.26), there results

$$P_D = \sum_{k=m}^{\infty} p_k = \sum_{k=m}^{\infty} p_0 \frac{(\lambda/m\mu)^k m^m}{m!} = p_0 \frac{(\lambda/\mu)^m}{m!} \frac{1}{(1 - \lambda/m\mu)}$$

or, after substituting for p_0 from (4.28),

$$P_D = \frac{\dfrac{(\lambda/\mu)^m}{m!} \dfrac{1}{(1 - \lambda/m\mu)}}{\displaystyle\sum_{k=0}^{m-1} \frac{(\lambda/\mu)^k}{k!} + \frac{(\lambda/\mu)^m}{m!} \frac{1}{(1 - \lambda/m\mu)}} \tag{4.29}$$

This equation for P_D is referred to as Erlang's C formula. Plots of P_D versus offered traffic per channel, λ/μ, are given in Fig. 4.18 for representative values of m, the number of servers. The references cited previously by Bellamy [8] and Briley [9] also give an extensive collection of results for the Erlang C formula.

Note that for delay systems, the calculation of blocking probability requires a sum over all numbers of messages in the system equal to or greater than m since messages are stored rather than rejected. Recall that the corresponding calculation of blocking probability for loss systems merely requires calculation of p_m since all subsequent messages are rejected after m are in the system.

Delay systems keep messages in storage if the system is blocked, and the stored messages are served later after some delay. This queueing delay can be calculated by first finding the average number of messages stored and then applying Little's formula to determine average time delay.

To find the average number of messages stored, note that none is stored until the number of arrivals exceeds m. Thus the average number stored, N_q, is given by

$$N_q = 1 \cdot p_{m+1} + 2 \cdot p_{m+2} + \cdots = \sum_{k=1}^{\infty} k \, p_{m+k}$$

Using the expression for p_k from (4.26) then gives

$$N_q = \sum_{k=1}^{\infty} k \, p_0 \left(\frac{\lambda}{\mu} \right)^{k+m} \frac{1}{m! \, m^k} = p_0 \left(\frac{\lambda}{\mu} \right)^m \sum_{k=1}^{\infty} k \left(\frac{\lambda}{m\mu} \right)^k$$

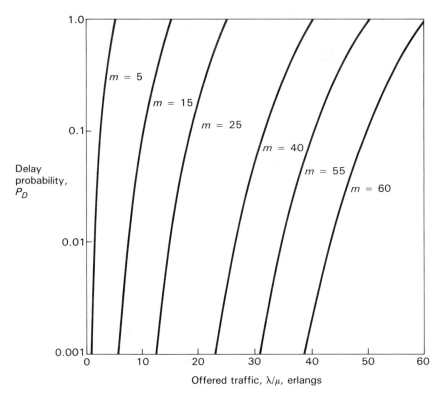

Figure 4.18   Delay Probability versus Offered Traffic for the LCD Model

Evaluation of the last sum then yields

$$N_q = p_0 \frac{(\lambda/\mu)^m}{m!} \frac{(\lambda/m\mu)}{(1 - \lambda/m\mu)^2} = \frac{\lambda/m\mu}{(1 - \lambda/m\mu)} P_D \qquad (4.30)$$

Finally, application of Little's Law, (3.8), gives the average queueing delay T_q as

$$T_q = N_q/\lambda = \frac{P_D}{m\mu(1 - \lambda/m\mu)} \qquad (4.31)$$

The parameter $1/\mu$, which is the average message transmission or holding time, can be expressed in terms of average message length $\overline{X}$, in bits, and line transmission rate, R, in bps, as

$$1/\mu = \overline{X}/R$$

In terms of these parameters, average queueing delay becomes

$$T_q = \frac{P_D}{m(1 - \lambda \overline{X}/mR)} \frac{\overline{X}}{R} \qquad (4.32)$$

4.5   Examples of PBX System Sizing

The characteristics of several types of switches and the analysis of blocking for certain conditions are discussed in detail in earlier sections of this chapter. The purpose of this section is to bring together some of the quantitative results to focus on the central design issue for digital PBXs, namely, system sizing (in effect, switch sizing) and blocking probability.

4.5.1   Sizing of PBXs

Sizing of PBXs is a relatively simple problem, typically with only one or two variables involved. Critical parameters vary with the type of switch to be sized. Switches are generally implemented as composite multistage switches of the space–time–space (STS) or time–space–time (TST) types, as previously discussed, and consideration is restricted to these two types.

SPACE–TIME–SPACE SWITCHES: Reference to Fig. 4.9 and the discussion of Subsection 4.4.3 provide the following information on STS switches:

- The multistage switch couples N TDM input bit streams to N TDM output bit streams; each TDM frame has C slots or channels; and
- The multistage switch has two space stages and k time slot interchange units (TSI).

For the complete switch to be nonblocking, $k = 2N - 1$. This value for k implies that each $N \times k$ space stage requires $Nk = 2N^2 - N$ crosspoints. Each space stage also requires a control store that contains the information necessary to specify the output connections for each slot in each of the N TDM streams. Thus, storage for NC control words is required per space stage. The length of the control word depends on the address space (see the following example).

Each TSI unit also requires a control store for each slot, or a total of C control words†. A TSI unit also needs a memory store to permit time slot interchange. Since up to a full frame delay is possible, the memory store must be capable of holding C data words, where a data word is the contents of a TDM slot. These requirements apply to each of the k TSI units.

TIME–SPACE–TIME SWITCHES: Subsection 4.4.3 also discusses TST switches, and the structure of such a switch is indicated in Fig. 4.10. These switches require

- $2N$ TSI units; and
- 1 $N \times N$ space stage switch.

---

†Note that the length of control words for a TSI unit is not necessarily the same as for a space stage.

As with the STS switch, both the input and output are N TDM bit streams with C slots per frame.

For TST switches to be nonblocking, the space stage must have l slots per frame, with $l = 2C - 1$. Calculations of the number of crosspoints required and of memory requirements are similar to those for STS switches. Note, however, that the storage required for a first-stage TSI unit is quite different from that of a third-stage unit.

Numerical Example

A STS switch has $N = 20$ input TDM streams, with $C = 24$ channels per line. If the switch is sized to be nonblocking, and if a data word is 8 bits long, calculate the total number of crosspoints needed and the total memory requirement.

Solution

For nonblocking, the number of TSI units, $k = 2N - 1 = 39$. Thus, for each of the space stages, $Nk = 20 \times 39 = 780$ crosspoints are needed. For the complete switch, the total number of crosspoints is $2(780) = 1560$.

The control store in each space stage is NC control words. A control word is as long as the longest address. Since $2^5 < 39 < 2^6$, the control word has at least 6 bits. Thus the control storage needed is $20 \times 24 \times 6 = 2880$ bits.

For each time stage, the memory storage is 24 data words, one from each channel and each 8 bits long. The control store for each unit needs addressing for each input channel. As $2^4 < 24 < 2^5$, storage of 24×5 bits is required. Thus, for each TSI unit, the storage required is $(24 \times 8) + (24 \times 5) = 312$ bits, and the total memory requirement is $2(2880) + 39(312) = 17,928$ bits.

4.5.2 Blocking Calculations

As discussed in Section 4.4, not all switches are nonblocking, and, as a measure for reducing cost and increasing efficiency, a switch or parts of a switch is sometimes allowed to block under certain conditions. A blocking system is designed to deal with some peak level of traffic intensity such as the average during the busy hour. The busy hour is a term used to designate a period of peak load chosen to represent what is likely to occur in reasonable system operation. Traffic larger than this peak amount is blocked, and, as discussed in Subsections 4.4.1 and 4.4.2, there are two common ways in which blocked calls are handled: by discarding messages after all circuits are full (LCC) or by storing overload messages until a circuit is open (LCD). The major design issues and parameters depend on which type of service is chosen.

LOST CALLS CLEARED (LCC): For this type of operation, a measure of quality is P_L, the probability that calls or messages are lost, which is called *grade of service* for telephone calls. This probability can be interpreted physically as the steady-state ratio of calls rejected to total number of calls. A value of P_L in the range of 10^{-2} to 10^{-3} is considered satisfactory in most applications.

Equation (4.22), developed in Subsection 4.4.2, relates P_L to the system parameters, λ, μ, and m, which are respectively the average arrival rate of messages to the system, the message service rate, and the number of channels available on the switch or concentrator. Note that (4.22) does not involve λ and μ separately, but only their ratio λ/μ, which has been identified as offered traffic in Erlangs.

A first design problem uses (4.22) directly and is to determine P_L, given a fixed offered traffic λ/μ and a fixed device capacity, m. Such a problem is solved graphically, using either Fig. 4.15 or the more extensive curves of Bellamy [8] and Briley [9], or through use of a computer program.

Two other design problems can be solved with versions of (4.22):

- Determine the offered traffic in Erlangs that produces a given P_L for a fixed device capacity; and
- Determine required device capacity, given P_L and the offered traffic in Erlangs.

Each of these problems can be solved with the graphs previously cited or through use of computer programs written for the specific problem.

Numerical Example

A remote switching unit in a PBX has 96 input channels, each with a bit rate of 64 kbps for either data or voice transmissions. The remote unit is connected to a nonblocking central switch over a full duplex T1 (24 channel) line. Each message has an average length of 100 bytes. Assuming that the average arrival rate is the same for each input channel, find the maximum average arrival rate so that the blocking probability for the PBX does not exceed $P_L = 0.01$.

Solution

The infinite source model, the results of which are plotted in Fig. 4.15, can be assumed to apply to a good approximation. Entering these curves with $P_L = 0.01$ and extrapolating to a value of $m = 24$ yields 15.5 Erlangs for the offered traffic. The average arrival rate per input channel, λ_i, is then computed as follows:

$$\mu = R/\overline{X} = 64 \times 10^3/100 \times 8 = 80$$

$$15.5 = \lambda/\mu = \lambda/80$$

$$96\,\lambda_i = \lambda = 1240$$

$$\lambda_i = 12.9 \text{ messages/second}$$

LOST CALLS DELAYED (LCD): For this type of operation, the messages are delayed when the number of arriving messages exceeds the number of output channels, m, for a device. Two measures of quality can be used for such systems: P_D, the probability of delay, and T_q, the average queueing delay. The probability, P_D, is given by (4.29) in terms of λ/μ and m. The average delay, T_q, is given by (4.31) in terms of P_D and the same parameters λ/μ and m.

Although the equations for LCD and LCC operation are different, P_D and T_q depend on the same parameters as does P_L. Thus there are the same three types of design problems as discussed for the LCC case: given any two of the variables P_D, λ/μ, or m, find the remaining one. Given all three parameters, T_q can be found from (4.31).

Numerical Example

A switching concentrator has 24 input channels, each with a bit rate of 9600 bps; how many output channels of the same bit rate are required to keep the probability of blocking, P_D, less than 0.2. The average input rate on each channel is 5 messages/second, and each message is 50 bytes long on the average.

Under the same conditions, what is the resulting average message delay?

Solution

First, compute the offered traffic as follows:

$$\mu = R/\overline{X} = \frac{9600}{50 \times 8} = 24$$

$$\lambda = 24 \times 5 = 120$$

$$\lambda/\mu = 120/24 = 5 \text{ Erlangs}$$

Now enter the curves of Fig. 4.18 with $P_D = 0.2$ and $\lambda/\mu = 5$. Interpolate to estimate $m = 9$ as the answer to the number of output channels. Substituting the values of P_D, m, and λ/μ into (4.31) then yields for average delay

$$T_q = \frac{0.2}{9 \times 24 \ (1 - 5/9)} = 2.1 \text{ msec}$$

4.6 Summary

This chapter discusses the use of digital PBXs as local networks. Such systems, which fall into a category by themselves, have many properties that are useful for local networks, but differ in many respects from the local area networks, which are the subject of the majority of this text.

A digital PBX uses circuit switching, setting up an end-to-end path through the network for each desired connection. Once a circuit is set up, traffic flows over the dedicated circuit. The availability of a path is the important performance issue for PBXs.

Digital switches operate on time-division multiplexed signals and must provide two translations: one in space—from one physical link to another—and one in time—from the time slot of one TDM signal to a time slot in another TDM signal. The chapter discusses in detail both time- and space-division switches as well as switches composed of a number of concatenated time- and space-division stages. The number of input–output circuits that can be provided by a switch is limited, so switch sizing is a pertinent design problem.

For economic reasons, switches can be designed to satisfy normal busy hour demands without the capacity to satisfy all peak requirements. This leads to the possibility of blocking if an end-to-end connection is not available when needed. This chapter provides an analysis of blocking, using queueing theory to derive appropriate equations. Examples are given to illustrate quantitative calculations for blocking.

Discussion of PBXs is limited to Chapter 4. The next chapter introduces local area networks, which are the subject of the remainder of the book.

References

[1] W. Stallings. *Local Networks: An Introduction*, Chapters 7 and 10. New York: Macmillan, 1984.

[2] "Voice/Data PBX Survey." *Datamation* (August 1983): 155–160.

[3] S. L. Junker and W. E. Noller. "Digital Private Branch Exchanges." *IEEE Communication Magazine* 21, no. 3 (May 1983): 11–17.

[4] G. M. Pfister and B. V. O'Brien. "Comparing the CBX to the Local Network—and the Winner is?" *Data Communications* (July 1982): 103–113.

[5] A. E. Joel, Jr. "Digital Switching—How it has Developed." *IEEE Transactions on Communications* COM-27, no. 7 (July 1979): 948–959.

[6] J. M. Kasson. "Survey of Digital PBX Design." *IEEE Transactions on Communications* COM-27, no. 7 (July 1979): 948–959.

[7] L. Kleinrock. *Queuing Systems*. Vol 1, *Theory*. New York: Wiley–Interscience, 1975.

[8] J. C. Bellamy. *Digital Telephony*. New York: Wiley–Interscience, 1982.

[9] B. E. Briley. *Introduction to Telephone Switching*. Reading, MA: Addison–Wesley, 1983.

Problems and Exercises

1. (a) Describe the operation of a space-division digital switch and a time-division digital switch.
   (b) How are they similar?
   (c) How do they differ?

2. A switch has input channels A, B, C, D and output channels W, X, Y, Z. Describe a blocking condition with the identifications given for the input and output lines.

3. The M/M/1 analysis given in Chapter 3 results in average queueing delay and the average number stored in a queue. Why is the additional analysis of Subsection 4.4.1 necessary?

4. Explain in detail the ways blocked calls can be processed.

5. Differentiate Eq. (4.2) with respect to n. Assign this derivative equal to 0, and find a cubic equation in n. Show that for large N the optimal value of n becomes $(N/2)^{1/2}$. Thus, find the maximum number of crosspoints for large N.

6. Consider a simple TS switch with three channels in each of two input streams and the same number of streams and channels coupling out of the time-division switches into the space-division switch. The output of the space-division switch also has two streams that contain three channels each.

   Show that the TS switch is blocking for any case such that two input channels from the same input stream must couple to the same output channel number in different output streams.

7. (a) Show that

$$\sum_{j=1}^{\infty} jx^j = x \sum_{j=1}^{\infty} \frac{d}{dx} x^j = x \frac{d}{dx} \sum_{j=1}^{\infty} x^j$$

   (b) Use the result of (a) to derive Eq. (4.30).

8. An example in the text calculates the number of crosspoints and the memory requirements for an STS switch. If this switch is replaced by a TST switch (other parameters remaining the same), calculate the requirements for the switch to remain nonblocking. Assuming that 100 bits of storage cost the same as 1 crosspoint, compare the cost of the two switches.

9. Rework problem 8 for a TST switch and the example in the text for an STS switch under the condition that the switches are to be sized for a 0.002 blocking probability at a channel utilization of 0.1. For this probability, the number of time stages in the STS switch is seven; the number of slots per frame input to the space stage of the TST switch is nine. Compare the cost of the two switches using the cost data of problem 8.

10. Consider a TST switch with two input and two output TDM streams, with two channels in each stream. The output of the first time-division switch (and the input to the space-division switch) also has two channels.
    (a) Show that this combination violates the general requirements for nonblocking of TST switches.
    (b) Find a blocking condition (i.e., find a combination of input–output channel connections that cannot all take place at once through the switch).
    (c) For the connections of (b), show that the addition of one more channel (for a total of three) at the output of the first time-division switches makes the TST switch nonblocking.

11. A remote switching unit for a PBX operates in a lost calls cleared mode. It is coupled to a nonblocking central switch over two full duplex T1 lines (a total of 48 channels). The concentrator has 98 input channels, each with a bit rate of 1.544 Mbps. Each message has a length of 1000 bytes, and all channels have the same average arrival rate, $\lambda_i = 75$ messages/second. Use an infinite source model as an approximation to find the probability that messages are lost.

12. Rework problem 11, assuming that the remote switching unit operates in a lost calls delayed mode. (Storage must be added to support the lost calls delayed mode.)

    For the modified system, find the probability of delay and the average queueing delay.

CHAPTER **5**

*I*ntroduction to Local Computer Networks

5.1   Definition and Functions

The transfer of data from one computer to another over a dedicated channel is discussed in Chapter 2. Multiplexing to allow the use of one channel to transmit several data streams is also presented as a way to make more efficient use of the channel. Computer networks, the subject of the remainder of the text, are an additional advance to provide not only more efficient use of communication channels but also the potential for sharing resources other than the channels themselves.

A computer network has been defined as an interconnected collection of autonomous computers. The adjective autonomous is used to imply that no one computer completely controls the others. The function of the network itself is to provide a path over which processes in the computers connected to the network nodes can exchange data, as shown in Fig. 5.1. Computer networks have been developed to make it possible to share facilities and distribute resources among the computers and other devices connected to the nodes of the network.

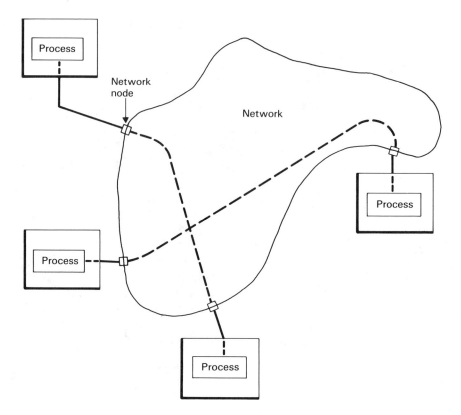

Figure 5.1   Computer Processes Communicating Through a Network

There are several types of computer networks, and in fact there are a number of ways of classifying such networks. Thurber and Freeman in several papers (for example, [1], [2]) discuss classifications in detail. For present purposes it is useful to consider a gross classification into two types, local and long-haul networks, based on network size and geographical extent.

Long-haul networks, typified by the ARPA network (see McQuillan and Walden [3]), cover a large geographical area, often extending over global or national regions. Local networks, which are the exclusive subject of the present text, are characterized by restricted physical dimensions, typically less than a few miles in extent.

The difference in physical dimensions has a pronounced effect on how the two types of networks are structured. Because of their limited physical extent, the transmission media, connecting the nodes of local networks, can be installed and owned by the network users. Thus it is economically feasible to use special-purpose, high-speed channels that can operate with very low error rates because of their low noise levels. Typical choices for transmission media are twisted-pair lines, fiber-optic links, 50-ohm coaxial cable (for baseband transmissions) and 75-ohm coaxial cable (for broadband transmissions).

In contrast to local networks, long-haul networks are generally restricted, for regulatory and economic reasons, to the use of telephone lines or possibly satellite links in conjunction with telephone lines. The difference in speed of the node-to-node links results in substantial differences in the types of structures and implementations, both hardware and software, that are used in the two cases. Further development in this text is restricted to local networks. Design problems for long-haul networks are discussed, for example, in the text by Schwartz [4].

To continue the development of local networks, the high bit rates that can be used on the node-to-node links enable many users to share the same channel. Often a single shared channel is used for the whole network. The access techniques, which regulate the use of the channel by the many users, are a key element in the design of local networks. Such techniques are classified in Section 5.3 and then discussed and analyzed in detail in Chapters 6–9.

Before continuing with the discussion of the technical characteristics of local networks, it is useful to consider some of the applications of such networks. As a first example, much recent attention has been given to the automated office, in which a local network plays the key role of interconnecting the workstations, computing equipment, printers, and so forth. Local networks can also interconnect workstations for software design teams or for computer-aided design projects. Such networks can interconnect cash registers and related equipment in point-of-sale systems. They can be used in local banking systems, libraries, university computing facilities, and, in short, almost any application requiring rapid communication between data processing or computing equipment as long as the equipment is located in the same general area.

A representative list of devices that may be interconnected by the local network in such applications as just listed includes: minicomputers, mainframe computers, disk storage devices, line printers, word processors, terminals, graphic terminals, optical character readers, and possibly voice and video equipment. Of course, the data rates for these diverse devices vary widely. A generic type of local network is sketched in Fig. 5.2.

Local networks are used to provide: relatively inexpensive communication between workstations and devices, distributed processing, rapid access to distributed data banks, and sharing of expensive devices and resources. Besides providing some or all of these functions, local networks can also implement a variety of user services such as speed conversion, code conversion, and data forwarding. Speed conversion enables slow-speed devices such as terminals, and fast devices such as computers, to communicate efficiently. Code conversion translates between different codes and character sets, and data forwarding involves local editing and assembling and transmitting appropriate increments of data.

Local area networks implement the transfer of data in discrete increments called packets. A packet can range from a few bits in length to several thousand bits in length, the extremes determined by the particular network.

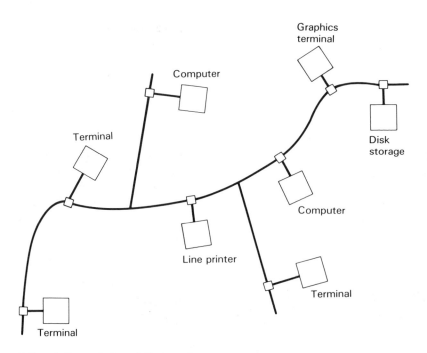

Figure 5.2   A Generic Local Network

For many of the devices used on local networks, a packet is a natural division of the data. Consider the output from a terminal, for example, that consists of blocks as typed in by the user. In a minority of cases, such as a file transfer from a computer, packetizing is artificial, but may be required for proper functioning of the network and to prevent any one user from monopolizing the facility. Each packet, transmitted on a local network, must carry with it certain overhead, which includes source and destination addresses and redundant bits for error control.

General discussions of computer networks are often structured to discuss network topology, transmission media, network access techniques, and network interfaces as major topics. Some mention of some of these topics has been made in the early parts of this section. Different transmission media have been described and it has been noted that local networks can normally use some type of channel that supports a high bit rate. Network interfaces are discussed in Chapters 7, 8, and 9 with reference to specific network types. Network topology and access techniques, which are methods for regulating the use of a channel, are closely related since topology determines some of the characteristics required in the access technique.

Section 5.2 discusses network structure and topology in some detail, with a few comments on access techniques. Section 5.3 follows with a classification of access methods. Detailed discussion and performance analysis of the major categories of access techniques takes place in Chapters 6–9. The next two sections deal respectively with characterization of network traffic and performance measures appropriate for local networks. Section 5.6 presents some networks that illustrate the main access methods.

5.2 Network Structure and Topology

The nodes of computer communication networks can be connected in a variety of ways. Figure 5.3 shows an unstructured topology that could result, for example, from an unplanned growth of a network. Such a topology may be satisfactory for what is called store-and-forward operation, which is commonly used in long-haul networks but infrequently in local area networks.

Store-and-forward operation can be explained as follows. When messages for transmission exceed some threshold length, they are subdivided at the source node into packets of a suitable length that consist of data-bits/characters and required overhead-bits/characters. Packets are transmitted from the source node to an adjacent node in the general direction of the final destination. The packets are received completely into temporary storage at the adjacent node where the packet address is read and where error control is exercised. A routing table (or some other strategy) is then used to determine to which adjacent node the packet is transmitted next. This step-by-step procedure is followed until the packet reaches its destination. Operation is

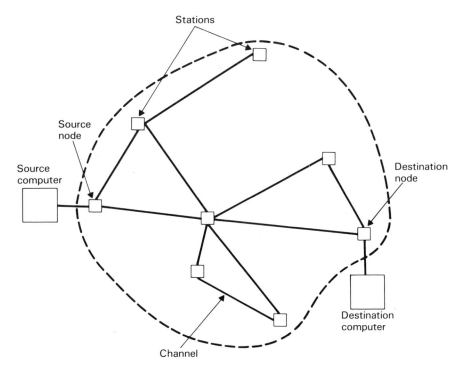

Figure 5.3 An Unstructured Topology

such that a number of packets with many different origination and destination nodes can be in the network at the same time.

Primary characteristics of the store-and-forward mode of operation result from the fact that each node or packet switch on the path of the packet must store the packet, check for any errors, read the address, and route the packet to the next node. The required operations produce a substantial delay at each node, plus an equipment cost associated with each operation. However, the method of transmission, from node to node, gives flexibility in placing nodes and in communicating between two nodes.

Local networks have a combination of requirements that make the store-and-forward type of operation undesirable. As previously noted, local area networks frequently connect a large number of relatively inexpensive pieces of equipment. Rapid communication between these devices is also often desired because the expense in both time delay and dollars associated with routing from node to node is considered excessive for local networks. Store-and-forward networks usually need to exercise error control on a link-by-link basis due to the noisy nature of the links used. On the other hand, end-to-end (source-to-destination) error control is sufficient for local area networks since error rates on the locally owned channels are generally low. Finally, there can be a frequent need in local networks for a broadcast type of message from one node to essentially all of the others. The need for such messages is relatively rare in long-haul networks.

The combination of requirements just stated favor not only a more structured topology than that shown in Fig. 5.3, but one that will support a simpler type of operation. Three topologies currently in common use have the desired characteristics: the star, the ring, and the bus. A fourth, a modified bus or tree, is also used. The four topologies are shown in Fig. 5.4. The central feature of all the topologies shown in the figure is the absence of a need for complex routing algorithms. This fact is most apparent in the bus and ring.

For the bus topology, a transmitting station sends its message in both directions over the bus and thus past all the nodes. Each station or node is passive, but has an ability to read the packet header as it passes by, and read into a buffer those complete packets for which the node is the destination. Packets can pass through the network at a rate determined only by the connecting channel. The time delays required in a store-and-forward network to read and store a packet, plus the time to determine a route to the next node and retransmit the packet, are no longer necessary.

For the ring network, communication is typically in one direction, for example, clockwise, around the ring. Again, as in the bus topology, packets potentially pass every station on the network, which allows each station or node to read addresses and select for complete reading the appropriate packets. Routing is unnecessary since all packets take the same path.

In typical implementations of ring networks, the stations are active rather than passive, as they often are in the bus configuration. For reasons discussed in detail in Chapter 8, each station on the ring delays each packet for one or more bit times and then retransmits it. The fact that each station is active

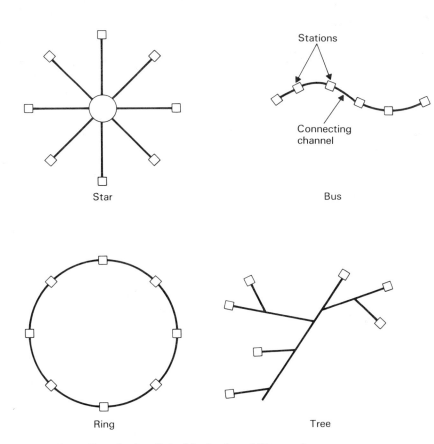

Figure 5.4   Four Topologies Suitable for Local Networks

provides the possibility that a station can remove from the ring those packets addressed to it.

There are a number of different access techniques that can be used with both the ring and bus topologies, and each different topology tends to require different techniques. Note that a structured topology is desirable for local networks to avoid the necessity for independent routing of each packet and to allow for a very rapid transfer of packets between the nodes of the network.

For the star topology, shown in Fig. 5.4, it is not so obvious that the advantages noted for the bus and ring can be achieved, and clearly a different access technique is required. To use the star topology for a local network, it is necessary to use the central node as a "traffic director" or switch. Traffic from one peripheral node to another is directed first to the central node where the destination address is read. The central node then relays, or retransmits, the traffic to its destination. To operate in this manner, all the links must be full duplex since transmission takes place in both directions. Polling networks, which are discussed in detail in Chapter 7, often use this topology.

From the brief comments just noted, it is apparent that the star topology, using some sort of central control, may not be as effective as the bus or ring in achieving the desirable features associated with routing. Analysis, to be given later, shows that this is in fact the case, but nonetheless this topology is used for other reasons and can be effective.

A final topology to be mentioned in conjunction with local networks is the tree, as shown in Fig. 5.4. A rooted tree topology is common for CATV networks, and trends seem to point in the direction of merging local network and CATV technologies. The links shown connecting the nodes for the tree in a CATV network are typically coaxial cable, which is used in a frequency-division-multiplex mode of operation. Transmission is in one direction only (half duplex) in each multiplexed band.

5.3 Channel Access Techniques

From the previous sections that discuss network structure and topology, it is clear that the method of control or of sharing a channel between multiple users is intimately related to other design choices, such as topology. In fact, as noted in Section 5.1, the choice of access technique is the major determining factor in local network performance. This section categorizes the major techniques in common use and discusses each briefly.

There are four major categories: fixed assignment, random assignment, demand assignment, and adaptive assignment.

For fixed assignment strategies, a fixed allocation of channel resources is made to each station on a predetermined basis. Two common schemes in this category are frequency- and time-division multiple access. For frequency-division multiple access (FDMA), each station is assigned a fixed frequency band in the common transmission medium. For time-division multiple access (TDMA), each station is assigned a time slot in a repetitive manner so that all stations are served periodically in some fixed order, as in synchronous time-division multiplex.

For the fixed assignment strategies, each station is allocated its assigned time slot or its assigned frequency band whether it has messages to transmit or not. Thus, for typical bursty computer data (bursty traffic is discussed in the next section), these schemes can be inefficient in the use of bandwidth, since there will be many times when a station does not use its allocation of channel resources, and they are wasted.

At the other extreme from fixed assignments are the random assignment methods. For the simplest of these methods, referred to as pure ALOHA, each station transmits whenever it is ready. If the channel happens to be free, the transmission is successful; if not, a collision occurs, and the colliding packets are retransmitted later. Such an access mechanism is well suited to bursty traffic since a station does not tie up the channel when it has no data to transmit. The drawback of pure ALOHA is that network performance deteriorates badly due to excessive collisions at medium and high traffic intensities.

The demand assignment and adaptive assignment strategies require a network control mechanism that operates in real time and attempts to allocate channel capacity to the multiple stations in an optimum or near-optimum fashion. Demand assignment methods are further classified as central control or distributed control. In either case, the control algorithm does not change with traffic conditions and is designed to allocate channel usage to stations with packets to transmit. Idle stations are ignored to make efficient use of the channel. Polling algorithms are illustrative of central control, whereas ring networks generally make use of distributed control.

Adaptive assignment methods attempt to refine further either random or demand assignment protocols. These strategies not only attempt to make efficient use of the channel by avoiding idle stations, but, in addition, they use algorithms that adapt to network conditions. Such adaptations can make a more efficient assignment of channel usage among those stations that require service. Adaptive assignment protocols are often limited-contention protocols since (rare) collisions are usually permitted at low loads to minimize access times. At high loads, however, these procedures usually adjust to some form of polling or TDM. A common feature of these methods is that some estimate of the network load is required by all stations. Examples of adaptive assignment procedures are given in Section 5.6.

There are many ways to implement the basic methods, and there also have been many attempts to refine these techniques and to incorporate the desirable features of different basic methods into hybrid methods. Franta and Chlamtac [5] list some 32 different strategies in a survey of the field.

An additional approach, which does not fall into the preceding categories, adapts a private branch exchange (PBX) or computerized branch exchange (CBX) into a local network. Such an approach is based on the use of the switch inherent in the PBX or CBX to set up direct connections, as needed, between the network users. A network of this type does not share channels in the same sense as the methods previously outlined and thus has decidedly different characteristics. The PBX approach to local networks is considered in Chapter 4 because, strictly speaking, a PBX is not a local area network. More complete reviews of the many alternatives for local networks can be found in the book by Franta and Chlamtac [5], the IEEE tutorial on local computer networks by Thurber and Freeman [6], and the recent text by Stallings [19]. Commercial or operating networks that fall into each of the four basic categories listed previously, including several subcategories, are described briefly in Section 5.6.

The central thrust of this text is to develop the basic principles of performance analysis for local networks. To accomplish this goal, it is necessary to focus on a subset of the possible access techniques, choosing those that are representative of major classes. The standards being developed by the IEEE 802 Committee and by the European Computer Manufacturers Association (ECMA) were consulted in choosing specific techniques to be discussed. The general field is covered by three classes of access techniques, which are discussed and analyzed in detail: polling methods in Chapter 7;

methods for ring networks in Chapter 8; and random access methods in Chapter 9. Time-division multiple access (TDMA) and frequency-division multiple access (FDMA) are discussed briefly in Chapter 6.

Fixed assignment methods are illustrated by the discussion of TDMA and FDMA. Polling is a basic method for demand assignment with central control. It is chosen as a basic method that is relatively easy to analyze, intuitively understandable, and one that is the basis of many access methods, such as token passing, BRAM (Broadcast Recognizing Access Method) and MSAP (Mini-Slot Alternating Priorities). The last two methods (see Franta and Chlamtac [5] for details) have not been implemented to date and so will not be discussed.

Ring networks and random access networks are two basic types that will have standards. Three types of ring networks are discussed in Chapter 8 to give relatively complete treatment to this basic structure. Chapter 9 discusses random access methods, through the development of increasingly more sophisticated strategies from elementary ALOHA to the carrier-sense multiple access with collision detection method that is becoming a standard for random access local area networks.

Although many principles and techniques used in adaptive assignment strategies are covered, adaptive strategies per se are outside the scope of this basic treatment of local networks.

5.4   Network Traffic

The major function of a local computer network, or of any computer communication network, is to provide a path for communication between user devices and processes connected to the network. The nature of the traffic offered by the user devices is a major factor in determining the performance of the network.

Unfortunately, the offered traffic load is a highly variable quantity affected by a large number of factors. A recent paper by Stuck [7] lists some two dozen local network services with their typical peak data rates. The peak data rates range from 100 bits/second for security systems to 30 megabits/second for noncompressed video. Eliminating these two services as extreme does little to reduce the range. A file server/block transfer is listed as 20 megabits/second and an optical character reader as 2.4 kilobits/second. Both of these devices are considered typical candidates for connection to a local network.

If consideration is given to a local network with, for example, 100 nodes connecting typical user devices, it is easy to imagine the extreme variability of the traffic offered to the network. Any one device may be inactive for long periods and then require a large data rate for a short time. The difference in extremes of the required data rates has been pointed out previously. Variations between different hours of day and night are certain to occur. Averages taken over different intervals such as weeks, days, hours, or seconds can show large differences. In short, defining typical steady-state distributions for network traffic is a difficult problem.

Some idea of the nature of local network traffic can be obtained by considering one interactive interchange between a user at a terminal and a computer. Fuchs and Jackson [8], in considering such an interchange, have identified six types of intervals in the pattern between connect and disconnect: idle time, computer burst segment, think time (i.e., time for the user to react to the computer message), user burst segment, user intercharacter time, and computer intercharacter time. This breakdown makes intuitive sense, and, although the exact details are unimportant, it is clear that the flow of bits or characters follows a complicated pattern with several random features.

Shoch and Hupp [9] have determined the distribution of several quantities from an operating prototype Ethernet with over 120 machines attached, specifically: load sampled over 6-minute and 1-second intervals, packet length distributions, and interpacket arrival times. Their results are shown in Figs. 5.5, 5.6, and 5.7.

Figure 5.5(a) shows load variations over 24 hours in samples taken at 6-minute intervals, whereas Fig. 5.5(b) shows load variations over a 4-minute

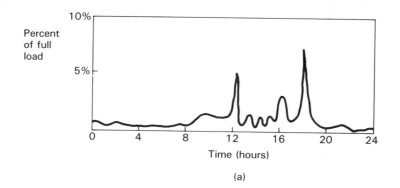

(a)

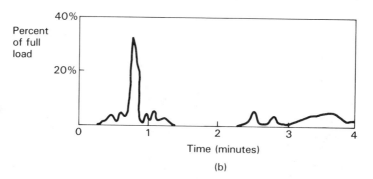

(b)

Figure 5.5 **Prototype Ethernet Load (Based on Shoch and Hupp [9])**
(a) On a typical day—smoothed data sampled at 6-minute intervals
(b) Over a 4-minute period—smoothed data sampled at 1-second intervals

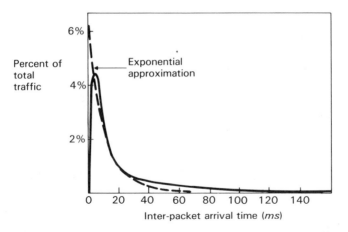

Figure 5.6 Inter-packet Arrival Time Distribution for the Experimental Ethernet (Based on Shoch and Hupp [9])

period in samples taken at 1-second intervals. Note that on a macroscopic basis, as represented by the 24-hour period, as well as on a microscopic basis, as represented by a 4-minute period, the traffic fluctuates relatively close to, but below, the average for long periods of time and then jumps to values much greater than the average for short periods of time. Note that the full range of Fig. 5.5(b) would be contained within one sample of Fig. 5.5(a). Users tend to use the network intermittently, with the interpacket arrival time in general much greater than the user transmission time. This type of load variation, which seems to be typical of a substantial portion of computer network traffic, is called *bursty*.

Figure 5.6 shows a distribution of interpacket arrival times. The data is strongly suggestive of an exponential distribution of arrival times, and a curve

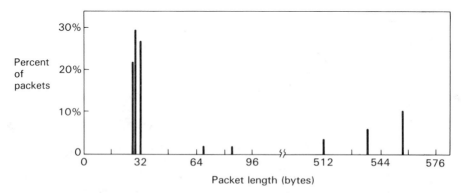

Figure 5.7 Distribution of Packet Lengths for the Experimental Ethernet (Based on Shoch and Hupp [9])

for such a distribution, with a mean of 39.5 ms chosen for a good fit, is shown dotted in the figure.

Finally, Fig. 5.7 shows a distribution of packet lengths. This data has a bimodal character, with a few discrete packet lengths in each portion of the distribution. The shorter packets are due to interactive (bursty) traffic, while the longer packets constitute bulk data transfer.

Faced with the extreme variability of traffic load at any given time or over any given interval, it is difficult to tailor network characteristics to specific traffic patterns. However, since bursty traffic patterns seem to be fairly typical, networks are designed to accommodate this property. For example, the choice of access techniques for the channel is frequently influenced by this type of traffic. For best efficiency, some sort of demand assignment is favored over methods that allocate channel resources on a fixed deterministic basis. Demand assignment makes it possible to allocate access to the channel when it is required, rather than on a regular schedule.

Apart from the identification of network traffic as bursty, it is difficult to make other characterizations. Furthermore, from the comments made previously, it is clear that network traffic is highly variable. A limited amount of data, such as that provided by Shoch and Hupp [9] and shown in Figs. 5.6 and 5.7, is available on interpacket arrival times and packet length distributions, but such data is for particular networks that connect particular devices and does not necessarily apply in general.

Since some description of network traffic must be used as a starting point for performance analysis, it is reasonable to approach the problem from another direction and determine what distributions for interpacket arrivals and packet lengths can give the most tractable analytic results. It seems apparent that the Poisson arrival process, which gives an exponential distribution of packet interarrival times, and the exponential or geometric message length distributions are the best candidates from this point of view.

For these favorable distributions, two logical questions arise:

1. How good are they in matching operating data? and
2. How robust are results computed from these distributions (i.e., how much do performance results change with changes in the nature of the distributions)?

Neither of these questions has been answered, in a general way, from measured results.

Fuchs and Jackson [8] have provided some data concerning these two questions, even though it is in a limited context. In a study of multiaccess computer communications for four systems (in the 1970 period), these authors found that arrival processes are adequately modeled as Poisson. The curve of Fig. 5.6, using the Shoch and Hupp [9] data, also seems to be reasonably approximated with an exponential interarrival distribution. The Fuchs and Jackson results are not as conclusive with respect to packet length distributions, although it could be inferred from their study that geometric distributions are an adequate approximation in many cases.

There is a line of qualitative theoretical reasoning that ties in with using Poisson arrivals and exponentially distributed message lengths as typical parameters in network studies. In a general sense, multiaccess networks can be regarded as single-server queueing systems. For such queueing systems, Kleinrock [21] makes the point that the behavior of the average waiting time for the M/M/1 queue is typical of most queueing systems. He justifies this statement with bounds that he derives on average waiting time for a single-server system with unrestricted distributions for arrival and service times (see Kleinrock [21], p. 34). In the more limited context of systems with Poisson inputs, the reader can verify that as the coefficient of variation for message lengths approaches 1, the average waiting times of the M/G/1 and M/M/1 queues tend to the same result.

Much more data needs to be studied to arrive at a definitive characterization of local network traffic, if indeed, given the extreme variability of such traffic, a single representative characterization can be said to exist. Given what is now available, however, a Poisson arrival process and an exponential or geometric distribution for message lengths seem to provide a good characterization of interactive data traffic in local area networks. Bimodal distributions for message lengths are possibly more accurate for modeling certain cases, but such a choice leads to much less tractable calculations.

As an additional note, the (discrete) geometric distribution is adequately approximated by a (continuous) exponential distribution if the mean of the geometric distribution is large with respect to the size of the basic quantum of the discrete distribution. This fact is used to justify use of the exponential distribution in most cases later in the book.

In the following chapters, which discuss different classes of local networks, the same fundamental traffic assumptions are made for all networks. It is assumed that the statistics of packets arriving at each station on the networks are identical and that the traffic to each station is adequately approximated as an independent Poisson process. It is also assumed that the statistical distribution of packet lengths is the same for all stations, and in most cases that this distribution is exponential. In other cases, it is assumed that packets have a constant length.

Even with these tractable assumptions, it is not always possible to develop useful models and, in several cases, only very approximate analytic results can be derived. The use of the same set of fundamental traffic assumptions with each network helps, however, to provide a fairly uniform treatment of the types of networks considered and allows some basis for a comparison of their performance characteristics.

5.5 Performance Measures

To carry out a quantitative study of local network performance, which is one major objective of this text, appropriate performance criteria must be defined. Although primary emphasis is on network performance, it is useful to begin the discussion of performance criteria at a higher level, namely at the user-to-user level.

Dollar cost is a major criterion of obvious importance to both the network user and designer. This criterion, like reliability, tends to be static in the sense that it is only indirectly related to how the system transmits packets. Cost is mentioned in discussing various types of networks, but is not used as an explicit design criterion.

5.5.1 User-level Criteria

Consider the diagram of Fig. 5.8, which shows a pair of typical users connected to a network.

An obvious and important performance measure from the user point of view is *response time,* which is the time to transmit a packet† correctly from, for example, user A to user B and receive a response, which can be a single acknowledgment. Response time consists of the following components:

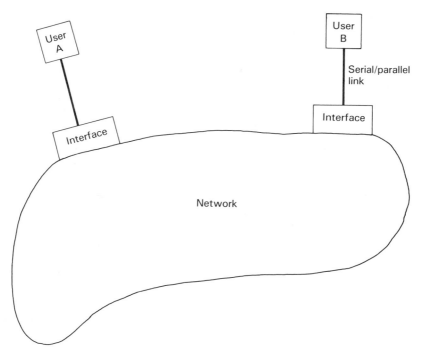

Figure 5.8   A Typical Pair of Users Coupled to a Network

---

†In cases for which a message, and not a packet, is the natural unit for a user, the behavior is more complicated. The unit for the first part of response time, as discussed, is the message transmission time. The time required in part 2 must be increased by the packetizing of the message in the station. Finally, response time must include the time for all the packets that comprise the message to move through the system, assuming that a single response to the whole message is sufficient.

1. The time for a packet from user A to traverse the serial or parallel link into the station interface;
2. The time the packet must wait in the interface buffer before being transmitted;
3. The time required to transmit the packet through the network, including propagation time;
4. The time the packet must wait in the interface associated with user B;
5. The time required to traverse the serial or parallel link to user B;
6. The time at user B to generate a response; and
7. The time for the response to proceed back through the system, following steps 1–5 as applied to the user B part of the network.

Response time depends on the state of the system at the time user A transmits its packet and is thus a random variable. Response time can be computed for steady-state conditions but is not restricted to such conditions. To have some general applicability, most performance measures are expressed as averages, rather than as variables that depend on the instantaneous state of the network. Thus, useful performance measures are defined as some sort of statistical average or moment of response time, or possibly as a function of such an average. Any "average" performance measure applies only for steady-state conditions.

The most common performance measure is simply average or mean response time. If variability about the average is to be considered, the standard deviation of response time is an additional measure of interest. A parameter that conveys still more information might be the percentage of response times that exceed a fixed value, usually tabulated as a function of the fixed value. The choice of performance criterion typically determines the difficulty and sophistication of the analysis used to determine performance. Of the three measures mentioned, mean response time can be obtained in general using the least complicated performance model.

Reliability is a performance measure of a different sort than response time, although it is nonetheless a criterion of concern to the user. Reliability is, of course, a measure of how vulnerable the system is to failures or improper operation. In a sense, reliability is a static measure that depends on the quality of component parts, the maintenance strategy used, the amount or lack of redundancy, and to some extent on the network geometry. This is in contrast to dynamic measures, such as mean response time, which depend on how the system functions in its task of transmitting packets. In the material to follow, comments are made on the relative reliability of several different types of networks. A detailed study of reliability is, however, beyond the scope of this book.

5.5.2 Network-level Criteria

As noted previously, emphasis in this text is on design of the network, which, with reference to Fig. 5.8, includes the network and its interfaces, but typically does not include the remainder of the system. A study of the network itself can focus on generic models for the several network types with the objective of comparative, general results. In contrast, since the network may be regarded as being embedded in a user-to-user system, user-level performance measures are more dependent on specific applications and specific types of equipment.

With reference to the several delays that make up response time for user-to-user interaction, note that delays of types 2 and 3, for the packet in the forward direction and for the response to the packet in the reverse direction, are due to the network and its interfaces. These time delays, due to waiting in the station buffer and passage through the network, are the parts of response time that are sensitive to dynamic network parameters such as load, since queueing for the shared channel is usually necessary.

On the other hand, the remaining components of response time tend to be less sensitive to load and depend more on application or device-oriented features such as the speed of the user/station links. When user inputs do not have to queue for use of the user/station links, delay in traversing these links is essentially constant and determined by the packet length divided by the link bit rate.

A feasible approach to determining the average response time for a specific user-to-user system can consist of two steps:

1. Determining the average one-way packet delay through the network and its interfaces as a function of load and possibly also of packet size; and
2. Using this information along with the (usually load-independent) delay for the user/station links to compute average user-to-user response time.

In this calculation, the delay due to the response packets traversing the network can be determined from network and interface delays.

Note that either the network delays or the delays due to the user/station links can dominate in the user-to-user response time. If the latter is the case, some network design issues, such as choice of the best access technique, may not be of critical importance. On the other hand, if network delays are significant, the best access technique is very important.

At the network level, throughput, another measure of performance, becomes significant. Throughput measures the number of bits per second or packets per second that can, on the average, be processed through the network. Obviously, given a specific channel and its attendant costs, it is desirable to use the channel as effectively as possible by obtaining the largest possible throughput. Several specific definitions of throughput are given in the next section.

Note that maximizing throughput and minimizing delay for a particular link or part of a network are generally conflicting goals, and thus an important characteristic of many networks is the delay–throughput tradeoff curve.

5.5.3 Specific Performance Criteria Definition and Notation

In the remainder of this text, two criteria, throughput and average delay at the network level, are used almost exclusively as performance metrics. These two variables are defined and discussed in detail in this section.

Throughput

Throughput, in bits/second, can be defined as the average number of bits passing a given point in a network per unit time. Since packets can be corrupted, it is usual to include only bits of error-free packets when measuring throughput. For a network or a part of a network in the steady state, it has been pointed out in Chapter 3 that the input and output rates are equal. Thus throughput is the average number of bits per second either entering or leaving a section of a network.

Frequently, throughput is normalized by dividing by the channel transmission rate (in bits per second) to obtain a number usually between 0 and 1. Normalized throughput, or simply throughput, is given the symbol S; this quantity is dimensionless. For example, if the average input rate to a portion of a network is λ packets per second, the channel transmission rate is R bits per second, and there are $\overline{X}$ bits per packet on the average, then unnormalized throughput is just λ packets per second, or $\lambda\overline{X}$ bits per second, and normalized throughput, S, is given by

$$S = \lambda\overline{X}/R \text{ (dimensionless)} \tag{5.1}$$

Throughput can apply to a complete network as well as to a single connecting link. When applied to a complete network, unnormalized throughput is the total number of bits per second entering (and leaving) the network. Thus, in atypical local area networks, when traffic enters and leaves the network over several different links or sections of the network, the total of the bit rates on the multiple paths can all add up to a normalized throughput greater than 1. Such is the case for register insertion rings, discussed in Chapter 8.

In cases for which the channel carries only one stream of traffic, as is typically for local area networks, another equivalent definition of normalized throughput, S, is the fraction of time the channel transmits good (i.e., error-free) packets—assuming steady-state operation, of course. For random access networks, such as discussed in Chapter 9, throughput is defined in normalized form directly as the average number of successful transmissions per packet transmission interval on the channel. A little thought shows that this definition is equivalent to the result of (5.1).

Normalized throughput is closely related to another measure called *channel utilization* or *efficiency*. Channel utilization is basically defined as the average fraction of time a channel is busy. If the channel carries only good packets when it is busy, and overhead is not considered, then (normalized) throughput and utilization are the same. The symbol ρ is used in this text for utilization under the conditions previously cited, and frequently ρ is also termed traffic intensity.

Channel utilization can be used in a more general way to account for overhead; used in this way, it is sometimes called *channel efficiency*. Utilization or efficiency, in this sense, can be defined as the fraction of time a channel transmits data as opposed to transmitting data plus overhead. Thus, if D is the number of data bits in a packet and H is the number of overhead bits in the packet, utilization is $S \times D/(D + H)$.

As a final comment on throughput, maximum throughput for random access networks is called *channel capacity*.

Average Transfer Delay

The second performance measure to be used is average transfer delay, T. Transfer delay is defined as the time from the arrival of the last bit of a packet into the station of a network until the last bit of this packet is delivered through the network to its destination station. Average transfer delay typically has a number of components that are specific to the different network types.

With reference to the general discussion of Subsection 5.5.1, average transfer delay accounts for delays 2 and 3 in the evaluation of response time. If average transfer delay is known as a function of packet length and load, it can be used sometimes along with information about the user/station link to compute average response time.

As with throughput, it is often convenient to normalize average transfer delay. In this case, the average channel transmission time, $\overline{X}/R$ seconds per packet, is the normalizing factor so that normalized average transfer delay, $\hat{T}$, is given by

$$\hat{T} = T/(\overline{X}/R) = RT/\overline{X} \text{ (dimensionless)} \tag{5.2}$$

5.6   Examples of Commercial and Experimental Local Networks

Local networks have evolved to the point that a significant number of different types are commercially available. In addition, there are many operating networks being used for experimental purposes. This section briefly discusses typical operating networks from each of the categories enumerated in Section 5.3. Note that the examples used for demand assignment with central control are not local area networks; they are used because they illustrate this assignment technique better than any local area networks known to the authors.

5.6.1   Fixed Assignment: Amdax CableNet

CableNet operates over a broadband coaxial cable. Equipment consists of an Executive, and a number of Data Exchange Interface Units (DAX), which have four ports for coupling devices to the network. A typical structure is shown in Fig. 5.9.

The executive uses time-division multiplex techniques to control access to the network. Communication is in one direction in each of two frequency bands: from the executive to the data exchange interface units in a band near 200 MHz and from the data exchange interface units to the executive in a band near 40 MHz. The required bandwidth for transmission in either band can be either 7 or 14 Mbps, depending on the equipment used.

The DAX ports can support data rates from 110 to 19,200 bps. The manufacturers claim that 16,000 devices can be used on a network.

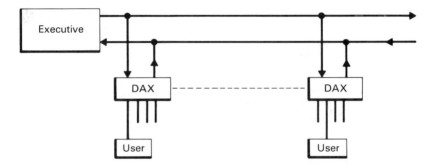

Figure 5.9   A Typical CableNet Installation (Based on Rahm [20])

A recent paper by Rahm [20] discusses an installation of CableNet at Dow Chemical Company and states that the following applications are supported: word/text processing, file retrieval electronic mail, form generation at terminals, color graphics, digitized voice, executive and secretarial workstations, computer control, dictation and recording, intelligent copiers, video and voice teleconferencing, and security systems.

5.6.2   Random Access: Xerox Fibernet and MITRE Cablenet

There are a number of commercially available networks that can be classified as random access. A partial list includes Net/One, LocalNet, and Cluster/One in addition to the two discussed in this section.

MITRE Cablenet, as described by Fowler [10], is a high-speed local area network built for company use and research. It uses existing CATV technology for most of its hardware. Connections to the cable are provided by specifically designed Bus Interface Units (BIU), which currently operate at a data rate of 825 kbps. The network uses carrier-sense multiple access with collision detection (CSMA/CD) to control station access to the cable. A representative diagram of an overall system is given in Fig. 5.10.

Each BIU can interface up to 11 terminals. Computers can be interfaced to the cable through either an RS-232 port into a standard BIU or a special BIU designed to operate at high transfer rates. Measured end-to-end data rates of up to 350 kbps have been observed.

Applications intended for MITRE Cablenet include: terminal-to-computer communications, computer-to-computer communications, office automation, intelligent workstations connected to shared resources, and gateways to other networks.

Xerox Fibernet (see Rawson and Metcalfe [11]) is an experimental optical-fiber local computer network that, when completed, will connect up to 19 stations at 150 Mbps through ½ km of optical fiber. It is constructed with a 19-port transmissive star coupler that uses injection lasers and avalanche photo diodes. An experimental test configuration is shown in Fig. 5.11. The channel access technique is Ethernet-like (Ethernet was also developed by

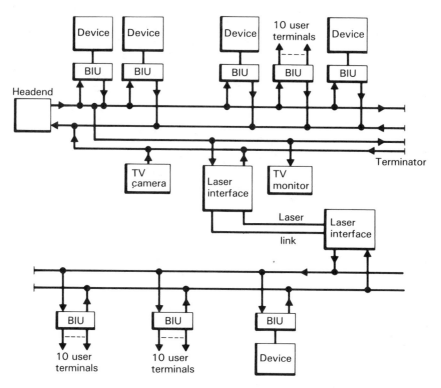

Figure 5.10   A Typical Cable Bus Configuration (Based on Fowler [10])

Xerox), namely, carrier-sense multiple access with collision detection (CSMA/CD). One unique feature of Fibernet is the extremely high bit rate that it can support. The lack of electrical interference on the optical cable is another significant advantage.

5.6.3   Demand Assignment with Central Control: Airline Reservations System (PARS), Stock Quotation System (NASDAQ)

Demand assignment with central control in the form of polling is employed frequently in a portion of larger systems such as the airline reservation system, PARS, or the stock quotation system, NASDAQ. In these two examples, the polling circuit extends over a larger area than is typical for local area networks; nevertheless, they illustrate the assignment method very clearly.

As discussed by Knight [12], access to the common communication channel for the PARS system can be diagrammed, as shown in Fig. 5.12. The terminal control units (TCUs) concentrate messages from a number of agent terminals. The TCUs are serviced by shared full duplex lines that operate at 2000, 2400, and 4800 bps. Polling is initiated from the computer center to the most distant TCU, and then the poll is passed from one TCU to another along the dotted

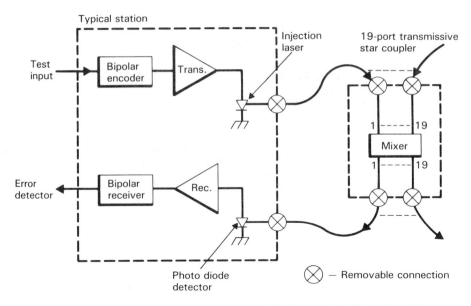

Figure 5.11   Xerox Fibernet Experimental Test Configuration (Based on Rawson and Metcalfe [11])

path. Message rates per line are around 1.5 mess/sec, and lines can service from 80 to 120 TCUs. The poll cycle (i.e., the time between successive polls of a TCU) is on the order of seven-tenths of a second.

In the NASDAQ system, as discussed by Schwartz et al. [13], each concentrator in the overall network polls a number of over-the-counter control units (OCUs), as shown in Fig. 5.13. The network of OCUs connected to their concentrator can be considered a local network.

The circuit that the OCUs share is an asynchronous full duplex 1600-bps circuit. The concentrator polls the OCUs in a cyclic manner. If an OCU has a

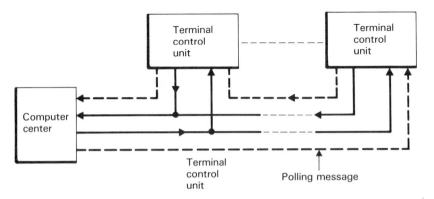

Figure 5.12   Channel Access in the PARS System (Based on Knight [12])

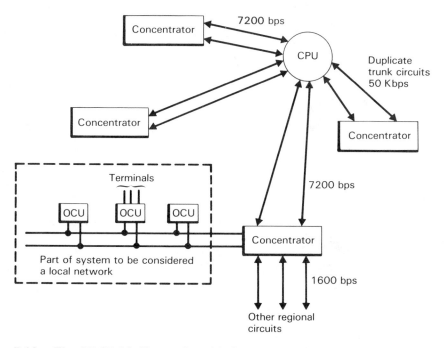

Figure 5.13   The NASDAQ Network, with Part of the System Considered as a Local Network Indicated (Based on Schwartz et al. [13])

message to transmit, it is transmitted when the OCU is polled. Only one message can be transmitted on a single poll. A one-character reply is sent to the concentrator if the OCU has no messages to send. The concentrator has a pool of 31 buffers for storing replies directed to the OCUs. These replies are transmitted to the appropriate OCUs in a nested fashion along with outgoing polling messages.

5.6.4   Demand Assignment with Distributed Control: Distributed Loop Computer Network (DLCN)

The Distributed Loop Computer Network is an experimental network that has been in use at Ohio State University since 1975. The network is discussed in a number of papers (see, for example, Liu [14] and Penney and Baghdadi [15]). The basic structure uses distributed control carried out by a shift register insertion access technique analyzed in Chapter 8. A block diagram that shows the shift registers and a typical configuration is given in Fig. 5.14.

The network is configured as a high-speed loop. Each station, as shown in the figure, has two shift registers and two switches that allow variable-length packets to be transmitted on a demand sharing basis. The DLCN is intended to be used as a distributed processing system that interconnects computers of a variety of sizes, terminals, and other peripheral devices.

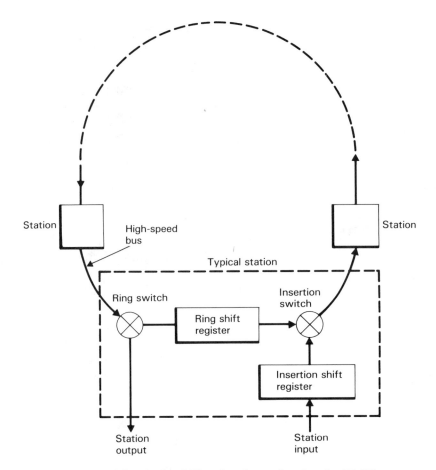

Figure 5.14   A Typical Station and Ring Configuration for the DLCN

Network services are said to include: processor-independent execution of jobs, uniform and flexible process-to-process communication, network-wide resource allocation, remote program calling and file access, and generalized process control structures.

5.6.5   Adaptive Assignment: The Adaptive Tree Walk Protocol

Adaptive assignment protocols have not in general been implemented, possibly because correctly operating, each station on the network requires some estimate of the current network load (i.e., how many other stations have data to transmit). A possible way to achieve this is to have a separate subchannel to use for signaling state changes. Such a subchannel can be obtained by traditional multiplexing techniques (i.e., TDM or FDM).

Due to the absence of implemented protocols, discussion in this section is limited to the Adaptive Tree Walk Protocol, developed by Capetanakis [16], which is typical of the many proposed limited-contention schemes. Two other protocols of note are the Urn Protocol, developed by Kleinrock and Yemini [17], and Parametric BRAM, discussed by Chlamtac et al. [18]. The urn method is pure random access at low loads and becomes synchronous TDM at heavy loads. On the other hand, parametric BRAM is essentially a polling scheme (BRAM) under heavy loads, but under light loads it permits collisions to occur to reduce access delays.

The Tree Walk Protocol is selected since it is relatively easy to explain and illustrates clearly the nature of an adaptive scheme. The protocol is best suited to a bus topology, although other physical structures, such as a ring, are possible. Access control to the channel is distributed and channel time is slotted so that transmissions can only commence at regular fixed-time instants.

Assume that the stations can be regarded as organized in a binary tree, as shown in Fig. 5.15 for an eight-station network. If the estimate of ready stations (i.e., stations with packets to transmit) is just one, then all stations (under node A) may attempt a transmission in the next slot. If, however, three or four stations are estimated as being ready, then stations under node D are permitted in the next slot. If none or just one of these stations (stations 0 and 1) transmits, then those stations under node E are permitted to transmit in the succeeding slot. If, however, a collision occurs between stations 0 and 1, then only station 0 has access in the next slot. Thus, this adaptive protocol behaves as a pure slotted contention scheme at low loads and becomes a synchronous TDM system at heavy loads.

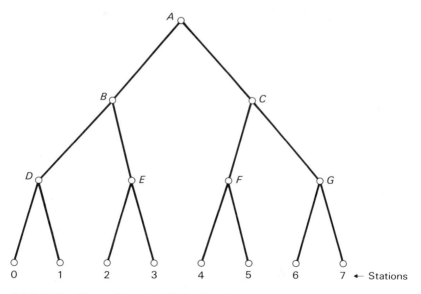

Figure 5.15   The Binary Tree for Eight Stations

5.7   Summary

This chapter introduces local computer networks by defining this class of networks, relating them to long-haul or wide-area networks and describing typical applications. A number of terms and concepts are introduced and discussed.

Major aspects of computer networks are identified as network topology, transmission media, access techniques, and network interfaces. All of these aspects are discussed in the context of local networks. Network traffic is also discussed and appropriate models to describe it in later work are given.

Performance measures necessary for a quantitative study of local area networks are reviewed in the chapter. Several criteria are discussed, including such user-to-user measures as response time. It is pointed out that average transfer delay, which measures delay across the network only, can serve as the major criterion for studying local area networks, since other types of delays tend to be independent of the network. Average transfer delay and normalized throughput, given the symbols T and S respectively, are chosen for use in the remainder of the text.

A final section of the chapter presents practical local networks illustrative of each of the categories discussed earlier.

Background required for beginning the quantitative study of performance of local area networks is completed with Chapter 5. The next chapter begins the quantitative study of performance.

References

[1] K. J. Thurber and H. A. Freeman. "Architecture Considerations for Local Computer Networks." *Proceedings of the 1st International Conference on Computing Systems* (1979): 131–142.

[2] K. J. Thurber and H. A. Freeman. "Local Computer Network Architectures." *Proceedings of COMPCON* (Spring 1979): 258–261.

[3] J. M. McQuillan and D. C. Walden. "The ARPA Network Design Decisions." *Computer Networks* 1 (August 1977): 243–289.

[4] M. Schwartz. *Computer-Communication Network Design and Analysis.* Englewood Cliffs, NJ: Prentice–Hall, 1977.

[5] W. R. Franta and I. Chlamtac. *Local Networks.* Lexington, MA: Lexington Books, 1981.

[6] K. J. Thurber and H. A. Freeman. *Local Computer Networks.* New York, NY: IEEE Computer Society Press, 1981.

[7] B. Stuck. "Which Local Net Bus Access is Most Sensitive to Traffic Congestion?" *Data Communications* (January 1983): 107–120.

[8] E. Fuchs and P. E. Jackson. "Estimates of Distributions of Random Variables for Certain Computer Communication Traffic Models." *Communications of the ACM* 13 (December 1970): 752–757.

[9] J. F. Shoch and J. A. Hupp. "Measured Performance of an Ethernet Local Network." *Communications of the ACM.* 23, no. 12 (December 1980): 711–720.

[10] T. B. Fowler. "A Wideband Cable Bus Local Area Network." *Proceedings of COMPCON* (Fall 1982): 405–414.

[11] E. G. Rawson and R. M. Metcalfe. "Fibernet: Multimode Optical Fibers for Local Computer Networks." *IEEE Transactions on Communications* COM-26 (July 1978): 983–990.

[12] J. R. Knight. "A Case Study: Airline Reservation Systems." *Proceedings of the IEEE* 60 (November 1972): 1423–1431.

[13] M. Schwartz, R. R. Boorstyn, and R. L. Pickholtz. "Terminal-oriented Computer Communication Networks." *Proceedings of the IEEE* 60 (November 1972): 1408–1423.

[14] M. T. Liu. "Distributed Loop Computer Networks." *Advances in Computers* 17 (1978): 163–221.

[15] B. K. Penney and A. A. Baghdadi. "Survey of Computer Communications Loop Networks: Part I." *Computer Communications* 2 (August 1979): 165–180.

[16] J. L. Capetanakis. "Tree Algorithms for Packet Broadcast Channels." *IEEE Transactions on Information Theory* IT-25 (September 1979): 505–515.

[17] L. Kleinrock and Y. Yemini. "An Optimal Adaptive Scheme for Multiple Access Broadcast Communication." *Proceedings of the ICC* (June 1978): 7.2.1–7.2.5.

[18] I. Chlamtac, W. R. Franta, and K. D. Levin. "BRAM: The Broadcast Recognizing Access Method." *IEEE Transactions on Communications* COM-27 (August 1979): 1183–1189.

[19] W. Stallings. *Local Networks, An Introduction.* New York: Macmillan, 1984.

[20] M. W. Rahm. "Cablenet: A User Prospective." *Proceedings of COMPCON* (Fall 1982): 337–342.

[21] L. Kleinrock. *Queueing Systems.* Vol. 2, *Computer Applications.* New York, NY: John Wiley & Sons, 1976.

Problems and Exercises

1. Give two topologies suitable for local area networks. Discuss your answers.

2. What assumptions are typically made concerning packet routing for store-and-forward networks? Why is routing not a significant problem for most local area networks?

3. Discuss the trade-offs between time-division multiple access and random access for use with local area networks.

4. Discuss the differences between store-and-forward operation and multiaccess operation. Which is the usual choice for local area networks?

5. The continuous (negative) exponential density function is given by

$$f(x) = \begin{cases} \lambda e^{-\lambda x}, & x > 0 \\ 0, & \text{otherwise} \end{cases}$$

The discrete probability function for the geometric distribution is given by

$$p(X_i) = \begin{cases} p(1-p)^{X_i}, & X_i = 0, 1, 2, \ldots \\ 0, & \text{otherwise} \end{cases}$$

The mean of the exponential distribution is $1/\lambda$, whereas that of the geometric distribution is $1/p$. For large and equal means, show that the two distributions are equivalent in the sense that the probability of X in any range is essentially the same for the two cases.

6. A network has a number of stations, each of which has an average input rate of 0.2 mess/sec. Messages are 10^4 bits in length with no overhead, no retransmissions, and network errors can be assumed to be negligible. The network stations share a channel of bit rate 10^6 bps.
   (a) What number of stations will produce a steady-state unnormalized throughput of 10 mess/sec?
   (b) What is the normalized throughput, S, that corresponds to 10 mess/sec?

7. Two types of error management are to be compared under error-free conditions.
   METHOD 1: fifty overhead bits are used for error correction in each 200-bit block; the remaining bits carry data. Blocks are transmitted in a continuous sequence.
   METHOD 2: ten overhead bits are used for error detection in each 200-bit block; the remaining bits carry data. When each block is received, a 5-bit acknowledgment message is sent back to the transmitter. A new block is transmitted after the acknowledgment is received from the previous block. Compare the methods by computing normalized throughput for both methods in terms of the channel bit rate R. (Note that the error-free comparison is unfair to method 1 since it does not degrade as the error rate increases. Method 2 degrades as error rate goes up because more and more retransmissions are required.)

8. A data message of 32K 8-bit characters is sent over a two-wire half duplex line in packets of length 2K bytes with 10 control characters per packet. The baud rate is 9600 Baud. Find the average message delay and channel utilization if
   (a) No acknowledgments are transmitted; or
   (b) If positive acknowledgments are transmitted and the next packet cannot be sent until all earlier ones are acknowledged.
   Assume that the turn-around time at each end is 150 ms, propagation delay is 30 ms, acknowledgment packets are 2 bytes (not data), and no errors are detected. Channel utilization is defined as the ratio of average time spent sending data to total time required.

CHAPTER **6**

*P*erformance of Basic Access Protocols

6.1 Introduction

As discussed in Chapter 5, the major categories of multiaccess procedures for local area networks are fixed assignment, random assignment, and demand assignment. A large number of specific procedures in each category has been developed in an attempt to achieve optimal results. The best procedures of each type have been highly refined and, because of their many interacting aspects, they are difficult to analyze.

To a major extent, the performance of all of the multiaccess procedures, as measured by throughput and delay versus load, fall within bounds that are given by the characteristics of several basic procedures. These procedures, which are relatively simple to analyze, require analytic solution methods that are illustrative of those used to analyze the more sophisticated procedures. Basic procedures, which serve the purpose of delineating the range of possible throughput and delay characteristics, are synchronous time-division and frequency-division multiplexing, pure ALOHA, and an idealized central control method, defined so that it is equivalent to an $M/D/1$ queue. The two multiplexing procedures give results characteristic of the fixed assignment methods. These procedures are relatively simple to analyze, and most can be used in practice.

The pure ALOHA method gives results that are at the extreme of the random assignment methods and hence gives worst-case throughput-load and delay-load characteristics for these methods. Pure ALOHA has application for multiple access radio links, but is not typically used for local networks.

The demand assignment methods require some sort of central control. For this class, an idealized central control method, which reduces to an $M/D/1$ queue, can be hypothesized. The idealized method is thus easy to analyze and is representative of the extreme results achieved by the demand assignment methods.

In the remaining portions of this section, the access methods listed previously are separately analyzed to determine throughput and delay curves, and then the methods are discussed and compared. The study of these basic methods shows the range of behavior that can be achieved by the multiaccess procedures. Since the analyses of the methods are relatively straightforward, this overall view is achieved with a minimum of computational complexity.

In this chapter, as well as in the following chapters on different classes of local networks, the fundamental traffic assumptions discussed in Chapter 5 are used for all networks. The basic assumption is that the traffic statistics of packets arriving at each station on the network are identical, and that each arrival process is Poisson and independent of all the other arrival processes. In the case of random access methods, the assumption of Poisson traffic is extended to include the retransmitted packets as well as new arrivals to the network.

6.2 Fixed Assignment Access Methods

For fixed assignment access methods, access to the common channel is independent of user demands and some portion of the resources of the channel (for example, time or bandwidth) is assigned to each user in a static, predetermined fashion.

In contrast to the random and demand assignment categories of local networks, the fixed assignment class has only a few different implementations. Furthermore, the analysis to determine average message delay is essentially the same for all implementations, and is relatively simple. Thus it is unnecessary to choose an extreme or idealized member of the fixed assignment class to demonstrate characteristic behavior in a tractable manner. The two basic methods, time-division multiple access (TDMA), and frequency-division multiple access (FDMA), are both analyzed; consequently, there is no need for a separate section on fixed assignment protocols. Note for completeness that a third method, code-division multiple access (CDMA), is also a member of the fixed assignment class.

The network model to be considered has M users, who are to share a common communication channel of bandwidth R Hertz, modulated at 1 bps/Hz. Packets of fixed length $\overline{X}$ bits arrive to each of the M stations at a rate of λ packets/sec. The arrival process of packets to each station is independent and Poisson, and queueing of packets is permitted at each station.

The operation of TDMA, also known as synchronous time-division multiplexing (STDM), is discussed in some detail in Chapter 2. The strategy results in dividing channel time into fixed-length frames that are in turn subdivided into fixed time slots, one for each station, as shown in Fig. 6.1(a). As discussed in Chapter 2, each frame needs some overhead for synchronization purposes. This is not shown in Fig. 6.1(a). A $T1$ frame, for example, needs one sync bit for every 192 information bits—an overhead of approximately 0.5% per frame. For other TDM schemes, the overhead may be more substantial.

As discussed in Chapter 2, one character is typically transmitted by each station when it has its turn to use the channel. For the sake of simplicity, it is assumed that each character is one packet of $\overline{X}$ bits in length. It turns out that this restriction on packet length to one character does not reduce the

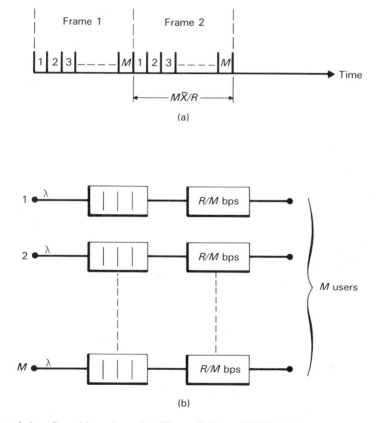

(a)

(b)

Figure 6.1   Considerations for Time-division Multiple Access
(a) Allocation of channel time
(b) Queueing model for evaluation of queueing delay

generality since the results obtained under this restriction are shown, in fact, to be completely general. Thus with a channel bit rate of R bps and M stations, each transmitting one packet per frame, the length of a frame is $M \overline{X}/R$ seconds.

Now consider a packet arriving at an arbitrary station. The delay in transferring the packet to its destination can be considered to have three components, excluding the propagation delay on the channel:

1. The actual transmission time, $\overline{X}/R$ seconds;
2. The queueing delay in the buffer of the station; and
3. A slot synchronization delay before a particular station gets its turn on the network.

The average slot synchronization delay for purely random arrivals is one-half of the frame time, or $M \overline{X}/2R$.

To evaluate the average queueing delay, the network can be modeled, as shown in Fig. 6.1(b), as M independent and separate M/D/1 queueing systems, each with a mean arrival rate of λ packets/sec. For each such queueing system, the effective bit rate of the channel, to a packet queueing at any station, appears to be R/M bps. Formulas for average delay and number in the network for an M/D/1 queue are derived in Chapter 3. In the present notation, $\overline{X}$ replaces $1/\mu$ for average packet length and R/M replaces C for channel bit rate. Equation (3.51) then gives the average queueing delay as

$$W = \frac{\rho}{2(1 - \rho)} \left(\frac{M\overline{X}}{R} \right) \tag{6.1}$$

where the utilization factor, ρ, of each queueing system is

$$\rho = \lambda(M\overline{X}/R) = M\lambda\overline{X}/R \tag{6.2}$$

The throughput of a network is defined in Chapter 5 as the fraction of time the channel is transmitting good packets. Network throughput, S, in the steady state is then the total input rate, $M\lambda$ packets/second, divided by the network capacity, $R/\overline{X}$ packets/second. Thus S is given by

$$S = M\lambda\overline{X}/R \tag{6.3}$$

From (6.2) and (6.3),

$$S = \rho \tag{6.4}$$

and (6.1) becomes

$$W = \frac{M S}{2(1 - S)} \left(\frac{\overline{X}}{R} \right) \tag{6.5}$$

The average transfer delay, T, is the sum of W, the transmission time, and the average synchronization delay, so that

$$T = \frac{\overline{X}}{R} + \frac{M\overline{X}}{2R} + \frac{M S}{2(1 - S)} \left(\frac{\overline{X}}{R} \right) \tag{6.6}$$

Lam [1] has shown that the result of (6.6) is general in the sense that it also applies when each packet contains an arbitrary, but fixed, number of characters.

It is often convenient to normalize the average delay into units of packet transmission times. Thus, T in (6.6) is normalized to $\hat{T}$ by dividing both sides of (6.6) by $\overline{X}/R$ to obtain

$$\hat{T} = 1 + \frac{M}{2} + \frac{MS}{2(1-S)} \tag{6.7}$$

Figure 6.2 shows $\hat{T}$ plotted against S for different values of M. Note that for large values of M greater than, for example, 20, (6.7) reduces to

$$\hat{T} = M\left[\frac{1}{2} + \frac{S}{2(1-S)}\right] \tag{6.8}$$

which implies that normalized average transfer delay increases in proportion to the number of stations for sufficiently large M and any choice of S.

Frequency-division multiplexing is also discussed in Chapter 2. In this case, each user is allocated a bandwidth of R/M Hz, as shown in Fig. 6.3(a) (as opposed to a time slot), and is free to transmit at will in this band. It is assumed that there is no loss of bandwidth due to guard bands and so forth, so that with modulation at 1 bps/Hz, the effective bit rate for each user is R/M bps.

Since each of the M channels operates independently, the FDMA network can be regarded for analysis purposes as M independent M/D/1 queueing systems, as shown in Fig. 6.3(b), in the same manner as for the TDMA network. The two cases, of course, differ in that the independent queueing systems for TDMA result from a fixed allocation of time slots, while for FDMA fixed frequency slots are assigned.

The input traffic to each independent queueing system for FDMA is λ packets/sec, and the effective bit rate is R/M, just as in the case of TDMA. Furthermore, network throughput, S—total network input rate divided by the channel capacity, both in packets per second—is the same for FDMA and TDMA. Thus the average queueing delay for a FDMA network is the same as for a TDMA network and is given by (6.5).

Average transfer delay is, however, different for the two cases. All channels for FDMA operate independently of each other, and hence there is no slot synchronization delay. On the other hand, actual packet transmission time is $M\overline{X}/R$, larger than for TDMA, since packets are always transmitted in the restricted bandwidth, R/M Hz, of a single channel.

Adding actual packet transmission time to queueing delay gives average transfer delay for a FDMA network as

$$T = \frac{M\overline{X}}{R} + \frac{S}{2(1-S)}\left(\frac{M\overline{X}}{R}\right) \tag{6.9}$$

This equation is normalized to

$$\hat{T} = M + \frac{MS}{2(1-S)} = \frac{M(2-S)}{2(1-S)} \tag{6.10}$$

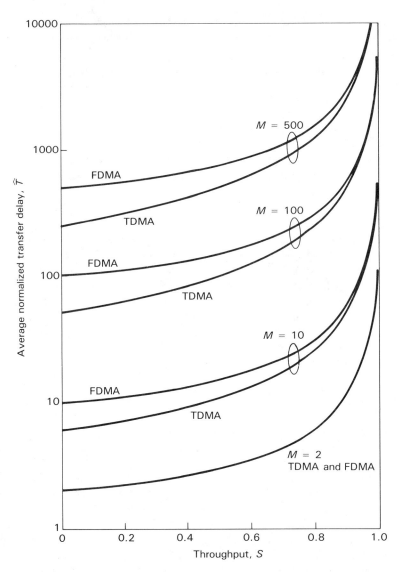

Figure 6.2   **Average Normalized Delay versus Throughput for TDMA and FDMA with the Number of Stations, _M_, as a Parameter**

using units of packet transmission time as $\overline{X}/R$ seconds. This choice is made to permit direct comparison to other access methods, including TDMA, although the average packet transmission time for FDMA is actually $M\overline{X}/R$ seconds.

Comparison of (6.10) to (6.7) for TDMA shows that

$$\hat{T}_{\text{FDMA}} = \hat{T}_{\text{TDMA}} + \frac{M}{2} - 1 \tag{6.11}$$

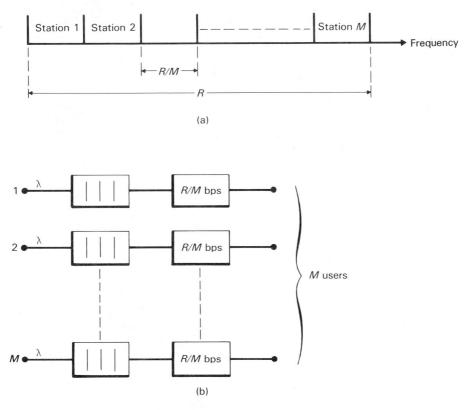

Figure 6.3   Considerations for Frequency-division Multiple Access
    (a) Allocation of bandwidth
    (b) Queueing model

Thus, for more than two stations, FDMA always gives greater average delay than TDMA. In fact, as (6.11) shows, the difference between the two average delays is independent of network load and is constant for fixed M.

The average normalized delay for FDMA is plotted against network throughput, S, in Fig. 6.2 for different values of M, along with the results for TDMA. As is evident from the figure and from (6.10), the minimum value of $\hat{T}$ is M. The figure shows that for $M = 2$, TDMA and FDMA give the same performance, and that as M gets larger, the differences between their average delays increases greatly.

6.3   The ALOHA Random Access Procedure

The ALOHA random access procedure (see Schwartz, [2]) illustrates a limiting form of distributed control that effectively allows every station to operate independently of the others. This procedure is chosen for the current study because it illustrates the behavior of the random access, or contention, procedures and is relatively easy to analyze.

Although ALOHA is seldom used for local networks, a number of practical procedures in current use for local networks have been derived from the ALOHA method by increasing the amount of interaction between stations. For example, to improve operating characteristics, several methods to be discussed use some form of synchronization and/or the ability to sense the carrier of other stations. To distinguish the basic ALOHA procedure from these other networks, it is often referred to as *pure* ALOHA.

A network that uses ALOHA is constructed so that each station is coupled to a single passive channel, such as a coaxial cable†, as shown in Fig. 6.4. An error-free channel is assumed, so that if only one station transmits in a given time interval, its packets are received without error at the receiving station; it then transmits an acknowledgment, often over a separate channel.

If two or more stations transmit so that their packets overlap in time, interference results, and errors are produced in the overlapping packets. Since these packets are in error, no acknowledgments are sent by the receiving stations. After an appropriate "time-out," which is at least as long as the maximum two-way propagation time of the cable, the original transmitting stations conclude that a collision has occurred and schedule retransmissions of the packets at later times. To avoid repeat collisions of the collided packets, the retransmission times are usually chosen at random by the stations involved.

To analyze the ALOHA access procedure, assume that P seconds are required for transmission of a packet. This time includes the maximum propagation time over the cable (i.e., between the most widely separated stations) and the time to process all the bits in the packet. Assume further that the total number of packets (new arrivals as well as retransmissions of packets

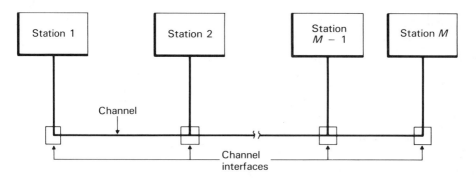

Figure 6.4   General Structure of an ALOHA-type Network

---

†The original ALOHA network used a radio channel.

that collided earlier) for transmission over the channel in some specified time has a Poisson distribution so that

$$P\{k \text{ arrivals in } t \text{ seconds}\} = \frac{(\Lambda t)^k}{k!}e^{-\Lambda t} \tag{6.12}$$

The mean of this distribution is Λt, which for t equal to one second gives Λ as the arrival rate to the network in packets per second.

An infinite population of users is inherent in the Poisson assumption. This is an approximation to a large but finite number of users in which each user generates packets very infrequently. Each user in the infinite population is assumed to have at most one packet that requires transmission at any time.

For analysis of the ALOHA procedure, throughput, S, and offered traffic, G, are usually defined as follows:

S—Average number of successful transmissions per packet transmission time, P; and
G—Average number of attempted packet transmissions per packet transmission time, P.

This definition of S defines throughput for random access channels. It has been argued in Chapter 5 that this definition of throughput is equivalent to that for the fixed assignment methods.

Now consider Fig. 6.5. The top part of the figure shows the time interval, P, required to transmit a reference packet. The lower part of the figure shows two packets that are at the extremes of just colliding with the reference packet shown. Examination of the figure shows that any packet that starts between these two extremes will overlap the reference packet and hence will collide with it. The vulnerable period can be seen to be of length $2P$.

A useful performance characteristic for the ALOHA access procedure is a relation between throughput and offered traffic (i.e., between S and G). Since S represents the number of good transmissions in an interval P, and G represents the number of attempted transmissions,

$$S = G P \{\text{good transmission}\} \tag{6.13}$$

The probability of a good transmission is the probability of no additional transmissions in the vulnerable period of length $2P$ about the time the transmission of the reference packet begins.

For a Poisson arrival process, the number of arrivals in an interval depends only on the length of the interval. Thus the actual instant the transmission of the reference packet begins is immaterial, and the probability of no collision (i.e., the probability of a successful transmission) is obtained as

$$P\{0 \text{ arrivals in an interval of length } 2P\} = e^{-2G} \tag{6.14}$$

by using $k = 0$, $t = 2P$ and $\Lambda = G/P$ in (6.12). Substituting the result of (6.14) into (6.13) then gives

$$S = G e^{-2G} \tag{6.15}$$

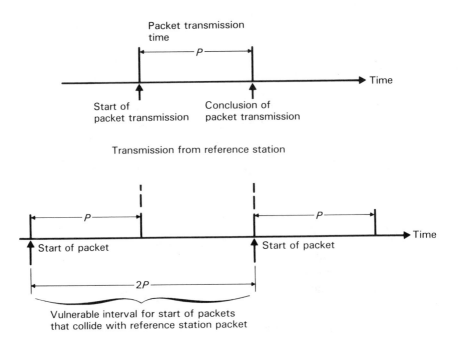

Packet transmission
time

Start of
packet transmission

Conclusion of
packet transmission

Time

Transmission from reference station

Start of packet

Start of packet

Time

Vulnerable interval for start of packets
that collide with reference station packet

Transmissions from all other stations

Figure 6.5   The ALOHA Vulnerable Period for a Reference Transmission

as the desired relation between throughput and offered traffic. A plot of (6.15) that shows S versus G is given in Fig. 6.6. The figure shows that S has a maximum value of $1/2e \simeq 0.184$ for $G = 0.5$. This can also be shown analytically.

An important assumption in the argument leading to (6.15) is that statistical equilibrium (i.e., steady-state conditions) exists. However, observation of Fig. 6.6 suggests that this assumption may not always be valid.

For example, consider the point of operation (G', S') on Fig. 6.6 where $G' > 0.5$. Equation (6.15) implies that this is a point of equilibrium, that is, the system is stable in the vicinity of this point. Now, if G increases slightly, due to statistical fluctuations in the offered load, the throughput S decreases as shown by the figure. A reduction in throughput for increasing load means that there are fewer successful transmissions due obviously to an increasing number of collisions. Thus the backlog, and hence the load on the network, G, is further increased. As a result, the point of operation moves further to the right, where the same scenario occurs again, and eventually the throughput goes to zero. This is known as channel saturation. Thus it is not possible to have a stable point of operation for values of G greater than 0.5.

An approximate analysis is now made to determine average packet delay exclusive of propagation time. For each packet, the average number of

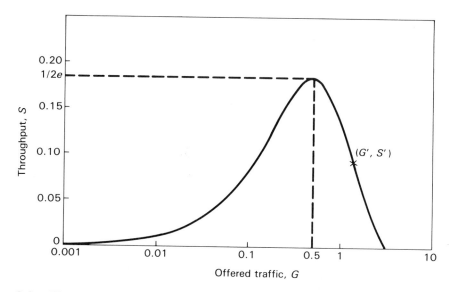

Figure 6.6   Throughput versus Offered Traffic for the Pure ALOHA Random Access Procedure

attempts per successfully transmitted packet is given by

$$G/S = e^{2G} \tag{6.16}$$

Thus, the average number of unsuccessful attempts per successfully transmitted packet is given by

$$G/S - 1 = e^{2G} - 1 \tag{6.17}$$

If a collision occurs, the station reschedules the colliding packet for some randomly chosen later time. This rescheduling causes a delay during which the packet is said to be in a state of *back off*. The average backoff delay is denoted B. Note that the assumption of a finite backoff time essentially violates the assumption of Poisson traffic. However, the approximation gives a loose lower bound on delay.

It is now possible to approximate the average transfer delay for packets in an ALOHA network. If propagation delays on the channel, and processing delays at the receivers are neglected, note that each unsuccessful attempt to transmit a packet requires $(P + B)$ seconds, on the average, and each successful attempt requires P seconds. Each completed transmission consists of one successful attempt plus an average of $(e^{2G} - 1)$ unsuccessful attempts. Thus the average transfer delay is given by

$$T = P + (e^{2G} - 1)(P + B) \tag{6.18}$$

The quantity B, the mean backoff delay, depends on the backoff strategy. Such strategies can be dynamic, in that they depend on network load, or static, in which case they are independent of load. A lower bound on average transfer delay, which does not depend on B, can be found by setting $B = 0$ to obtain

$$T_{min} = Pe^{2G} \tag{6.19}$$

As in the case of FDMA and TDMA, it is desirable to normalize the delay expressions to units of packet transmission times, in this case by dividing by P. Dividing both sides of (6.18) and (6.19) by P results respectively in

$$\hat{T} = e^{2G} + (e^{2G} - 1)\, B/P \tag{6.20}$$

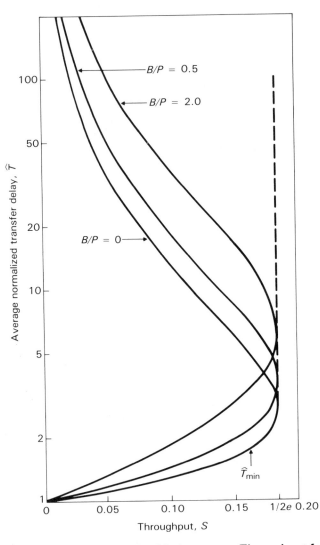

Figure 6.7 Average Normalized Delay versus Throughput for the ALOHA Random Access Procedure

*Chapter 6 **Performance of Basic Access Protocols***

and

$$\hat{T}_{min} = e^{2G} \tag{6.21}$$

To relate $\hat{T}_{min}$ to S, rather than G, it is necessary to solve the transcendental equation (6.15) for G in terms of S; this intermediate result is not particularly useful. There is no difficulty, however, in computing $\hat{T}_{min}$ versus S from (6.15) and (6.21); this is done to obtain the curve of $\hat{T}_{min}$ versus S, given in Fig. 6.7. The figure shows that S reaches its maximum, 0.184, for $\hat{T}_{min} = e = 2.718$. Figure 6.7 also shows $\hat{T}$ versus S for a number of nonzero values of B/P, assuming that B is constant (a static backoff strategy). These curves are computed in the same way.

The analysis in deriving this last result, and hence Fig. 6.7, again assumes that steady-state conditions exist. Since this assumption is not valid for $G > 0.5$, at least, the curve for $\hat{T}_{min}$ greater than 2.718 is not part of the actual steady-state operating range of the network. Since channel saturation always occurs for offered loads in excess of 0.5, delays become infinite, so performance for an ALOHA channel in this range is as shown by the dashed line in Fig. 6.7.

6.4   Idealized Central Control

Any central control network can be represented by the diagram of Fig. 6.8. The control computer determines which of the M stations can access the channel at any time; the controller uses some appropriate algorithm, the exact nature of which is determined by the type of central control.

An ideal type of operation can be hypothesized by assuming that transfer of the channel from one station to another can be accomplished, under direction of the control computer, instantaneously, without cost. That is to say, whenever a station has data to transmit, the control computer knows this instantaneously and assigns the channel to that station: immediately, when the channel is idle, or immediately after the channel becomes idle in the event it was busy initially. Waiting packets are queued at their stations in buffers assumed to have infinite capacity. If two stations have queued packets, the station with the first arrivals is assigned the channel first. (Ties are arbitrated in some specified manner.)

An approximation to ideal operation of this sort might be achieved by some type of control algorithm in a network for which propagation time is negligible. Obviously, however, ideal central control networks are an extrapolation of practical networks and do not actually exist. The performance of an ideal central control network serves as a bound on what is possible with practical equipment. Such performance is determined for the following specific conditions:

1. The arrival process at each station is Poisson with a mean of λ packets/sec arriving at each station;

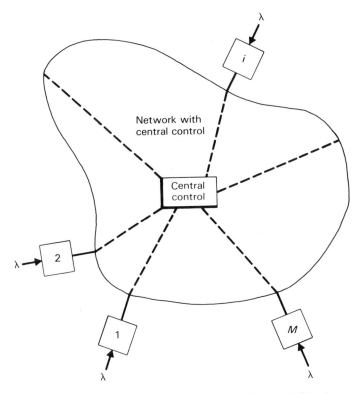

Figure 6.8   Idealized Network for Multiaccess Channel Sharing

2. Packets have a constant length $\overline{X}$ bits;
3. There are M stations;
4. The channel has a bit rate of R bps; and
5. Propagation time is assumed to be negligible so that distance between stations has no effect on operation.

As additional notation, the total input to the network, given by λM, is denoted Λ (packets/second).

Since packets do not interfere, and since no cost is associated with transferring the use of the channel from one station to another, the whole distributed network behaves as a single queue, with all of the station queues merged into one queue. The throughput and delay–traffic intensity curves for a single queue apply for the complete ideal network.

Note that a constant packet length has been specified in the assumptions so that the ideal central control network behaves as an $M/D/1$ queue.† It was shown in Chapter 3 that an $M/D/1$ queue has the least delay, for fixed traffic intensity, of any in the $M/G/1$ class. Such a queue then gives a lower bound

---

†A number of authors, such as Franta and Chlamtac [3], show M/D/1 queueing results as a limiting form of behavior for specific access procedures.

curve for the delay–traffic intensity relationship for any $M/G/1$ queue. Any practical network has delays in addition to those experienced by the single equivalent queue, and thus the results for the idealized case serve as a lower bound for delay versus traffic intensity for any local area network.

The analysis of the idealized central control network reduces to use of the expressions derived in Chapter 3 for the $M/D/1$ queue. In the present notation, the arrival rate to the queue is $\Lambda = \lambda M$, and the constant channel processing rate is $R/\overline{X}$, both in packets/sec. Equations (3.50) and (3.49) then give the average number in the equivalent queue, N_q, and the average delay, T, as

$$N_q = \frac{\rho^2}{2(1 - \rho)} \tag{6.22}$$

and

$$T = \frac{\overline{X}}{R} + \frac{\rho}{2(1 - \rho)} \frac{\overline{X}}{R} \tag{6.23}$$

where the utilization factor, ρ, equals $\Lambda(\overline{X}/R)$.

As previously mentioned, a network is typically characterized in terms of throughput, S, rather than traffic intensity, ρ. As discussed in Chapter 5, one definition of throughput is the fraction of time the channel transmits good packets. Traffic intensity for a queueing system is defined as the fraction of time the server, or the channel in the case of a network, is busy. The assumptions for the idealized central control network imply, however, that only good packets are transmitted. Thus for this case, when the channel is busy, it is transmitting good packets, and hence, ρ and S are equal.

Substituting S for ρ in (6.23) relates average transfer delay and throughput for the ideal network as

$$T = \frac{\overline{X}}{R} + \frac{S}{2(1 - S)} \frac{\overline{X}}{R} \tag{6.24}$$

This result is normalized into units of packet transmission times by dividing both sides of (6.24) by $\overline{X}/R$ to obtain

$$\hat{T} = T/(\overline{X}/R) = 1 + \frac{S}{2(1 - S)} = \frac{2 - S}{2(1 - S)} \tag{6.25}$$

where $\hat{T}$ denotes normalized average transfer delay.

An expression for the number of packets waiting in all of the station buffers, as a function of throughput, follows from (6.22) if S is substituted for ρ. The result is

$$N_q = \frac{S^2}{2(1 - S)} \text{ packets} \tag{6.26}$$

The relationships of the normalized quantities $\hat{T}$ and N_q to throughput, S are shown in Fig. 6.9.

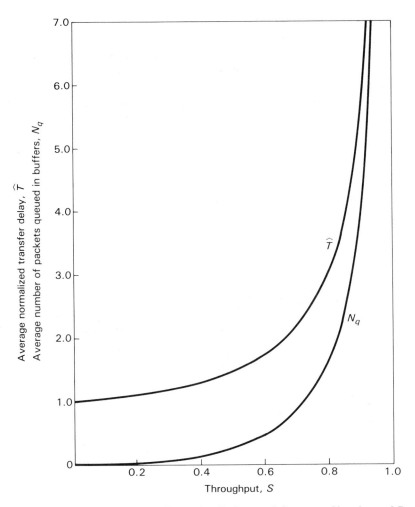

Figure 6.9 Average Normalized Transfer Delay and Average Number of Packets Waiting in All Station Buffers versus Throughput for the Idealized Central Control Network

As discussed in Section 6.3, offered load for random access networks is regarded as input packets plus retransmitted packets on some reference time interval. However, for networks such as the idealized central control type being discussed and the fixed assignment methods discussed previously, there are no retransmitted packets. Furthermore, in the steady state, the input and output packet rates are equal for the complete network. Thus the definition of G given in Section 6.3 reduces to that of S so that

$$G = S \tag{6.27}$$

Equation (6.29) is valid as long as the input packet rate does not exceed the maximum output packet rate, which is $R/\overline{X}$ (μC in the notation of Chapter 3). If G becomes equal to or greater than 1, the channel is saturated (blocked),

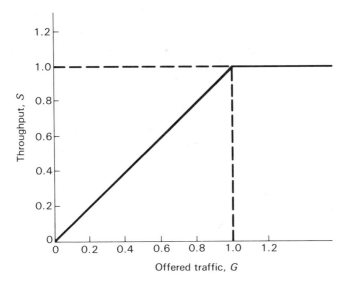

Figure 6.10   Throughput versus Offered Traffic for the Idealized Central Control Network

and the network can remain in the steady state with throughput equal to 1 only if packets are dropped. Assuming that the idealized central control network always operates in the steady-state condition, the relation of S to G is as shown in Fig. 6.10. Under the same assumptions, this relationship also holds for the fixed assignment methods. The curve of S versus G in the figure is useful for comparison to S–G curves for random access networks as discussed previously and in Chapter 9.

As a final comment on the idealized central control network, note that throughput, S, and the average number of packets waiting, N_q, are for the whole network. The assumptions, however, make the average behavior of all stations the same. Thus, per-station throughput, s, and average number of packets waiting per station, n_q, can be expressed as

$$s = S/M \tag{6.28}$$

$$n_q = N_q/M \tag{6.29}$$

and substituted into Eq. (6.26) if a per-station result is desired.

Total transfer delay, T, as used in Eq. (6.24), is average delay suffered by a packet entering and exiting at arbitrary stations. Thus this quantity does not have a per-station counterpart.

6.5   Comparison of Basic Capacity Assignment Strategies

Sections 6.2–6.4 develop the basic relations for average transfer delay versus throughput and throughput versus offered traffic for the different strategies chosen as representative of the range of possibilities for multiaccess procedures. The results are given both as analytical expressions and as curves in the sections cited.

A logical first step in comparing the strategies is to plot the results for each method on a common graph. This is done in Fig. 6.11 for normalized delay versus throughput and in Fig. 6.12 for throughput versus offered traffic. (FDMA is omitted from the curves because it is directly related to TDMA— see Eq. (6.11).)

The curves for normalized delay show that ideal central control has the least delay for any value of throughput. This is to be expected since this method assumes no overhead cost and hence produces no further delays for sharing the channel. The delay is also unaffected by the number of stations under the ideal conditions. Since the environment is assumed error-free and no packets are lost, throughput and offered traffic are equal until saturation occurs when throughput is equal to 1.

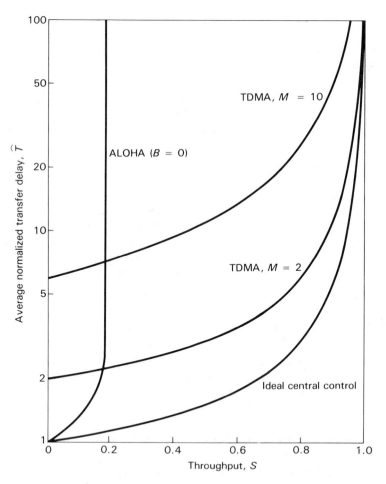

Figure 6.11 Comparison of Average Normalized Transfer Delay versus Throughput for the Basic Multiaccess Strategies

Chapter 6 ***Performance of Basic Access Protocols***

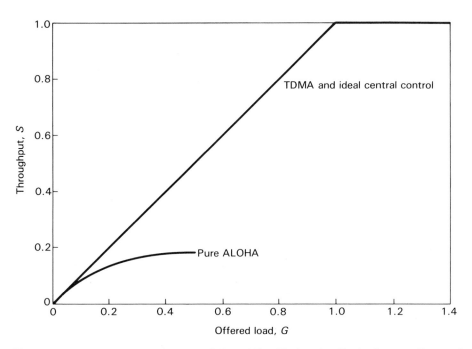

Figure 6.12   Throughput versus Offered Traffic for the Basic Access Strategies

Delay for ideal central control can serve as a lower bound on average delay for any practical method since actual implementations always require overhead to share the channel. Note that the least possible normalized delay is 1 for $S = 0$. This corresponds to an actual delay of $\overline{X}/R$, the time required for a channel of rate $R/\overline{X}$ packets per second to process a packet. Since there are no packets in storage, there is no waiting for the channel. The delay curve increases from 1 as throughput increases from 0 along the curve of a single $M/D/1$ queue. As throughput goes up, the average waiting time, and hence average delay, increases since there are times when packets enter the network stations faster than they can be processed over the channel. Of course, on the average the input rate is equal to the output rate as long as the offered traffic G is less than 1.

The FDMA and TDMA access procedures illustrate the effect of a deterministic allocation of channel capacity, in terms respectively of fixed bandwidth and of fixed time slots, to each station. Such networks can be constructed, and the models developed accurately represent the important characteristics of the methods.

Since each station has its assigned capacity, whether it needs it or not, delay is significantly affected by the number of stations. In fact, with throughput equal to 0 so that there is no load on the network, normalized delay is $1 + M/2$ for TDMA, which indicates that in addition to the one normalized unit of delay always required to transmit the packet, an effective waiting time of $M/2$ packet transmission times is also incurred. In the case of FDMA, the minimum normalized delay is M packet transmission times. As shown by Eq.

(6.13) FDMA delays are, on the average, $(M/2 - 1)$ packet transmission times larger than corresponding TDMA delays. In both cases, the increase of delay with load is similar to that for ideal central control.

For the assumptions used, the fixed assignment access procedures do not lose or degrade packets; therefore, the throughput versus offered traffic has ideal characteristics.

The ALOHA method, which illustrates the extreme of the random access procedures, differs significantly in its characteristics from both the ideal central control and the TDMA procedures. The method can be implemented. The model developed gives the throughput versus offered load characteristic as $M \rightarrow \infty$ and also gives a lower bound on delay as a function of throughput.

The ALOHA network requires no central control and no overhead is explicitly built into the procedure. As a result, at small values of throughput, the normalized delay is close to that of the ideal central control. For such loads there are few collisions, on the average, and each station effectively uses the channel as it is needed. As throughput is increased, however, more and more collisions occur, and delay increases drastically because of the need to retransmit packets that have suffered collisions.

The effect of retransmissions on the throughput versus offered traffic characteristics is also pronounced, as Fig. 6.12 shows. Again, for small values of offered traffic, throughput increases almost along the ideal curve. However, as the load is increased further, throughput increases, then levels off, and finally drops to 0 in the saturation region as collisions completely take over the channel. It has been shown that ALOHA performance is not overly sensitive to the actual number of stations, but depends more on the total load on the channel. However, the stability of ALOHA and other random access networks depend to quite an extent on the number of stations.

Although useful in terms of defining what is possible, the basic methods discussed are related to other practical procedures in quite different ways. The ideal central control procedure is, as its name implies, ideal; it cannot be implemented. It serves only to give bounds on what is possible. Several classes of practical central control access procedures exist, and their performance, as well as that of other types of access procedures, can be profitably compared to this ideal.

The TDMA access procedure is a practical procedure, so the results presented for it can be achieved. Furthermore, it turns out that there are few variations on the TDMA and FDMA procedures as pure deterministic methods of assigning channel capacity. Thus these methods are not at the extreme of a practical class, but are entirely representative of the class.

Frequency-division multiplexing is also practical, although delays somewhat larger than TDMA are produced. It is, however, possible to achieve performance close to that predicted. In broadband networks, FDMA is often used to delineate bands within a wideband channel. Other access procedures can then be used for independent systems that operate within each band.

The ALOHA method can also be implemented as a practical random access procedure. It is, however, a member of a large class of practical procedures, and its performance is the poorest in this class. Performance characteristics of other random access procedures can vary drastically from that of the ALOHA, which gives the least desirable performance for both average delay and throughput versus offered load.

As a final general comment, a number of access procedures have been developed in an attempt to combine all or some of the characteristics represented by the several different methods. The objective of these hybrid methods is to obtain performance as close as possible to that of ideal central control. A good discussion of access methods for local area networks at the level of this chapter, along with a survey of the literature, is given by Hayes [4].

6.6   Summary

This chapter begins the quantitative analysis of local area network performance by discussing several basic multiaccess procedures chosen to illustrate the extremes of possible behavior. Four methods are discussed: time-division multiple access, frequency-division multiple access, a random access procedure, and an idealized central control method. Each of the methods is analyzed to obtain expressions for average normalized transfer delay versus throughput and throughput versus offered traffic.

The methods of Chapter 6, particularly ALOHA and ideal central control, illustrate extremes of behavior. Chapter 7 begins the discussion of more practical methods with an analysis of polling.

References

[1] S. S. Lam. "Delay Analysis of a Time Division Multiple Access (TDMA) Channel." *IEEE Transactions on Communications* COM-25, no. 12 (December, 1977): 1489–1494.
[2] M. Schwartz. *Computer Communication Network Design and Analysis,* 287–292. Englewood Cliffs, NJ: Prentice–Hall, 1977.
[3] W. R. Franta and I. Chlamtac. *Local Networks,* 215–217. Lexington, MA: Lexington Books, 1981.
[4] J. F. Hayes. "Local Distribution in Computer Communications." *IEEE Communications Magazine* 19 (March 1981): 6–14.

Problems and Exercises

Problems 1, 2, and 3 pertain to a local network with 10 stations that uses a cable with a capacity of 10^6 bits/second. The network processes packets with 12 8-bit characters.

1. (a) Determine the average message delay, in seconds, for a TDMA network with values of throughput given by $0, 0.2$, and 0.6. Use a few more values and plot $\hat{T}$ versus S.
   (b) Repeat for an ideal central control network.
   (c) Repeat for an FDMA network.

2. Use suitable values of S to evaluate the bound on delay for an ALOHA network. Why is it not possible to use values of S above some limit less than 1?

3. What is the limit on average input rate λ packets/second (assumed to be the same for each station), so that average message delay is less than 0.1 seconds? Obtain a result for TDMA and for an ideal central control network.

4. *Capacity* for a random access network is defined as maximum throughput, S, for any value of G. Determine capacity analytically for ALOHA.

5. Equation (6.9) is an expression for the average transfer delay for an FDMA network with *constant* length packets.
   (a) Follow the approach used in the text to derive an expression for the average transfer delay of an FDMA network that has *exponentially distributed* packet lengths. Denote the mean packet length as $\overline{X}$.
   (b) Normalize the average transfer delay to find

   $$\hat{T} = T/(\overline{X}/R)$$

   (c) Compare $\hat{T}$ for fixed and exponentially distributed packet lengths at the minimum and maximum values of S.

6. A random access network uses the ALOHA access protocol. The packet transmission time is 10^{-3} sec for an average packet length of 1000 bits.
   (a) What average input rate to each of 100 stations will result in the maximum possible network throughput?
   (b) What is the maximum unnormalized throughput in packets/second for the whole network?
   (c) Under these conditions, estimate the average number of retransmissions.

Network for Problem 7:

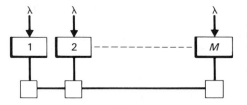

- R — bit rate (bps) of common bus;
- Constant length packets, $\overline{X}$ bits/packet;
- λ — average input rate, packets/second, at each station; and
- M — number of stations

7. (a) What is the largest value of λ that the network can accommodate using each of the protocols discussed in Chapter 6. Express the answer in terms of R, $\overline{X}$, and M.
   (b) For a throughput, S, of one-half of the maximum possible, determine the average transfer delay (not normalized) for each of the protocols of Chapter 6 for $M = 100$, $\overline{X} = 100$ bits/packet, and $R = 10^7$ bits/sec. The bound T_{min} can be used for ALOHA.

8. An idealized central control network services 10 stations and is constructed with a line of bit rate $R = 9600$ bps.
   (a) At a throughput of $S = 0.5$, what is the total average message delay for 500-bit messages?
   (b) How much of this delay is waiting time in the buffer?

9. The delay–throughput curves of Fig. 6.7 show that minimum average delay in the stable throughput range is obtained for $B = 0$. Explain why this backoff strategy is never used and the fallacy inherent in these curves.

10. (a) Assuming that a guardband of g Hz is necessary for each channel in an FDMA system, derive an expression for the average transfer delay with 1 bps/Hz modulation. Give expressions for the maximum throughput that can be obtained with this system and the fractional increase in the minimum transfer delay due to the guardbands.
    (b) For a channel of total bandwidth 2 MHz and 100 channels, calculate the transfer delay for: 1000 bit packets, an arrival rate of 5 packets/sec, and guardbands of (i) 0 Hz; (ii) 2 KHz; and (iii) 10 KHz.

11. It is often possible to write the normalized transfer delay $\hat{T}$ for a multiaccess network in the form

$$\hat{T} = A \frac{Z - S}{P - S}$$

where S is the throughput, P is the pole of the delay function (i.e., the value of S at which the delay goes to infinity) and A is some multiplicative constant.
    (a) Use the equations derived in this chapter to find A, Z, and P for the FDMA, TDMA, and ideal central control schemes.
    (b) Find estimates of A, Z, and P for ALOHA; use the three points: $S = 0$, the point for which delay goes to infinity for a suitably large number of stations, and an intermediate point found with Fig. 6.7. Take $B = 0.5 \, P$.

12. (a) A TDMA frame has extra bits to ensure frame synchronization. Let the fractional overhead per frame be y. Use the same notation as in the text to derive an expression for the average normalized transfer delay for a TDMA system in terms of the throughput, S, the number of stations, M, and the overhead factor, y. What is the maximum throughput when the overhead is included in the analysis?
    (b) For a TDMA network with 50 stations and a normalized throughput of 0.4, calculate the error introduced by neglecting frame overhead when the overhead is (i) 0.5%; and (ii) 10%. In each case calculate the maximum throughput possible.

CHAPTER *7*

*P*olling Networks

7.1 Introduction

Polling networks represent the most straightforward method of combining line sharing with resource sharing. This type of network falls into the class of central control networks in the terminology introduced in Chapter 5. Typically a central computer controls the network; this computer may also serve as a clearinghouse for messages between terminals.

Figure 7.1 gives a general representation of a polling network. Such networks are used to interconnect a variety of devices. An early application was to interconnect a number of agent terminals in, for example, an airline reservation system to each other and to a central computer. In principle, however, the devices connected by a polling network can range from terminals or terminal clusters connected through a terminal interchange to devices such as printers, storage disks, graphics terminals, and even main-frame computers.

The basic feature of a polling network is the action of the central computer in polling each location, or station, on the network in some predetermined order to provide access to the channel. As each location is polled, the connected device, if it has data to transmit, uses the full data rate of the connecting channel to transmit its backlog to the central computer. In between polls, the connected devices accumulate messages, but do not transmit until polled. Transmissions between stations take place through the

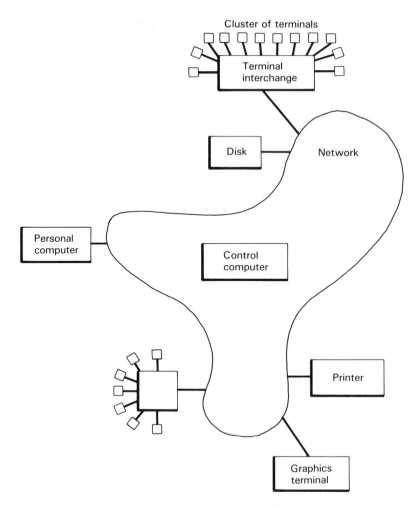

Figure 7.1 A General Representation of a Polling Network

central computer, which receives all incoming packets and transmits them to the appropriate locations.

The lines coupling the polled stations to the central computer are typically high speed and can be either half duplex or full duplex. If the lines are full duplex, the central computer can communicate outgoing messages to their destination stations over one-half of the full duplex connection and simultaneously receive incoming messages from the currently polled station over the other half. If the lines are half duplex, they must be shared between incoming and outgoing traffic, and a small amount of time is required each time the line is turned around at the central control.

Polling networks can operate in either of two modes, identified as *roll-call* and *hub* polling. In both modes the network is controlled by the central computer, and the opportunity to transmit is systematically rotated from one station to another. For roll-call polling, the central computer initiates the polling sequence by sending a polling message to a chosen station. After this station has transmitted its backlog of messages, it so notifies the central computer with a suffix to its last packet. After receiving this suffixed packet, the central computer sends a poll to the next station in the polling sequence, and the process is continued.

For hub polling, the central computer sends out the polling message to the initial station in the same manner as for roll-call polling. When this station has

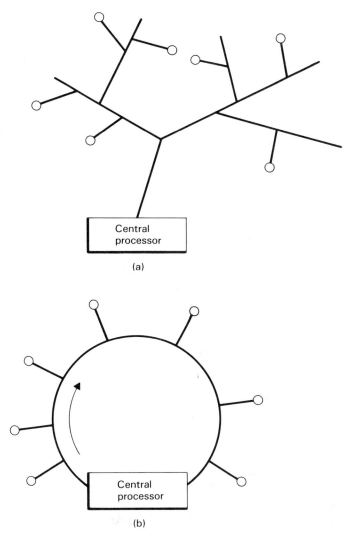

(a)

(b)

Figure 7.2   Typical Topologies for Polling Networks
(a) Tree topology
(b) Ring topology

completed its transmission, it suffixes a *go-ahead* to the end of its transmission as before, but for hub polling a *next-station address* is also required. (Such an address is optional for roll-call polling.) This address and the equipment that enable all stations to monitor incoming traffic to the central computer constitute additional features required for hub polling.

With hub polling, after a station completes its transmission, the next station in the polling sequence (which is continually monitoring incoming traffic to the central computer) reads the go-ahead, recognizes its own address, and begins transmitting immediately. Use of the monitor function in this way for hub polling can speed up the polling operation. In essence, transmission of the go-ahead to the central computer and of the poll from the central computer to the next station in the polling sequence is, in effect, replaced in hub polling by transmitting a go-ahead directly from one station to another.

Polling networks can be configured in ring, bus, star, or tree topologies. Ring and tree types are illustrated in Fig. 7.2. Roll-call polling is straightforward for any of these topologies. Implementation of the monitor function for hub polling may not be obvious in all cases. For ring topologies, however, polling can be implemented in an obvious manner if the polling sequence progresses between adjacent stations. For other topologies, some sort of *bridge* and additional monitor wiring is often required to enable each station to monitor incoming traffic.

The preceding comments cover the rudiments of the operation of polling networks. The basic concepts are enlarged in the next section of this chapter. Detailed discussions can also be found in Schwartz [1] and in Hayes [2]. Later subsections analyze the performance of both roll-call and hub polling within the same analytic framework, and present design equations and performance charts. More advanced analyses can be found in Schwartz [1], Spragins [4], [5], and Konheim and Meister [6]. The chapter concludes with a brief discussion of adaptive polling.

7.2 Operation of Polling Strategies

The details of the operation of polling networks are now examined, using the fairly typical example shown in Fig. 7.3, along with the packet formats of Fig. 7.4. For roll-call polling, the following sequence of operations is typical:

- The central computer sends out a polling packet to station *i* in the polling sequence;
- Station *i* synchronizes on bits and characters;
- Station *i* reads and interprets the station address and the go-ahead contained in the polling packet (see Fig. 7.4(a));
- Station *i* transmits all its backlogged messages to the central computer for distribution to the central computer and other stations;
- Station *i* appends a go-ahead, and possibly a next-station address, to its last packet (see Fig. 7.4(c));

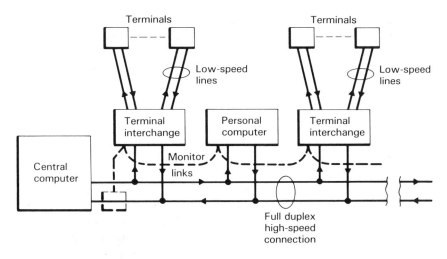

Figure 7.3   A Typical Polling Network

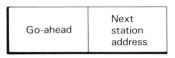

Bit sync	Character sync	Go-ahead	Station address	Check characters	End of packet

(a)

Bit sync	Character sync	Station address	Terminal address (if required)	Information content	Check characters	End of packet

(b)

Go-ahead	Next station address

(c)

Figure 7.4   Typical Packet Formats for Polling Networks
(a) Polling packet for roll-call polling
(b) Format for data packets
(c) Suffix to last data packet transmitted

- The central computer synchronizes on bits and characters;
- The central computer reads and interprets the incoming packets, including the final go-ahead and next-station address; and
- The central computer sends out a poll to station $(i + 1)$.

The eight steps are repeated for each station until all have been polled; then the whole process is repeated again, starting with station i.

Since the high-speed connection is duplex for the example, the central computer can transmit to some stations on the outgoing line while other stations are transmitting to the computer on the incoming line. Terminals can feed messages into storage at each terminal interchange while the interchange is communicating with the central computer. Operation can be asynchronous in both directions, or the central computer can maintain synchronous operation on the outgoing line while the stations communicate asynchronously on the incoming line. (If synchronous operation is maintained on the outgoing line from the central computer, the second step in the polling sequence is unnecessary.) If a station has no messages, it either does not reply to the polling packet or sends back a go-ahead with the next-station address.

For hub polling, the dotted monitor connections in Fig. 7.3 must be used, and each station must affix a next-station address after the go-ahead on the end of its transmission. Given these changes, the central computer is no longer explicitly required in transferring the poll between stations. This is now accomplished by each station continually observing the incoming data to the central computer over the monitor connection (shown generically in Fig. 7.3 with dashed lines) and responding to the go-ahead when it recognizes its own address.

The typical packet formats shown in Fig. 7.4 contain overhead. Several bits are necessary in polling and data packets for bit and character synchronization. The polling packet used by the central computer for roll-call polling contains a go-ahead to initiate data transfer from the designated station. Both polling and data packets have standard CRC characters and an end-of-packet flag. For both polling types, the go-ahead suffix to the last data packet is necessary, whereas the next-station address is optional for roll-call and required for hub polling.

Now consider the diagrams of Fig. 7.5, which depict two different monitoring situations for hub polling. The monitor can be implemented very simply, as shown by the dashed connection in Fig. 7.5(a) for a bus topology, if operation of the network is restricted so that the station physically most distant from the central computer is used to initiate the polling sequence, and the stations are polled in their physical order. In such a case, each station can monitor the incoming line directly. This simple implementation can also be used on a ring of the type shown in Fig. 7.2(b) if the stations are polled in the same sequence as they are physically located on the ring.

Outside of such special cases, more complex monitoring connections that use bridges are required. An example for a multidrop network is shown in Fig. 7.5(b), in which station $(i + 1)$ follows station i in the polling sequence. Note

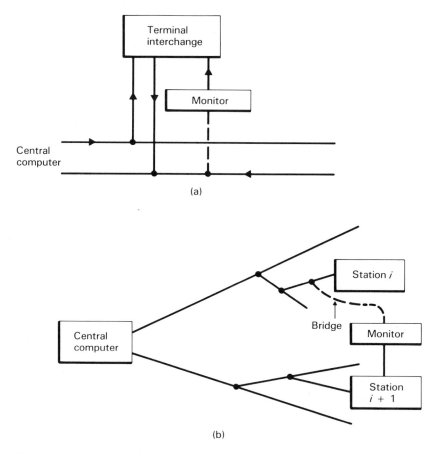

(a)

(b)

Figure 7.5   Monitoring for Hub Polling
(a) Simple case
(b) A multidrop configuration

that for each station to monitor its predecessor in the polling sequence, more complex wiring is generally required.

The essential features of polling networks, such as the one shown in Fig. 7.3, are contained in the schematic diagram of Fig. 7.6. The figure illustrates the logical structure of a polling network for any topology and for both hub and roll-call polling. The logical structure described is used for further discussion of polling. In addition, it is assumed for simplicity that all traffic is from terminals to the central computer. This is the most common type of operation, but extension of the analysis to other cases is possible if such cases need to be considered.

Messages arrive at random at each station and are stored in a buffer until the station is polled. When the station is polled, it uses all of the capacity of the channel to the central computer to transmit to the central computer until its

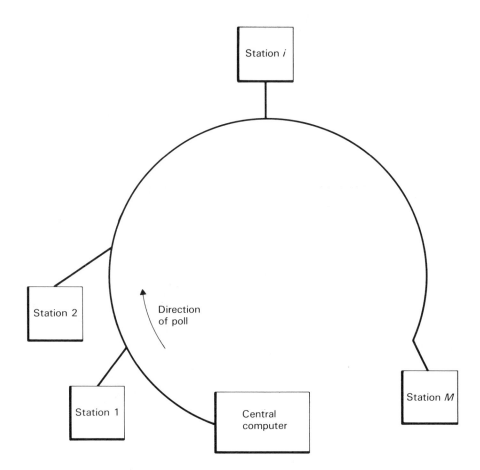

Figure 7.6   Schematic Diagram of a Polling Network

buffer is perceived to be empty. Thus the station transmits until the last complete packet has been transmitted. When its buffer is empty, the station sends out a go-ahead with a next-station address. The next station is then polled, either explicitly by the central computer for roll-call polling, or implicitly by that station monitoring the line traffic and detecting the go-ahead with next-station address, in the case of hub polling.

A time called *walk time* and designated w is required to transfer the poll from one station to another and synchronize the station for transmission to the central computer. The walk time includes all the time required by all functions necessary to transfer the poll. This includes channel propagation delay, transmission time of polling and response packets, modem synchronization time (if modems are needed), and so forth. Walk time is less for hub polling than roll-call polling, but both types can be analyzed with the same basic model.

The total time required to poll each station and return to the starting station in the polling sequence is called *cycle time*. Cycle time, t_c, is a random variable because the amount of data to be transmitted by each station depends on how much data is received since the last poll. The average cycle time, T_c, is an important parameter for describing the operation of polling networks.

Other measures of the performance of polling networks, in addition to average cycle time, are:

- Average queue length at each station, N, measured in packets;
- Average time, W, that packets must wait in the station buffer before being transmitted; and
- Average transfer delay, T, from packet entry into the station buffer until delivery to the central computer.

Response time, as defined and discussed in Chapter 5, is also useful in measuring performance from the user point of view. Response time, or the time required for a user to transmit a message and receive a response, typically depends on higher-level protocols and is thus not specifically considered in this chapter, which treats polling as a basic access strategy. It is worth noting, however, that response time often includes not only the average transfer delay from a station buffer to the central computer, but also the average transfer delay from the central computer back to the station. This latter time is straightforward to compute since it involves the delay from the central computer to a terminal interchange on a channel dedicated to the central computer and for which there are no access problems to complicate the calculation.

The behavior of several of the basic variables for polling networks is illustrated with the diagram of Fig. 7.7. The figure shows a typical pattern of

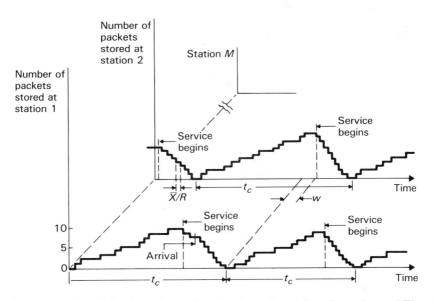

Figure 7.7 **Number of Packets Stored at Stations 1 and 2 as Functions of Time in the Steady State**

the number of packets stored at two representative stations in a polling network as a function of time in the steady state. The channel bit rate is assumed to be R, and the packets have a constant length, $\overline{X}$. Thus transmission of a ready packet over the channel takes $\overline{X}/R$ seconds.

Consider station 1 first, and note that the number of packets stored increases by one with each arriving packet while the station is waiting to use the channel. When the station finally receives the poll, at the point in the figure marked "service begins," it begins to transmit packets out of its buffer at a constant rate, $\overline{X}/R$, determined by the packet length and the capacity of the channel to the central computer. Packets still arrive and are stored while those previously stored are being transmitted. When the buffer at station 1 is perceived to be empty, the opportunity to transmit is transferred to station 2. After the walk time, w, station 2 begins to transmit, and the process continues.

7.3 Performance Analysis

A straightforward analysis of a polling network can be made to determine average cycle time, but sophisticated techniques, beyond the scope of the present treatment, are required for a rigorous determination of average transfer time and average number of packets stored in the station buffers. A derivation of an expression for average transfer time can be made in a heuristic manner, however, and such a derivation will be presented. A rigorous analysis to determine all three performance measures has been made by Konheim and Meister [6], and their results are used to verify the results of the heuristic derivation.

The following conditions are assumed in determining the desired quantities:

1. The arrival processes to each station are statistically equivalent Poisson processes with equal average arrival rates, λ packets/second;
2. The walk time, w, between stations is constant and is the same for every consecutive station pair;
3. The channel propagation times between stations are equal and are included in the walk time; and
4. The packet length distributions, for random length packets, are the same for packets arriving at each station.

Other network parameters are the number of stations, M, and the channel bit rate, R, in bits/second.

7.3.1 Average Cycle Time

Let N_m be the average number of packets with average length $\overline{X}$ bits stored at a typical station when the go-ahead poll arrives at this station. The common channel with capacity R is then available to the station to transmit data, and

$N_m \overline{X}/R$ seconds are required to empty the station buffer. To be more precise, N_m, in the expression for time to empty the station buffer, should include not only the packets stored at the time service begins, but also those that arrive during the time the station is receiving service.

After the station buffer is emptied at one station, access to the channel is transferred to another station in a time equal to the walk time, w. The length of an average cycle can thus be expressed as

$$T_c = M[N_m \overline{X}/R + w] \tag{7.1}$$

since the average time to empty a station buffer and transfer to the next station is the same for each of M stations.

The average number, N_m, of packets that must be transmitted to empty a station buffer in the steady state is determined by the average arrival rate, λ packets/second, and the average cycle time T_c as

$$N_m = \lambda T_c \tag{7.2}$$

Thus (7.2) and (7.1) can be combined and simplified to yield an expression for T_c, as

$$T_c = \frac{Mw}{1 - M\lambda \overline{X}/R} \text{ seconds} \tag{7.3}$$

The quantity $M\lambda \overline{X}/R$, which is the ratio of the total average arrival rate to the network to the total capacity of the network (both in packets/second), was defined earlier as throughput, S. Thus

$$S = M\lambda \overline{X}/R \tag{7.4}$$

and a final expression for average cycle time is

$$T_c = \frac{Mw}{1 - S} \text{ seconds} \tag{7.5}$$

For (7.3) and (7.4) to be valid, the network must operate in a steady-state manner. This in turn requires that the offered load to the network, $M\lambda$ packets/second, must be less than the channel service rate, $R/\overline{X}$, in the same units. An equivalent requirement is that throughput, S, must be less than 1.

Equation (7.5), for average cycle time, agrees with the result obtained by Konheim and Meister.

7.3.2   Delay Analysis

As stated previously, a basic performance measure for polling networks is the average time, W, an arriving packet at a typical station must wait before reaching the head of the queue in the station buffer. This average waiting delay can be divided into two component delays:

1. The waiting delay, W_1, in the station buffer while other stations are being served (i.e., while the station is inactive and awaiting its turn to be polled); and

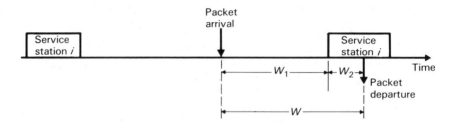

Figure 7.8   Division of Waiting Times for a Typical Packet

2. The waiting delay, W_2, in the station buffer while that particular station is being served.

Figure 7.8 shows the physical relationship between the different waiting periods, and they are related mathematically by

$$W = W_1 + W_2 \tag{7.6}$$

All three of the variables in (7.6) are random variables, and in general W_1 and W_2 are not independent. Konheim and Meister [6] use advanced techniques to derive an exact expression for W. The approach used here is a heuristic one designed to give some insight without the necessity for rigorous mathematics. Several assumptions and heuristic arguments are used. It is assumed that W_1 and W_2 can be evaluated independently, and that W_1 can be obtained through consideration of a cycle with average parameter values rather than with a more rigorous approach with all parameters of the cycle random. An additional heuristic argument is used to evaluate W_2.

The pattern of activities for a polling network in a cycle with average parameters is shown in Fig. 7.9. From the point of view of a station i, the cycle consists of the time station i is being served and the remaining time, during which it is idle (waiting to be polled). The following calculation shows the relative size of the average values of these times, W_2 and W_1.

The average number of packets that must be transmitted over the channel by a particular station while it is being served is expressed in Eq. (7.2) as $N_m = \lambda T_c$. The corresponding average service time for the station is N_m times the channel service rate in packets/second or $\lambda T_c \overline{X}/R$. Defining the parameter, ρ,

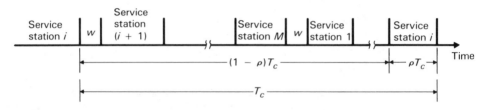

Figure 7.9   A Cycle for a Polling Network, with Average Times Indicated

as

$$\rho = \lambda \overline{X}/R \qquad (7.7)$$

the average service time per station can be expressed as ρT_c, as shown in Fig. 7.9. The remaining part of the "average" cycle during which the station is idle is then, of course, $T_c(1 - \rho)$.

Now consider packets arriving at random during the time, $T_c(1 - \rho)$, which is the average length of time that station i is waiting to be served. The packets arrive from a Poisson process, and for such "random" arrivals it is intuitive, when the number of packets is large, that the average time, W_1, that these packets must wait for service is given by

$$W_1 = \frac{(1 - \rho) T_c}{2} \text{ seconds} \qquad (7.8)$$

(i.e., one-half of the idle interval).

In fact, it can be shown (see Ross [7], p. 17) that the arrival times are distributed independently and uniformly on the interval $[0, T_c(1 - \rho)]$ so that (7.8) is an exact result for ρ and T_c constant, as is the case for an average cycle. When it is known that exactly one packet has arrived during an interval of fixed length, it is easy to show that the time of arrival has such a uniform distribution.

The delay W_1 can be expressed in terms of more basic parameters by using (7.3) for T_c and (7.7) for ρ to obtain

$$W_1 = \frac{Mw(1 - \rho)}{2(1 - M\rho)} \qquad (7.9)$$

The second component, W_2, of the total average delay experienced by arriving packets is the average time packets must wait to reach the head of the queue in the station buffer after the station begins receiving service. This component of delay is identified along with the first component in Fig. 7.8. An expression for W_2 is now obtained using a heuristic argument.

This second component of delay, for packets at any station, is a delay experienced when the station in question is receiving service. To obtain an expression for this delay, consider an equivalent network for which there is no walk time so that some station is always being served if there are packets in the network. (In queueing notation, if the server never goes idle with queued packets in the network, the server is called *work conserving*.) It is reasonable to regard this complete equivalent network as a distributed M/G/1 queue with M stations and total arrival rate $M\lambda$. In other words, the M individual queues can be regarded as a single lumped queue with the arrival rate aggregated.

An expression for the average time delay, T, for an M/G/1 queue is given by Eq. (3.40) in terms of σ_y^2, the variance of the service time. Although not shown in this text, this equation is not dependent on the order of service provided that the server is work conserving.

To apply (3.40) in the present case, note that average service time is given by $1/\mu C$ (or $\bar{X}/R$ in the present notation). It is more convenient to express W_2 in terms of moments of service time rather than variance. Thus if X is a random variable that represents packet length in bits, then its first and second moments are denoted $\bar{X}$ and $\bar{X^2}$. It follows that service time for a packet is X/R, and hence its variance is $(\bar{X^2}/R^2 - (\bar{X}/R)^2)$. Finally, substitution in (3.40) yields

$$W_2 = \frac{(M\lambda)\,\bar{X^2}/R^2}{2(1 - M\rho)} \tag{7.10}$$

Throughput for the distributed queue, or for the network in the present application, is given by

$$S = M\lambda\,\bar{X}/R \tag{7.11}$$

in conformity with (7.4) and (7.7), and thus W_2 can be expressed as

$$W_2 = \frac{S\,\bar{X^2}}{2\bar{X}R(1 - S)} \tag{7.12}$$

This expression for W_2 from the *zero walk time* network is added to the expression for W_1 to find the total delay W. Thus, using (7.9) and (7.12), W can be expressed as

$$W = \frac{Mw(1 - S/M)}{2(1 - S)} + \frac{S\bar{X^2}}{2\bar{X}R(1 - S)} \tag{7.13}$$

Two distributions of packet lengths that are often of interest are constant and exponential. For these two cases, the second moment of packet length becomes $(\bar{X})^2$ and $2\,(\bar{X})^2$ respectively, so that W for these cases is given by

Constant packet lengths

$$W = \frac{Mw(1 - S/M)}{2(1 - S)} + \frac{S\bar{X}}{2R(1 - S)} \tag{7.14}$$

Exponential packet lengths

$$W = \frac{Mw(1 - S/M)}{2(1 - S)} + \frac{S\bar{X}}{R(1 - S)} \tag{7.15}$$

These results for average waiting time, derived heuristically, can be compared to precise results obtained by Konheim and Meister [6]. The physical assumptions for the Konheim and Meister model differ from those used in the heuristic derivation in two respects; Konheim and Meister use:

1. A synchronized, slotted network with the requirement that transmission of data can take place only at the beginning of a "slot"; and
2. Walk time is assumed to be a random variable.

By setting the variance of the walk time equal to zero, the second of these assumptions is reduced to the constant walk-time assumption used in the heuristic analysis. Since most polling networks operate asynchronously, it is reasonable to delete a quantization term in the Konheim and Meister result before comparison to the heuristic result. If this is done (along with setting the variance of walk time equal to zero), the two results agree exactly.

Numerical Example 7.1

Consider a metropolitan area network with a single central processor located at the headend of a broadband CATV system that has a tree topology. The following are specified:

- Maximum distance from headend to a subscriber station—20 kilometers;
- Access technique—roll-call polling;
- Length of polling packet—8 bytes;
- Length of go-ahead—1 byte;
- Data rate of channel—56 Kbps;
- Number of subscribers—1000;
- Packet length distribution for packets from subscriber to headend—exponential;
- Mean packet length—200 bytes; and
- Propagation delay—6 μsec/km.

(a) Find the mean waiting delay for arriving packets at the stations if each user generates an average of one packet per minute;
(b) If the channel data rate is reduced to 9600 bps, what is the longest possible mean packet length that will not overload the system? and
(c) For mean packet lengths of two-thirds the result of (b), determine the mean waiting delay.

Solution

It is first necessary to determine the mean walk time for all stations. Components of walk time for roll-call polling are: transmission time of go-ahead, propagation delay from a subscriber to the headend processor, transmission delay of the polling packet, propagation delay from the headend to the next subscriber polled, and modem synchronization delay at the subscriber.

Maximum one-way propagation delay for a packet from the subscriber to the headend is given by

$$20 \times 6 = 120 \ \mu sec$$

(This maximum delay is assumed for transmission between any subscriber and the headend.) Polling packet and go-ahead transmission times are, respectively, $8 \times 8/56 = 1.14$ milliseconds and $8/56 = 0.14$ milliseconds. Walk time can then be determined as the sum of transmission delays for the go-ahead and polling packets, propagation delays from a station to the headend and from the headend to the next station, and modem synchronization time so that

$$w = 0.14 + 1.14 + 2 \times 0.120 + 10 = 11.52 \text{ milliseconds}$$

Throughput per station, total throughput, and average waiting delay, W, can now be determined from the appropriate expressions:

(a) Throughput/station $= \rho = \dfrac{\lambda \overline{X}}{R} = \dfrac{1/60 \times 200 \times 8}{56 \times 10^3} = 4.76 \times 10^{-4}$

Total throughput $= S = M\rho = 1000 \times 4.76 \times 10^{-4} = 0.476$

$$W = \frac{1000\,(11.52 \times 10^{-3})(1 - 4.76 \times 10^{-4})}{2\,(1 - 0.476)} + \frac{0.476 \times 200 \times 8}{56 \times 10^3\,(1 - 0.476)}$$

$\qquad = 10.99 + 0.026 = 11.02$ seconds

(b) $S_{max} = \dfrac{1000\,(1/60 \times 8 \times \overline{X}_{max})}{9600} < 1$

$\overline{X}_{max} < 72$ bytes

(c) $\overline{X} = 2/3 \times 72 = 48$ bytes

$\qquad$ Throughput/station $= \rho = \dfrac{\lambda \overline{X}}{R} = \dfrac{1/60 \times 48 \times 8}{9600} = 6.67 \times 10^{-4}$

$\qquad$ Total throughput $= S = 2/3\, S_{max} = 0.067$, or $S = M\rho = 0.667$

Polling packet and go-ahead transmission times change because of the new channel bit rate, so that the walk time changes and is given by

$$w = \frac{8 \times 8}{9.6} + \frac{8}{9.6} + 2 \times 0.12 + 10 = 17.74 \text{ milliseconds}$$

Finally, W is given by

$\qquad W = 26.62 + 0.01 = 26.63$ seconds

Note that the first term in W is dominant, as is generally the case if walk time is large.

7.3.3 Average Number Stored in a Station Buffer

Having evaluated the average packet delay at a typical station, it is easy to find the average number of packets stored in a station buffer. Using Little's Law directly with the average packet delay given by (7.13), the average number stored, N, is given by

$$N = \frac{Mw\lambda(1 - S/M)}{2(1 - S)} + \frac{S\lambda \overline{X^2}}{2\overline{X}R(1 - S)} \qquad (7.16)$$

At this point, note that the result given by Konheim and Meister [6] is slightly different from Eq. (7.16). Their analysis assumes that accumulation of data is in increments of data units rather than packets, where a data unit is a small unit of data such as a byte or character. As a result, the average number of packets as given by their analysis is somewhat greater because partially arrived packets are included in the result. In fact, the first term in their result is the same as that in (7.16), whereas their second term is slightly larger because no S (less than 1) appears in their numerator. However, this second term is in general much smaller than the first.

As an alternative to using Little's Law directly, the following argument may be used to give an intuitive feel for how the queue size varies in a station buffer. The approximate analysis begins, as in the previous section, by partitioning the number of packets stored in the station into two parts:

1. Those packets that arrive while a station is inactive; and
2. Those packets that arrive while the station is being served.

The average number of packets received by a station during its total inactive period is equal to the arrival rate, λ, times the length of the idle period, $(1 - \rho)T_c$, or $\lambda(1 - \rho)T_c$. As previously discussed, the arrival times of these packets, from a Poisson process, are uniformly distributed over the idle interval, and thus the average number in the queue is given by one-half of the number at the end of the idle period, or

$$N_1 = \frac{\lambda(1 - S/M)T_c}{2} = \frac{\lambda(1 - S/M)Mw}{2(1 - S)} \tag{7.17}$$

(Note that N_m, which is used in Subsection 7.3.1 to derive average cycle time, is essentially twice N_1.) Since these packets are the majority of those transmitted during the active period for the station, N_1 is a good approximation of the average number of packets stored in the buffer over the complete cycle. Figure 7.10(a) shows the build up of packets in a typical station buffer during the idle period and their transmission when the station receives service.

Packets that arrive during the service period are not accounted for by N_1, and such packets increase the average number stored in the station buffer. It is difficult to develop a heuristic argument that results in a quantitative expression for this increase in the average number stored caused by packets arriving during the service period. However, as suggested in Fig. 7.10(b), these arrivals do not have a large effect on the average number queued, particularly if $\rho \ll 1$ and M is large.

The expression for N given in (7.16) reduces to those in (7.18) and (7.19) for the special cases of constant and exponentially distributed packet lengths

Constant

$$N = \frac{S^2/M}{2(1 - S)} + \frac{Mw\lambda(1 - S/M)}{2(1 - S)} \tag{7.18}$$

Exponential

$$N = \frac{S^2/M}{(1 - S)} + \frac{Mw\lambda(1 - S/M)}{2(1 - S)} \tag{7.19}$$

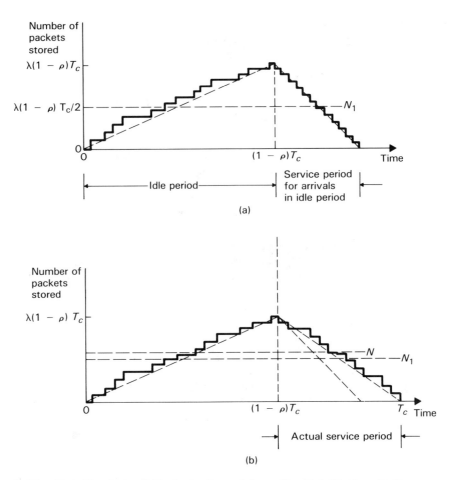

Figure 7.10 The Number of Packets Stored in a Typical Station Buffer as a Function of Time

(a) No arrivals during service period

(b) Arrivals during service period

Since $S < 1$, the first term is often small in comparison to the second if M is, for example, 10 or more. This statement is consistent with the earlier claim that N_1 is a good approximation for N.

Numerical Example 7.2

Consider the metropolitan area network discussed in Example 7.1. The average number of messages queued at each station is to be determined for parts (a) and (c) of the problem stated.

Solution

(a) Values for w, ρ, and S are the same as determined in Example 7.1 part (a); namely, $w = 11.52$ milliseconds, $\rho = 4.76 \times 10^{-4}$, and $S = 0.476$. Equation (7.19) then gives N as

$$N = \frac{(0.476)^2/1000}{(1 - 0.476)} + \frac{1000 \times 11.52 \times 10^{-3} \times 1/60\,(1 - 0.476/1000)}{2\,(1 - 0.476)}$$

$$= 4.32 \times 10^{-4} + 0.183 = 0.183 \text{ packets/station.}$$

(c) Values for w, ρ, and S are also the same as in Example 7.1 part (c): $w = 17.74 \times 10^{-3}$ seconds, $\rho = 0.0667 \times 10^{-4}$, $S = 0.667$. Equation (7.19) gives

$$N = 1.33 \times 10^{-3} + 0.444 = 0.445 \text{ packets/station}$$

Note that the second term (N_1) dominates in both cases, as is usually the case for large Mw.

7.4 Performance of Polling Networks

The basic equations developed in Section 7.3 can be used to obtain design curves for polling networks. Average waiting time, average transfer delay, and average number stored at the stations are performance variables related to throughput with walk time and number of stations as parameters. The assumptions stated at the beginning of Section 7.3 and used to derive the basic equations still apply, of course. An additional restriction to constant length packets is also used for most of the work to keep the number of curves to a reasonable number. Curves for other packet length distributions can be developed as needed, although the results show only minimal sensitivity to this parameter.

Consider delay first. Equation (7.14) gives the basic expression for average waiting time, W. Average transfer delay, T, defined as the total average time between packet arrival at a station and its delivery to the central computer, can be expressed in terms of W as

$$T = \overline{X}/R + \tau_{\text{ave}} + W \text{ seconds} \tag{7.20}$$

where $\overline{X}/R$ is the average time to transmit the packet over the channel and τ_{ave} is the average propagation delay from a station to the central computer. The parameter τ_{ave} can often be expressed as $\tau/2$, where τ is defined as the end-to-end propagation delay for a bus network, as the maximum delay from any station to the central computer for a tree network, and as the propagation delay around the ring for a ring network.

Using (7.14) for W, T can be expressed in terms of basic parameters as

$$T = \overline{X}/R + \tau_{\text{ave}} + \frac{Mw(1 - S/M)}{2(1 - S)} + \frac{S\overline{X}}{2R\,(1 - S)} \text{ seconds} \tag{7.21}$$

It is often convenient to normalize T, which is in seconds in (7.21), by dividing it by the time to transmit a packet over the channel, $\overline{X}/R$. The normalized variable, $\hat{T}$, which has units of packet transmission times, then becomes

$$\hat{T} = T/(\overline{X}/R) = 1 + \frac{R\tau_{\text{ave}}}{\overline{X}} + \frac{wRM(1 - S/M)}{2\overline{X}(1 - S)} + \frac{S}{2(1 - S)} \tag{7.22}$$

This equation can be further simplified by defining normalized propagation delay, a, as

$$a = \tau R / \overline{X} \tag{7.23}$$

and normalized walk time, $\hat{w}$, as

$$\hat{w} = wR / \overline{X} \tag{7.24}$$

For $\tau_{ave} = \tau/2$, the final normalized equation is given as

$$\hat{T} = 1 + a/2 + \frac{M\hat{w}(1 - S/M)}{2(1 - S)} + \frac{S}{2(1 - S)} \tag{7.25}$$

packet transmission times.

The average number of packets stored at a station, as given in (7.18), can be written in normalized units as

$$N = \frac{S^2/M}{2(1 - S)} + \frac{S\hat{w}(1 - S/M)}{2(1 - S)} \text{ packets} \tag{7.26}$$

(Note that for this equation, $\hat{w}$ is the only variable that is normalized.) Similarly, the average cycle time, T_c, from (7.5) can be normalized and written as

$$\hat{T}_c = \frac{M\hat{w}}{1 - S} \text{ packet transmission times} \tag{7.27}$$

When the number of stations is moderately large (for example, $M > 20$), the expressions for average delay and average number stored at each station simplify to

$$\hat{T} = 1 + a/2 + \frac{M\hat{w}}{2(1 - S)} + \frac{S}{2(1 - S)} \text{ and} \tag{7.28}$$

$$N = \frac{S^2/M}{2(1 - S)} + \frac{S\hat{w}}{2(1 - S)} \tag{7.29}$$

Further simplifications are obtained if a is much less than 1 and $M\hat{w}$ is much greater than 1. Since S is always strictly less than 1, the following results are obtained.

$$\hat{T} = \frac{M\hat{w}}{2(1 - S)} = \frac{\hat{T}_c}{2} \text{ and} \tag{7.30}$$

$$N = \frac{S\hat{w}}{2(1 - S)} \tag{7.31}$$

The information contained in the general expressions for normalized average transfer delay and average number stored at the stations, as given by

(7.25) and (7.26), is displayed in Figs. 7.11–7.13 for the condition that $a = 0$.

Figure 7.11 shows the relationship between $\hat{T}$ and $M\hat{w}$ for several choices of S. The relation is linear, as can be noted from (7.28). The quantity $\hat{T}_c/2$, as given by (7.30), is also plotted on the graph of Fig. 7.11, although it does not differ from the plot of $\hat{T}$ enough to be detected as a separate curve. The approximate equality between $\hat{T}_c/2$ and $\hat{T}$ can be verified by comparing (7.30) and (7.28). Note that for $a = 0$, as is being assumed, $\hat{T}$ can be expressed as $(2 - S + M\hat{w})/(2(1 - S))$. The term $2 - S$ is negligible for $M\hat{w}$ on the order of 10 or larger, and hence under these assumed conditions $\hat{T}_c/2 \simeq \hat{T}$.

Figure 7.12 shows $\hat{T}$ and $\hat{T}_c/2$ versus S for 10 and 100 station networks with different walk times. This figure verifies the conclusion, stated previously, that $\hat{T}_c/2$ is an excellent approximation for $\hat{T}$ if $M\hat{w}$ is sufficiently large. Figure 7.13 shows how the average number of packets stored at a single station varies with throughput for different values of M and $\hat{w}$.

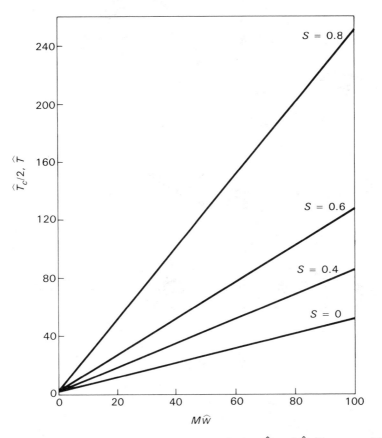

Figure 7.11   Normalized Average Transfer Delay $\hat{T}$ and $\hat{T}_c/2$ versus $M\hat{w}$ for $a = 0$ and Several Values of S (Curves for $\hat{T}$ and $\hat{T}_c/2$ differ only at very small values of $M\hat{w}$)

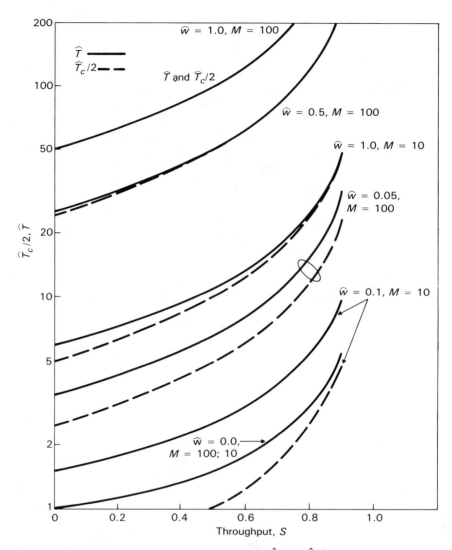

Figure 7.12   Normalized Average Transfer Delay $\hat{T}$ and $\hat{T}_c/2$ versus Throughput, S, for $M = 10$ and 100 and Several $\hat{w}$

Several comments on the design of polling networks can be made from examinations of the equations and plots given previously. Normally it is desirable to keep $\hat{T}$ and N as small as possible. Since both of these parameters tend to be linear, increasing functions of $M\hat{w}$ for large values of the latter, the number of stations should be restricted when $\hat{w}$ is large and, correspondingly, if a large number of stations is required, efforts should be made to keep $\hat{w}$ small.

Both $\hat{T}$ and N increase with S. Thus, as throughput increases, performance in terms of delay deteriorates, and more storage is required at the network

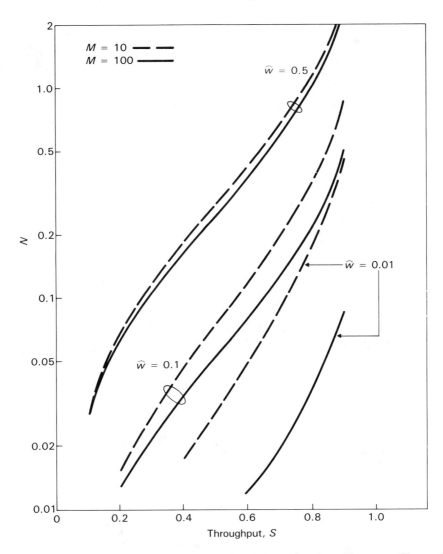

Figure 7.13 Average Number of Packets Stored per Station, **N**, versus Throughput, **S**, for Several Values of **M** and **ŵ**

stations. Note, however, that over the range of parameters used in the curves, the number of packets stored per station never exceeds the order of one.

From an analysis point of view, cycle time, T_c or $\hat{T}_c$, is much easier to compute than other delay parameters. Thus advantage can be taken of the fact that $\hat{T}_c/2$ is a good approximation for $\hat{T}$ over much of the practical range of $M\hat{w}$.

Finally, note that for walk and propagation times equal to 0, $\hat{T}$ reduces to the expression obtained in Chapter 6 for the ideal central control type network.

7.5 Adaptive Polling

The performance analysis of polling, given in the previous section, shows that average transfer and waiting times are determined to a major extent by the number of stations polled and the walk time between stations. Even when the network is lightly loaded (i.e., S is small), it is still necessary to poll each of the M stations, and hence average waiting time, for example, remains significant. In fact, for small S, W, as given by (7.13), can be approximated as

$$W \simeq Mw/2 \tag{7.32}$$

In an effort to decrease average transfer and waiting delays for light loading, an adaptive polling technique has been proposed by Hayes [8]. This technique requires that the stations be connected in a logical tree structure so that stations can be probed in groups, rather than each station separately, to determine which ones have data to transmit.

The tree structure is shown in Fig. 7.14. The controller carries out the probing procedure by separating the stations into two groups that are probed one at a time by a signal broadcast to all stations in that group. A station with data to transmit returns a positive response to the probe arrival. After receiving a positive response from a group, the controller separates that group

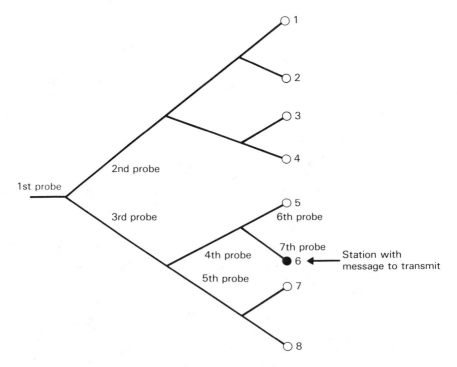

Figure 7.14 Illustration of Probing (for 8 stations)

into two subgroups and probes each of these in turn. The procedure of probing, halving the group, and probing again is continued until each individual station with data to transmit is located. Only then does data transmission commence. The sequence of transmissions is determined by the central control.

Figure 7.14 illustrates a case in which one station out of eight has data to transmit. The sequence of seven probes shown in the figure is a typical sequence for locating the ready station. Note that even though a positive response is received to the fourth probe, probe 5 as shown is necessary because the central controller does not know that only one station has data to transmit.

In general, if the number of stations, M, is expressed as 2^n, $(2n + 1)$ probes are necessary to locate a single ready user. (These probes not only locate the user, but tell the central control that there are no other ready users.) This number results from noting that there are two probes associated with every subdivision of the station groups, and that n subdivisions are necessary. The additional "1" arises because an initial probe is used to determine if any of the stations has data to transmit. If there are, for example, two ready users, then the number of probes is at least $(2n + 1)$; the exact number of probes depends on the relative location of the two users in the logical tree.

The number of probes in a probing strategy compares favorably with the $M = 2^n$ polls required per cycle for a standard polling protocol. For example, in the case of a single ready user, if $M = 16$, and hence $n = 4$, standard polling requires 16 polls, whereas the probing strategy requires only $2 \times 4 + 1 = 9$ probes. For $M = 256$ and $n = 8$, the comparison of 256 to 17 shows even more savings.

When more than one station has ready packets, however, the advantage of probing may not be as great. Indeed, at the extreme, if all stations have ready packets, the number of probes necessary to locate all ready users is $(2^{n+1} - 1)$, approximately twice as many as polling.

A compromise between pure polling and pure probing has been proposed to achieve improvements over conventional polling for most loading conditions. This adaptive technique begins a cycle, for example, by probing four groups of two in turn rather than one group of eight. Information from previous cycles concerning the number of busy users can be used to determine how many groups to probe at the beginning of each cycle. Clearly, under extremely heavy loads, this adaptive technique reverts to pure polling.

Figure 7.15 shows the relationship between the average number of polls per cycle, $\overline{P}$, and the probability, p, that an individual station has a message to transmit. The probability, p, can be approximated, assuming Poisson arrivals at each station, by the equation

$$p = 1 - e^{-\lambda T_c} \tag{7.33}$$

Equation (7.33) is obtained by noting that $e^{-\lambda T_c}$ is the probability of no arrivals from a Poisson process, with average arrival rate λ in the average time of a cycle, T_c.

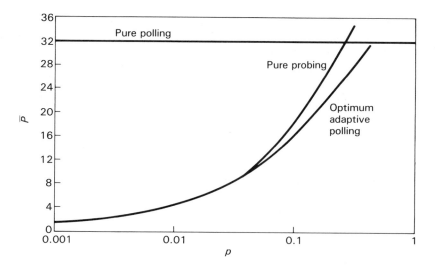

Figure 7.15 **Performance of Probing and Polling Strategies for M = 32 Stations, Showing the Mean Number of Probes per Cycle, $\overline{P}$, versus the Probability, p, that an Individual Station has a Message to Transmit (from Hayes [8])**

The figure shows how $\overline{P}$ varies with p for pure polling, pure probing, and an optimum adaptive strategy discussed by Hayes [8] and Lam [9].

Knowing the average number of polls per cycle, $\overline{P}$, for adaptive polling, the general result for average waiting time can be used to determine this quantity for the adaptive polling technique. Thus, substituting $\overline{P}w$ for Mw in (7.13) results in

$$W = \frac{\overline{P}w(1 - S/M)}{2(1 - S)} + \frac{S\overline{X^2}}{2\overline{X}R(1 - S)} \tag{7.34}$$

as the average waiting time for the adaptive polling technique. Note that the maximum value of $\overline{P}$ is M. Also note that when only one of the M stations is ready, the number of probes or polls is $2n + 1$, as stated previously. Since $n = \log_2 M$, it follows that $\overline{P}$ for this case is simply $2(\log_2 M) + 1$.

7.6 Summary

This chapter begins with a description of the mechanics of polling systems, pointing out that they are an example of a central control network. Roll-call and hub type polling netwcrks are described in detail.

Parameters used to characterize the performance of polling networks are cycle time, average waiting time in network buffers, average transfer delay, and average number of packets stored in a station buffer. Expressions for each of these quantities are obtained in terms of throughput, number of stations, and walk time.

Walk time is discussed in some detail and is defined as the time required to transfer control of the channel from one station to another. Components of walk time for hub polling are the time to transmit go-aheads, the propagation delay, and, if modems are used, modem synchronization. For roll-call polling, the time to transmit polling packets must be added.

Results of normalized equations for $\hat{T}_c/2$, average number stored per station, N, and average transfer delay, $\hat{T}$, are plotted versus throughput. The last two quantities are also plotted versus the product of number of stations and walk time, $M\hat{w}$. One conclusion from the equations and curves is that for relatively large $M\hat{w}$, $\hat{T}_c/2$ is a good approximation for $\hat{T}$. Several other conclusions relative to designing polling networks are drawn. A final subsection discusses adaptive polling.

The next chapter is concerned with ring networks that use distributed control.

References

[1] M. Schwartz. *Computer-Communication Network Design and Analysis.* Englewood Cliffs: Prentice–Hall, 1977.

[2] J. F. Hayes. "Local Distribution in Computer Communications." *IEEE Communications Magazine* 19 (March 1981): 6–14.

[3] J. F. Hayes. *Modeling and Analysis of Computer Communications Networks.* New York: Plenum Press, 1984.

[4] J. D. Spragins. "Loop Transmission Systems—Mean Value Analysis." *IEEE Transactions on Communications* COM-20, pt. II (June 1972).

[5] J. D. Spragins. "Simple Derivation of Queueing Formulas for Loop Systems." *IEEE Transactions on Communications* COM-25 (April 1977): 446–448.

[6] A. G. Konheim and B. Meister. "Waiting Lines and Times in a System with Polling." *Journal of the Association of Computing Machinery* 21 (1974): 470–490.

[7] S. M. Ross. *Applied Probability Models with Optimization Applications.* San Francisco: Holden–Day, 1970.

[8] J. F. Hayes. "An Adaptive Technique for Local Distribution." *IEEE Transactions on Communications* COM-24 (August 1978): 1178–1186.

[9] S. S. Lam. "Multiple Access Protocols." In *Computer Communications,* vol. 1, *Principles,* ed. W. Chou. Englewood Cliffs, New Jersey: Prentice–Hall, 1983.

Problems and Exercises

1. Define and compare the following variables: walk time, cycle time, and transfer delay.

2. Compare average transfer delay for a TDMA network and a polling network for $M = 10$ stations, normalized walk time, $\hat{w} = 1$, and your choice of S values. Would

you expect the comparison to be valid for other values of the parameters? Explain. Neglect propagation delay.

3. Consider a "first-cut" design of a metropolitan area network that uses polling. Walk time can be approximated by using twice the maximum one-way propagation delay between the headend computer and any station, one modem sync time, and the time to transmit a polling packet. Data for the network is as follows:
   - Maximum distance between headend and any station—25 km;
   - Propagation time—6 μsec/km;
   - Modem sync time—19 milliseconds;
   - Polling packet—five 8-bit bytes;
   - Bit rate of channel—56 kilobits/sec;
   - Average packet length—75 bytes; and
   - Average input rate to each station—1 packet/minute.
   (a) Find walk time.
   (b) Use a tractable approximation for average transfer delay and find the maximum number of stations so that this delay is less than one second.
   (c) If transfer delay is unimportant, what maximum number of stations is possible, assuming that the network must function?

4. A polling network is to be constructed with hub polling and the parameters listed below:
   - Propagation time—negligible;
   - Go-ahead message—two 8-bit bytes;
   - Sync time for go-ahead—10 milliseconds;
   - Average packet length—100 bits;
   - Average input to each station—1 packet/minute; and
   - Number of stations—300
   (a) Compute the walk time.
   (b) What channel bit rate is necessary for operation of the network to be possible?
   (c) What is the average transfer delay for a channel with bit rate $R = 1200$ bps? Approximate answers are satisfactory.

5. For the network of problem 4, with $R = 1200$ bps, what is the average number of packets stored at each station?

6. Assume 10 stations 1000 feet apart with one station 1000 feet from a central computer. Each station is to service five terminals whose average traffic varies from a minimum of 1 message/hour to a maximum of 10 messages/minute. Each message is twenty 8-bit bytes, and the same messages are transmitted by the stations to the central computer. The terminals transmit into a buffer at the station over a 300-bps line, where they are stored until the station can transmit to the central computer. The *total* average delay for messages from a *terminal* to the central computer must not exceed 2 seconds.
   Design a polling system, using reasonable values for all variables.

7. A number, M, of stations are connected in tandem 200 meters apart with 200 meters between the nearest station and the central computer. The connections are all made with 19.2 kbps lines. Data messages to the central computer are thirty 8-bit characters long. Each station serves 30 terminals, each of which generates Poisson traffic with a mean arrival rate, λ_i, of 1 mess/sec. Modem synchronization time is 10 milliseconds, propagation delay is 6 milliseconds/km, polling packets are six 8-bit characters, and the go-ahead is two 8-bit characters.

(a) For hub polling, express average cycle time, total transfer delay, and average number of messages stored in terms of M. Plot each of these quantities versus M.

(b) How many stations can be used if total average transfer delay for messages from the stations to the central computer must be less than 0.1 seconds? Consider both hub and roll-call polling.

(c) Consider using $T_c/2$ as an approximation to total average transfer delay. Why is this reasonable? Plot $T_c/2$ versus M on the graph of (a).

(d) What is the minimum value of total average transfer delay as throughput approaches 0? Given the configuration of stations, how can this be reduced?

(e) Total load on the polling network can be expressed as $\Lambda = M \sum_{i=1}^{30} \lambda_i$. What absolute limit does Λ place on the number of stations?

8. Packets arrive from a Poisson process to a station. Given that exactly one packet arrives in an interval of length τ, show that the arrival time of the packet is uniformly distributed over the interval.

9. Consider an eight-station network, using probing as the access method. If exactly two stations have packets to transmit, how many probes on the average are required? For a 2^n station network, how many different locations for the two stations are possible?

10. Repeat problem 9 for the case that three stations are ready to transmit.

CHAPTER *8*

*R*ing Networks

8.1   Introduction

The classification ring network is based on network geometry rather than access protocol, which is used to delineate polling, discussed in Chapter 7, and random access, described in Chapter 9. The ring classification is often used, however, and it is appropriate since the ring structure results in a number of distinctive operational features and, to a certain extent, determines characteristics of the access protocols.

A ring network, such as shown in Fig. 8.1, can be characterized as a sequence of point-to-point links between stations, closed on itself. All messages travel over a fixed route from station to station around the loop, passing through network interfaces at each station. Typically, each station is active in the sense that it regenerates the message and can identify addresses, but the interface unit does not usually store messages, as in a store-and-forward network. However, new messages awaiting transmission on the ring can, of course, be stored in the station. Each station passes the message on after a short delay of a few bit times. For most ring networks, messages may circulate past each station so that operation is of a broadcast type, although this is not always the case. For a typical ring network, the connecting links are high-speed buses, messages are passed in only one direction around the ring, and propagation delays are small.

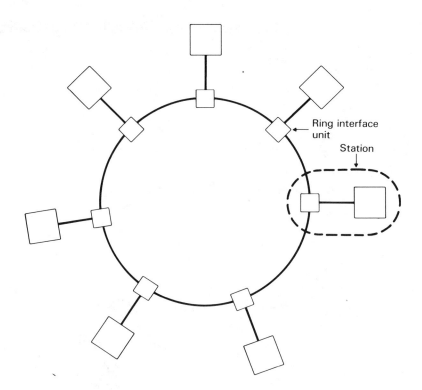

Figure 8.1   A Typical Ring Structure

The ring structure brings both advantages and disadvantages. Advantages are:

- Implementation is simple because transmission paths are fixed;
- Routing algorithms are not required;
- Stations introduce only a small delay to a packet circulating on the ring;
- Multiple addressing is straightforward;
- Rings can cover a relatively large distance because the message can be regenerated at each station; and
- Efficiency does not degrade rapidly with load.

Disadvantages, on the other hand, include:

- Operation depends on each station's network controller, so if an interface fails, the network is essentially broken;
- The ring must be broken to add or delete stations; and
- Propagation delay is proportional to the number of stations.

A number of different types of ring networks have been designed, and a smaller but still significant number of different types have been implemented. Penney and Baghdadi [1], for example, in a survey paper list a dozen types of ring networks, all of which differ in some respect. Of the many different types of rings that have been suggested, three types seem to have commercial promise: token rings, slotted rings, and register insertion rings. Attention is restricted in this text to these three types, which also cover most of the major variations in approach.

The basic approach used by the three types of rings to be studied can be stated concisely. Token rings control ring access through use of a token passed from station to station. Operation of such rings is closely related to that of hub polling, discussed in Chapter 7. Slotted rings circulate a number of relatively small fixed-sized slots that, when empty, are available for use by any station. The operation is in some sense analogous to a circulating conveyor belt that carries packets from one station to another. Finally, register insertion rings have two shift registers at each station node. These shift registers operate as switches to control traffic into and out of the ring and also operate as extensions to the ring, making possible longer packets than can be used with the slotted ring.

The remaining sections of this chapter discuss the three types of rings in detail and analyze their performance. Since storage at the nodes is usually not a problem for ring networks, performance is reflected primarily in packet delay. Thus performance analysis for ring networks consists of determining packet delay, and how it is affected by the various parameters of the network.

8.2   Token Rings

8.2.1   Basic Operation

A token ring has the basic structure of all ring networks, as illustrated in Fig. 8.1. Each station interface has the components shown in Fig. 8.2(a): a line driver and a receiver for coupling to the ring, and appropriate transmitter and receiver for communicating with devices located at the station. Operation of the interface is controlled by a controller, as shown in the figure. Bits from the ring enter the interface in one direction in a serial fashion, are read in the interface, and then, after a delay of several bits, are retransmitted over the ring either unchanged or after some modification.

Logical operation of the interface, under instructions from the controller, is shown in Fig. 8.2(b). Note that there are two modes, listen and transmit. Stations are normally in the listen mode, in which the station can detect its address on traffic circulating on the ring and read the contents of packets addressed to it.

Access to the ring for transmissions is controlled by a *token,* which is a dedicated bit or bit structure that can be in one of two possible states: busy or idle. When the ring is first activated, an idle token circulates around the ring from station to station. A station with data to transmit reads the idle token and changes it to the busy state before retransmitting it. The busy token is then incorporated as part of the header of data transmitted on the ring by the

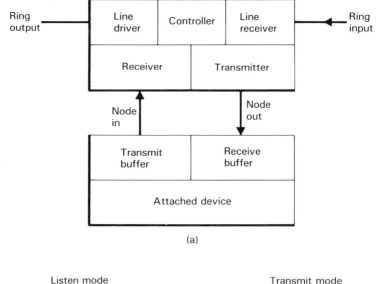

(a)

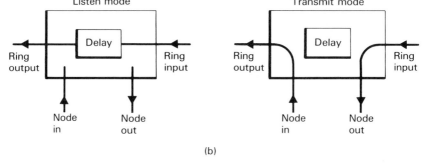

(b)

Figure 8.2   Station/Ring Interface
(a) Interrelation of components
(b) Logical operation

station. Thus other stations on the ring can read the header, note the busy
token, and refrain from transmitting.

In an elementary system, the token can be a dedicated pattern of several
bits or a single bit transmitted in a format different from that used for data
bits. In more sophisticated practical systems, such as specified in the IEEE
802 standard, the token is one element of a physical control field, which can be
several bytes long.

As an illustration of a dedicated bit pattern for a simple token, the token
could consist of a sequence of eight 1's. For this pattern, or for any dedicated
bit pattern, it is necessary to ensure that the same pattern does not occur in a
run of data. This is accomplished by monitoring the data and using *bit
stuffing,* a procedure that breaks up any data pattern that duplicates the token
by adding, or "stuffing," extra bits. When stuffing has been used, the receiver

must be able to identify the stuffed bits so that they can be removed before error detection.

Continuing the illustration of an 8-bit token pattern, a station with a ready packet would need to read all 8 bits of the token to ascertain that it is free. The station interface could then make use of the station delay to change the last bit of the token to a 0 to indicate "busy" before retransmission. The token pattern at the station output is then the busy pattern of seven 1's and a 0. Since there is no need to store the first 7 bits of the token pattern, the station node in this case introduces only a 1-bit delay.

A long dedicated bit pattern, with the associated stuffing required, can be inefficient. An alternative is to make use of special bits for the token, or special bits to mark the beginning and ending of a control field. An elementary manner for accomplishing this with Manchester encoded bits is shown in Fig. 8.3. Figure 8.3(a) shows the standard Manchester encoding for data bits; any

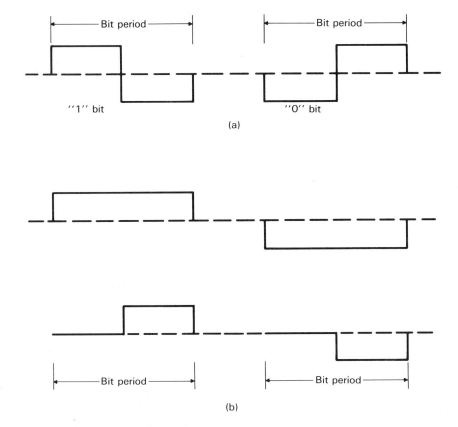

Figure 8.3 **Manchester Encoded Data Bits with the Violations Shown as Control Bits**
(a) Manchester encoded data
(b) Violations that can be used as control (token) bits

one of the patterns shown in Fig. 8.3(b) could be used for the token or to delineate the control field. The use of Manchester encoding, with violations for control bits, not only makes for more efficient operation, but also provides clocking pulses for the receiver to use for synchronization.

State-of-the-art token ring networks, such as proposed in the IEEE 802 standard, embed the token in a physical control field that carries out additional network functions. For example, Andrews and Schultz [2] propose a control field that sets a priority mode, a priority reservation, and several other indicators along with the token. The formats of the physical control field, the free token packet, and the complete packet, as proposed by Andrews, are given in Fig. 8.4.

Once the station has captured a free token and thus gained access to use of the ring, there are two types of operation: exhaustive service and nonexhaus-

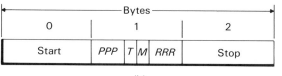

Bits				Bits	
0–2	3	4	5–7	0–1	2–7
PPP	T	M	RRR	FF	CCCCC

PPP = Priority mode   T = Token   M = Monitor count

RRR = Priority reservation   FF = Packet format   CCCCC = Control indicators

(a)

Bytes			
0	1		2
Start	PPP	T	M	RRR	Stop

(b)

Bytes							
0	1–2	3 – 8	9 – 14	D⩾0	(15 + D) – (18 + D)	19 + D	20 + D
Start	Starting control field	Destination address	Source address	Data	Packet check sequence	Stop	Ending control field

(c)

Figure 8.4   Formats for Token Ring Communications as Proposed by Andrews [2]

(a) Starting control field
(b) Free token packet
(c) Complete packet format

Chapter 8   Ring Networks

tive service. For exhaustive service, the station retains use of the ring until it has transmitted all the data stored in the transmit buffer of the device attached to the ring at the station (see Fig. 8.2(a)). For nonexhaustive service, the station is allowed to transmit only a specified number of bits each time it captures the ring.

For operation under light and medium loads, the two types of operation are essentially equivalent, and the exhaustive type of operation is assumed in the remainder of this section.

Now consider the flow of packets around the ring. Bits are processed serially out of each station interface. The input to each station is the output of the previous station delayed by the propagation delay between the two stations. In the listen mode, each station passes on the packet received at its input after a delay referred to as the *station latency*. The station latency is a minimum of one bit and can range up to a dozen or so bits in rings, such as that described by Andrews and Schultz [2], that use control fields with several features.

Bits and packets are processed around the ring in a synchronous fashion, with synchronization achieved, for example, by use of Manchester encoding. If all stations are in the listen mode, the token circulates around the ring in a time equal to the sum of the propagation delays plus the sum of the station latencies. This composite time is called *ring latency*.

When one or more stations has data to transmit, one of the stations captures the ring and transmits its data in an output packet. As previously noted, the transmitting station produces a modified token (or more generally, an appropriate control field) as the header for the packet to indicate to other stations that the ring is no longer free. (Note that the token is considered to be a part of the transmitted packet.) The amount of data in the packet can be arbitrary (assuming exhaustive service). The transmitting station is responsible for removing its packet from the ring and for generating a new free token when its transmission is over.

There are several times when a new free token can be generated. The variations give rise to what are referred to as *multiple-token, single-token,* and *single-packet* operation.

For multiple-token operation, the transmitting station generates a new free token and places it on the ring immediately following the last bit of transmitted data. As its name implies, this type of operation permits several busy tokens and one free token on the ring at one time. For more than one token to be on the ring, packet lengths and station latencies must be related so that busy tokens do not progress far enough around the ring to be removed by their originating stations before the new free token is generated.

In contrast to multiple-token operation, single-token operation requires that a transmitting station wait until it has erased its own busy token before generating a new free token. If a packet is longer than the ring latency, however, the station will receive (and erase) its busy token before it has finished transmitting data. In this case, the station must continue transmitting data and generate a new free token only after the last data bit has been transmitted. This is, of course, the same as multiple-token operation. Thus single- and multiple-token operation differ only in cases for which the packet is shorter than the ring latency.

For single-packet operation, a station does not issue a new free token until after it has circulated completely around the ring and erased all of its transmitted packet. This type of operation is the most conservative of the three in ensuring that two transmissions do not interfere. Both single-packet and single-token operation ensure that there is only a single token on the ring at any given time. Single-packet operation goes one step beyond single-token operation in requiring that the complete packet, including the busy token, be erased before generating a new free token.

Figure 8.5 illustrates the three types of operation for a four-station ring with a station latency of 1 bit time and a negligible propagation delay. The table shows a sequence of discrete bit times, with time increasing from top to bottom. For each case it is assumed that station 1 initially captures the ring after receiving a free token at discrete time $t = 1$. In all cases, station 1 outputs a busy token one bit period after receiving the free token. Note that for such a four-station ring, the output of station 4 is the input to station 1. Note also that

Discrete time	Multiple token					Single token					Single packet					Discrete time
	In #1	Out #1	Out #2	Out #3	Out #4	In #1	Out #1	Out #2	Out #3	Out #4	In #1	Out #1	Out #2	Out #3	Out #4	
0																0
		□			□	□				□	□				□	
2		■				■						■				2
		d	■			d	■					d	■			
4		d	d	■		d	d	■				d	d	■		4
	■	d	d	d	■	■	d	d	d	■	■	d	d	d	■	
6	d	d	d	d	d	d	d	d	d	d	d	d	d	d	d	6
	d	d	d	d	d	d	d	d	d	d	d	d	d	d		
8	d	□	d	d	d	d	□	d	d	d			d	d	d	8
	d		□	d	d	d		□	d	d			d	d		
10	d			□	d	d			□	d	d				d	10
	■				■	■				■		□				
12	d	■			d	d	■			d			□			12
	d	d	■		d	d	d	■		d				□		
14	□	d	d	■	□		d	d	■		■				■	14
		□	d	d		□	d	d	□		d	■				
16			□	d		□			d		d	d	■			16
				□					□		d	d		■		
18	□				□	□					d	d				18
							□			□	d					
20											□				□	20
												□				
22													□			22
														□		
24											□				□	24
26																26

Ring diagram:

```
        [1]
 In #1        Out #1
Out #4  ┌──────┐
  [4]───┤      ├───[2]
        └──────┘
Out #3        Out #2
        [3]
```

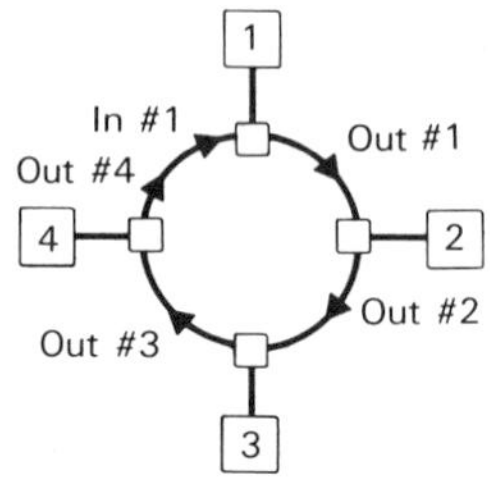

□ = Free token
■ = Busy token
d = Data bit

Figure 8.5 Illustration of the Three Operational Modes for a Four-station Ring

station 1 receives its busy token and transmitted data beginning at discrete time $t = 5$ after token and data have traversed the ring with a ring latency of four bit periods. The data that originates in station 1 is, of course, erased when it returns to this station.

In all three types of operation, station 1 initially transmits a packet of total length six bit times; after this transmission, station 4 transmits a packet of total length three bit times (which is less than the ring latency). However, the time at which station 4 captures the ring and the time at which a free token is subsequently generated depends on the mode of operation, as shown in Fig. 8.5.

For multiple-token operation, station 1 produces a free token at discrete time $t = 8$ after outputting its last data bit. As shown in Fig. 8.5, station 2 could capture the ring as soon as discrete time $t = 9$. Since stations 2 and 3 have no data to transmit, station 4 captures the ring at $t = 11$. Note that multiple tokens subsequently exist on the ring at $t = 14$. Of course, there can never be more than one free token on the ring (unless some fault condition exists). The free token finally arrives back at station 4 at time $t = 17$.

Single-token operation is identical to multiple-token operation as long as the total packet length in bit times is greater than or equal to the ring latency. However, when this is not the case, ring operation differs; Fig. 8.5 shows that station 4 captures the ring at $t = 11$ and starts transmitting a packet of total length three bit times. A new free token, however, is not generated until $t = 15$, one bit time after the busy token returns. This free token subsequently completes a further circuit of the ring at $t = 19$.

Single-packet operation results in a free token generated by station 1 at discrete time $t = 11$, after the station has received and erased its last data bits. Subsequently, a new free token is generated by station 4 at $t = 20$, which then arrives back at station 4 at $t = 24$.

This section on basic operation of token rings is concluded with a summary of the delays encountered by a packet in such a network. A quantitative model for delay analysis is developed in the next section.

A packet arriving at a station enters the transmission buffer, where it experiences the first increment of delay while waiting for the station to capture the ring. Once the station captures the ring, the packet has three more types of delay before it arrives at its destination station:

1. The delay due to latency in each station the packet traverses;
2. The propagation delay associated with each increment of the ring the packet traverses; and
3. The transmission time or the time to process all the bits in the packet over the links of the ring.

8.2.2   Delay Analysis

This section deals with the derivation of expressions for the average transfer delay suffered by packets on token-passing networks. Expressions are obtained for multiple-token, single-token, and single-packet operation, the three cases discussed in Section 8.2.1. A paper by Bux [3] serves as the basis for most of the analysis.

To obtain tractable results, it is necessary to make several assumptions:

- The inputs to the ring are balanced in the sense that arrivals are equally likely at any station;
- The arrival process to each station is Poisson, with average arrival rate λ packets/second;
- The average distance between the sending and receiving station is one-half the distance around the ring;
- The stations are spaced so that the propagation delays between consecutively serviced stations are equal and given by τ/M, where τ is the total ring propagation delay and M is the number of stations;
- The packet length distribution is the same for each station, with mean length $\overline{X}$ bits and second moment $\overline{X^2}$ (bits)^2; the random variable X denotes the length of an arbitrary packet; and
- Service at each station is exhaustive (i.e., the station transmit buffer is emptied each time the station captures the ring).

Additional notation is:

- Channel bit rate, R bits/second;
- Latency per station, B bits;
- Round-trip propagation delay for the ring, τ; and
- Ring latency, τ'.

To determine the transfer delay for token-passing rings, note the similarity between token passing and hub polling, as discussed in Chapter 7. Both methods transfer use of the common channel from station to station. The fact that hub polling typically requires a central controller, whereas token passing does not, is not relevant to performance analysis. In all other respects, operation is essentially the same. The walk time in polling corresponds to the time interval that begins at the instant a station finishes its transmission of data, and concludes when the next station receives a free token.

In the next several subsections, the polling equations are adapted to the three types of token passing. The starting point is a general expression for the average waiting time in a polling network, given by Eq. (7.13) of Chapter 7. This equation is given as

$$W = \frac{Mw(1 - S/M)}{2(1 - S)} + \frac{S\overline{(X/R)^2}}{2(\overline{X}/R)(1 - S)} \tag{8.1}$$

where the last term has been expanded to place in evidence the presence of the mean square of the service time.

As is indicated in Eq. (7.20) for polling networks, average transfer time, T, is obtained by adding the following to the average waiting time:

1. $\overline{X}/R$, the average time to transmit a packet; and
2. τ_{ave}, the average propagation delay from a station to the central computer in the polling network.

The result, as given in (7.20), is

$$T = \overline{X}/R + \tau_{\text{ave}} + W \tag{8.2}$$

To adapt (8.2) for token rings, note that $\overline{X}/R$, the average time to transmit a packet, is unchanged. For a ring network, however, the average delay corresponding to τ_{ave} in the polling network is $\tau'/2$, one-half of the ring latency. This result follows from the assumption that packets travel, on the average, halfway around the ring from source to destination station. The ring latency is given by

$$\tau' = \tau + MB/R \text{ seconds} \tag{8.3}$$

so that $\tau'/2$, which could be termed the average ring latency, is given by

$$\tau'/2 = \tau/2 + MB/2R \text{ seconds} \tag{8.4}$$

Thus average transfer time for a ring network can be expressed as

$$T = \overline{X}/R + \tau'/2 + W \tag{8.5}$$

where W must also be adapted to token rings.

To adapt (8.1) to token rings, three parameters must be evaluated:

1. The walk time;
2. The network throughput; and
3. Moments of the service time, $\overline{X}/R$ and $\overline{X^2}/R^2$ in (8.1).

The walk time for all token rings consists of a propagation delay τ/M plus the station latency B/R seconds. Thus

$$w = B/R + \tau/M = \tau'/M \tag{8.6}$$

Moments of the service time not only appear explicitly in (8.1), but the mean service time is implicit in the network throughput, S. For ring networks, the service time can potentially include any time interval during which the ring is inactive in the course of completing one packet transmission and becoming available for another transmission. Specifically, for a ring network, the service time X/R in (8.1) is replaced by the total time consumed by the ring in processing a packet and in becoming free to process the next packet. This time is called the "effective service time," E. The same interpretation of service time must be used to compute network throughput. Thus S in (8.1) is replaced by S' given by

$$S' = M\lambda\overline{E} \tag{8.7}$$

The notation S is reserved for

$$S = M\lambda \overline{X}/R$$

as used previously.

The modifications to the polling equations result in the following general equation for average transfer time for a token-ring network.

$$T = \frac{\overline{X}}{R} + \frac{\tau'}{2} + \frac{\tau'(1 - S'/M)}{2(1 - S')} + \frac{S'\overline{E^2}}{2\overline{E}(1 - S')} \tag{8.8}$$

Multiple-token Operation

As discussed in Subsection 8.2.1, this mode of operation assumes that a new free token is generated immediately after the last bit of the packet leaves the transmitting station. This type of operation is the same as for a polling network—if any station has packets to transmit, the channel remains busy transmitting them except for the walk time intervals already accounted for in the polling expression. Thus the average effective service time is just $\overline{X}/R$, and its second moment is simply $\overline{X^2}/R^2$. Equation (8.8) then gives average transfer delay for multiple-token operation as

$$T = \frac{\overline{X}}{R} + \frac{\tau'}{2} + \frac{\tau'(1 - S/M)}{2(1 - S)} + \frac{S\overline{X^2}}{2\overline{X}R(1 - S)} \tag{8.9}$$

Maximum throughput is determined as the largest throughput for which the average transfer delay remains finite. Thus from (8.9) the upper bound on S is 1 for multiple-token operation. Of course, this upper bound cannot be achieved because $S = 1$ implies infinite average delay, which violates the basic premise that the network operates under stable, stationary conditions.

Average transfer delay for multiple-token operation and the special cases of fixed length packets and exponentially distributed packet lengths can be derived from (8.9) to obtain:

Fixed length packets $(\overline{X^2} = (\overline{X})^2)$

$$T = \frac{\overline{X}}{R} + \frac{\tau'}{2} + \frac{\tau'(1 - S/M)}{2(1 - S)} + \frac{S\overline{X}/R}{2(1 - S)} \tag{8.10}$$

Exponentially distributed packet lengths $(\overline{X^2} = 2(\overline{X})^2)$

$$T = \frac{\overline{X}}{R} + \frac{\tau'}{2} + \frac{\tau'(1 - S/M)}{2(1 - S)} + \frac{S\overline{X}/R}{1 - S} \tag{8.11}$$

Single-token Operation

In this mode, a new free token is not generated until the transmitting station has received its own busy token back after the token has circulated completely around the ring. Thus there is never more than one token on the ring.

If the packet transmission time, X/R, is greater than the network latency, τ', the station is still transmitting a packet when its busy token returns after circulating around the ring. Thus it cannot generate a new free token until it has finished transmitting data, and operation becomes identical to that of multiple-token operation, as discussed previously.

On the other hand, if $X/R < \tau'$, single-token operation can differ considerably from multiple-token operation because the effective service time is greater than X/R due to periods when the ring is tied up waiting for the busy token to return to its originating station. In considering this case, it is convenient to define a normalized ring latency delay, a', by the equation

$$a' = \frac{\tau'}{\overline{X}/R} \tag{8.12}$$

For later reference, note that a' is related to the normalized propagation delay, a, (defined in Chapter 7 as $\tau/(\overline{X}/R)$) by the equation

$$a' = a \left(1 + MB/\overline{X}\right) \tag{8.13}$$

Because the relationship of τ' to X/R is critical, the cases of fixed and exponentially distributed packet lengths are considered separately.

For fixed length packets $\overline{X} = X = $ constant. Thus, as noted previously, if $\overline{X}/R$ is greater than τ', or $a' < 1$, single-token operation is the same as multiple-token operation, and average transfer delay, T, is given by (8.9). When $a' > 1$, however, the single-token becomes different from the multiple-token operation since average effective service time is greater than $\overline{X}/R$ and is in fact equal to τ'. This is the case because the ring cannot be used to transmit a new packet until the busy token of the previous packet has circulated completely around the ring.

With $\overline{E} = \tau'$, (8.7) gives S' as

$$S' = M\lambda\tau' = M\lambda(\overline{X}/R)\, a' = S a' \tag{8.14}$$

The appropriate substitutions can now be made in (8.8) to express average transfer delay for single-token operation with fixed packet lengths and $a' > 1$ as

$$T = \frac{\overline{X}}{R} + \frac{\tau'}{2} + \frac{\tau'(1 - Sa'/M)}{2(1 - Sa')} + \frac{Sa'\tau'}{2(1 - Sa')} \tag{8.15}$$

Note that the maximum achievable throughput on the ring is 1 for $a' < 1$ and $1/a'$ for $a' > 1$; the result, of course, depends on a' as determined by the packet length $\overline{X}$ and the network parameters R, τ, M, and B.

In the case of exponentially distributed packet lengths, the result is somewhat more complicated because packet length, X, becomes a random variable, and a probability distribution must be assigned to effective service time. If $X/R < \tau'$, effective service time is just τ', the time required for a transmitting station to receive its busy token after transmission around the ring. On the other hand, if $X/R > \tau'$, effective service time is X/R.

Since X has an exponential distribution function with mean $\overline{X}$, and since R is a constant, the distribution function of X/R is

$$F_{X/R}(y) = \begin{cases} 1 - e^{-Ry/\overline{X}}, & y \geq 0 \\ 0, & y < 0 \end{cases} \tag{8.16}$$

from which it follows that the distribution function of the effective service time, E, is given by

$$F_E(y) = \begin{cases} 0, & y < \tau' \\ 1 - e^{-Ry/\overline{X}}, & y \geq \tau' \end{cases} \tag{8.17}$$

These distribution functions are shown in Fig. 8.6.

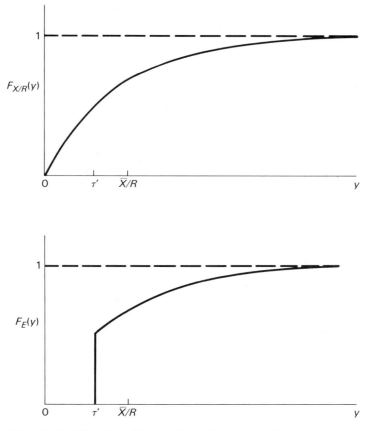

Figure 8.6 **Probability Distribution Functions for *X/R* and for Effective Service Time, *E***

The evaluation of the first and second moments of effective service time is straightforward and the results are

$$\overline{E} = \overline{X}/R\, e^{-a'} + \tau' \tag{8.18}$$

and

$$\overline{E^2} = (\tau')^2 + 2(\overline{X}/R)^2\, e^{-a'}\,(1 + a') \tag{8.19}$$

The results of (8.18) and (8.19) along with S' as computed from (8.7) can be substituted in (8.8) to obtain average transfer delay as

$$T = \frac{\overline{X}}{R} + \frac{\tau'}{2} + \frac{\tau'\,[1 - S(e^{-a'} + a')/M]}{2\,[1 - S(e^{-a'} + a')]}$$

$$+ \left(\frac{\overline{X}}{R}\right)\frac{S\,[(a')^2 + 2(1 + a')e^{-a'}]}{2\,[1 - S(e^{-a'} + a')]} \tag{8.20}$$

Note that the maximum throughput obtainable is given by $1/(e^{-a'} + a')$.

Single-packet Operation

In this mode of operation, a new free token is not generated until the sending station has received and erased all of the packet it has transmitted. Thus there is never more than one packet circulating on the ring. In this case there is a delay of τ' seconds after the end of each packet so that the effective service time is always $X/R + \tau'$. The average and second moment of this service time can be easily obtained as

$$\overline{E} = \overline{X}/R + \tau' \tag{8.21}$$

and

$$\overline{E^2} = \overline{(X/R)^2} + 2\tau' \overline{X}/R + (\tau')^2 \tag{8.22}$$

Equation (8.21) and (8.22), along with (8.7) for S', can be used in (8.8) to express average transfer delay for single-packet operation as

$$T = \frac{\overline{X}}{R} + \frac{\tau'}{2} + \frac{\tau'[1 - (1 + a')S/M]}{2[1 - (1 + a')S]} + \frac{S[\overline{X^2} + (R\tau')^2 + 2\overline{X}R\tau']}{2[1 - (1 + a')S] R\overline{X}} \tag{8.23}$$

For fixed length and exponentially distributed packet lengths, the result simplifies slightly to:

Fixed length packets

$$T = \frac{\overline{X}}{R} + \frac{\tau'}{2} + \frac{\tau'[1 - (1 + a')S/M]}{2[1 - (1 + a')S]} + \frac{S\overline{X}/R (1 + a')^2}{2[1 - (1 + a')S]} \tag{8.24}$$

Exponentially distributed packet lengths

$$T = \frac{\overline{X}}{R} + \frac{\tau'}{2} + \frac{\tau'[1 - (1 + a')S/M]}{2[1 - (1 + a')S]} + \frac{S\overline{X}/R[(1 + a')^2 + 1]}{2[1 - (1 + a')S]} \tag{8.25}$$

In this case the upper bound to the ring channel throughput is $1/(1 + a')$.

Typical calculations, using the delay formulas worked out in Section 8.2.2, are shown in the following example.

Example 8.1

(a) For both constant and exponential packets, evaluate the mean transfer delay for a single-token ring that has the following parameters:

- Ring length of 1 km;
- Bit rate of 4 Mbps;
- Mean packet length of 1000 bits;
- Forty stations on ring;
- Poisson arrival process to each station with 10 packets/second arrival rate; and
- Station bit latency of 1 bit.

Repeat this calculation for a ring in which the latency per station is 10 bits.

(b) If the number of stations on the ring is increased from 40 to 120 with the ring length the same, evaluate the mean transfer delay for the cases of 1- and 10-bit station latency. All the other network parameters are unchanged.

Solution

(a) Assuming a propagation delay of $5\mu s/km$,

$$\tau' = 5 + \frac{40 \times 1}{4 \times 10^6} = 15 \; \mu s$$

$$a' = \tau' \, R/\overline{X} = 0.04$$

$$S = M\lambda\overline{X}/R = 0.1$$

Thus, using (8.9) for the constant length packets

$$T = 250 + 7.5 \; + 8.29 \; + 13.89 = 279.68 \; \mu s$$

Using (8.20) for the exponentially distributed packets,

$$T = 250 + 7.5 + 8.31 + 27.78 = 293.59 \; \mu s$$

When the latency is 10 bits in each station

$$\tau' = 5 + \frac{40 \times 10}{4 \times 10^6} = 105 \; \mu s$$

$$a' = 0.42$$

Using (8.9) again for the fixed length packets,

$$T = 250 + 52.5 + 58.19 + 13.89 = 374.58 \; \mu s$$

Using (8.20) for the exponential packets gives

$$T = 250 + 52.5 + 58.72 + 28.61 = 389.83$$

(b) $M = 120$ and latency, $B = 1$ bit. This gives

$$\tau' = 5 + \frac{120 \times 1}{4 \times 10^6} = 35 \; \mu s$$

$$a' = \tau' \, R/\overline{X} = 0.14$$

$$S = M\lambda\overline{X}/R = 0.3$$

Fixed packets

$$T = 250 + 17.5 + 24.94 + 53.57 = 346.01 \; \mu s$$

Exponential packets

$$T = 250 + 17.5 + 25.04 + 107.67 = 400.21 \; \mu s$$

When the latency is 10 bits per station, the parameters become

$$\tau' = 5 + \frac{120 \times 10}{4 \times 10^6} = 305 \; \mu s$$

$$a' = 1.22$$

Fixed packets (using (8.15) since $a' > 1$)

$$T = 250 + 152.5 + 239.80 + 88.04 = 730.34 \ \mu s$$

Exponential packets

$$T = 250 + 152.5 + 278.54 + 192.45 = 873.49 \ \mu s$$

8.2.3 Performance Studies

The emphasis in this subsection is on comparing the three different modes of operation for token passing and the sensitivity of these modes to network parameters, in particular, the ring latency. Exponentially distributed packet

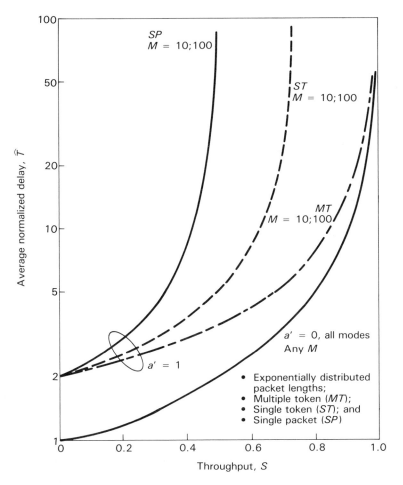

Figure 8.7 **Average Normalized Transfer Delay versus Throughput for Different Operational Modes and for Different Numbers of Stations**

lengths feature prominently in the performance curves because this distribution permits a good comparison of the relative merits, as far as performance is concerned, of multiple or single tokens on the ring.

As in earlier work, the average transfer delay is normalized in units of mean transmission time by writing $\hat{T} = T/(\overline{X}/R)$. The results of the previous section are tabulated in normalized form as follows:

Fixed length packets

MULTIPLE TOKEN

$$\hat{T} = 1 + \frac{a'}{2} + \frac{a'(1 - S/M)}{2(1 - S)} + \frac{S}{2(1 - S)} \tag{8.26}$$

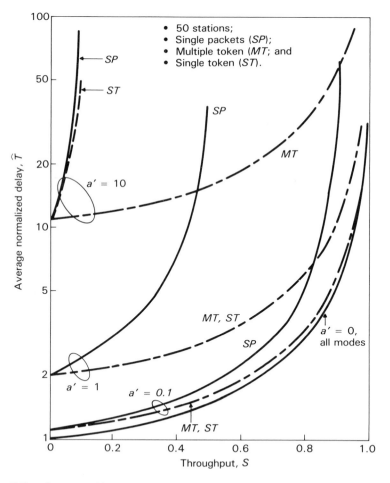

Figure 8.8 **Average Normalized Transfer Delay versus Throughput for Different Operational Modes and Fixed Length Packets**

SINGLE PACKET

$$\hat{T} = 1 + \frac{a'}{2} + \frac{a'[1 - (1 + a')S/M]}{2[1 - (1 + a')S]} + \frac{S(1 + a')^2}{2[1 - (1 + a')S]} \tag{8.27}$$

SINGLE TOKEN

$a' \leq 1$: same as for multiple token

$$a' > 1: \hat{T} = 1 + \frac{a'}{2} + \frac{a'(1 - Sa'/M)}{2(1 - Sa')} + \frac{S(a')^2}{2(1 - Sa')} \tag{8.28}$$

Exponential packets

MULTIPLE TOKEN

$$\hat{T} = 1 + \frac{a'}{2} + \frac{a'(1 - S/M)}{2(1 - S)} + \frac{S}{1 - S} \tag{8.29}$$

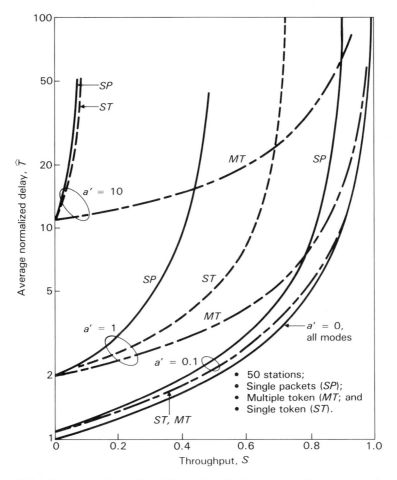

Figure 8.9 **Average Normalized Transfer Delay versus Throughput for Different Operational Modes and Exponentially Distributed Packet Lengths**

SINGLE PACKET

$$\hat{T} = 1 + \frac{a'}{2} + \frac{a'[1 - (1 + a')S/M]}{2[1 - (1 + a')S]} + \frac{S[(1 + a')^2 + 1]}{2[1 - (1 + a')S]} \qquad (8.30)$$

SINGLE TOKEN

$$\hat{T} = 1 + \frac{a'}{2} + \frac{a'[1 - S(e^{-a'} + a')/M]}{2[1 - S(e^{-a'} + a')]} + \frac{S[(a')^2 + 2(1 + a')e^{-a'}]}{2[1 - S(e^{-a'} + a')]} \qquad (8.31)$$

Note that under extremely low load, ($S = 0$), the average delay in all cases listed becomes

$$\hat{T} = 1 + a' \qquad (8.32)$$

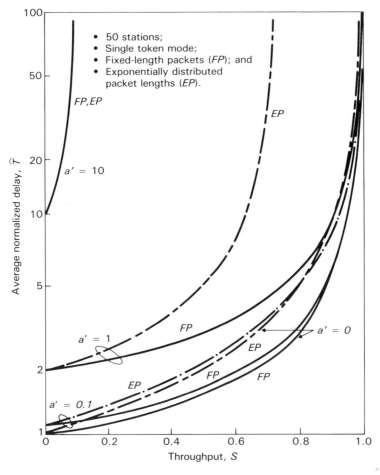

Figure 8.10 **Average Normalized Transfer Delay versus Throughput for Fixed and Exponentially Distributed Packet Lengths**

and thus

$$T = \overline{X}/R + \tau + MB/R \qquad (8.33)$$

Also, under conditions in which a' is very much less than 1, which occurs, for example, with long packets and short latencies, the average normalized delay for fixed length packets in all cases is closely approximated by

$$\hat{T} = 1 + \frac{S}{2(1 - S)} = \frac{1 - S/2}{1 - S} \qquad (8.34)$$

whereas for exponentially distributed packet lengths, the corresponding result in all cases is

$$\hat{T} = 1 + \frac{S}{1 - S} = \frac{1}{1 - S} \qquad (8.35)$$

The performance of each of the three modes of operation is now compared and their sensitivity to different network parameters is studied. Figure 8.7 compares the performance of the three modes with exponentially distributed packet lengths for fixed a' ($a' = 1$) and for 10- and 100- station networks. This figure shows that the number of stations on the network has negligible effect on the average delay, provided, of course, that the load per station is adjusted to maintain the total network load S constant. As expected, the curve for $a' = 0$ shows that the same performance is obtained for all modes when the ring latency is very much shorter than the average packet length.

Figures 8.8 and 8.9 show the effect on performance of different ring latencies for fixed and exponentially distributed packet lengths respectively. Both figures show that the most conservative mode, single-packet operation, always provides the poorest performance, whereas the multiple-token mode is never inferior to either of the other two modes. Clearly, however, single-token

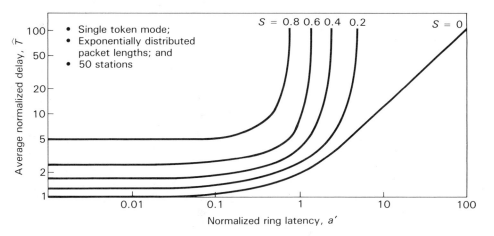

Figure 8.11 **Average Normalized Transfer Delay versus Normalized Ring Latency for Different Network Loads**

operation provides about as good a performance level, provided a' is small. However, as a' is increased, the multiple-token method is superior.

The sensitivity of delay to packet length distribution is studied in Fig. 8.10 for single-token operation. Whereas constant length packets always give shorter delays than corresponding exponentially distributed packets, the differences are not significant for small values of a'. Interestingly, when the normalized ring latency is relatively large, the two distributions give effectively the same average delay.

Finally, the sensitivity of performance to a' for different ring loads is shown in Fig. 8.11 for exponentially distributed packet lengths and the single-token operational mode. The figure indicates that the ring operates ideally as long as the ring latency is much less than the average packet length. However, performance degrades rapidly when a' exceeds some point in the range 0.5 to 5, depending on the network load.

8.3   Slotted Rings

8.3.1   Basic Operation

Slotted rings share with other types of rings the basic structure shown in Fig. 8.1. Bits are transferred in serial fashion in one direction from station to station around the ring. Slotted rings are distinguished by the fact that a constant number of bit positions grouped into fixed-lengths slots circulates continuously around the ring. This type of operation requires that the ring latency, measured in bits, must equal (or be greater than) the total number of bit positions in the circulating slots. In some respects, there is a useful analogy to a circulating conveyor belt marked off in sections allotted to bits.

Bit spaces in the circulating slots are grouped into several minipackets that can be used by the stations to transmit data. For typical operation, each minipacket contains a bit in the header that indicates whether the slot positions are in use or empty. If the slot is empty, it is available for use by a station with data to transmit. A station with data to transmit may not immediately find an empty slot, in which case it must wait until one appears.

The fact that the ring latency determines the total number of bits in the circulating slots has an important influence on the design of a slotted ring, as the following calculation shows. Assume 10 Mbits/sec channel operation so that a bit time is 0.1 μsec. A typical channel propagation delay is 5 μsec per kilometer of cable so that one kilometer of cable can support 50 bits. If each station interface introduces, for example, a 1-bit delay, it is clear that a large number of stations and/or a long cable is required to support more than one slot on the ring. For example, using the preceding numbers, 50 stations connected by 2 kilometers of cable produce a ring latency of 150 bits. This ring can then support three slots of exactly 50 bits, four slots of 35 bits with a 10-bit gap, or a number of other slot and gap combinations.

It is desirable to keep gaps as short as possible. One way to accomplish this is to introduce artificial delays through the use of shift registers in the ring interfaces. In the previous example, by way of illustration, five slots of 35 bits could be accommodated by the introduction of an artificial delay of 25 bit times, which is 2.5 μsec. This insertion of artificial delays is sometimes called *padding*.

Because of the restrictions just noted, slotted rings are designed to transmit relatively few bits at a time from each station, but to transmit them in a manner that minimizes access delay and that can have other advantages with respect to acknowledgments, monitoring, and so forth.

Numerous slotted or *empty-slot* ring designs have been suggested. Three of the better known are: the Farber Ring (Farber and Larson [4]); the Pierce Ring (Pierce [5]); and the Cambridge Ring (Needham and Herbert [6]). There are, of course, many minor variations in the proposed designs. Of the three rings just cited and many others described in the literature, the Cambridge Ring seems to be the principal one with commercial application. Therefore, further descriptive detail relates specifically to the Cambridge Ring, although it is representative of any slotted ring.

A block diagram of a typical Cambridge Ring is given in Fig. 8.12. Note that sections of the ring are coupled by repeaters that can also couple to the

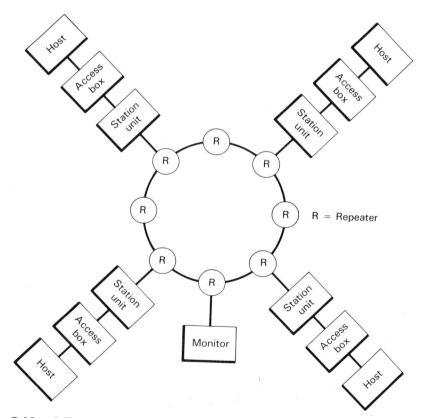

Figure 8.12   A Typical Cambridge Ring

station units, which in turn interface to the hosts served by the ring through access boxes. The present Cambridge Ring uses links that support a data rate of 10 Mbits/sec. Most sectors use twisted pairs of ordinary telephone cable with repeaters no more than 100 meters apart. Sectors may use fiber optic or coaxial cable for longer links. The monitor station shown in Fig. 8.12 is used to set up and maintain ring framing and to perform several checks to detect obscure errors and faulty equipment.

The interface to the ring consists of parts of the repeater, the station unit, and the access box. The station unit contains independent transmission and reception modules, both of which are coupled to the repeater. The access box contains circuits that interface the station unit to a particular host.

The reception module contains monitor circuits that continuously read the sequence of digits received from the repeater. As long as the station is not busy with a previously received minipacket, the sequence of received digits flows into a receiving shift register at the same time that digits are being processed out over the ring by the repeater. When the monitor detects that a packet is addressed to its station, the register stops shifting, and the minipacket is stored in the receiver register until it is cleared by a signal from the access box. If further minipackets addressed to the station arrive before the receiver register is cleared, they must be marked to indicate that the station is busy.

The transmission module in the station unit contains a shift register that is coupled in parallel to the access box. Data and destination bytes are written in parallel into this register, with source and control bits added automatically. A signal from the access box can send the contents of the transmit register onto the ring to fill the first empty packet slot. The transmit register may retain a copy of the transmitted minipacket.

A minipacket format is shown in Fig. 8.13. The total length is only 38 bits with just 2 bytes or 16 bits of data. The largest Cambridge Ring circulates four such minipackets and a short gap, which consists of several gap digits. The station unit has framing circuits that synchronize on the gap digits and the leading 1's in each minipacket.

The two response bits in the minipacket make four response signals possible after the minipacket has circulated completely around the ring. These are: destination absent, packet accepted, destination deaf, destination busy. These

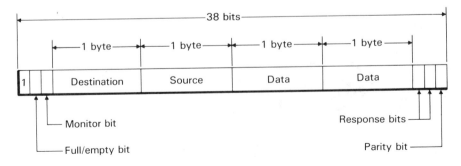

Figure 8.13   Minipacket Format for the Cambridge Ring

response bits are read by the transmitting station before it takes action to discard its copy of the transmitted minipacket or to retransmit the minipacket. Note that use of the response bits in the manner just described makes separate acknowledgment packets unnecessary.

Each minipacket also contains four control bits, as shown in Fig. 8.13: the first bit is always a 1 so that a station in normal operation can never receive a long unbroken stream of 0's. The monitor bit is used by the monitor station, and the indicator bit gives the state of the slot, that is, full or empty.

Because the minipackets are so short, normal length packets, which the stations must process to service the attached hosts, must be transmitted in a number of minipacket segments. To prevent hogging of the ring by one station while it transmits a large segment of data, slotted rings typically require that the full–empty indicator for the following minipacket be changed to empty after a station transmits the last bit of a minipacket. Such a requirement guarantees fair sharing of the ring among all stations.

The operation of a slotted ring is illustrated in Fig. 8.14 for two conditions:

1. Only one station has a large data packet to transmit; and
2. Two stations have large data packets to transmit and hence share the ring.

The ring is assumed to have only four stations, each with a latency of one bit. Propagation delay is ignored and the 4-bit latency is used to support one slot on the ring. The first bit of the 4-bit slot is used as the full/empty indicator.

Operation of the ring is somewhat similar to that of a token ring, and Fig. 8.14 is constructed in the same manner as Fig. 8.5, which describes the token ring. Two aspects of slotted ring operation can be determined from the figure. Each column in the table gives ring activity as a function of discrete time, as seen from the point of view of a particular station. On the other hand, each row of the table shows the outputs from each station at a particular discrete time.

When only station 1 is transmitting, the station receives an empty-slot indicator and captures the ring at discrete time 1 in the table, transmits its minipacket, and then releases the ring by inserting an empty-slot indicator at discrete time 5. Note that four empty slots must pass, until discrete time 8, before station 1 receives its own empty-slot indicator and is able to transmit another minipacket. Observe the station 1 column in the table and note that the station can only transmit one-half of the time even though it has a backlog of data. Thus from the point of view of station 1, the maximum ring bit rate is only $R/2$.

The right-hand half of Fig. 8.14 shows slotted ring operation when stations 1 and 3 have data to transmit. It is a useful exercise to trace through the details of this part of the figure to see how two stations share the ring.

One point to note is that, even though the ring bit rate is only $R/2$ as seen by a particular station, the full ring is never completely idle when more than one station has data to transmit, and thus the full bit rate R is used by the collection of stations. To confirm this, note the outputs of all four stations at specific times by examining the rows in the table.

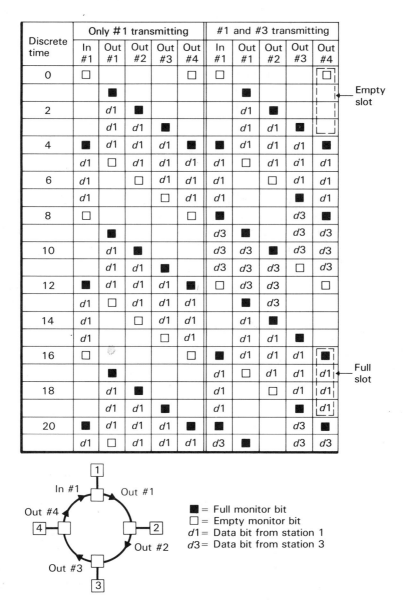

Discrete time	Only #1 transmitting					#1 and #3 transmitting				
	In #1	Out #1	Out #2	Out #3	Out #4	In #1	Out #1	Out #2	Out #3	Out #4
0	□				□	□				□
		■					■			
2		d1	■				d1	■		
		d1	d1	■			d1	d1	■	
4	■	d1	d1	d1	■	■	d1	d1	d1	■
	d1	□	d1	d1	d1	d1	□	d1	d1	d1
6	d1		□	d1	d1	d1		□	d1	d1
	d1			□	d1	d1			■	d1
8	□				□	■			d3	■
		■				d3	■		d3	d3
10		d1	■			d3	d3	■	d3	d3
		d1	d1	■		d3	d3	d3	□	d3
12	■	d1	d1	d1	■	□	d3	d3		□
	d1	□	d1	d1	d1		■	d3		
14	d1		□	d1	d1		d1	■		
	d1			□	d1		d1	d1	■	
16	□				□	■	d1	d1	d1	■
		■				d1	□	d1	d1	d1
18		d1	■			d1		□	d1	d1
		d1	d1	■		d1			■	d1
20	■	d1	d1	d1	■	■			d3	■
	d1	□	d1	d1	d1	d3	■		d3	d3

■ = Full monitor bit
□ = Empty monitor bit
d1 = Data bit from station 1
d3 = Data bit from station 3

Figure 8.14   Illustration of a Four-station Slotted Ring Under Two Loading Conditions (Ring Latency is 4 Bits)

In summary, a main characteristic of slotted rings is that data must be transferred in short minipackets that cause undesirable properties such as a large overhead-to-data ratio and the necessity to break up normal packets into a number of minipackets. On the other hand, the slotted ring type of operation does not permit ring hogging, eliminates the need for separate acknowledgment packets, makes close monitoring possible, and keeps access delays at a minimum.

8.3.2 Delay Analysis

In this subsection, a heuristic argument is given to derive an expression for the average transfer delay in a slotted ring network with exponentially distributed packet lengths. A much more sophisticated analysis, provided by Bux [3], yields the same result for packets of arbitrary length distributions. The Bux argument requires knowledge of fairly complicated queueing systems, such as processor-sharing models and so-called "mixed" queueing networks (see Kleinrock [7] and Baskett et al. [8]). The heuristic argument presented gives the correct result for exponentially distributed packet lengths, and reference can be made to Bux [3] for proof that the result carries over to more general cases.

The assumptions used to develop the model are essentially the same as used for the token ring network:

- Independent Poisson arrival processes to each station with rate λ packets/second;
- The packet lengths are exponentially distributed with mean $\overline{X}$ bits;
- The end-to-end propagation delay around the ring is τ seconds and the ring latency is τ' seconds;
- The bit rate on the channel is R bps;
- There are M stations on the network; and
- The minipacket length is much less than the packet length.

The latter assumption is, of course, peculiar to slotted rings. It can also be noted that τ and τ' are related in the same way as for rings discussed in Section 8.2, i.e.,

$$\tau' = \tau + MB/R \tag{8.36}$$

where B is the station latency in bits.

Since the time for a slot to circulate around the ring is very small (in comparison with a packet transmission time), the network can be modeled to a good approximation as a distributed M/M/1 queueing system with arrival rate $M\lambda$ and average service time $\overline{X}/R$. To adapt the M/M/1 model to the actual operation of the slotted ring, the channel bit rate, as seen by any particular station, is effectively $R/2$. This point is illustrated in conjunction with Fig. 8.14, and the effect is caused by the strategy used to prevent hogging of the ring by any particular station.

The full bit rate, R, however, is used in computing throughout because, as also illustrated in conjunction with Fig. 8.14, the ring is never completely idle when more than one station has data to transmit. Thus throughput is given by

$$S = M\lambda \overline{X}/R \tag{8.37}$$

as in other similar cases such as polling.

Average transfer delay for an M/M/1 queueing system is given by (3.43) in Chapter 3 as

$$T = \frac{\overline{X}/R}{1 - \rho} \tag{8.38}$$

where ρ is the utilization factor of the queueing system.

To adapt (8.38) to the slotted ring, ρ is replaced by S, R is replaced by $R/2$, and one-half of the ring latency, $\tau'/2$, is added to this delay. The latter is needed because an average ring latency of $\tau'/2$ is assumed for transfer between source and destination stations, as is the case for token rings.

These changes yield

$$T = \frac{2}{1 - S}\left(\frac{\overline{X}}{R}\right) + \frac{\tau'}{2} \tag{8.39}$$

Whereas this heuristic argument is valid only for packets with exponentially distributed lengths, Bux [3] has shown that (8.39) gives the mean transfer delay for packets with arbitrary packet length distribution, assuming that minipackets are much shorter than full packets. (This is a consequence of the processor-sharing model that Bux develops.)

An important feature of the slotted ring that the preceding results do not place in evidence is the large amount of overhead used in each minipacket. This overhead has a serious effect on both the mean transfer delay and on the ring throughput, and must be accounted for in the final model.

Let L_h be the number of header bits contained in each slot. Header in this context is anything that is not actual data—for example, addressing information, indicator bits, response bits, and so forth. Let L_d be the number of data bits in each slot. Then $(L_h + L_d)$ is the length of each slot in bits. Define the overhead factor

$$h = L_h/L_d \tag{8.40}$$

From this, it is clear that a packet of length X bits is increased to $(1 + h)X$ bits in a slotted ring. Thus, it is necessary to replace $\overline{X}$ by $(1 + h)\overline{X}$ and, using (8.37), S by $S(1 + h)$.

Introducing these changes into (8.39) then gives average transfer delay for the slotted ring as

$$T = \frac{2(1 + h)}{1 - S(1 + h)}\left(\frac{\overline{X}}{R}\right) + \tau'/2 \tag{8.41}$$

From (8.41), note that the maximum throughput is $1/(1 + h)$ (i.e., $L_d/(L_h + L_d)$), which is often much less than 1.

Recall at this point that every type of local area network, whether polling, contention or whatever, also requires a certain amount of packet overhead. However, it is usually a small fraction of the complete packet length and so does not seriously affect the performance measures evaluated. In fact, for all the networks other than the slotted ring, the relative amounts of overhead do not differ very much, so comparisons between the performance measures are only slightly affected by overhead.

In the case of slotted rings, however, there is usually more overhead than real data, so the overhead cannot be ignored. As a case in point, the overhead factor, h, for the current version of the Cambridge Ring is $22/16 = 1.375$. It is relatively easy to re-evaluate the performance measures for those networks for which overhead is not considered so as to show its effect, if this additional accuracy is required.

To conclude this section, it is interesting to note that for a slotted ring the parameters that define the slot size are related by

$$\tau' = \frac{m(L_h + L_d)}{R} + g = \tau + MB/R \qquad (8.42)$$

where m is the number of slots on the ring, the gap is g seconds, and the right-hand equality is that given by (8.36).

Often a slotted-ring design begins with the specification of all but g, τ', and m of the eight variables in (8.42). In such a case, the number of slots, m, is adjusted to minimize the gap, g. If the station latencies are not sufficiently large to provide the value of τ', required by the left-hand expression in (8.42), additional padding delays can be added in the stations to increase B.

Some of the ideas just introduced can be illustrated by the following example.

Example 8.2

A slotted ring is 1 kilometer long, has 50 stations attached, and has a bit rate of 10 Mbps. Each slot contains 3 bytes of data, a source byte, a destination byte, and another byte, that includes the monitor and indicator bits. It may be assumed that each station latency is 1 bit.

(a) How many slots can this ring hold without adding any artificial delays? What is the gap time? If packets of length 1200 bits are to be transmitted on this ring, find the mean transfer delay when packets arrive at each station at a rate of (i) 1 packet/second, (ii) 40 packets/second.

(b) Increase the number of stations on the network to 100. (i) How many slots can the ring now hold without adding artificial delays? (ii) What is the gap time? Again, evaluate the mean transfer time for the same arrival rates and same packet length.

Solution

(a) The propagation delay for a 1-kilometer channel can be taken to be 5 μs. Using (8.36), the ring latency τ' is given by

$$\tau' = 5 \times 10^{-6} + 50 \times 1/(10 \times 10^6) \text{ seconds} = 10 \ \mu s$$

The length of each slot is 6 bytes. Thus, using (8.42),

$$\tau' = m(48)/(10 \times 10^6) + g$$

Clearly, $m = 2$ is the largest integer that makes τ' less than or equal to 10 μs. As a result, the gap g equals 0.4 μs.

The overhead factor, h, is given by

$$h = L_h/L_d = 24/24 = 1$$

$$\overline{X}/R = 1200/(10 \times 10^6) = 120 \ \mu s$$

(i)

$$S = M\lambda \overline{X}/R = 6 \times 10^{-3}$$

Thus, (8.41) gives

$$T = \frac{2}{1 - 6 \times 10^{-3} \times 2} \cdot (120) \ 2 + \frac{10}{2} = 490.8 \ \mu s$$

(ii)

$S = 0.24$ giving

$T = 928.1 \ \mu s$

(b) The ring latency for the case of 100 stations is given by

$$\tau' = 5 \times 10^{-6} + 100 \times 1/(10 \times 10^6) = 15 \ \mu s$$

Now, it is possible to have three slots on the ring with a gap time of 0.6 μs. The other variable affected by the change in the number of stations is S:

(i)

$$S = M\lambda \overline{X}/R = 1.2 \times 10^{-2}$$

$$T = \frac{2}{1 - 1.2 \times 10^{-2}(2)} \cdot (120) \ 2 + \frac{15}{2} = 499.3 \ \mu s$$

(ii)

$S = 0.48$

$T = 12007.5 \ \mu s$

Since the maximum throughput is $(1 + h)^{-1} = 0.5$, loads close to this level produce very large delays.

8.3.3 Performance Studies

In this subsection, an expression for the average transfer delay normalized to units of packet transmission times is obtained. The sensitivity of this delay to changes in the amount of overhead per slot is studied for packets of arbitrary length.

Normalizing the average transfer delay, given in (8.41), to $\hat{T}$ yields

$$\hat{T} = \frac{2(1 + h)}{1 - S(1 + h)} + \frac{a'}{2} \tag{8.43}$$

where a' is the normalized latency as discussed in the section on token rings. As previously stated, this equation applies for arbitrary message length distributions.

Note that under very low load conditions ($S = 0$), (8.43) gives

$$\hat{T} = 2(1 + h) + a'/2 \tag{8.44}$$

which is more than twice the minimum delay of most other networks. This is obviously due not only to the large amount of overhead present in each slot, but also to the anti-hogging rule that produces empty slots circulating even when a station has data to transmit.

Normalized latency a' appears in Eq. (8.43) only as an additive constant. Thus, in studying the sensitivity of the performance of slotted rings to

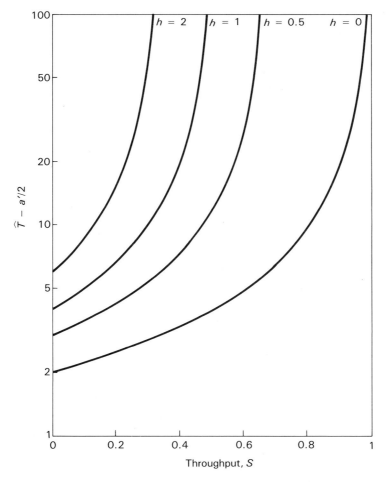

Figure 8.15   Average Normalized Transfer Delay, Less Average Latency Delay, versus Throughput for Different Overhead and Arbitrary Packet Length Distribution

overhead, it is possible to permit a' to be arbitrary. Figure 8.15 is a graphical representation of (8.43), plotting $(\hat{T} - a'/2)$ against S. It is assumed that there is no gap on the ring and that h and a' may be varied independently of each other. From the curves it is clear that the overhead should be minimized to achieve optimum performance.

The parameters h and a' may not always be independent, as is assumed in the curves of Fig. 8.15, since varying the station latency, and hence a', often affects the overhead factor, h. This effect is indirect. The parameter a' determines the maximum number of slots on the ring. Since the number of required overhead bits per minipacket is typically fixed, a suitable slot length and number of slots are chosen to provide a negligible gap. The number of data bits, L_d, is then determined by the slot length and overhead. The overhead factor for this choice of number of slots is given by Eq. (8.40).

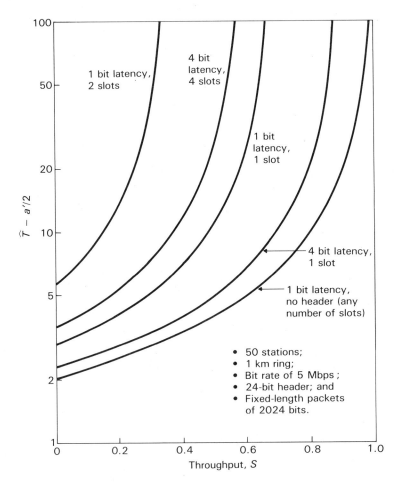

Figure 8.16 **Average Normalized Transfer Delay, Less Average Latency Delay, versus Throughput for Different Station Latencies and Numbers of Slots**

To observe the effect of interaction between h and a', the curves in Fig. 8.16 are plotted for different station latencies with correspondingly different numbers of slots. As in Fig. 8.15, it is assumed that there is a negligible gap and no artificial delays, so the amount of data transmitted in each slot depends on the ring latency and the number of slots. For example, for a two-slot ring with a station latency of 4 bits, and the parameters as specified in the figure, 88 data bits can be transmitted in each minipacket, with an overhead factor of 0.273. The value of a' for this particular case is easily shown to be 0.111. The parameters a' and h, required in Eq. (8.43), can be worked out in a similar manner for the other curves in the figure.

The results of Fig. 8.16 are also useful because they can be compared to simulation results determined by Bux [3]. For the parameters used in the cases of station latency of 4 bits per station, Bux has both theoretical curves and results from simulation studies over a range of loads. The results in Fig. 8.16, from Eq. (8.43), compare very favorably with Bux's simulation results and thus to some extent validate the heuristic model.

The principal conclusion that can be drawn from Fig. 8.16 is that fewer slots result in shorter average transfer delay for a specified station latency.

8.4 Register Insertion Rings

8.4.1 Basic Operation

Register insertion rings share the general structure of Fig. 8.1 with token and slotted rings, as previously discussed. As in other cases, the distinctive features of the register insertion ring become apparent from the station interface. As shown in the diagram of Fig. 8.17, the interface is distinguished from those of other types of ring networks by the presence of three shift registers. The

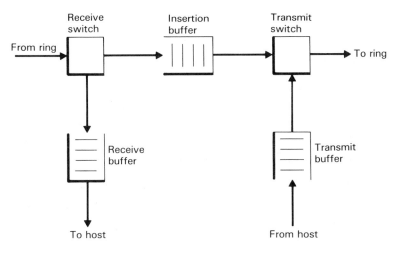

Figure 8.17   A Register Insertion Ring Interface

addition of these shift registers into the ring effectively increases the capacity of the ring in terms of the total number of bits it can hold at any one time. Thus, in some respects, register insertion rings can be regarded as a refinement of slotted rings to increase the length of the packets that can be transmitted.

Operation of the interface can be described as follows. With the receive and transmit switches closed on the ring positions, bits circulate around the ring through the insertion buffer in the same fashion as for a slotted ring. When a station has a packet to transmit, it is loaded serially into the transmit buffer. Now, to insert the new packet onto the ring, the ring must be broken by the transmit switch, which removes the insertion buffer from the ring and connects the transmit buffer. While bits are being transferred serially from the transmit buffer onto the ring, bits circulating on the ring are lost unless they can be stored in the insertion buffer. Thus the transmit buffer must be prevented from switching in unless there are at least as many spare storage positions in the insertion buffer as there are bits in the incoming packet. If this condition is met, however, the new packet can be injected, and circulation around the ring (now enlarged by the positions used in the insertion buffer) continues.

The position of the receive switch is determined by the address of each packet. Packets arriving at their destination are fed serially into the receive buffer of the station and are thus removed from the ring.

Register insertion rings can be designed to transmit packets with random length distributions and maximum packet size limited by the transmit and insertion buffers. When the insertion buffer is empty, the input pointer, shown in Fig. 8.18, points to the rightmost bit position, which means that all the bit positions, including and to the left of where it is pointing, are empty. When the transmit switch is at position B and bits arrive from the ring, they are stored in the buffer, which moves the pointer to the left. When the ring is again

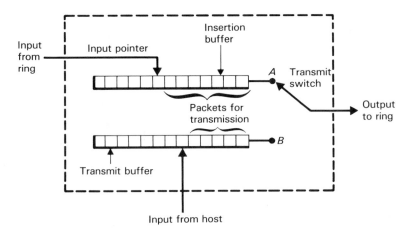

Figure 8.18   Storing of Packets in the Ring Interface

Chapter 8   ***Ring Networks***

available to the insertion buffer, the switch is moved to position *A*, and bits are immediately shifted out onto the ring. Operation in this way allows the insertion buffer to "breathe," in a manner of speaking, expanding the capacity of the ring when required and reducing this capacity when empty bit positions reappear.

When an insertion buffer has spare capacity and packets are available for transmission, as in Fig. 8.18, selection of the switch position depends on whether the ring uses *station priority* or *ring priority*. Station priority allows the transmit buffer to transmit first, whereas ring priority gives preference to the insertion buffer. Control is exercised by the switch software and is normally a fixed feature of the network.

A practical implementation of the station priority type of register insertion ring is the Distributed Loop Computer Network (DLCN) developed by Liu [9]. For the DLCN, the station is restricted to have priority only so long as the size of the packet to be transmitted from the transmit buffer is less than the remaining capacity of the insertion buffer. If this is not the case, the insertion buffer is given priority. This flow control feature is necessary for proper operation and also tends to prevent one station from hogging the ring.

The packet format for the DLCN network is given in Fig. 8.19. Control bits are included to indicate message type and whether broadcast or single-destination-type operation is intended. Lost message detection, lockout prevention, and several other features are also provided.

As a final comment on the basic operation of register insertion rings, the feature of removing packets at the destination station, instead of the transmitting station, opens the possibility of using parts of the ring for two or more simultaneous communication paths. For example, Fig. 8.20 shows how three station pairs exchange packets at the same time. When routing allows this type of use, network throughput can exceed 1, although utilization of any part of the ring channel itself is, of course, strictly less than 1.

8.4.2 Delay Analysis

This subsection deals with the derivation of an expression for the average transfer delay that packets undergo on a register insertion ring. It is shown that under certain conditions, this mean delay is the same for ring priority and station priority, as discussed in the previous section. The analysis follows

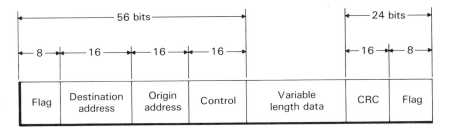

Figure 8.19 Packet Format for the DLCN Network

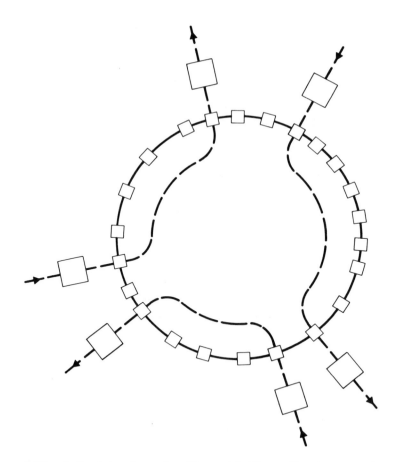

Figure 8.20   A Register Insertion Ring with Three Simultaneous Packet Transmissions

primarily the work of Thomasian and Kanakia [10], with some help from a paper by Bux and Schlatter [11].

For ease in reference, the general ring structure of Fig. 8.1 and the register and insertion ring interface of Fig. 8.17 are reproduced in Fig. 8.21, specifically for a four-station network.

The station latency, τ_i', for station i includes the propagation delay τ_i between successive stations $(i - 1)$ and i, and the number of bits, B, read by station i. Thus

$$\tau_i' = \tau_i + B/R \tag{8.45}$$

A major factor in B is the number of bits used for address recognition. In the model to be developed, it is assumed that τ_i' is the same for all station pairs so that

$$\tau_i' = \tau'/M = \tau/M + B/R \tag{8.46}$$

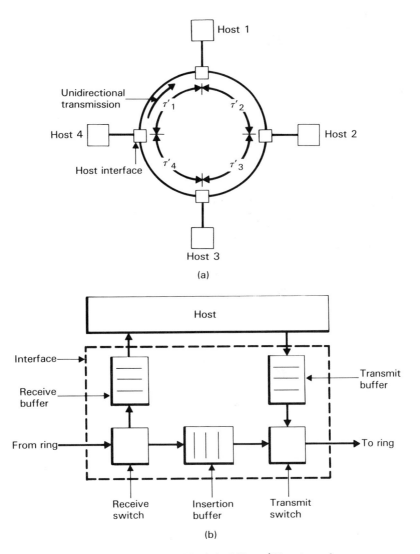

Figure 8.21   Four-station Ring with Model of Host/Ring Interface

where τ is the total ring propagation delay, τ' is the total ring latency, and M is the number of stations on the ring. The value of B must be at least $\log_2 M$ plus one bit for regeneration, or $(1 + \log_2 M)$.

As in other networks, the performance criterion of interest for register insertion ring networks is the average transfer delay on the network measured from the time the packet is completely stored in the transmit buffer to the time the packet is completely received by the receive buffer. The times required to move packets between the transmitting host and the transmit buffer, and between the receive buffer and the destination host are not part of the calculated transfer delay.

The path for a particular packet involves the tandem connection of a number of station interfaces between the transmitting and receiving stations. A general model for such a connection requires a tandem connection of queues for which an analytical solution can be obtained only under very stringent assumptions. Unfortunately, the assumptions that make the tandem-queues model tractable are not realistic with respect to how the network actually functions. Thus an alternate, approximate approach, based on a form of what Kermani and Kleinrock [13] call *virtual cut-through*, is used in the analysis.

Consider the four-station network of Fig. 8.21 again. Assume that a particular tagged packet is being transmitted from station 1 to station 3. Under optimum conditions for the tagged packet, it can be transmitted immediately out of the transmission buffer of station 1 and on to the ring. If the insertion buffer of station 2 is connected to the ring, but with its pointer at the rightmost position (see Fig. 8.18), no delay is suffered in this buffer, and the packet arrives in the receive buffer of station 3 after a delay of only (τ_2' + τ_3') plus the packet transmission time. This is, of course, the minimum delay.

On the other hand, the tagged packet could suffer delays in leaving the transmit buffer of station 1, or in waiting in the insertion buffer of station 2. The insertion buffer of station 2 could also introduce a transit delay if the pointer is not at the rightmost position. Whether or not these delays occur, of course, depends on the packet flows through other parts of the ring.

A model of the four-station network that can be used to account for the packet delays is shown in Fig. 8.22. The *latency boxes*, labeled τ_i' in the figure, account for all the station latencies. The transmit and insertion buffers appear as labeled. Under the optimum conditions (for the tagged packet considered previously in transmission from station 1 to station 3) the insertion buffers are connected to the ring, but no bit positions are used by the ring. Thus the tagged packet moves directly from the transmit buffer in station 1 with no delay into the latency box of station 2, and through it immediately into the latency box of station 3 with no delay. The packet then moves out to the host at station 3. One packet transmission time plus τ_2' plus τ_3' is the total delay for the packet.

The model of Fig. 8.22 can be used in quantitative analyses under general conditions, subject to the following assumptions:

1. The arrival processes to each transmit buffer are Poisson, with the same mean arrival rate λ_t for all M stations;
2. All stations have the same distribution of packet lengths (in bits), with first and second moments $\overline{X}$ and $\overline{X^2}$ respectively;
3. The latency for each station is a constant τ'/M;
4. All stations have the same transmission pattern: station i transmits to station $(i + j)$ Mod M† with probability $q_j, j = 1, 2 \ldots M - 1$; this assumption results in what is called a *balanced ring* and implies that the

---

†Mod M denotes the remainder after division by M (e.g., 1 Mod 2 = 1, 5 Mod 2 = 1, 32 Mod 2 = 0).

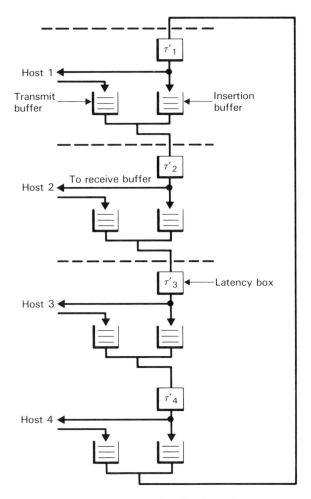

Figure 8.22   Model of Four-station Register Insertion Ring

probability of transmitting between two stations depends only on the separation of the two stations;

5. The capacity of both insertion and transmit buffers is infinite; this assumption of infinite capacity of the insertion buffers is critical for the station priority case; and

6. The interarrival times and service times are independent; thus, the chain of station elements, shown in Fig. 8.22, can be broken up into independent submodels for each station. This assumption, which results in a very tractable model, has been shown by comparison to simulation results to give reasonably accurate, although somewhat pessimistic, results. A more accurate model is provided by Bux and Schlatter [11].

Note that all the quantities, λ_t, $\overline{X}$, $\overline{X^2}$, τ'/M and the q_j, $j = 1, 2, \ldots M - 1$, are typically specified in defining the operating conditions for the ring.

Figure 8.23 gives the submodel that applies to all station interfaces, subject to the stated assumptions that make all interfaces equivalent as far as the model is concerned. Note that in addition to λ_t, the submodel involves a traffic parameter, λ_r, that is the average packet flow into the insertion buffer from the ring. It is assumed that this input process to the insertion buffer is Poisson with an average value of λ_r packets/second. In special cases this representation can be exact. In general, however, it is an approximation that is reasonable and quite realistic.

The relationship of λ_r to λ_t is determined from the complete network diagram of Fig. 8.22, using the probabilities q_j, $j = 1, 2, \ldots M - 1$, which determine the traffic pattern for the network. Note that the average arrival rates λ_r and λ_t carry over from the complete network diagram of Fig. 8.22 to the submodel of Fig. 8.23. The quantity λ_t, the average arrival rate to a particular station, is specified as an independent variable that, following assumption 1, is the same for all stations.

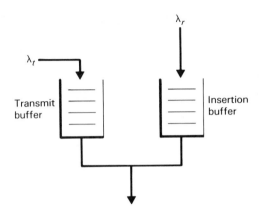

Figure 8.23   Submodel of a Single Host Interface

The submodel of Fig. 8.23 can be regarded, as far as waiting time is concerned, as a head-of-the-line nonpreemptive priority M/G/1 queueing system. "Service" in this submodel, and in the model of Fig. 8.22, is different from the normal M/G/1 queue in that service is defined to occur only in the receive buffer of the destination station. Service is modeled in this way because, for a ring-type transmission, bits move in "lock step" around the ring and suffer a transmission-type time delay only once, as in virtual cut-through. For other buffers, after the head-of-the-line is reached, a packet can move to another insertion buffer queue after passing through a latency box. Note also from Fig. 8.22 that a packet does not go through the insertion buffer of either the source or the destination station.

The submodel of Fig. 8.23 is now used to determine expressions for the average waiting times, W_t in the transmit queues and W_r in the insertion queues, under both ring and station priority conditions.

To begin the analysis, let ρ_r and ρ_t be defined as

$$\rho_r = \frac{\lambda_r \overline{X}}{R} \tag{8.47}$$

and

$$\rho_t = \frac{\lambda_t \overline{X}}{R} \tag{8.48}$$

Now the M/G/1 nonpreemptive priority queueing expressions from Chapter 3 can be used to derive the average waiting times W_r and W_t. The results naturally depend on which buffer is given priority. Thus there are two cases.

CASE 1: RING PRIORITY (Priority to the insertion buffer): The mean waiting times in the transmit queue and the register insertion queue are given respectively by

$$W_t = \frac{\lambda_r + \lambda_t}{2(1 - \rho_r - \rho_t)(1 - \rho_r)} \frac{\overline{X^2}}{R^2} \tag{8.49}$$

and

$$W_r = \frac{(\lambda_r + \lambda_t)}{2(1 - \rho_r)} \frac{\overline{X^2}}{R^2} \tag{8.50}$$

CASE 2: STATION PRIORITY (Priority to the transmit buffer): For this case, the expressions are interchanged to account for the interchange in priority, to give

$$W_t = \frac{(\lambda_r + \lambda_t)}{2(1 - \rho_t)} \frac{\overline{X^2}}{R^2} \tag{8.51}$$

and

$$W_r = \frac{(\lambda_r + \lambda_t)}{2(1 - \rho_r - \rho_t)(1 - \rho_t)} \frac{\overline{X^2}}{R^2} \tag{8.52}$$

Having determined the waiting times with the submodel of Fig. 8.23, it is now necessary to return to a consideration of the complete network to determine λ_r and which buffers actually produce delays.

First, it is clear that a packet must wait in only one transmit buffer, the one at the station at which it originates. Now, consider how many insertion buffers, on the average, a packet passes through in traveling from its source station to its destination station. Denote this number as α and recall that the insertion buffers at the source and destination stations are not traversed by the packet. Recall also that the parameter q_j, $j = 1, 2, \ldots, M - 1$ is the probability that a packet originating at station i is routed to station $(j + i)$ Mod M, which is j stations away. There are $j - 1$ stations between source and destination, and the packet must go through the insertion buffer at each of these stations. Thus the average number of insertion buffers, α, traversed by the packet is given by

$$\alpha = \sum_{j=2}^{M-1} (j-1)\, q_j \qquad (8.53)$$

It now remains to evaluate λ_r in terms of other parameters. This can be done by relating λ_r to q_j and λ_t, as is illustrated with the four-station diagram of Fig. 8.24. Traffic at rate λ_t enters each of the four stations. The probabilities q_j specify in effect the fraction of traffic that enters at a particular station and then exits at each of the remaining stations. The net traffic on the ring at the input to an insertion buffer is λ_r. For example, λ_r for station 1 is the sum of the traffic entering at stations 2, 3, and 4, less the traffic that exits before reaching the insertion buffer of station 1, as shown in Fig. 8.24. Thus

$$\lambda_r = (1 - q_1)\lambda_t + (1 - q_1 - q_2)\lambda_t + (1 - q_1 - q_2 - q_3)\lambda_t$$

But

$$q_1 + q_2 + q_3 = 1$$

so that the last term is 0 and the first two terms can be expressed as

$$\lambda_r = \lambda_t\,[q_2 + 2\,q_3] = \lambda_t \sum_{j=2}^{M-1} (j-1)\, q_j \qquad (8.54)$$

Although derived for the four-station case ($M = 4$), the second form of (8.54) is a general result that, when combined with (8.53), yields

$$\lambda_r = \alpha\lambda_t \qquad (8.55)$$

The delays previously discussed are now collected into an expression for the average transfer delay for the register insertion ring. First of all, packets experience only one transmission delay and wait in only one transmit buffer for any path around the ring, to produce an average delay of $W_t + \overline{X}/R$.

The specified traffic patterns, given by q_j, $j = 1, 2, \ldots M - 1$, lead to a value of α through use of (8.53). By its definition, α gives the average number of insertion buffers traversed by packets moving around the ring. Thus the average delay due to insertion buffers is $\alpha\, W_r$.

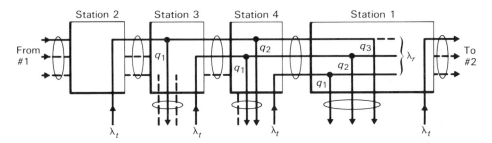

Figure 8.24   A Four-station Network Showing the Origins of the Components of the Traffic λ_r at Station 1

The final delay to be accounted for is the average delay due to station latencies. Recall that a packet path does not include insertion buffers at the source station or the destination station. Reference to a diagram such as given in Fig. 8.22 shows, however, that the packet path includes latencies at each intermediate station and at the destination station. Therefore, the average number of station latencies traversed by packets is $(\alpha + 1)$, and the average delay due to latencies is $(\alpha + 1)\, \tau'/M$.

Adding all the delays gives an expression for average transfer delay as

$$T = \overline{X}/R + (\alpha + 1)\, \tau'/M + W_t + \alpha\, W_r \tag{8.56}$$

The quantity $(W_t + \alpha\, W_r)$ can now be evaluated for the two priority schemes. Let ρ be defined as

$$\rho = \lambda_t \overline{X}/R \tag{8.57}$$

so that from (8.48), $\rho_t = \rho$, and from (8.47), $\rho_r = \alpha\rho$.

CASE 1: RING PRIORITY: Using (8.49), (8.50), and (8.55), $(W_t + \alpha\, W_r)$ can be expressed as

$$W_t + \alpha\, W_r = \frac{\lambda_t(1 + \alpha)}{2(1 - \alpha\rho)[1 - \rho(1 + \alpha)]}\frac{\overline{X^2}}{R^2} + \frac{\alpha\lambda_t\,(1 + \alpha)}{2(1 - \alpha\rho)}\frac{\overline{X^2}}{R^2}$$

which reduces to

$$W_t + \alpha\, W_r = \frac{\lambda_t\,(1 + \alpha)^2}{2(1 - \rho - \alpha\rho)}\frac{\overline{X^2}}{R^2} \tag{8.58}$$

CASE 2: STATION PRIORITY: A similar calculation that uses (8.51), (8.52), and (8.55) yields

$$W_t + \alpha\, W_r = \frac{\lambda_t\,(1 + \alpha)}{2(1 - \rho)}\frac{\overline{X^2}}{R^2} + \frac{\alpha\lambda_t\,(1 + \alpha)}{2[1 - \rho(1 + \alpha)]\,(1 - \rho)}\frac{\overline{X^2}}{R^2} \tag{8.59}$$

which reduces to

$$W_t + \alpha\, W_r = \frac{\lambda_t\,(1 + \alpha)^2}{2(1 - \rho - \alpha\rho)}\frac{\overline{X^2}}{R^2} \tag{8.60}$$

a result identical to (8.58) for the ring priority.

Thus, for the balanced ring, both priority schemes give the same average transfer delay

$$T = \overline{X}/R + (\alpha + 1)\, \tau'/M + \frac{\lambda_t\,(1 + \alpha)^2}{2(1 - \rho - \alpha\rho)}\frac{\overline{X^2}}{R^2} \tag{8.61}$$

As in other types of networks, throughput, S, can be defined as

$$S = M\rho \tag{8.62}$$

and average transfer delay can be written in terms of S as

$$T = \frac{\overline{X}}{R} + \frac{(\alpha + 1)\, \tau'}{M} + \frac{\lambda_t\,(1 + \alpha)^2}{2[1 - S\,(1 + \alpha)/M]}\frac{\overline{X^2}}{R^2} \tag{8.63}$$

From (8.63), note that maximum network throughput is $M/(1 + \alpha)$, a number that can be greater than 1. However, maximum utilization, or throughput, for the channel between successive stations is 1.

Equation (8.63) can now be evaluated for specific packet length distributions. For exponentially distributed packet lengths, (8.63) becomes

$$T = \frac{\overline{X}}{R} + \frac{(\alpha + 1)\tau'}{M} + \frac{\lambda_t (1 + \alpha)^2}{[1 - S(1 + \alpha)/M]} \frac{(\overline{X})^2}{R^2} \tag{8.64}$$

whereas for fixed length packets, it becomes

$$T = \frac{\overline{X}}{R} + \frac{(\alpha + 1)\tau'}{M} + \frac{\lambda_t (1 + \alpha)^2}{2[1 - S(1 + \alpha)/M]} \frac{(\overline{X})^2}{R^2} \tag{8.65}$$

Several different traffic patterns are now considered. Two extreme cases are:

1. All packets generated by host i destined for host $(i + 1)$ Mod M; and
2. All packets generated by host i destined for host $(i - 1)$ Mod M.

In case 1,

$$q_j = \begin{cases} 1, & j = 1 \\ 0, & \text{otherwise} \end{cases} \tag{8.66}$$

showing that packets travel only to the next station. Thus, $\alpha = 0$ (i.e., the insertion buffers are always empty), and M separate transmissions may exist on the ring. In this case, Eq. (8.63) gives

$$T = \frac{\overline{X}}{R} + \frac{\tau'}{M} + \frac{\lambda_t}{2(1 - S/M)} \frac{\overline{X^2}}{R^2} \tag{8.67}$$

In case 2,

$$q_j = \begin{cases} 1, & j = M - 1 \\ 0, & \text{otherwise} \end{cases} \tag{8.68}$$

showing that packets travel the maximum distance around the ring. Thus, (8.53) gives $\alpha = M - 2$, and the ring becomes very heavily utilized. In this case, (8.63) gives

$$T = \frac{\overline{X}}{R} + \frac{(M - 1)\tau'}{M} + \frac{\lambda_t (M - 1)^2}{2[1 - S(M - 1)/M]} \frac{\overline{X^2}}{R^2} \tag{8.69}$$

and the maximum throughput becomes $M/(M - 1)$.

Finally, a fairly typical traffic pattern is considered. Assume the probabilities q_j are such that $\alpha = (M/2) - 1$, as is the case when a station transmits to each of the other stations with equal likelihood so that

$$q_j = 1/(M - 1), \qquad j = 1, 2, \ldots, M - 1 \tag{8.70}$$

In such a case, the average transfer delay becomes

$$T = \frac{\overline{X}}{R} + \frac{\tau'}{2} + \frac{\lambda_t M^2}{8(1 - S/2)} \frac{\overline{X^2}}{R^2} \tag{8.71}$$

and the maximum throughput is 2. This particular case with equally likely destination probabilities is often referred to as the symmetric traffic case.

8.4.3 Performance Studies

Since ring and station priority systems for balanced rings give the same average transfer delay, T, and the same channel utilization, ρ, there is no need to distinguish between these two systems in this section. In contrast to other types of rings, the traffic pattern is a critical factor in the performance study of register insertion rings. The traffic pattern is accounted for in the model developed through its effect on the variable α, the average number of insertion buffers traversed by a packet.

As in other performance studies, the average transfer delay is normalized to units of packet transmission times, and thus (8.63) gives

$$\hat{T} = 1 + \frac{(\alpha + 1)a'}{M} + \frac{(1 + \alpha)^2}{2[1 - S(1 + \alpha)/M]} \frac{\lambda_t \overline{X^2}}{(\overline{X}) R} \tag{8.72}$$

Note that for any type of packet length distribution, the maximum throughput is $M/(1 + \alpha)$.

For the cases of fixed and exponentially distributed packet lengths, the result in terms of normalized quantities becomes

Fixed length packets:

$$\hat{T} = 1 + \frac{(\alpha + 1)\,a'}{M} + \frac{(1 + \alpha)^2\,S/M}{2[1 - S(1 + \alpha)/M]} \tag{8.73}$$

Exponentially distributed packet lengths:

$$\hat{T} = 1 + \frac{(\alpha + 1)\,a'}{M} + \frac{(1 + \alpha)^2\,S/M}{1 - S(1 + \alpha)/M} \tag{8.74}$$

In the symmetric traffic case in which $\alpha = (M/2) - 1$, (8.73) becomes

$$\hat{T} = 1 + \frac{a'}{2} + \frac{MS}{8(1 - S/2)} \tag{8.75}$$

while (8.74) becomes

$$\hat{T} = 1 + \frac{a'}{2} + \frac{MS}{4(1 - S/2)} \tag{8.76}$$

The effect of the traffic pattern on delay is shown in Fig. 8.25. In this figure, the two extreme traffic patterns, which correspond to $\alpha = 0$ and $\alpha = M - 2$, are considered along with the symmetric traffic case, which corresponds to

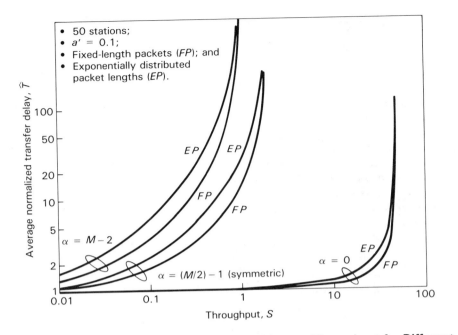

Figure 8.25   Average Normalized Transfer Delay versus Throughput for Different Traffic Patterns

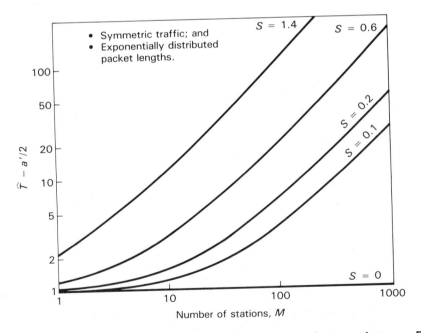

Figure 8.26   Average Normalized Transfer Delay, Less Average Latency Delay, versus Number of Stations for Different Ring Loads

$\alpha = (M/2) - 1$, for both fixed and exponentially distributed packet lengths. The curves show that the traffic pattern has a major effect on the performance of register insertion rings. Although fixed length packets give essentially one-half of the delay of exponentially distributed packet lengths, the packet length distribution is seen from the curves to be of secondary importance.

It is also clear from (8.73) and (8.74) that the larger the number of stations, M, the more pronounced is the difference between the extreme traffic patterns represented by $\alpha = 0$ and $\alpha = M - 2$ since for the former, maximum attainable throughput is M, whereas for the latter it is only $M/(M - 1)$.

Figure 8.26 shows the effect on average transfer delay of the number of stations on a symmetric balanced ring. In these curves, a' is kept constant whereas the number of stations is varied, even though in general the normalized ring latency a' depends on M. The curves are for exponentially distributed packet lengths. Results for fixed packet lengths are very similar.

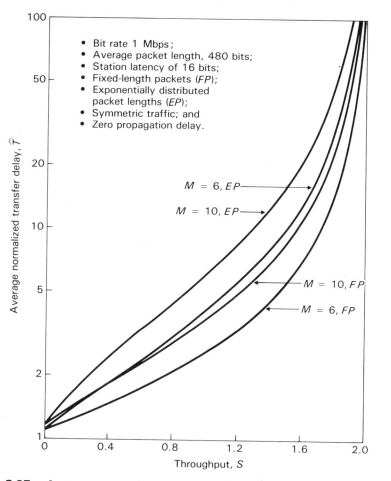

Figure 8.27 shows curve with:
- Bit rate 1 Mbps;
- Average packet length, 480 bits;
- Station latency of 16 bits;
- Fixed-length packets (FP);
- Exponentially distributed packet lengths (EP);
- Symmetric traffic; and
- Zero propagation delay.

Curves labeled: $M = 6, EP$; $M = 10, EP$; $M = 10, FP$; $M = 6, FP$.

Axes: Average normalized transfer delay, $\hat{T}$ (vertical); Throughput, S (horizontal).

Figure 8.27 Average Normalized Transfer Delay versus Throughput for Different Packet Length Distributions and Different Numbers of Stations

Examination of the curves in Fig. 8.26 shows that average transfer delay (less average ring latency) tends to be proportional to M for M large, and that direct proportionality begins for smaller M at larger throughputs. This result is of course confirmed by examination of Eq. (8.76), from which the curves are plotted. Note also that the differences between the curves for various throughput values is more pronounced for large values of M.

A final set of curves, in Fig. 8.27, shows delay versus throughput for exponentially distributed and fixed length packets with symmetric traffic and two choices for the number of stations. For these curves, station latency is fixed so that ring latency changes with the number of stations. This implies that the address length is large enough for all ring sizes under consideration. For the parameters listed in Fig. 8.27, a' is 0.167 and 0.2 for the six- and 10-station rings respectively. These values were chosen to correspond to those used by Liu et al. [12] in a simulation study of a DLCN ring.

The curves show how average transfer delay and throughput are related as the number of stations vary, with fixed-station (as opposed to ring) latency. The delay results presented are somewhat higher than those of Liu.

8.5 Comparative Performance of Ring Networks

This chapter has described the operation and developed models for the performance of three different classes of ring networks: the token passing, the slotted, and the register insertion type rings. In keeping with the main thrust of the book, the emphasis has been on developing tractable models that describe the performance of the networks to a reasonable approximation.

This chapter concludes with a comparative assessment of performance since all three types of networks considered have the same geometry and common parameters, such as station and ring latency. In addition, all have been analyzed from a unified point of view. At the same time, the comparative assessment should not be construed to be a definitive study of the relative merits of the three ring classes. There are two reasons for this statement. First, the models of performance are approximate and have been developed to illustrate the major aspects of performance with models as tractable as possible. Second, and possibly more important, the tractable performance models are not intended to reflect aspects such as cost, reliability, higher-level protocols, and so forth, which can have an important effect on the choice of practical networks.

In spite of these reservations, the following is a useful and accurate first-order comparison of the performance of the three methods. The comparison is based on Figs. 8.28 and 8.29, which compare single-token rings, slotted rings with no gaps, and register insertion rings with symmetric, balanced traffic characteristics. Fig. 8.28 assumes that the normalized ring latency, a', is 1 for all three rings, while Fig. 8.29 has a' equal to 0.1. In both figures, 10- and 100-station rings with these latencies are considered. In all cases, identical Poisson traffic to each station, equal physical separation of consecutive

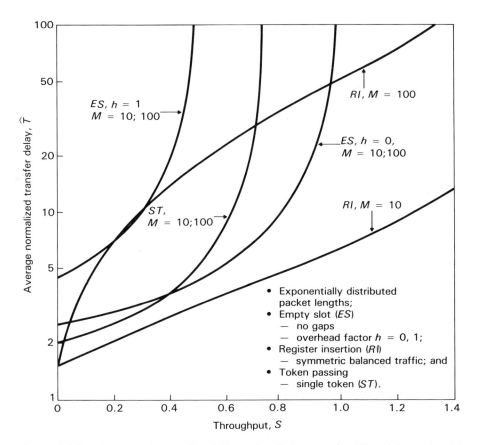

Figure 8.28 Average Normalized Transfer Delay versus Throughput for 10 and 100 Station Rings Using Different Access Methods, all with a Normalized Ring Latency of 1

stations, and exponentially distributed packet lengths are assumed so that the appropriate equations derived in each performance-studies section can be used directly. In the case of slotted rings, overhead factors of 0 and 1 are considered in the figures.

Figure 8.28 shows that for a 10-station ring and $a' = 1$, register insertion provides the best results, but that when the number of stations is 100, register insertion gives the worst results. In the latter case, token passing is best at low loads, whereas slotted rings are better at larger loads provided that the overhead per minipacket is very small.

Figure 8.29 shows that for a 10-station network and $a' = 0.1$, token passing is best at low loads, whereas register insertion is superior for high loads. However, when the number of stations is increased to 100 with the same ring latency, token passing is best under all load conditions.

In conclusion, the following general comments can be made about each type of ring. In terms of performance, register insertion rings are desirable when

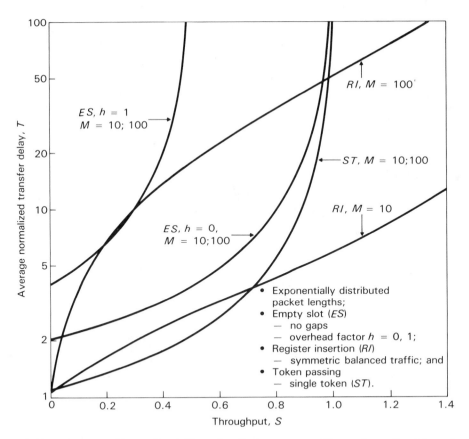

Figure 8.29 Average Normalized Transfer Delay versus Throughput for 10 and 100 Station Rings Using Different Access Methods, all with a Normalized Ring Latency of 0.1

the number of stations is small, or for extremely low loads for an arbitrary number of stations. Token-passing rings seem to have the best performance under a variety of conditions; station latencies should be as short as possible, however, to maximize the ring throughput and to make the minimum transfer time as small as possible. Finally, slotted rings are competitive with other rings when the ring has a large number of stations and the ring propagation delay is large; obviously, the overhead per minipacket must be kept to a minimum for best results.

Another point of comparison between the three access methods is the minimum average transfer delay that occurs under very low loads ($S = 0$). If the case of symmetric traffic is considered, the minimum delays for single-token, empty slot, and register insertion rings are respectively $1 + a'$, $2 + a'/2$ and $1 + a'/2$. In the first two methods considered, a packet arriving at a station generally cannot be transmitted at once—it must wait for either a free token or an empty slot.† However, such is not the case for the register insertion ring, in which a packet is put onto the ring at once if the ring is available. As such, the register insertion ring may be regarded as having a form of random access protocol.

These comparisons are based on the assumption that a' for all rings is the same. This is not necessarily true. A register insertion ring, with packets removed at the destination station, requires a minimum of a 7-bit station latency for addressing if the network has 100 stations ($100 < 2^7$). On the other hand, a 1-bit latency may be sufficient for slotted and token rings. This aspect can be taken into account, but a more detailed parametric study is required. Propagation delay, packet length, and channel bit rate are additional factors that must be specified. The preceding discussion is intended to make general comparisons based on as few specific parameter choices as possible.

8.6   Summary

This chapter discusses local area networks that use a ring geometry and access protocols appropriate to such a choice. The major types discussed are: token rings, slotted rings, and register insertion rings. Token rings can be further classified as multiple token, single token and single packet on the basis of how the token is used.

Typical frame formats are given and discussed for each major network type, and brief comments are made on implementations. The operation of the access protocols is described for each category, and a performance equation that relates average transfer delay to throughput is derived for each case.

Comparative performance of the ring types is discussed in Section 8.5. Unfortunately, there is no clear-cut best choice among the various types. It is possible, however, to identify ranges of traffic load and other parameters over which each type of network has advantages.

The next chapter deals with another class of access methods called *random access protocols*. Such protocols are frequently used with a tree- or bus-type geometry.

References

[1] B. K. Penney and A. A. Baghdadi. "Survey of Computer Communications Loop Networks: Parts 1 and 2." *Computer Communications* 2 (1979): 165–180, 224–241.

[2] D. W. Andrews and G. D. Schultz. "A Token-ring Architecture for Local Area Networks." *Proceedings of COMPCON,* (Fall 1982): 615–624.

---

†Whereas this delay has been modeled in the single-token case, it has not been taken into account in the slotted ring; an extra normalized delay of $a'/2m$, where m = number of slots on the ring, must be added.

[3] W. Bux. "Local-area Subnetworks: A Performance Comparison." *IEEE Trans. Communications* COM-29, no. 10 (October 1981): 1465–1473.

[4] D. J. Farber and K. C. Larson. "The System Architecture of the Distributed Computer System—The Communications System." *Proceedings of Symposium on Computer-Communications and Teletraffic.* Polytechnic Institute of Brooklyn. (April 1972): 21–27.

[5] J. Pierce. "How Far Can Data Loops Go?" *IEEE Transactions on Communications* COM-20 (June 1972): 527–530.

[6] R. M. Needham and A. J. Herbert. *The Cambridge Distributed Computing System.* London: Addison–Wesley, 1982.

[7] L. Kleinrock. *Queueing Systems.* Vol. 2, *Computer Applications.* New York: Wiley, 1976.

[8] F. Baskett, K. M. Chandy, R. R. Muntz, and F. G. Palacios. "Open, Closed and Mixed Networks of Queues with Different Classes of Customers." *Journal of the Association of Computer Machinery* 22 (1975): 248–260.

[9] M. T. Liu. "Distributed Loop Computer Networks." In *Advances in Computers,* ed. M. C. Yovits, 163–221. New York: Academic Press, 1978.

[10] A. Thomasian and H. Kanakia. "Performance Study of Loop Networks Using Buffer Insertion." *Computer Networks* 3 (1979): 419–425.

[11] W. Bux and M. Schlatter. "An Approximate Method for the Performance Analysis of Buffer Insertion Rings." *IEEE Transactions on Communications* COM-31 no. 1. (January 1983): 50–55.

[12] M. T. Liu, G. Babic, and R. Pardo. "Traffic Analysis of the Distributed Loop Computer Network (DLCN)." *Proceedings of the National Telecommunications Conference* (December 1977): 31:5–1 – 31:5–7.

[13] P. Kermani and L. Kleinrock. "Virtual Cut-Through: A New Computer Communication Switching Technique." *Computer Networks* 3 (December 1979): 267–286.

Problems and Exercises

1. Consider the curves given in Fig. 8.8 for token ring networks with 50 stations. Use the curves to find the average transfer delay for a network under the following conditions:

   Channel bit rate $= 10^6$ bits/sec;
   Latency per station $= 1$ bit;
   Length of ring $= 5$ km;
   Average packet length $= 75$ bits/packet;
   Average arrival rate/station $= 50$ packets/second; and
   Single-packet operation.

2. (a) In terms of throughput, what is the most significant advantage of a register insertion ring?

   (b) What is the largest value of S possible for a single-packet ring with fixed length packets? Give the answer in terms of symbols for the basic parameters.

   (c) For which kind of ring network is the traffic pattern critical in performance analysis? Why is this the case?

3. On a graph similar to Fig. 8.16, plot the curve for 2 bits latency and four slots. Use the other data given in Fig. 8.16.

4. (a) Complete the following table to show the position of the free token, the busy token, and data bits at the discrete times t_1-t_{11} for multiple-token, single-token, and single-packet token rings. There are three stations symmetrically located on a ring with negligible propagation delay as shown, and each station has 2 bits latency. Station 1 is the only station with data to transmit, and it has 3 data bits, d_1, d_2, and d_3, to transmit.
   (b) From the point of view of station 1, what is the average throughput over the observation interval (i.e., t_1-t_{11})?

| Station | Station outputs | | | | | | | | |
| Time | Multiple token | | | Single token | | | Single packet | | |
	1	2	3	1	2	3	1	2	3
t_0		□				□			□
t_1									
t_2									
t_3									
t_4									
t_5									
t_6									
t_7									
t_8									
t_9									
t_{10}									
t_{11}									

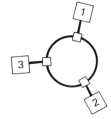

Notation to be used:
□ = Free token
■ = Busy token
d_i = Data bit

5. A token ring uses single-token operation and has fixed-length packets of length

500 bits. Other parameters are as follows:

> Channel bit rate = 10^6 bps;
> Number of stations = 100;
> Station latency = 4 bits; and
> Propagation delay for complete ring = 10 μsec.

(a) Find the average transfer delay in seconds if $S = 0.5$.
(b) Repeat for multiple-token operation.
(c) Repeat for single-packet operation.

6. One hundred stations are connected to a local area ring network with a channel bit rate $R = 10^7$ bps. The network transmits constant length packets of 100 8-bit bytes in length. Each station has a Poisson arrival process with the same arrival rate λ.
(a) What is the largest value of λ possible for any token or slotted ring network?
(b) What is the largest value of λ possible for a register insertion ring under all possible traffic patterns?
(c) What is the largest value of λ for a register insertion ring under symmetric traffic conditions?

7. (a) Tabulate analytic expressions for average transfer delay in seconds when throughput is essentially 0 for all the ring methods: multiple and single token, single packet, slotted, and register insertion with symmetric traffic.
(b) Assume that station latency is as small as possible, subject to the following parameter values:

> Propagation time = 0;
> Number of stations = 100; and
> Fixed packet length = 500 bits.

Which method gives the smallest delay for these conditions?

8. A token-ring network is to be designed to connect M stations that are 200 kilometers apart. The connections are to be made with 2400 bps lines. Each station services 30 terminals, each of which generates Poisson traffic with a mean rate, λ_i, of 1 message/minute. Propagation delay is 5 μsec/km. Packets have a mean length of 30 8-bit characters. Two cases are to be considered: Case 1—1-bit token ($B = 1$); Case 2—10 bits for overhead and token ($B = 10$)
(a) Express average transfer delay versus M, and plot the result for fixed-length packets, multiple-token operation, and Cases 1 and 2.
(b) How many stations can be used if average transfer delay is to be less than 1 second? Work this problem for multiple token, fixed-length packets, and Case 1.
(c) For values of S approaching 0, compare average transfer delay for fixed- and exponential-packet lengths. Consider all three types of operation (single token, multiple token, and single packet) and both Cases 1 and 2.
(d) Total load on the network can be expressed as

$$\Lambda = M \sum_{i=1}^{30} \lambda_i$$

What absolute limit does Λ place on the number of stations?

9. A token-ring network has three stations, each with a latency of 2 bits. Propagation delay is negligible. The token is 1 bit long. Station 1, the only station with data to transmit, must transmit 3 data bits. Packets are of constant length and, in this case, the packet consists of a 1-bit token and 3 data bits.
(a) For multiple-token and single-token operation, express the average effective service time, $\overline{E}$, as a *number of bit times*.

(b) Use the results of (a) to determine for each of the two cases the number of free bit positions on the ring between the last data bit in the packet and the new free token.

(c) Express the results of (b) in general terms with the appropriate symbols (i.e., $\bar{E}, \bar{X}, R, M$, etc.).

10. Consider the three types of networks whose performances in terms of mean normalized transfer delay are given in Fig. 8.28. Take $M = 10$, $h = 1$, with other parameters as given in the figure.

(a) What is the best choice of access protocol for a value of throughput of 0.6?

(b) Approximate the performance of a polling network in a reasonable manner, and choose the parameters so that the polling network and the register insertion network ($M = 10$) gives the same delay for $S = 0.5$. Which, of all the access protocols (those in the figure, plus polling), gives the smallest $\hat{T}$ for $S = 0.8$? $S = 0.2$?

(c) What is the average transfer delay (in seconds) for the polling network with $S = 0.2$, average packet length 100 bits/packet, and channel bit rate $= 10^4$ bits/second?

11. A slotted ring has a total propagation delay of 10 μsec, a bit rate of 10 Mbps, and 100 stations, each with a latency of 2 bits/station. Determine two possible minipacket lengths and specify the gap, if any.

12. (a) Determine a general expression for the maximum number of stations a register insertion ring can support for stable operation.

(b) A register insertion ring has the following parameters:
λ/station = 1 packet/second;
$\bar{X}$ = 100 bits/packet; and
$R = 10^6$ bps.

Determine the maximum possible number of stations for each of the traffic distributions:
 (i) Symmetric;
 (ii) All traffic to the next station in the direction of traffic flow around the ring; and
 (iii) All traffic completely around the ring to the last station before the transmitting station.

13. Unlike the token and slotted rings, the register insertion ring has no inherent acknowledgment mechanism. One way acknowledgments can be provided is to allow packets to continue around the ring past the destination station (where the contents of the packet are read) back to the originating station. For a balanced symmetric network, let A be the ratio of the average network queueing delay with this acknowledgment scheme to the corresponding delay without any acknowledgment scheme.

(a) Show that A is an explicit function of throughput S only; show graphically how A varies with S.

(b) For exponentially distributed packets, show how the average queueing delays, with and without the acknowledgment scheme, vary with S. Take λ_t to be constant at 1 packet/second.

14. A register insertion ring has four stations connected. All stations have identical traffic characteristics and generate the same traffic pattern. Compare the following traffic patterns (probabilities are specified in Table 8.1) and determine the maximum throughput possible in each case.

Table 8.1   Traffic Patterns

		Case (a)		
Source \ *Destination*	*1*	*2*	*3*	*4*
1	—	1/2	1/3	1/6
2	1/6	—	1/2	1/3
3	1/3	1/6	—	1/2
4	1/2	1/3	1/6	—

		Case (b)		
Source \ *Destination*	*1*	*2*	*3*	*4*
1	—	1/6	1/3	1/2
2	1/2	—	1/6	1/3
3	1/3	1/2	—	1/6
4	1/6	1/3	1/2	—

15. In register insertion rings, a station latency of $(1 + \log_2 M)$ bits is often necessary: 1-bit regeneration delay and $\log_2 M$ bits to read an address on an M-station network (assuming that M is a power of 2).
    (a) Find a general expression in terms of M and other parameters for the average normalized transfer delay under balanced symmetric traffic conditions.
    (b) Contrast this delay with that on a comparable multiple-token ring network, where the station latency is just 1 bit, by finding the conditions under which each access method gives the lower delay at very low loads.
    (c) Consider a ring with a total propagation delay of 10 μseconds, a channel bit rate of 1 Mbps, and packets exponentially distributed with mean 1000 bits. Under very low load conditions, for what number of stations does the token-passing access method give less delay? Since register insertion rings under symmetric traffic conditions have a maximum throughput of 2, the delay–throughput curves for the two access methods must intersect at least at one point. Find the crossover point(s) for rings of 8 and 32 stations.

*R*andom Access Networks

9.1   Introduction

In Chapter 6, the concept of a random access network is introduced in the discussion of the ALOHA network. Recall that ALOHA networks share a common channel, often configured with a bus-type geometry, and have some characteristics in common with the ring networks just discussed in Chapter 8. For the ring networks, however, channel access is managed by a token, by the presence of empty slots, or by an insertion register, so that only one station transmits at a time. Random access networks, on the other hand, are characterized by the absence of a channel-controlled access mechanism. To some extent, a station is free to broadcast its packets at a time determined by the station itself, with never any certainty that another station is not simultaneously attempting a transmission. In fact, for pure ALOHA, a station is free to broadcast whenever it has a packet to send.

Random access procedures are well matched to the needs of bursty users since the entire bandwidth of a channel can be used by a station once it successfully gains access. Under light load conditions, a user can, on the average, successfully access the channel after only a short waiting period. Other advantages are that no central control is required, stations can be added or deleted easily, and most malfunctions are localized to single stations and do not affect the whole network.

As discussed in Chapter 6, the price to be paid for the advantages of simplicity and short delay times in random access networks is potential interference between users as they compete for the use of the common channel. Two or more users may decide to transmit at almost the same time so that their signals overlap on the channel, and all are garbled. Such an overlap of signals is called a *collision,* and the time during which the channel is occupied by corrupted or partially corrupted signals is variously called a *collision interval,* a *contention interval,* or a *contention period.*

Random access procedures were first developed for long radio links and for satellite communications. The pure ALOHA protocol was one of the first such procedures, and it uses the simple expedient of allowing stations to transmit whenever they have packets ready. Efforts to improve the performance of pure ALOHA led to more sophisticated techniques designed to reduce the number of collisions and the length of collision intervals. Slotted ALOHA is an illustration of such a refinement. For slotted ALOHA, all stations must be synchronized, and all packets must be the same length. Furthermore, synchronization requires the distribution of timing information over the whole network. With these modifications, a significant decrease in the length of contention intervals can be achieved because packets are forced to collide either completely or not at all. For long radio and satellite links, with corresponding long propagation delays, it is difficult to achieve improvements in performance over slotted ALOHA.

Other types of networks, such as relatively compact terrestrial radio networks with stations closer together, have much shorter propagation delays. For such networks, it is feasible for a station that has a packet to transmit to "listen" to the channel to determine if it is busy before a transmission is attempted. If the channel is sensed to be busy, the station can defer its transmission until the channel is sensed to be idle. This process is called *carrier sensing,* and networks that use the process are called *carrier-sense multiple access* (CSMA) networks. Implementation of CSMA protocols requires hardware at each station for sensing the presence of signals on the channel when the station itself is not transmitting.

Carrier sensing is useless for satellite channels since the propagation delays involved are usually many times greater than the packet transmission time. In such applications, the sensed channel state provides information about the channel that is of little value because of the propagation delay between the transmitting and the receiving stations.

For networks with propagation delays much shorter than packet transmission times, CSMA-type protocols can provide smaller average delays and higher throughputs than the ALOHA methods since the carrier sensing can reduce the number of collisions and the length of collision intervals. Section 9.4 defines, analyzes, and compares several different forms of CSMA: nonpersistent, 1-persistent, and *p*-persistent.

The advent of local networks initiated an area of application and characteristics that favor carrier-sense procedures and refinements on these procedures. Local networks often use a channel medium, such as coaxial cable, that permits a station to monitor the signal on the cable while the station itself is transmitting. This is called *listen while transmitting*. If an interfering signal is detected during the monitoring period, the transmission can be aborted immediately. This modification reduces the length of collision intervals since corrupted transmissions can be detected and aborted quickly. The modified operation gives a distinct improvement over CSMA and ALOHA procedures that depend on either the receipt of a positive acknowledgment in a specified time interval after the packet has been transmitted to identify good transmissions, or the lack of such an acknowledgement to determine that a transmission has been corrupted.

With the addition of the *collision-detect* feature, the protocol is called *carrier-sense multiple access with collision detection* (CSMA/CD). Most commercial implementations of the CSMA/CD protocols for local networks, such as Ethernet, seem to favor 1-persistent CSMA/CD over other variations. Because of the superiority of CSMA/CD, it is favored over CSMA in most applications of random access procedures to local networks; ALOHA procedures are seldom if ever used in such networks.

In Chapter 8, expressions have been developed for both the throughput and delay performance of the different types of access methods for ring networks. A reasonable objective for the present chapter would be a parallel development for the random access methods. Unfortunately, the delay analysis for both CSMA and CSMA/CD protocols is generally very difficult, and in some cases not even numerical solutions are possible. Because of this difficulty in obtaining analytical results for delay, it is not possible to use a direct approach to this aspect of performance. Expressions for throughput can, however, be obtained in a direct manner for all random access protocols of interest.

Slotted ALOHA is the only protocol in the random access class for which a delay analysis can be made within the mathematical framework chosen for this text. Thus, although slotted ALOHA is not an important protocol for local networks, an analysis of it is presented in some detail to illustrate possible solution methods and give insight into the behavior and factors that affect the performance of any random access network. More specifically, as is shown in the discussion of delay for nonpersistent CSMA/CD, the results for slotted ALOHA indicate clearly the general effects on performance of various network parameters for any type of random access protocol.

Stability is another issue for random access protocols, and here too the results of an analysis of slotted ALOHA can be used to infer results for more complicated protocols.

The next section of this chapter covers the design of random access networks in terms of topology and station structure. The discussion of slotted

ALOHA, mentioned previously, is contained in Section 9.3. Section 9.4 is concerned with CSMA protocols (without collision detection). Analytic expressions for throughput versus load are obtained for nonpersistent CSMA, both slotted and nonslotted. Similar results for other CSMA protocols are also given but not derived. This section also compares performance characteristics of the different CSMA protocols with respect to throughput–load and delay–throughput tradeoffs.

The final section, Section 9.5, deals with CSMA/CD procedures. Basic operation of such networks is discussed, and throughput analyses are given for nonpersistent and slotted nonpersistent CSMA/CD. The section concludes with sensitivity studies and a comparison of the performance of CSMA/CD relative to other access methods.

9.2 Basic Properties of Random Access Networks

The most common geometric configurations of local area networks that use random access protocols are the bus and the tree; the choice is often determined by whether the transmissions are baseband or broadband. Baseband transmissions tend to be used on all-passive bus networks. Such transmissions travel in both directions from a station along a bus, which may be coaxial cable, twisted pair, or a fiber-optic link. The bus is terminated at both ends to prevent the signal from reflecting back along the bus. Figure 9.1(a) shows how a baseband signal from station A reaches stations B and C on the bus.

Broadband networks, on the other hand, use active repeaters or amplifiers to interconnect segments of passive transmission media such as coaxial cable. The repeaters are used to extend the range of the transmitted signals and to direct their paths, in most cases in only one direction, along a particular segment of the network. The tree topology and the technology associated with cable television (CATV) are often used for broadband networks.

Many broadband networks use a frequency translator and repeater in a headend located at the apex of the tree. Stations transmit in one frequency band "upstream" to the headend, and signals addressed to other stations on the network are retransmitted "downstream" by the frequency translator in another frequency band. Proper termination of each branch of the tree is again required to prevent signal reflection. Figure 9.1(b) shows how a broadband signal from station A reaches stations B and C. An alternative to a frequency translator is dual cables—one for upstream and another for downstream—as diagrammed in Fig. 2.37 of Section 2.4.

In both the broadband and baseband transmission schemes, all transmissions are of the broadcast type (i.e., every station on the bus can potentially receive every transmission). From the performance point of view, the major difference between baseband and broadband schemes is the greater propagation delays inherent in broadband networks due to the unidirectionality of the transmissions. Since propagation delay is an explicit parameter in perfor-

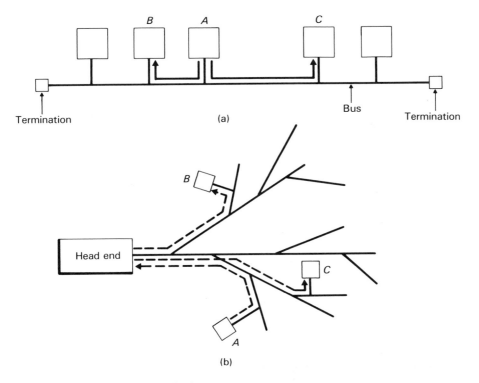

Figure 9.1 **Transmission Paths**
(a) On a baseband bus network
(b) On a broadband tree network

mance results, the same model can be used to study performance of baseband and broadband networks. In the remainder of this chapter, discussions of implementations are limited to baseband networks since these are less complex and easier to understand.

Figure 9.2 shows a coaxial cable with M stations connected to form a baseband random access network. Each station has three major components: the network processor, the transceiver interface, and the transceiver. The user device at each station, which can be a computer or some peripheral device such as a terminal, couples into the network processor through either a serial or parallel connection. The network processor packetizes the incoming data, implements the access protocol algorithm, and generally exercises control over the station. Although the network processor controls the station, it does so with information obtained locally at the station. Control information transmitted over other channels in addition to the cable is not required. Thus, control of random access networks is completely distributed among the stations.

A packet that is ready to be transmitted is transferred in parallel from the network processor to the transceiver interface, where it is stored in a buffer.

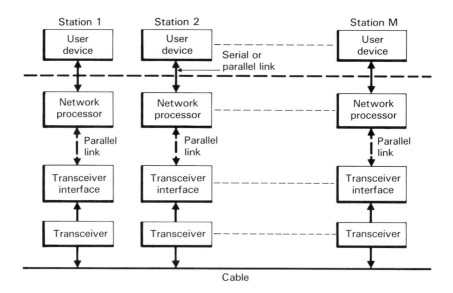

Figure 9.2   A Typical Bus Structure for a Contention-type Local Network

When a station is allowed to transmit by its access protocol algorithm, a ready packet is transferred serially out of the interface buffer through the transceiver for transmission over the cable. The signal for transmission over the cable has a characteristic analog waveform to represent each bit. Distinctive features of this analog waveform, such as zero crossings, are used by the transceiver to convert the analog signal back to its digital counterpart. Thus a combination of analog signals on the cable from two or more stations results in a distorted waveform that cannot properly be converted back to digital form. As noted, such a distortion is called a *collision* and all colliding signals lose their information content.

Signals transmitted over the cable are sensed by every station on the network. Thus each packet must carry overhead bits to indicate the address of the desired destination.

Monitoring equipment is required in the transceivers to implement CSMA and CSMA/CD protocols. For CSMA, each transceiver must be able to sense the signals of other stations while they are not transmitting. Furthermore, for CSMA/CD, each transceiver must be able to monitor the cable both before and during its own transmissions.

Signals propagate along a typical coaxial cable at approximately 65% of the speed of light, thus about 5 nanoseconds (ns) are required to propagate over a one-meter length of cable (or 5 μs per kilometer). For any of the protocols that use information derived from signals received on the cable, such propagation delay times are important.

To illustrate, consider the station configuration shown in Fig. 9.3 and assume instantaneous carrier sensing. If station B transmits a signal, it propagates in both directions over the cable. Station A receives the signal

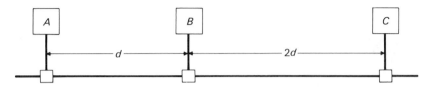

Figure 9.3   A Typical Station Configuration

approximately $5d$ ns after it is transmitted, and station C receives the signal still later, after approximately $10d$ ns. If station A happened to transmit at the same instant as station B, even an ideal signal detector at B would not detect the signal from station A until $5d$ ns had passed. At this point, station B is aware that its transmission has collided with that of station A. For operation at 10 Mbps, $0.05d$ bits are processed by station A before a collision is detected. Table 9.1 shows several values for d.

Examination of the table shows the range of values for d for which collision detection is effective. For a large station separation, such as would be the case for a satellite link with d, for example, 10^5 meters or longer, thousands of bits would be transmitted before a collision could be detected. Collision detection is not effective for such large station separations. On the other hand, for small values of d, collisions can be detected and transmissions aborted before a significant number of bits has been transmitted. This is typically the case for local networks for which d is small and propagation time is a relatively small fraction of packet transmission time.

The interaction of stations on a CSMA network, particularly when collision detection is used, depends on both the relative location of stations and the times at which packet transmissions are initiated. For example, let d in Fig. 9.3 be 100 meters and assume that stations A and B both have packets ready to transmit 1.2 μs after station C starts a transmission, as shown in Fig. 9.4. The propagation delay between B and C is 1 μs, and thus B has sensed the bus to be busy and defers when its packet is ready for transmission at $t = 1.2$ μsec. The propagation delay between A and C is 1.5 μs, so A, unaware of C's transmission, transmits 1.2 μs after C. After a further interval of just 0.3 μs, the transmission from C arrives at A, and collision detection takes place.

Table 9.1   Number of Bits Transmitted by Station B
Before a Collision Can be Detected at
Station A

d(meters)	Number of bits
20	1
200	10
2000	100
2×10^4	1000

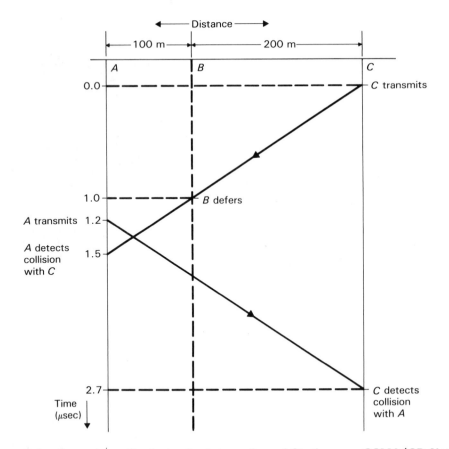

Figure 9.4 **Example to Illustrate the Interaction of Stations on CSMA/CD Networks**

However, station C, though it was the first to transmit, is not aware of a collision until the packet from A reaches C. This occurs 2.7 μs $(1.2 + 1.5)$ after C initially starts transmitting.

This example illustrates station interaction when the transmissions of only two stations overlap. When three or more transmissions collide, network behavior can get quite complicated.

After this general introduction to random access protocols, one of the basic random access protocols, slotted ALOHA, is described and analyzed in more detail in the next section.

9.3 Slotted ALOHA

Slotted ALOHA is a refinement over the pure ALOHA access procedure discussed in Chapter 6. The slotted ALOHA procedure requires that time be segmented into slots of a fixed length, P, exactly equal to the packet transmission time, $\overline{X}/R$, where $\overline{X}$ is the packet length, and R is the bit rate of the channel. Every packet transmitted must fit into one of these slots by beginning and ending in precise synchronization with the slot segments. To accomplish synchronization, a packet arriving to be transmitted at any given station must be delayed until the beginning of the next slot. In contrast, for pure ALOHA, a packet transmission can begin at any time. Clearly, slotted ALOHA requires additional overhead to provide the synchronization required between different stations in the network.

Although slotted ALOHA was developed for satellite channels, it can be used on local area networks even though it is not very efficient. As previously noted, the primary reason for the detailed analysis of slotted ALOHA, given later in this section, is the insight provided into the behavior of other more sophisticated protocols that are more suitable for use with local networks. The basic operation of all the random access protocols is quite similar. Their major differences lie in the ways in which the channel is monitored.

Before beginning the detailed analysis of slotted ALOHA, a general description of station operation and of the basic access procedure is given. A bus-type structure such as that given in Fig. 9.2 is assumed.

An active station on an ALOHA network can, in general, be in one of two states: transmitting or backed off. In the transmitting state, a packet is delivered in a time $P = \overline{X}/R$. The backed-off state results after a collision that involves a packet from the station in question. To avoid repeated collisions, collided packets are rescheduled at later times chosen independently and at random.

A common method for rescheduling collided packets is to select an integer, k, from the integers $0, 1, 2, \ldots, K - 1$, under the condition that selection of each integer is equally likely with a probability $1/K$. The backoff time for a chosen integer, k, is then set at k packet times or kP seconds.

In the slotted ALOHA access procedure, a ready packet is transmitted at the beginning of the next slot after its arrival. If the packet is successfully received (i.e., a collision does not occur), then a positive acknowledgment is sent (assumed to be transmitted over a separate error-free channel) and received by the sending station after a delay determined by the two-way propagation time of the channel and the processing time in the receiver. If a collision occurs, no acknowledgment is sent, and after a fixed time-out equal to the maximum two-way propagation time, quantized to slots, the sending station selects a backoff time for retransmitting the packet. The station remains backed off, or in a waiting state, until the packet is retransmitted. After retransmission, the packet is either successful or collides, so the behavior previously described is repeated. A flow diagram for the slotted ALOHA access process is given in Fig. 9.5.

9.3.1 Throughput Analysis

In this subsection, expressions for the throughput, S, in terms of the offered load, G, are derived for slotted ALOHA, first for an infinite population of users and then for a finite population. It is shown that the infinite population

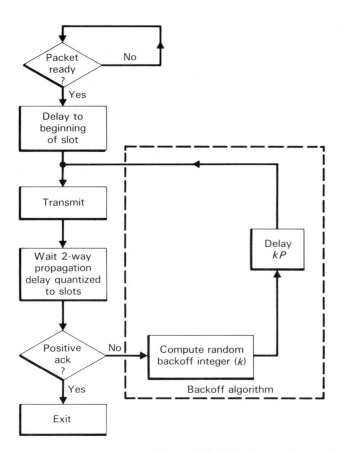

Figure 9.5   Flow Diagram for Slotted ALOHA Access Procedure

model is a good approximation to the finite population case when there are at least 20 users.

The infinite population analysis closely parallels the analysis given for pure ALOHA in Section 6.3 of Chapter 6. Throughput, S, and offered traffic, G, are again defined respectively as the average number of successful transmissions and attempted transmissions per packet transmission interval. Of course, the packet transmission interval, P, is the slot time and is a constant for all packets. As in Chapter 6, the infinite population model assumes that arrivals to the network, both new arrivals and retransmissions due to collisions, form a Poisson process with mean arrival rate, Λ packets/second. Since G denotes the average number of arrivals (attempted transmissions) in the packet interval of P seconds, it follows that

$$\Lambda = G/P \text{ packets/sec} \tag{9.1}$$

The relation for throughput versus offered load for slotted ALOHA is derived in essentially the same manner as for pure ALOHA in Section 6.3.

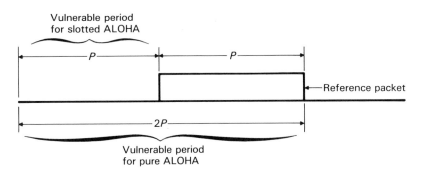

Figure 9.6   Vulnerable Periods for Pure and Slotted ALOHA

The difference in operation is apparent from the diagram of Fig. 9.6, which shows the vulnerable period for transmitted packets. In the case of slotted ALOHA, with packets synchronized to slots, it is clear from this figure that the vulnerable period is reduced to P seconds since only packets transmitted in the same slot with the reference packet can interfere with it. The figure also shows the vulnerable period of pure ALOHA which, as indicated in Chapter 6, is $2P$.

Throughput and offered traffic are related in the same manner as given by Eq. (6.13) for pure ALOHA:

$$S = G \, P \, \{\text{successful transmission}\} \tag{9.2}$$

The probability of a successful transmission is the probability of no other arrivals in the vulnerable period of length P. Since the arrival process is Poisson

$$P \, \{\text{no arrivals in an interval of length } P\} = e^{-\Lambda P} \tag{9.3}$$

Using (9.1) for Λ and (9.3) in (9.2) gives

$$S = G \, e^{-G} \tag{9.4}$$

which can be compared to the result for pure ALOHA from Eq. (6.15), rewritten as

$$S = G \, e^{-2G} \tag{9.5}$$

Figure 9.7, which plots results from (9.4) and (9.5), shows the relationship between S and G for both ALOHA methods. Note that the maximum throughput for slotted ALOHA is $1/e \approx 0.368$ (twice that of pure ALOHA), and that the maximum occurs for $G = 1$. This result can be obtained analytically through differentiation of S with respect to G.

In Eq. (9.5), it is assumed that the number of users is infinite. Since the number of users for any physical network is always finite, it is of considerable interest to develop a revised model for such a case. Consideration of the finite population case can also determine under what conditions, if any, the infinite population model gives a reasonable approximation.

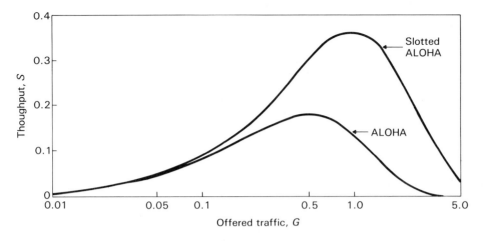

Figure 9.7   Throughput versus Offered Traffic for ALOHA and Slotted ALOHA

Consider a network with M independent stations that use a slotted ALOHA access procedure. The transmissions of each user are now modeled as a sequence of independent Bernoulli trials. The assumption is made that all transmissions originate from the same arrival process, and the model does not account for backoff delays due to collisions.

This choice of distribution for transmissions from each user is consistent with that made earlier for the infinite population case. A result from probability theory states that the distribution of a sum of M independent Bernoulli random variables, each with a parameter G/M, approaches a Poisson distribution, with parameter G, as M approaches infinity (see Parzen [9]). Thus, as the number of users becomes large, the model assumed for the finite number of users approaches the model previously chosen for an infinite population.

Now let S_i be the probability of station i successfully transmitting a packet in any slot. Then $1 - S_i$ is the probability of not successfully transmitting a packet in any slot interval. Similarly, let G_i and $1 - G_i$ respectively be the probabilities of station i attempting and not attempting a transmission in any slot. Note that S_i and G_i are also the steady-state average throughput and offered traffic for station i.† The transmissions referred to can be either new packets arriving from outside the network or retransmitted packets that collided in earlier attempts. Since G_i refers to an attempted transmission and S_i to a successful transmission, it follows that $S_i \leq G_i$ for all i.

---

†This follows from use of the relative-frequency concept of probability so that

$$P \{\text{station } i \text{ successfully transmits}\} = S_i = \frac{\text{number of slots used by}}{\text{good transmissions from station i}}{\text{total number of slots}}$$

where the number of slots is large and average throughput is defined in Section 6.3.

A relation between S and G results from the following reasoning. The probability that station j has a successful transmission is the probability that station j is the only station to attempt a transmission in a particular slot. Thus, since attempted transmissions are independent from station to station,

$$S_j = G_j \prod_{\substack{i=1 \\ i \neq j}}^{M} (1 - G_i) \tag{9.6}$$

This equation is general, allowing for different transmission probabilities, G_i, for each station.

It is often desirable to consider the special case in which statistically independent stations share the load equally. Then $S_i = S/M$, $G_i = G/M$, and (9.6) becomes

$$S = G (1 - G/M)^{M-1} \tag{9.7}$$

Using the limit expressed by

$$\lim_{n \to \infty} \left[1 + \frac{X}{n} \right]^n = e^X \tag{9.8}$$

(9.7), for $M \to \infty$, reduces to

$$S = Ge^{-G} \tag{9.9}$$

Equation (9.9) is, of course, identical to (9.4) for the infinite population case.

It is of interest to continue the examination of the case of M statistically independent identical stations, with M finite. Maximum throughput, S_{max}, for this case is obtained by differentiating (9.7) with respect to G and putting the result equal to 0. After simplification, this gives

$$0 = (1 - G/M) - G \left(\frac{M - 1}{M} \right)$$

which results in $G = 1$ as the value of G for maximum throughput, independent of M. Substitution of $G = 1$ into (9.7) yields

$$S_{max} = (1 - 1/M)^{M-1} \tag{9.10}$$

Table 9.2 gives maximum throughput for different values of M. It can reasonably be concluded from this set of values that the infinite population model, for which $S_{max} = 0.368$, is a good approximation to the more realistic finite population case when the number of stations is greater than 20. Note too that maximum channel throughput, S_{max}, is equal to offered load G only for $M = 1$. In fact, as Table 9.2 shows, S_{max} decreases rapidly with increasing M toward $1/e$ as more stations are added to the network.

9.3.2 Delay Analysis

As previously noted, derivation of average transfer delay–throughput relationships for contention networks is generally a difficult, and sometimes impossi-

Table 9.2   Maximum Throughput versus Number of Stations for Slotted ALOHA

M	1	2	5	10	20	100	∞
S_{max}	1	0.5	0.410	0.387	0.377	0.370	0.368

ble, task. For slotted ALOHA, it is possible, however, to derive useful expressions for delay using reasonably accurate network models. The approach taken is that developed by Lam [1] and summarized by Kleinrock [2]. The derivations are relatively straightforward and use only arguments based on elementary probability theory.

The development has two distinct parts. The basic relations for average transfer delay and throughput versus offered load are derived in this section in terms of certain basic parameters, including the average number of retransmissions. An expression for the average number of retransmissions in terms of throughput, offered traffic, and a backoff parameter is then derived separately in an appendix to this chapter. As shown in this appendix, this second step involves a number of straightforward but tedious calculations of probabilities. Although there are a number of parts to the calculation, the overall analysis deserves serious study because it gives valuable insight and illustrates the approach that must be taken to compute delay for any type of contention network, including those in common use for local area networks.

As could be expected, the delay–throughput characteristics for random access networks are sensitive to the handling of the retransmission of packets that have collided. The analyses given in Chapter 6 for ALOHA, and earlier in this chapter for slotted ALOHA, account for retransmissions only by increasing the offered traffic. These analyses assume that both new and collided packets come from the same process and do not account for the delays that collided packets experience. The analysis to follow accounts for newly arrived and retransmitted packets as separate variables. The result is an average transfer delay–throughput relation and also a throughput-offered load expression more accurate than Eqs. (9.4) or (9.7).

Operation of the access protocol follows the description and flow chart given in the introductory part of this section and in Fig. 9.5. The following assumptions and definitions are made in the subsequent analysis:

- The population of users is infinite;
- New arrivals to the network come from a Poisson process with mean arrival rate S packets/slot or Λ packets/second, where $S = \Lambda P$;
- The total arrival process of packets to the network, including new arrivals and retransmissions, is Poisson with mean arrival rate G packets/slot;
- Each station has at most one packet ready for transmission, including any previously collided packets;
- End-to-end propagation delay for the complete bus is τ seconds;
- A transmitting station learns whether or not its transmission is successful

after a time rounded to r slots, where r is the smallest integer greater than $2\tau/P$, and all stations are assumed to require this same number of slots; and

- The processing time of the receiver is negligible in comparison with propagation delay.

To begin the analysis, consider Fig. 9.8(a), which shows a typical packet transmission sequence, including a potential retransmission after a collision. After an initial transmission, which requires P seconds, the station must wait r slots, or rP seconds, to determine if the transmission is successful or has collided. If a collision has occurred, a retransmission is scheduled for a randomly chosen later time. To determine the backoff, an integer k is selected at random from the set $0, 1, 2, \ldots, K-1$, with each integer equally likely. The delay, or backoff, is then set at kP and the retransmission takes place P +

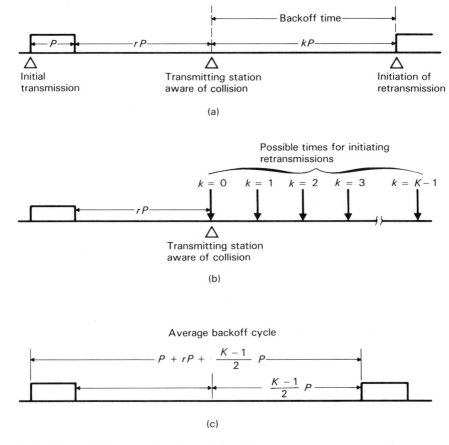

Figure 9.8   Timing Diagrams for Slotted ALOHA

(a) A specific packet transmission sequence

(b) Possible packet retransmission times

(c) Average backoff cycle

$rP + kP$ seconds after the initiation of the first transmission. As shown in Fig. 9.8(b), the randomly selected integer, k, can set the backoff delay to any value from 0 to $K - 1$ packet times. Note that the average backoff time, $\overline{kP}$, is given by

$$\overline{kP} = \frac{1}{K} \sum_{k=0}^{K-1} kP = \left(\frac{K-1}{2}\right) P \tag{9.11}$$

An average backoff cycle (defined as the total time required to transmit a packet, determine that it has collided, and wait the backoff time) thus requires $P + rP + (K - 1) P/2$ seconds [which reduces to $rP + (K + 1) P/2$], as shown in Fig. 9.8(c).

Now consider the total transfer delay experienced by a packet in a network that uses a slotted ALOHA protocol. Such a delay has four components:

1. The waiting time after arrival until the beginning of the next slot;
2. The delay due to retransmissions;
3. The packet transmission time; and
4. The propagation delay.

The average of each of these component delays is now determined and summed to give the average transfer delay. For item 1, the arrival process for new packets is assumed to be Poisson, and thus all arrival times during a slot are equally likely. The average waiting time between arrival and the beginning of the slot is thus $P/2$ seconds. Relative to item 3, the packet transmission time is, of course, P seconds.

The average delay for each retransmission cycle was determined to be $[rP + (K + 1)P/2]$ seconds. The total average delay caused by retransmissions, required as item 2, depends on how many retransmission cycles are required. If H denotes the average number of retransmission cycles, then $H [rP + (K + 1)P/2]$ is the average time required for all retransmissions.

Finally, consider the propagation delay, item 4. Packets for transmission between any pair of stations must be propagated over the length of cable that connects the stations. Average transfer delay requires the average of such delays over all station pairs, a result that depends on the station configuration along the bus. If the stations are uniformly distributed along the bus, as might be the case for a local network, the average separation of stations is approximately one-third the bus length, or the average propagation delay is approximately $\tau/3$ seconds.

The four components of average transfer delay can now be added to obtain

$$T = P + P/2 + \tau/3 + H\left[rP + \left(\frac{K+1}{2}\right)P\right] \tag{9.12}$$

To complete the determination of average transfer delay, the average number of retransmissions, H, must be determined in terms of the other network parameters, S, G, and K. As a first step in determining H, define the probabilities q_n and q_t as follows:

> q_n—The probability of a successful transmission, given that the transmission is with a new packet; and
>
> q_t—The probability of a successful transmission given that the transmission is a retransmission.

The probability, p_i, that a given packet requires exactly i retransmissions can now be expressed in terms of q_n and q_t as

$$p_i = (1 - q_n)(1 - q_t)^{i-1} q_t, \qquad i \geq 1 \tag{9.13}$$

The average number of retransmissions is determined from p_i by the equation

$$H = \sum_{i=1}^{\infty} i \, p_i \tag{9.14}$$

Substituting (9.13) into (9.14) then gives, after some algebraic simplification,

$$H = \frac{1 - q_n}{q_t} \tag{9.15}$$

Substitution of (9.15) into (9.12) gives an expression for average transfer delay in terms of q_n and q_t:

$$T = P + P/2 + \tau/3 + \left(\frac{1 - q_n}{q_t}\right)\left[rP + \left(\frac{K + 1}{2}\right)P\right] \tag{9.16}$$

As in discussions of other protocols, it is useful to obtain a normalized transfer delay, $\hat{T}$, by dividing the unnormalized quantity by the packet transmission time, P. Thus, dividing both sides of (9.16) by P yields

$$\hat{T} = 1.5 + a/3 + \left(\frac{1 - q_n}{q_t}\right)[r + K/2 + 0.5] \tag{9.17}$$

where $a = \tau/P$ is the normalized end-to-end propagation delay.

Determination of q_n and q_t in terms of S, G, and K is a straightforward, but relatively tedious, application of elementary probability theory. To avoid being sidetracked from the main analytic thrust, this determination is discussed in an appendix to the chapter. The results of the calculation are the following:

$$q_t = \left[\frac{e^{-G/K} - e^{-G}}{1 - e^{-G}}\right]\left[e^{-G/K} + \frac{G}{K}e^{-G}\right]^{K-1} e^{-S} \tag{9.18}$$

and

$$q_n = \left[e^{-G/K} + \frac{G}{K}e^{-G}\right]^{K} e^{-S} \tag{9.19}$$

It is also shown in the appendix that both q_t and q_n become equal to e^{-G} in the limit as $K \to \infty$.

Returning now to the general discussion, it follows from (9.2) that S/G is the probability of a successful transmission. Thus G/S is the average number of times a packet must be transmitted until success, and it follows from the definition of H that

$$1 + H = G/S \tag{9.20}$$

Using (9.15) in (9.20) and solving for S then gives

$$S = G\left[\frac{q_t}{1 + q_t - q_n}\right] \tag{9.21}$$

which is a more accurate relation between S and G than that given by (9.4). Equation (9.21) reduces to (9.4), as it should, for infinite K, as can be seen by substituting the limiting values of q_n and q_t in (9.21). As previously noted, both of these quantities approach e^{-G} as $K \to \infty$.

Equations (9.18), (9.19), and (9.21) are a set of nonlinear simultaneous, transcendental equations from which, in principle, q_t and q_n can be eliminated to relate S to G for fixed values of K. Unfortunately, an analytic solution to these equations is difficult, if not impossible, to obtain. A numerical solution is, however, relatively straightforward and can be carried out as follows. Multiply the right-hand side of (9.21) by e^S/e^S. Then use (9.18) and (9.19) to express $e^S q_n$ and $e^S q_t$ as functions of G and K. Substitute the results into (9.21) to get

$$S B(G, K) + S e^S = A(G, K) \tag{9.22}$$

where $A(G, K)$ and $B(G, K)$ are respectively $G e^S q_t$ and $(e^S q_t - e^S q_n)$, both of which depend only on G and K. A sequence of numerical values can now be substituted for G and K and, for each choice, $A(G, K)$ and $B(G, K)$ can be determined. The solution is completed by solving (9.22) for S by trial and error for each computed pair of $A(G, K)$ and $B(G, K)$.

Numerical results for S versus G obtained in this manner are plotted in Fig. 9.9 for $K = 2$, 5, and 20. The limiting case of $K \to \infty$ is also included in the figure. Table 9.3, which lists values of $H = (1 - q_n)/q_t$ as a function of S for different values of K and G, is also obtained as a byproduct of the calculation.

In the curves of Fig. 9.9, note that the maximum throughput occurs for $G = 1$ for all values of K. The maximum throughput improves as K increases, reaching a peak value of $S = 1/e \simeq 0.368$ for $K \to \infty$. Most of the variation with K occurs before $K = 20$, and this value produces a result very close to the limiting case.

Turn now to normalized average transfer delay as given by (9.17), and note that this quantity depends on the normalized end-to-end propagation delay, a, on r, which is the smallest integer greater than $2a$, on K, the backoff time parameter, and on $H = (1 - q_n)/q_t$, which is tabulated in Table 9.3. To obtain typical results, a is set to 0.01 and r to 1. For these choices, and with

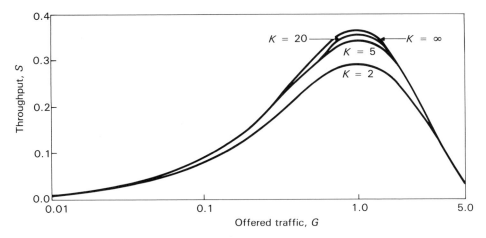

Figure 9.9 **Throughput versus Offered Traffic for Slotted ALOHA**
$(K = 2, 5, 20,$ and $\infty)$

corresponding values of K, S, and H chosen from Table 9.3, curves of T versus S are constructed with Eq. (9.17). The resulting curves are given in Fig. 9.10.

In Fig. 9.10, it is possible to choose a T–S contour by varying K, which minimizes T for fixed values of S. Such an optimum curve is shown as a dashed line in the figure. Note that because of stability, as discussed briefly in Chapter 6 and in more detail in the next section, the optimum curve does not follow a given K contour past the knee, but moves up to the curve for the next value of K as the knee of a given curve is passed. If it were desirable to devise a dynamic backoff strategy that approximated the optimum curve, the backoff for small S should be small and it should increase as S increases, in keeping with the way in which K varies along the optimum curve.

To conclude this section, it is useful to derive an expression for the average number of stations that are backlogged (i.e., have a packet awaiting transmis-

Table 9.3 $H = (1 - q_n)/q_t$ **Tabulated as a Function of S**

	K = 2		K = 5		K = 20		K = 40		K = 100	
G	S	H	S	H	S	H	S	H	S	H
0.1	.084	.1948	.088	.1278	.09	.1101	.09	.1073	.091	.1068
0.2	.1435	.3855	.158	.2659	.162	.2304	.163	.2259	.163	.2226
0.5	.247	1.0174	.286	.7470	.299	.6689	.301	.6583	.302	.6519
1.0	.294	2.4028	.347	1.8777	.363	1.7485	.365	1.7314	.368	1.7269
1.5	.276	4.4281	.322	3.6491	.332	3.5077	.335	3.5001	.335	3.4900
3.0	.145	19.6493	.152	18.6665	.15	18.9456	.15	19.0280	.15	19.0694
5.0	.036	136.8246	.034	143.4445	.034	146.7928	.033	146.9229	.034	147.3268

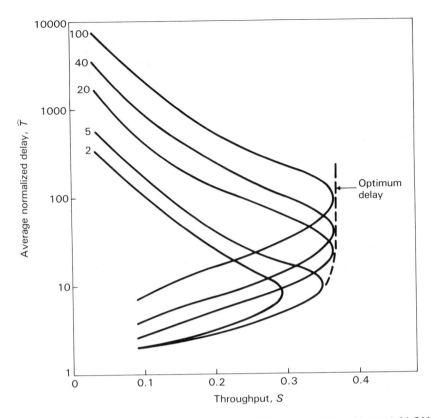

Figure 9.10 Average Normalized Delay versus Throughput for Slotted ALOHA
$(a = 0.01, r = 1, K = 2, 5, 20, 40, 100)$

sion). The average backoff delay, or the average time for all retransmissions of a packet, has been determined in conjunction with the derivation of Eq. (9.12) and is given by $H\,[rP + (K + 1)P/2]$. The average number of retransmissions, H, has also been discussed, and representative values are tabulated versus S in Table 9.3.

Since backoff delay is equivalent to queueing delay in a queueing system, Little's Law can be used to determine the average number, n, in the backlog. The arrival rate to a station is given by S/P packets/second. The product of this arrival rate with the average backoff delay is thus the average number in the backlog so that

$$n = \frac{S}{P} H \left[rP + \left(\frac{K + 1}{2} \right) P \right] \tag{9.23}$$

Equation (9.23), of course, reduces to

$$n = SH \left[r + \frac{1}{2} + \frac{K}{2} \right] \tag{9.24}$$

Curves of n versus S can be constructed from (9.24) using Table 9.3 for appropriate values of H. Such curves are used in the discussion of stability in Subsection 9.3.3.

As a final comment, simulation studies indicate that the delay performance of slotted ALOHA depends principally on the mean retransmission delay of a packet and is not sensitive to actual probability distributions of retransmission times (see Lam [1]). Thus the mean retransmission delay, $P(K - 1)/2$ seconds, is of much greater importance in determining the delay performance of slotted ALOHA than is the fact that each possible backoff integer is equally likely.

9.3.3 Stability Considerations

In Subsection 9.3.2, a set of analytic expressions is derived to relate average transfer delay to throughput, and throughput to offered traffic. The results are plotted in Figs. 9.7, 9.9, and 9.10. A study of Figs. 9.7 and 9.9 shows that two values of offered traffic, G, seem to exist for each value of throughput, S. Similarly, Fig. 9.10 indicates two different average delay values for each value of throughput. This apparent contradiction is explained by stability considerations for the slotted ALOHA protocol.

A major assumption in all of the analyses is that of statistical equilibrium. It is now shown that this assumption is not always justified, and that both the number of stations, M, and the mean backoff time are major factors in determining stability. Another factor of importance is the average number of stations in the backlog, n. This quantity is related to throughput, S, by Eq. (9.24).

Before stability is discussed, a comment on one of the assumptions is in order. Most of the analysis in earlier sections assumes that the population of users is infinite. Such an assumption is used to obtain the expression for n in (9.24).

It is shown, for at least one model in Subsection 9.3.1, that the infinite population model adequately approximates finite user population behavior, provided that the number of stations, M, is reasonably large, for example, greater than 20. In fact, other studies show that the approximation of a reasonably-sized finite population of users by an infinite one tends to be valid for many relationships of interest in the design of local networks, including those with more complicated protocols than slotted ALOHA. Thus the relationship between the average number of stations in the backlog and throughput, Eq. (9.24), and other results from Subsection 9.3.2, are used as an approximation to the finite user population case, even though the result is derived with the assumption of an infinite population of users.

To approach the stability question, consider the average backlog–throughput relation of (9.24). Since this equation is derived under assumed equilibrium conditions, throughput is the normalized input and output packet rate because they are equal. The relationship is to be used, however, to afford insight into a dynamic rather than an equilibrium situation. First, the relation, as previously noted, is used to approximate behavior for any suitably large value of M, the number of users. Second, (9.24) is viewed as giving the relationship between average backlog and the normalized *output* packet rate.

An equation is now developed for a normalized *input* packet rate such that the simultaneous solution of the new equation with (9.24) produces an equilibrium value of throughput when normalized input and output packet rates are equal.

The new equation results from the following reasoning. For a finite population of M users with an average of n stations backlogged and waiting, $(M - n)$ stations can generate new packets. Let the probability of one free station generating a packet be denoted σ. It then follows that the total input packet rate, S, from the $(M - n)$ free stations is given by

$$S = (M - n)\,\sigma \tag{9.25}$$

With M and σ constant, (9.25) defines a straight line in the (n, S) plane. The slope of this line is $-\sigma$, and its intercepts on the n and S axes are respectively M and $M\sigma$. At equilibrium, the input packet rate as given by (9.25) must be equal to the output packet rate as given by (9.24) and plotted in Fig. 9.11.

The simultaneous solution of (9.25) and (9.24) can be achieved by using the straight line of (9.25) as a load line superimposed on a member of the family of curves from Fig. 9.11, as shown for typical cases in Fig. 9.12. The intersections of the throughput–backlog curve and the load line are the points at which the two values of S are equal; hence these points specify possible operating, or equilibrium, values of throughput. Four possible cases are shown in Fig. 9.12.

Before considering these cases, it is appropriate to define stability in the context of slotted ALOHA and other contention networks. A random access protocol is said to be stable when its load line intersects (nontangentially) the throughput curve in exactly one place. The following arguments show why this definition makes sense. Otherwise, the channel is said to be unstable. (This definition is due to Kleinrock and Lam [3].) Note in Fig. 9.12 that cases (a) and (c) represent stable conditions, whereas (b) and (d) are unstable.

The figures indicate that a channel may have up to three possible equilibrium points. An equilibrium point is said to be stable if it is possible for operation to remain at or about that point for a finite period of time. It is said to be globally stable if it is the only stable equilibrium point. If there are more than one stable equilibrium points, each is said to be locally stable. Finally, an equilibrium point is said to be unstable if operation immediately drifts away from it.

It is now useful to consider the four cases separately. In Fig. 9.12(a), M is relatively small, the system is lightly loaded, and the backlog is small at the equilibrium operating point P. To show that this operating point is stable, consider what happens if a statistical fluctuation in input traffic moves the point of operation from P to A, where the backlog is much larger. The throughput is temporarily at A and the input is at B. Since A is greater than B, the output is instantaneously greater than the input, which reduces the

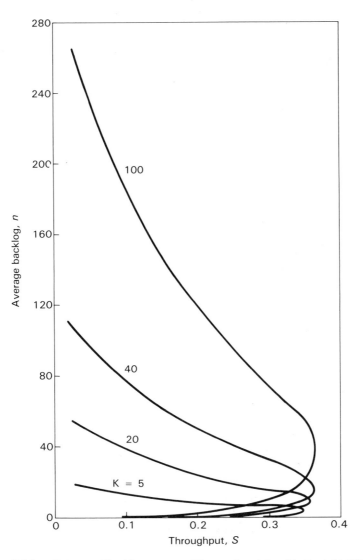

Figure 9.11 **Average Backlog versus Throughput for Slotted ALOHA**
($K = 5, 20, 40, 100$)

backlog so that the point of operation moves back towards P. Similarly, any decrease in input load causes the output to decrease, thereby increasing the backlog. Thus P is stable, and since no other stable point exists, it is globally stable and it follows that the channel is stable.

Now consider the second case for which the number of stations, M, is increased, keeping σ constant, so that the load line is shifted to the position shown in Fig. 9.12(b). There are now three possible points of equilibrium. However, only two of them are locally stable, and the third is unstable. First

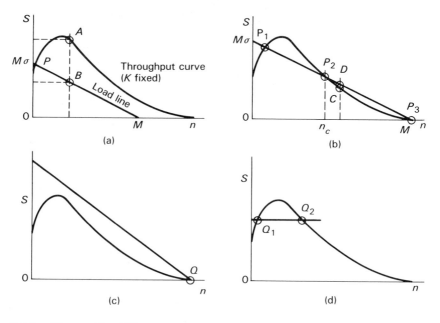

(a)

(b)

(c)

(d)

Figure 9.12   Channel Stability:

    (a) Stable

    (b) Unstable but locally bistable

    (c) Stable but overloaded

    (d) Unstable

consider P_1. For small changes in load either way, the argument given for the case of Fig. 9.12(a) is valid, so P_1 is locally stable. At P_2, the situation is different. If the backlog increases momentarily to C, the output drops faster than the input (because C is below D); thus the backlog is further increased, and the point of operation moves towards P_3. On the other hand, a momentary change to the left of P_2 drives the point of operation towards P_1. Finally, P_3 can be shown to be locally stable in the same manner as P_1.

    Thus, in this case, the channel has a bistable nature with one of the stable points, P_1, giving large throughput and small delay, and with the other, P_3, giving almost zero throughput and very large delay. This latter point corresponds to channel saturation and is clearly a very undesirable operating condition. Both P_1 and P_3 are locally stable, but neither is globally stable. At each of these points, quasistationary conditions prevail for some finite period of time, but eventually the backlog changes to the other condition. In the case of P_1, this occurs when the backlog, due to some statistical fluctuation, becomes greater than the critical backlog, n_c (the backlog at P_2). Similarly, equilibrium switches from P_3 to P_1 when n becomes instantaneously less than n_c. Thus the channel flip-flops between the two locally stable states. In practice, the network operates in one or the other of the stable states for a very long period of time. However, the channel must eventually switch its

*Chapter 9   **Random Access Networks***

equilibrium point. Since the network is essentially blocked at P_3, a bistable channel as shown in Fig. 9.12 is not acceptable to a network designer or user. With no globally stable point of operation, a channel is obviously unstable.

Figure 9.12(c) shows what happens when the number of users is increased further with σ still constant. Now the channel is completely overloaded, and even though the network is globally stable, equilibrium occurs at channel saturation, Q.

To consider the infinite population case, let the product of M and σ have the value of $M\sigma$ used in Fig. 9.12(a). Now increase M, thereby decreasing σ, with $M\sigma$ held constant. As $M \rightarrow \infty$, the load line becomes horizontal, as shown in Fig. 9.12(d). Although only two possible equilibrium points, Q_1 and Q_2, are shown, a third exists at $n = \infty$. The point Q_1 is again locally stable, Q_2 is unstable, and the point at infinity is also locally stable. Thus, the infinite population slotted ALOHA is unstable.

It is always possible to stabilize an unstable channel for a practical network by increasing the backoff factor K. Consider Fig. 9.13, in which with backoff K_1, the channel is unstable, with two locally stable equilibrium points. Now increase K_1 to K_2, which makes the channel stable. However, the point of operation is now Q_1, instead of P_1, which means that stability has been achieved at the cost of reduced throughput and increased average backlog and delay.

As a general comment, the results of Subsection 9.3.2 are not sufficient to characterize the performance of slotted ALOHA completely because stability must be taken into consideration. The curves obtained in that section do, however, give the locus of possible operating points and indicate how the parameters are interrelated. Of course, in an ideal situation of fixed constant load in the steady state, the results do give a complete characterization.

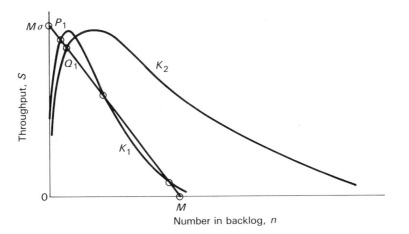

Figure 9.13   **Stabilizing a Slotted ALOHA Channel by Increasing the Backoff Time**

For unstable channels, a measure of channel stability has been defined by Kleinrock and Lam [3]. Since the slotted ALOHA channel is essentially unstable, it is necessary that the network be able to adapt to different loading conditions, minimizing delays as much as possible and providing stable throughput. A number of such adaptive control procedures have been proposed, notably by Lam and Kleinrock [4].

9.4 Protocols that Use Carrier Sensing

Carrier-sense multiple access (CSMA) protocols are refinements on the pure and slotted ALOHA protocols, with the refinements achieved through use of additional hardware at each station to sense the transmissions of other stations. The carrier-sense information is used to minimize the length of collision intervals. For carrier sensing to be effective, however, propagation delays must be less than packet transmission times. If such is not the case, the carrier-sense information is received too late to be effective in accomplishing its purpose. As might be expected, the ratio of propagation delay to packet transmission time becomes an important parameter in performance studies of CSMA.

Access procedures that make use of carrier sensing have most of the characteristics of slotted ALOHA, with additional decisions made on the basis of the carrier-sense information. There are several ways in which this information is used, and this gives rise to two general classes of CSMA protocols: nonpersistent and p-persistent. Operation for each of these classes can be slotted or nonslotted.

For slotted operation, CSMA protocols quantize time into slots of τ seconds, where τ is normally the end-to-end propagation delay of a bus or the maximum round-trip delay for any station on a broadband tree network. This choice of slot size should be contrasted to that of packet transmission time as used by slotted ALOHA. Like the slotted ALOHA, however, all stations for slotted CSMA operation must synchronize and are forced to start transmission only at the beginning of a slot. The information that packets have been sensed on the bus is used at the beginning of the slots.

In the remainder of Section 9.4, nonpersistent CSMA, both slotted and nonslotted, is analyzed to obtain throughput–load relationships. Similar results are presented without proof for other forms of CSMA. The results for the different methods are compared, and the sensitivity of the maximum throughput to normalized propagation delay is studied. The section concludes with some consideration of delay and stability in CSMA networks.

9.4.1 Persistent and Nonpersistent CSMA Protocols

The CSMA protocols share with other contention-type networks the physical block diagram of Fig. 9.2, which assumes baseband-type operation. The transceiver contains the carrier-sense hardware, which serves the function often described as *listen before transmit*.

The several CSMA protocols can be described with the flow chart of Fig. 9.14, which is an extension of that given in Fig. 9.5 for slotted ALOHA to include a "carrier-sense strategy" box. The diagram also shows a dashed delay box, which is included for slotted operation along with a quantization of all variables to slots.

As a reference point, the flow chart of Fig. 9.14 becomes that of Fig. 9.5 for slotted ALOHA if the carrier-sense box is replaced by the direct connection shown in the figure, and if slotting to packet transmission times is used.

The CSMA protocols differ from slotted ALOHA only by the inclusion of decisions based on carrier sensing. The several CSMA procedures differ among themselves in how the decisions are made. In all cases, as the figure

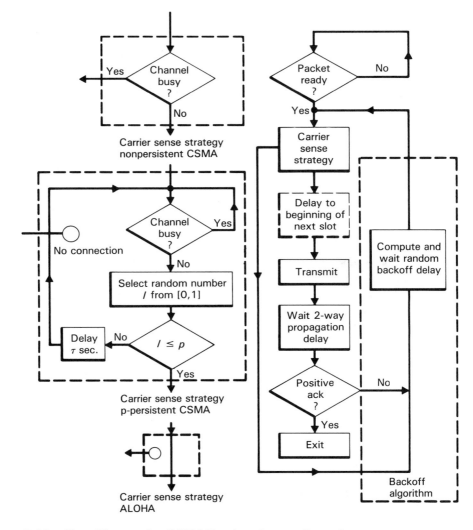

Figure 9.14   Flow Diagram for CSMA Random Access Procedures

shows, when a station learns that its transmission is unsuccessful, it reschedules the transmission of the packet to a later time by using some specified backoff algorithm. After the backoff, the station again senses the channel and repeats the algorithm specified by the protocol. If, at some point, a station has a packet ready for transmission, it is termed a ready station, irrespective of whether the packet is new (just generated) or a retransmission.

Nonpersistent CSMA is considered first, using the appropriate carrier-sense box in Fig. 9.14. With this protocol, interference between packet transmissions is minimized because a packet that finds the channel busy is always rescheduled. When a station becomes ready, the channel is sensed, and the following algorithm is carried out.

1. If the channel is sensed idle, the packet is transmitted; or
2. If the channel is sensed busy, the station uses the backoff algorithm to reschedule the packet to a later time. After the backoff, the channel is sensed again, and the algorithm is repeated.

A special case of the p-persistent CSMA protocol is now considered for $p = 1$. Reference should be made to the appropriate carrier-sense strategy in Fig. 9.14. The 1-persistent protocol never allows the channel to go unused when there is a ready station. The algorithm proceeds as follows. A ready station senses the channel and then:

1. If the channel is sensed idle, the packet is transmitted (in the flow chart of Fig. 9.14, the random number selected is always between 0 and 1, and the test always results in "YES"); or
2. If the channel is sensed busy, the station keeps on sensing the channel (i.e., persists) until the channel goes idle, and then it transmits the packet (again with probability 1).

Finally, the general case of p-persistent CSMA is considered. The idea behind making p other than 1 is to reduce the number of collisions in the following way. When two (or more) stations become ready during a busy interval, with 1-persistent CSMA they all wait until the end of the transmission in progress; when it ends, all transmit. Clearly, a collision must then occur (with probability 1). By reducing p so that it is less than 1, the probability of such a collision occurring is reduced.

For general p-persistent operation, a ready station operates as follows after the channel is sensed:

1. If the channel is sensed idle, then with probability p, the station transmits the packet, or with probability $(1 - p)$, the station waits τ seconds, where τ is the end-to-end propagation delay on the bus, and the algorithm is repeated; or
2. If the channel is sensed busy, then the station persists in sensing the channel until it becomes idle, and then it operates as in step 1.

As noted, slotted versions of all the preceding protocols can be considered by quantizing time into slots of length τ seconds and by synchronizing stations so that transmissions can begin only at the start of a slot.

9.4.2 Throughput Analysis of Nonpersistent CSMA

This subsection gives an approximate analysis of nonpersistent CSMA comparable in accuracy to that given in Subsection 9.3.1 for slotted ALOHA. The basic assumptions are as follows:

- The number of users is infinite and the arrival process from this infinite population is Poisson; the process includes both new and previously collided packets;
- The propagation delay is assumed to be τ seconds between any two stations, where τ is the maximum one-way propagation delay on the bus;
- All packets have the same length and the same transmission time, P seconds. In the case of slotted protocols, considered in Subsection 9.4.3, P is an integer multiple of τ seconds;
- At any point in time, each station has at most one packet ready for transmission, including any previously collided packets;
- Carrier sensing takes place instantaneously, and there are no turn-around delays in switching from transmitting to receiving;
- The channel is noiseless so that failure of transmission is due to collisions only; and
- The overlap of any fraction of two packets results in destructive interference so that both packets must be retransmitted.

With respect to the assumption about propagation time between stations, the number of collisions for any station pair tends to be exaggerated when this time is set to the maximum time. Thus the results obtained from the model for the value of throughput for a given value of offered traffic tend to be pessimistic (i.e., on the high side). It has been shown, however, that this assumption does not in general seriously affect the results obtained with the model.

Relative to the assumptions as a group, the major restrictions result from the facts that the number of users is assumed to be infinite and that no distinction is made between newly generated and retransmitted packets. These restrictions are, of course, present in the model developed in Subsection 9.3.1 for slotted ALOHA.

For slotted ALOHA, a more accurate model was also developed from which it is possible to judge the accuracy of the simpler model. It was shown for slotted ALOHA that the simpler model is reasonably accurate for M greater than 20. Unfortunately, it is not feasible within the level of the present text to develop models for CSMA of the type developed in Subsection 9.3.2 for slotted ALOHA. Nevertheless, it is not unreasonable to conclude that the models to be developed for CSMA protocols display roughly the same accuracy, and that they depend on M and other parameters in much the same manner as for slotted ALOHA.

To begin the analysis, recall that G denotes the average number of attempted transmissions, successful and otherwise, for P seconds of channel time, and that S, the throughput, is defined as the number of successful transmissions in the same packet time. Assuming statistical equilibrium, it then follows that S/P is the average arrival rate of newly generated packets to the network (in packets/second) and G/P is the total average arrival rate of packets to the network (in packets/second) both newly generated and retransmitted.

Nonpersistent CSMA can be analyzed with the help of Fig. 9.15. The packet labeled 0 is assumed to arrive for transmission at a reference station at a time, t, when the channel is idle to all users. Since the channel is sensed idle, the packet is transmitted immediately and requires the packet transmission time of P seconds. With the given assumptions, the propagation delay to any other station is τ seconds. Therefore, for τ seconds, the other stations do not sense packet 0, and if these stations have arrivals in the time interval $[t, t + \tau]$, they initiate packets as shown in the figure. Packet n is the last packet that arrives for transmission at a random time Y less than $(t + \tau)$.

After time $(t + \tau)$, all stations have sensed the packets on the channel and,

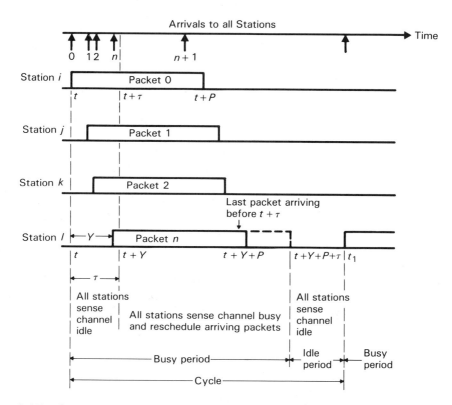

Figure 9.15   Components of a Cycle Containing an Unsuccessful Busy Period for Nonpersistent CSMA

Chapter 9   Random Access Networks

according to the nonpersistent CSMA protocol, further arriving packets, such as packet $(n + 1)$, defer and are rescheduled for transmission at a later time. Transmission of packet n is completed by time $(t + Y + P)$. All stations sense the end of this packet by time $(t + Y + P + \tau)$, but up until this time, all packets for transmission are rescheduled for a later time.

After time $(t + Y + P + \tau)$, all stations sense the channel as idle, and the next arrival at t_1 initiates a packet transmission to start another cycle. The intervals $[t, t + Y + P + \tau]$ and $[t + Y + P + \tau, t_1]$ are called a *busy period* and an *idle period* respectively. A cycle consists of a busy period and an idle period, although an idle period can have zero length because of the way the busy period is defined (with the extra τ).

The busy period shown in Fig. 9.15 is an unsuccessful transmission period. On the other hand, if no packets arrive to other stations in the interval $[t, t + \tau]$, no collision occurs, $Y = 0$, and the busy period is a successful transmission period, as shown in Fig. 9.16.

From this argument, it is clear that the vulnerable period for CSMA protocols is the maximum one-way propagation delay, τ seconds. This compares very favorably, provided $\tau < P$, with vulnerable periods of P and $2P$ for slotted and pure ALOHA respectively.

Throughput is now calculated for the nonpersistent CSMA channel just described. Let U denote the time during a cycle that the channel is used without collisions and $\overline{U}$ denote its average value. If $\overline{I}$ and $\overline{B}$ denote the average length in time of the idle period and the busy period respectively, then throughput can be expressed as

$$S = \frac{\overline{U}}{\overline{I} + \overline{B}} \tag{9.26}$$

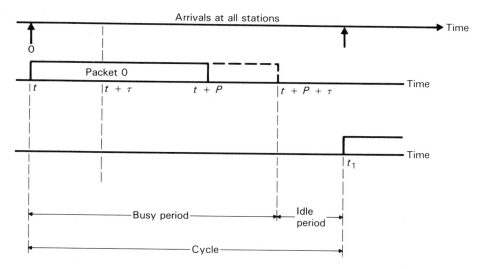

Figure 9.16 Components of a Cycle that Contains a Successful Busy Period for CSMA

This equation follows from the facts that all cycles are statistically similar, assuming steady-state conditions exist, and that throughput is the ratio of average time transmitting successful packets to total time. $\overline{U}$, $\overline{I}$, and $\overline{B}$ remain to be evaluated.

A good transmission occurs for packet 0 if no other packet is transmitted to interfere with it. The probability of this event, P_s, is equal to the fraction of time good transmissions occur. Each packet transmission, good or bad, is of length P seconds. Therefore, the average time in a cycle when the transmission is successful, $\overline{U}$, is given by

$$\overline{U} = P \cdot P \{\text{packet 0 is a good transmission}\} = P \, P_s \tag{9.27}$$

The probability that packet 0 is a good transmission is equal to the probability that no packets arrive in the vulnerable interval $[t, t + \tau]$. Arrivals are distributed with a Poisson distribution with average arrival rate (from both new and retransmitted packets) G/P packets per second. Thus

$$P_s = P \{0 \text{ arrivals in } \tau \text{ seconds}\} = e^{(-G/P)\tau} \tag{9.28}$$

and

$$\overline{U} = P e^{-G\tau/P} \tag{9.29}$$

The busy period has a random length, B, given by

$$B = Y + P + \tau \tag{9.30}$$

where $Y = 0$ in the case of a successful transmission (see Figs. 9.15 and 9.16). The average value of B, $\overline{B}$, thus becomes

$$\overline{B} = P + \tau + \overline{Y} \tag{9.31}$$

since Y is the only random quantity on the right-hand side of (9.30). The distribution functions of Y and then $\overline{Y}$ are computed from further consideration of the arrival process. The distribution function of Y, $F_Y(y)$, is defined as

$$F_Y(y) = P \{Y \leq y\} \tag{9.32}$$

Since $t + Y$ is the time of the last packet arrival in the interval $[t, t + \tau]$, $P\{Y \leq y\}$ is equal to the probability of no arrivals in the interval $[y, \tau]$. (Recall that the first arrival is packet 0 at time τ to initiate the reference cycle.) The probability of no arrivals in $[y, \tau]$ is computed from the Poisson arrival distribution as

$$F_Y(y) = P \{0 \text{ arrivals in } (\tau - y) \text{ seconds}\} = e^{-G(\tau-y)/P} \tag{9.33}$$

for $0 < y \leq \tau$. The distribution function of Y is sketched in Fig. 9.17. Note that there is a "jump" of size $e^{-G\tau/P}$ at $y = 0$, which indicates that the probability of no packet arriving in $(t, t + \tau]$ is $e^{-G\tau/P}$. This is, of course, the probability that packet 0 is successful.

Using standard techniques, the average value of Y is evaluated as

$$\overline{Y} = \tau - \frac{P}{G} (1 - e^{-G\tau/P}) \tag{9.34}$$

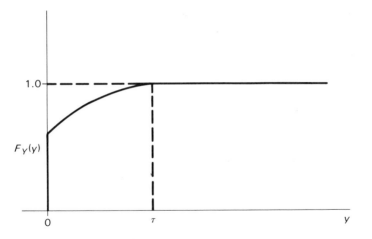

Figure 9.17   Probability Distribution Function for the Random Variable _Y_

and then from (9.31), the average busy period is

$$\overline{B} = P + 2\tau - \frac{P}{G}(1 - e^{-G\tau/P}) \tag{9.35}$$

Note that for very small G, (9.35) gives an average busy period of $(P + \tau)$, the length of a successful transmission period.

To complete the evaluation of throughput using (9.26), it remains to evaluate the average duration of an idle period, $\overline{I}$. Since the arrival process is Poisson, the interarrival times are exponentially distributed with mean P/G seconds. Such a process has what is termed the *memoryless property* (i.e., in observing a memoryless channel, the average wait for a new arrival from any randomly chosen point in time is the same and equal to the mean of the interarrival time distribution).

The idle period is just the time interval between the end of a busy period and the next arrival to the network. With the end of a busy period as the point in time at which the channel is observed, the mean idle period becomes

$$\overline{I} = P/G \tag{9.36}$$

Applying (9.26) and using the expressions found for $\overline{U}$, $\overline{B}$, and $\overline{I}$, the throughput is obtained as

$$S = \frac{Pe^{-G\tau/P}}{P + 2\tau - \dfrac{P}{G}(1 - e^{-G\tau/P}) + P/G} \tag{9.37}$$

which reduces to

$$S = \frac{G\,e^{-G(\tau/P)}}{G(1 + 2\tau/P) + e^{-G(\tau/P)}} \tag{9.38}$$

The expression of (9.38) contains the parameter τ/P, the ratio of propagation time to transmission time for one packet. As in earlier chapters, this parameter is given the symbol a so that

$$a = \tau/P \tag{9.39}$$

and

$$S = \frac{G\,e^{-aG}}{G\,(1 + 2a) + e^{-aG}} \tag{9.40}$$

Curves of the final relationship between S and G are given in Fig. 9.18 for several values of a. From (9.40), it follows that throughput for $a = 0$ is given by

$$S = G/(1 + G) \tag{9.41}$$

Note from this equation that a throughput of unity can be obtained, theoretically, for an infinite offered traffic. From Fig. 9.18, it is clear that as a becomes small, throughput approaches closer to this limiting value for large values of G. This is the case since carrier sensing gives better information about the true state of the channel at the position of a given station when a is a small quantity.

9.4.3 Throughput Analysis for Slotted Nonpersistent CSMA

This subsection presents the approximate analysis of slotted nonpersistent CSMA, which parallels that for nonslotted nonpersistent CSMA given in Subsection 9.4.2. The basic assumptions used in the analysis are those listed in

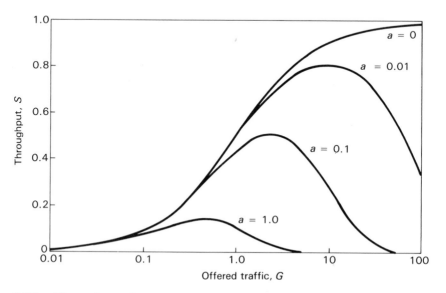

Figure 9.18   Throughput, S, versus Offered Load, G, for Nonpersistent CSMA

Subsection 9.4.2 with, of course, the additional quantization of time into slots of length τ.

A diagram for slotted nonpersistent CSMA, corresponding to Fig. 9.15 for the unslotted case, is given in Fig. 9.19. The analysis proceeds in much the same manner as for the unslotted case. The channel is assumed idle prior to the first slot, and at least one packet for transmission is assumed to arrive during the first slot so that packet 0 is initiated at the beginning of the second slot, as shown in the figure. If arrivals occur at more than one station during the interval of the first slot, these arrivals also cause packets to be transmitted at their respective stations, as shown. Packets are assumed to require a transmission time P, which is an integer number of slots. During the slots that are occupied by the packet 0, and possibly other packets, stations with arriving packets sense the channel to be busy, and their packets defer to be transmitted at a later time.

As can be observed from Fig. 9.19, each busy period is exactly $(P + \tau)$ seconds in length, irrespective of whether it is a successful or unsuccessful transmission period. As in the nonslotted case, the busy period is longer than the packet transmission time by the amount τ, which allows the end of the transmission to be sensed at all stations. Any arrivals during the added slot are

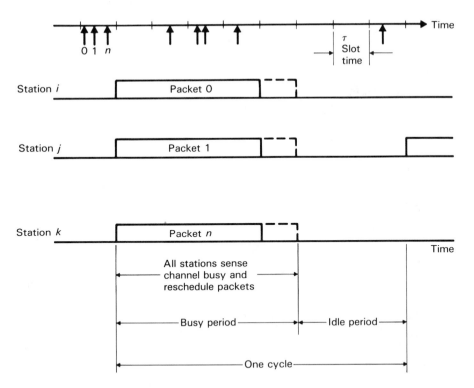

Figure 9.19 **Various Relationships Used in the Analysis of Slotted Nonpersistent CSMA**

processed with carrier-sense data taken at the beginning of the next slot when the channel is idle. Thus, as in the unslotted case, it is possible to have a cycle with an idle period of length zero. In general, the idle period consists of an integer number of slots with no arrivals, concluded by a slot with at least one arrival to initiate a new busy period.

The slotted protocol can be analyzed in the same manner as the unslotted by computing $\overline{U}, \overline{I}, \overline{B}$, and then S, using Eq. (9.26). For this case, the probability, P_s, that packet 0 is a good transmission is the probability of only one arrival during the last slot of the idle period, given a busy period (i.e., that some arrival occurs). The conditional probability, P_s, can be expressed as

$$P_s = P \text{ \{one arrival in interval } \tau \mid \text{some arrival occurs\}}$$

$$= \frac{P \text{ \{one arrival in interval } \tau \text{ \textit{and} some arrival occurs\}}}{P \text{ \{some arrival occurs\}}} \tag{9.42}$$

The numerator and denominator of (9.42) can be evaluated with the assumed Poisson arrival distribution. Note first, however, that the probability of the event "one arrival in τ \textit{and} some arrival occurs" is equal to the probability of the event "one arrival in τ." Thus, using the Poisson statistics

$$P \text{ \{one arrival in } \tau\} = G(\tau/P)e^{-G(\tau/P)} = aGe^{-aG} \tag{9.43}$$

and

$$P \text{ \{some arrival occurs\}} = 1 - e^{-G(\tau/P)} = 1 - e^{-aG} \tag{9.44}$$

From (9.42), P_s is then determined as

$$P_s = aGe^{-aG}/(1 - e^{-aG}) \tag{9.45}$$

Knowing P_s, $\overline{U}$ can be determined from (9.27) as

$$\overline{U} = P \cdot P_s = P[aGe^{-aG}/(1 - e^{-aG})] \tag{9.46}$$

The average busy period, $\overline{B}$, is easy to obtain for the slotted case since it is always $(P + \tau)$ seconds (see Fig. 9.19). Thus

$$\overline{B} = P + \tau \tag{9.47}$$

The length of the idle period, $\overline{I}$, is always an integer number of slots since a packet can only be transmitted at the beginning of a slot. Furthermore, for an idle slot to be followed by a transmission, one or more arrivals must occur in the idle slot. For the Poisson process, the number of arrivals in disjoint intervals (slots in this case) are independent random variables.

With this background, consider the last slot of a busy period. If there is at least one arrival during this slot, then the next slot will begin a new busy period, and the length of the idle period is zero. This type of reasoning is now extended, using appropriate notation, to determine expressions for the probabilities of idle periods of any length.

Let J denote the length of an idle period in slots. Then, from the preceding reasoning

$$P\{J = 0\} = P\text{ \{at least one arrival in } \tau\}$$

$$= 1 - e^{-G\tau/P} = p \tag{9.48}$$

where p is defined as the probability of at least one arrival in a slot. As a next step, consider $J = 1$. The probability that $J = 1$ is given by

$$P\{J = 1\} = P\text{ \{no arrival in } \tau\}\, P\text{ \{at least one arrival in } \tau\}$$

$$= (1 - p)\, p \tag{9.49}$$

using an obvious extension of the approach used to obtain (9.48). A continuation of this argument shows that

$$P\{J = j\} = (1 - p)^j p \tag{9.50}$$

which defines a geometrically distributed random variable with a mean given by

$$\bar{J} = \frac{1 - p}{p} = \frac{e^{-aG}}{1 - e^{-aG}} \tag{9.51}$$

The average idle period, $\bar{I}$, in seconds, is equal to τ times $\bar{J}$ so that

$$\bar{I} = \tau \bar{J} = \frac{\tau e^{-aG}}{1 - e^{-aG}} \tag{9.52}$$

Now, using the expressions for $\bar{I}$, $\bar{B}$, and $\bar{U}$, given respectively by (9.52), (9.47), and (9.46), S can be expressed as

$$S = \frac{\bar{U}}{\bar{B} + \bar{I}} = \frac{aGe^{-aG}}{1 - e^{-aG} + a} \tag{9.53}$$

It follows from (9.53) that in the limit as $a \to 0$, S is given by $G/(1 + G)$, the same result as is obtained for the nonslotted case.

A family of throughput versus offered load curves is plotted in Fig. 9.20, using (9.53), with a as a parameter.

9.4.4   Additional CSMA Results and Performance Studies

In the previous two subsections, analytic results that relate throughput and offered load have been obtained for slotted and nonslotted nonpersistent CSMA, using a model that is tractable and gives reasonable accuracy. Essentially the same assumptions can be used to obtain results for slotted and nonslotted 1-persistent CSMA. The analyses parallel those given previously; however, some of the details are more tedious. Since the basic approach is well illustrated by the analyses of nonpersistent CSMA in Subsections 9.4.2 and 9.4.3, the results for 1-persistent CSMA are stated in the following equations without proof.

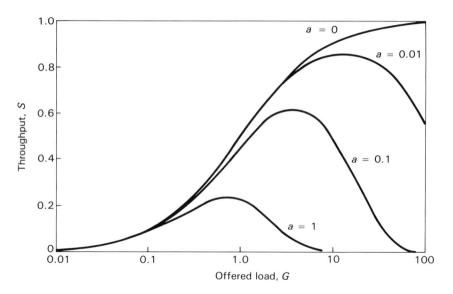

Figure 9.20 Throughput, *S*, versus Offered Traffic, *G*, for Slotted Nonpersistent CSMA

The results, as derived by Kleinrock and Tobagi [5], are

1-persistent CSMA

$$S = \frac{G[1 + G + aG(1 + G + aG/2)]\, e^{-G(1 + 2a)}}{G(1 + 2a) - (1 - e^{-aG}) + (1 + aG)\, e^{-G(1 + a)}} \tag{9.54}$$

Slotted 1-persistent CSMA

$$S = \frac{G\, e^{-G(1 + a)}\, [1 + a - e^{-aG}]}{(1 + a)(1 - e^{-aG}) + a\, e^{-G(1 + a)}} \tag{9.55}$$

Figure 9.21 presents a plot of the throughput versus load performance of all the protocols for which analytical expressions are given in the text up to this point for a fixed value of normalized propagation delay $a = 0.01$. The protocols represented are pure and slotted ALOHA, and both nonslotted and slotted nonpersistent and 1-persistent CSMA. The equations that give the results that are plotted are, respectively, (6.15), (9.4), (9.40), (9.53), (9.54), and (9.55).

The curves show that for small values of offered traffic, *G*, the persistent methods have the best throughput, whereas at large values of offered traffic, the nonpersistent methods win out. Studies done by Kleinrock and Tobagi [5] show that the *p*-persistent CSMA protocols for $0 \le p < 1$, which are not shown in Fig. 9.21, have an *S–G* performance somewhat between 1-persistent CSMA and nonpersistent CSMA.

The equations used to obtain the curves in Fig. 9.21 can also be used to plot

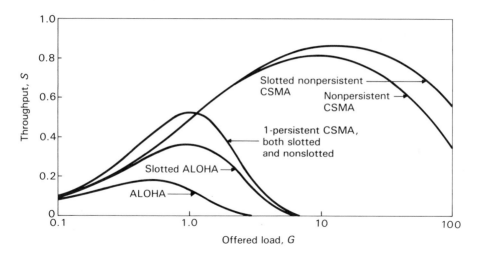

Figure 9.21 Comparison of the *S* versus *G* Characteristics of ALOHA, Slotted ALOHA, and Nonpersistent, Slotted Nonpersistent, and 1-persistent CSMA, both Slotted and Nonslotted, all for *a* = 0.01

channel capacity versus normalized propagation delay. (Recall that channel capacity is defined as the maximum value of throughput over all offered loads.) The curves of channel capacity versus *a*, which are given in Fig. 9.22, show that each class of protocol has a distinctive variation of capacity with *a*. The capacity of the ALOHA methods is independent of *a* and is the largest for all the protocols examined when *a* is large. This can be explained by the fact that, with large propagation delays relative to packet transmission times, carrier sensing provides information too late to improve operation. In fact, for *a* large enough, for example, (*a* > 1), operation is degraded because using badly outdated information in the manner dictated by the access protocol is worse than having no information at all.

The curves of Fig. 9.22 also show that capacity of 1-persistent CSMA is less sensitive to normalized propagation delay for small *a* than is nonpersistent CSMA. However, for small *a*, nonpersistent CSMA has larger capacity than has 1-persistent CSMA, although the situation reverses as *a* approaches the range of 0.3–0.5.

The parameter, *p*, of the *p*-persistent protocol can be chosen for maximum throughput for each value of *a*, and the optimum *p*-persistent capacity can then be examined versus *a*. The result is a curve that lies between the slotted and nonslotted nonpersistent CSMA curves for much of the range of *a* in Fig. 9.22. For *a* greater than, for example, 0.2, the optimum *p*-persistent CSMA gives slightly larger capacity than slotted nonpersistent CSMA.

The problems that arise in attempting to determine the average delay versus load for CSMA are the same as those that arise for pure and slotted ALOHA. The assumption that the total offered channel traffic forms a Poisson process implies that the average retransmission delay is infinite, or at

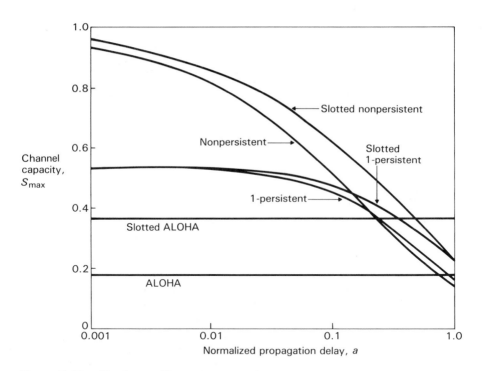

Figure 9.22   Maximum Throughput or Capacity versus Normalized Propagation Delay for Different CSMA Protocols

least large compared to the packet transmission time, P. This of course leads to arbitrarily large average transfer delays. Thus the tractable approach used to obtain the analytic S-G relationships, for example, in Subsections 9.4.2 and 9.4.3, cannot be used to find average transfer delay.

As in the case of slotted ALOHA, an alternate and much more difficult calculation is required to obtain average transfer delay. Tobagi and Kleinrock [6] have used an embedded Markov chain technique to find the average delay–throughput relationship for slotted nonpersistent CSMA. Their model assumes that each backoff delay is chosen independently from an exponential distribution. Even though this protocol is the most tractable of the CSMA protocols, the relationship found is not a simple closed-form analytic expression.

As might be expected, the results of this analysis of slotted nonpersistent CSMA are similar to the curves of Fig. 9.9 for slotted ALOHA, except that the throughputs achieved are much greater, and average delays are much smaller. In the same manner as for slotted ALOHA, an optimum performance envelope to minimize the average delay for each value of throughput can be obtained for the CSMA case.

Since analytical approaches are so intractable, it is usually necessary to employ simulation to find the delay–throughput tradeoffs for contention networks. For this purpose, Kleinrock and Tobagi [5] have developed a simulation model that uses many of the assumptions of the infinite population model given in Subsection 9.4.2. The simulation model departs from these assumptions in two respects: only the newly generated packets are derived independently from a Poisson process, and the retransmission times are chosen independently from a uniform distribution.

Figure 9.23 gives the Kleinrock–Tobagi simulation curves for the throughput-average delay tradeoffs for the ALOHA and CSMA procedures for $a = 0.01$. For each value of throughput, the average delay is optimized with respect to the mean backoff time. Figure 9.9 shows that the optimum p-persistent CSMA protocol gives the best performance; however, nonpersistent CSMA is almost as good.

This section concludes with the question of stability of CSMA protocols. Tobagi and Kleinrock [6] have shown that the model discussed in Subsection 9.3.3 for slotted ALOHA also applies to the CSMA protocols. They show, with particular reference to slotted nonpersistent CSMA, that the same instability problems occur in CSMA as occur in slotted ALOHA. They show further, however, that in practical situations, as long as M is smaller than, for

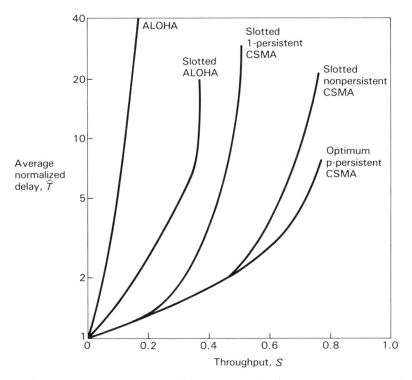

Figure 9.23 **Average Normalized Delay versus Throughput for Different Random Access Protocols (From simulation studies by Kleinrock and Tobagi [5])**

example, 1000, CSMA, with proper backoff strategies, provides essentially true stable performance.

9.5 Protocols that Use Carrier Sensing with Collision Detection

Protocols that use carrier-sense multiple access with collision detection (CSMA/CD) represent a further improvement on those random access procedures discussed previously. Collision detection, also called "listen while transmit," makes it possible to detect a collision shortly after it occurs and thus abort flawed packets promptly, minimizing the channel time occupied by unsuccessful transmissions.

The CSMA/CD protocols are implemented with the same type of physical structure as the protocols discussed previously and shown in the diagram of Fig. 9.2. To implement the additional feature of collision detection, the transceiver must include hardware not only for transmitting and monitoring the channel before transmitting, but, in addition, monitoring while transmitting. For a baseband system, such as is being assumed, the collision detection monitor observes the analog waveform directly from the channel. Thus, when signals from two or more stations are present simultaneously, the composite waveform is distorted from that for a single station in such a manner that collisions can usually be identified by larger than normal voltage amplitudes on the cable.

The CSMA/CD protocols essentially add to basic CSMA procedures the listen-while-transmit feature. Thus these protocols can have the same variations as CSMA: slotted and unslotted; and nonpersistent and p-persistent. For all these variations, the additional feature of collision detection gives improved performance for local networks that use a short bus with bit rates such that the normalized propagation delay is small. As will be established, under these conditions the addition of collision detection produces throughput versus offered load characteristics for CSMA/CD that are superior to those of other types of random access protocols.

Not all local networks have a small normalized propagation delay, however. Thus CSMA/CD is not always the logical choice, and the issue of choosing a random access protocol can become more complicated. Nevertheless, CSMA/CD is perhaps the most useful of the random access procedures for local networks.

The next subsection of the text discusses the basic CSMA/CD operation, including refinements such as collision consensus reinforcement and dynamic backoff schemes. This is followed by a subsection that details throughput analyses for nonpersistent CSMA/CD, both slotted and nonslotted. A similar result for a 1-persistent protocol is also given without proof. A final subsection discusses the sensitivity of throughput to network parameters and compares the throughput–load and delay–throughput tradeoffs for CSMA/CD with those of the other protocols.

9.5.1 Basic Operation

The basic operation of the CSMA/CD protocol can be explained with the aid of the flow diagram of Fig. 9.24. Figure 9.24(a) shows the algorithm for CSMA, discussed in Subsection 9.4.1. To implement CSMA/CD-type operation, the portion of the algorithm enclosed in the double dotted line is replaced by the collision detection-type logic shown in Fig. 9.24(b).

As shown in the figure, the logic of the algorithm is the same as that for CSMA through the transmit operation. After the packet is transmitted, CSMA/CD employs hardware to listen while the transmitted packet is in transit over the cable. If no collisions are detected, a packet is successfully transmitted, and the algorithm is exited. On the other hand, if a collision is detected, the packet is promptly aborted, a jamming signal is transmitted, and the collided packet is backed off in the same manner as for CSMA. The jamming signal and several backoff algorithms are discussed after a more formal statement of the CSMA/CD algorithm. With CSMA, a negative acknowledgment (or lack of a positive acknowledgment) is required to inform a transmitting station of a collision. With CSMA/CD, no such feedback is necessary.

Stated concisely, in the CSMA/CD algorithm, a ready station takes the following action.

- If the channel is sensed idle:
  - —For nonpersistent and 1-persistent CSMA/CD, the packet is transmitted; and
  - —For p-persistent CSMA/CD, the packet is transmitted with probability p, and is delayed by the end-to-end propagation delay, τ seconds, with probability $(1 - p)$;
- If the channel is sensed busy, then:
  - —For nonpersistent CSMA/CD, the packet is backed off and the algorithm is repeated;
  - —For 1-persistent CSMA/CD, the station defers until the channel is sensed idle and then transmits a packet; and
  - —For p-persistent CSMA/CD, the station defers until the channel is idle and then, with probability p, transmits a packet, and with probability $(1 - p)$ delays transmission by τ seconds. In the latter case, after the τ seconds delay, the procedure is repeated;
- If a collision is sensed, the station aborts the packet being transmitted and transmits a jamming signal. The stations of all colliding packets then abort their transmission and backoff; and
- At the time a backed-off packet is to be retransmitted, the algorithm is repeated.

The jamming signal, referred to in the algorithm, is not an essential feature of CSMA/CD, but it is used by common implementations such as Ethernet. The jamming signal serves as a collision consensus enforcement strategy in that a station experiencing interference transmits a jamming signal to ensure that all other stations know of the collision and backoff.

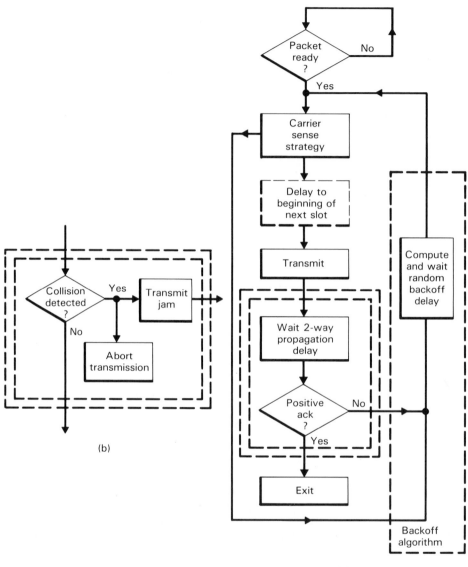

(b)

(a)

Figure 9.24 **Flow Diagram for CSMA/CD. The Box in the Dotted Lines Replaces the Corresponding Box for CSMA; The Carrier Sense Options are the same for CSMA as in Fig. 9.14**

(a) CSMA operation

(b) Collision detect refinement

Commercial CSMA/CD networks seem to favor the l-persistent CSMA/CD protocol using a backoff algorithm such as that used by Ethernet. The Ethernet backoff algorithm is called a *truncated binary exponential type,* one version of which allows an initial attempt plus 15 retransmissions, each delayed by an integer r times the base backoff time. The integer r is selected at random from the discrete distribution, uniform on the set of integers $\{0, \ldots, 2^{k-1}\}$, where k is the minimum of the number of attempted transmissions to date and the integer 10. After 16 attempts, the packet is discarded. The base backoff time is a suitably chosen time increment, often twice the end-to-end propagation delay.

The backoff algorithm just described is an example of a dynamic backoff strategy, so named because the distribution from which the backoff time is selected changes with the number of collisions. The term *linear incremental backoff* is sometimes used to identify any dynamic backoff strategy for which the mean backoff time is linearly proportional to the number of collisions experienced by a particular packet.

As an alternative to the dynamic strategies, the distribution from which the backoff times are selected can remain fixed. For example, as previously discussed, the pure and slotted ALOHA methods use a fixed uniform distribution for determining the backoff times. An exponential distribution with fixed mean is another popular example.

A description of what happens on the channel during a collision interval (an unsuccessful busy period) is important in understanding the operation of a random access procedure. (Recall that a typical collision interval is examined for CSMA in Section 9.4 using Fig. 9.15.) For CSMA/CD using jamming, a one-dimensional time plot such as used for CSMA is inadequate for illustrating behavior and thus the two-dimensional diagram of Fig. 9.25 is employed.

As is the case for CSMA, CSMA/CD has a vulnerable period τ seconds long. In other words, if a station begins transmitting, another station will not detect the transmission (and hence defer or back off, depending on the protocol) until after the propagation delay of τ seconds. For most general analyses, τ is taken to be the maximum end-to-end propagation delay of the channel. However, if two specific stations are considered, as in Fig. 9.25, τ, now denoted τ_{AB}, can be the specific propagation delay between the two stations.

After a colliding signal arrives at a station that is already transmitting, the collision detection circuitry requires a time, denoted ϵ, to detect the presence of a collision. The timing diagram of Fig. 9.25 shows ϵ along with other parameters.

Now consider the timing diagram in more detail. Distance along the bus is on the horizontal axis with the spacing between two stations A and B indicated. The increasing time axis is drawn from top to bottom. Station A begins a transmission at time t_0 to start the cycle, as shown at the top of the figure. The signal propagates to station B, but, before it arrives, station B initiates a transmission at the time $(t_0 + Y)$, where Y is a random variable. Shortly after station B begins to transmit, the signal from A arrives and ϵ

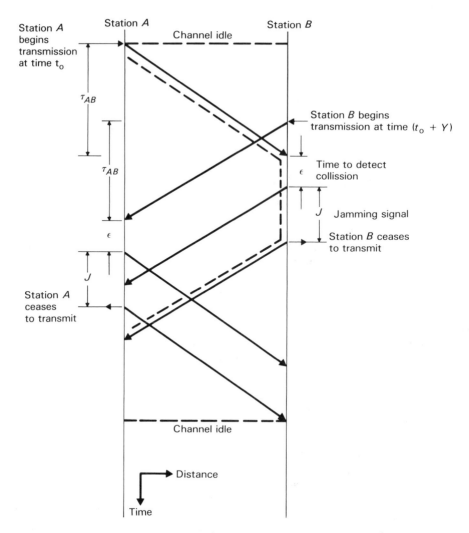

Figure 9.25   Timing Diagram for CSMA/CD, Showing Contention

seconds later, B detects the collision. Station B then sends out a jamming signal for J seconds. The signal from B reaches A after τ_{AB} seconds, A detects a collision (ϵ seconds after receiving the signal from B), and then A initiates its own jamming signal of J seconds duration.

In examining the figure, note that station A is the first to transmit, transmits for the greater part of the collision interval, and transmits longer than station B. In spite of this, both stations view the channel as active for exactly the same length of time, namely, $(J + 2\tau_{AB} + \epsilon)$ seconds, which is independent of Y, the length of the time interval when only A is transmitting. (The component parts of this time interval for station A are shown as dashed lines in Fig. 9.25.)

Busy periods and idle periods can be defined for the composite CSMA/CD channel in the same manner as for CSMA. In making the definitions, keep in mind that the state of the overall channel may be different from what is perceived by an individual station because of the propagation delay. An idle period exists when no station perceives the channel to be busy. If the channel is not idle, it is busy. A busy period is a collision interval, if more than one station is attempting to transmit in the period. Otherwise, the busy period is a successful busy period. In Fig. 9.25, note that a collision interval exists from the time station A begins to transmit until station B receives the last part of the jamming signal from station A.

The effect of ϵ and a specific station-to-station propagation delay, τ_{AB}, are shown in Fig. 9.25. These refinements are omitted in Fig. 9.26 to concentrate on more basic effects. Figure 9.26(a) shows a contention interval for CSMA for comparison to that for CSMA/CD given in Fig. 9.26(b). In both parts of the figure, the time the first transmission begins, t_0, is set to zero.

From Fig. 9.26(a), note that CSMA has a contention interval of length $(P + Y + \tau)$, where P is the time to transmit a packet. Figure 9.26(b) for CSMA/CD shows that the contention interval is reduced to $(Y + J + 2\tau)$, if, of course, $J + \tau < P$, which is normally the case.

As a final point, for emphasis, Fig. 9.26(b) shows that each station that participates in the collision observes the channel as busy for a time $(J + 2\tau)$ seconds. Other stations, however, may see the channel as busy from the time station A begins to transmit, at time 0, until station B ceases to transmit, at time $(Y + J + 2\tau)$. This latter time is defined to be the length of the contention interval and is appropriate for use in throughput analysis. From the point of view of station A, the first station to transmit, an extra τ has been added to ensure that all stations see the jam signal.

9.5.2 Throughput Analysis for CSMA/CD

In this subsection, a throughput analysis is given for nonpersistent CSMA/CD for the infinite population model. For the same model, similar results are presented for slotted nonpersistent and slotted 1-persistent CSMA/CD.

The infinite population model for CSMA/CD protocols has essentially the same set of assumptions as those given in Subsection 9.4.2 for CSMA, with the following additions:

- The time, ϵ, to detect a collision is negligible; and
- The jamming time, J, is the same for all stations.

The same basic approach can be used to determine the relationship between throughput and offered traffic for CSMA/CD as is used for CSMA. Thus it is necessary to evaluate $\overline{U}$, $\overline{B}$, and $\overline{I}$ in the expression

$$S = \frac{\overline{U}}{\overline{B} + \overline{I}} \tag{9.56}$$

Recall that use of (9.56) assumes that all channel time consists of cycles that contain busy periods of length B and idle periods of length I.

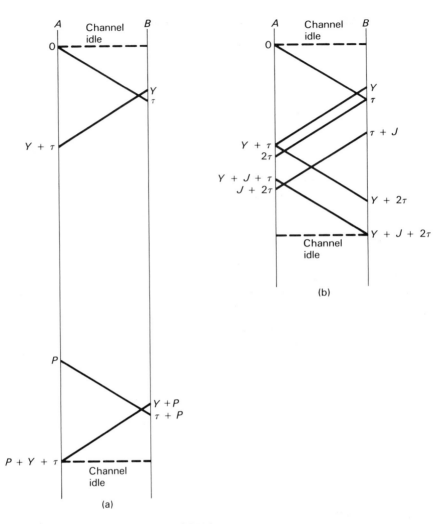

Figure 9.26   Contention Interval for CSMA
        (a) Without collision detection
        (b) With collision detection (and $\epsilon = 0$)

Consider first the evaluation of $\overline{B}$, the average length of the channel busy period. Since a busy period can be either a successful transmission period or a contention period, $\overline{B}$ is given by

$$\overline{B} = P_s(P + \tau) + (1 - P_s)\overline{C} \qquad (9.57)$$

where P_s is the probability of a successful transmission, $\overline{C}$ is the average length of a contention period, and the other symbols have the significance assigned previously.

A basic step in continuing the analysis is the evaluation of the average length of a contention period, $\overline{C}$. To aid in this determination, consider Fig.

9.27, which is an extension of Fig. 9.26 to three colliding transmissions. Recall that it was convenient to assume a propagation delay of τ between every pair of stations. To accomplish this physically for three stations, a ring or star configuration with all the stations equally spaced is required. The geometry shown in Fig. 9.27 is adequate, however, for showing delays between station I and the other two stations, which is what is required here. In the figure, a transmission from station I, used as a reference packet, commences at time zero, while stations II and III begin transmissions at times Y and Z respectively, with Z less than Y.

The figure shows that the length of a contention period, C, which is the time interval during which at least one corrupted transmission is propagating on the bus, is given by

$$C = Z + J + 2\tau \qquad (9.58)$$

From this, it is evident that it is the time of transmission of the first packet to collide with the reference packet that determines the length of the contention period. This is the reverse of CSMA (see Figs. 9.26(a) and 9.15), in which it is the time of transmission of the last colliding packet that determines the length of the contention period. This is crucial to the following analysis.

Before proceeding, note that it is necessary in the analysis of CSMA/CD to differentiate between successful and unsuccessful transmission, or contention, periods. This is not necessary for CSMA because Eq. (9.30), an expression for

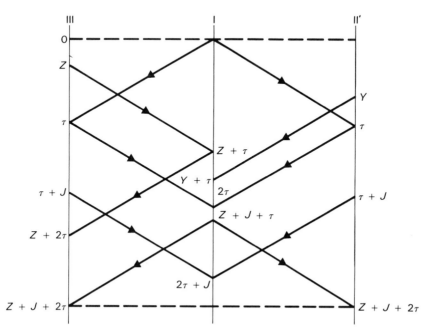

Figure 9.27   Three Colliding Transmissions in a Collision Period for CSMA/CD

the busy period B, includes successful transmissions as a special case. This is not possible for CSMA/CD.

To continue with the analysis, the average length of the contention period, $\overline{C}$, can be obtained immediately from (9.58) by

$$\overline{C} = J + 2\tau + \overline{Z} \tag{9.59}$$

as Z is the only random variable. It is now necessary to compute the distribution function of the random variable Z and then evaluate $\overline{Z}$.

To calculate the distribution function of Z, consider Fig. 9.27 again. This figure represents a typical contention period that begins with the transmission of a reference packet, assumed to be from station I, and continues until the network is idle to all stations. Packets are assumed to be transmitted as soon as they arrive, if, at the arrival time, the channel is sensed to be idle. Thus, with respect to Fig. 9.27, stations II and III immediately transmit any packets that arrive in the vulnerable interval $[0, \tau]$.

The time Z is the arrival time of the first packet that collides with the reference packet from station I. What is needed is the distribution function $F_Z(z)$ of Z defined as $P\{Z \le z\}$, with $0 \le z \le \tau$. To compute this probability, it is useful to think of Z as the time of arrival of the first packet in the interval $[0, \tau]$, given that there is at least one arrival in this interval. The conditioning on at least one arrival ensures that a contention period is being considered. The arrival at station I of the reference packet that initiates the contention period does not need to be counted as an arrival in the same sense as the colliding packet, since all channel time is partitioned into nonoverlapping periods, either successful, contention, or idle, and this partitioning is taken as a basic structure in the analysis.

To continue the analysis, $F_Z(z)$ can be expressed as

$$F_Z(z) = P\{Z \le z\} = 1 - P\{Z > z\} \tag{9.60}$$

The probability, $P\{Z > z\}$, is the probability of no arrivals in $[0, z]$, given that there is at least one arrival in $[0, \tau]$. This probability can be expressed as

$$P\{Z > z\} = \frac{P\{\text{no arrivals in } [0, z]\} \, P\{\text{at least one arrival in } [z, \tau]\}}{P\{\text{at least one arrival in } [0, \tau]\}} \tag{9.61}$$

by using basic properties of conditional probability and independent events, along with the fact that the arrival process is Poisson and thus has independent increments.

Expressing each of the probabilities in (9.61) for a Poisson process with average arrival rate G/P packets/second yields

$$P\{Z > z\} = \frac{e^{-Gz/P}\,[1 - e^{-G(\tau - z)/P}]}{1 - e^{-G\tau/P}} \tag{9.62}$$

Finally, using (9.60),

$$F_Z(z) = (1 - e^{-Gz/P})/(1 - e^{-G\tau/P}), \quad 0 \le z \le \tau \tag{9.63}$$

This distribution function is sketched in Fig. 9.28.

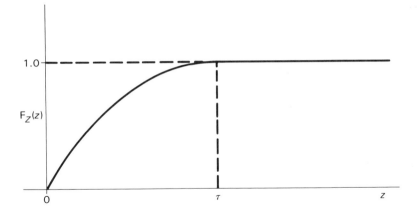

Figure 9.28 **Distribution Function for the Random Variable Z**

The expected or average value of Z, $\overline{Z}$, can be evaluated from $F_Z(z)$ in a straightforward manner, and the result can be expressed as

$$\overline{Z} = \tau \left[\frac{1}{g} - \frac{e^{-g}}{1 - e^{-g}} \right] \tag{9.64}$$

where

$$g = G\tau/P = a\,G \tag{9.65}$$

and a is the normalized propagation time previously defined. The parameter g is the offered channel traffic per propagation period, τ, since G is the offered channel traffic per packet time, P. (Note that slotted CSMA/CD protocols often use τ as the slot time, which makes g the offered channel traffic per slot.)

The average length of the contention period, $\overline{C}$, can now be expressed, using (9.64) in (9.59) to obtain

$$\overline{C} = J + \tau \left\{ 2 + \frac{1}{g} - \frac{e^{-g}}{1 - e^{-g}} \right\} \tag{9.66}$$

To determine the average length of the busy period $\overline{B}$, from Eq. (9.57), the probability of a successful transmission, P_s, is required in addition to $\overline{C}$. This probability is the probability of having no arrivals to the channel in the vulnerable period $[0, \tau]$. Thus

$$P_s = e^{-G\tau/P} = e^{-g} \tag{9.67}$$

and

$$\overline{B} = e^{-g}(P + \tau) + (1 - e^{-g})\left[J + \tau \left(2 + \frac{1}{g} - \frac{e^{-g}}{1 - e^{-g}} \right) \right] \tag{9.68}$$

To complete the calculation of S from Eq. (9.56), note that

$$\overline{U} = P_s P = P e^{-g} \tag{9.69}$$

and that the average idle period, $\bar{I}$, for CSMA/CD is the same as for nonslotted CSMA:

$$\bar{I} = P/G = \tau/g \qquad (9.70)$$

Using these results in (9.56) gives

$$S = \frac{Pe^{-g}}{(P + \tau)e^{-g} + \left\{J + \tau\left[2 + \dfrac{1}{g} - \dfrac{e^{-g}}{1 - e^{-g}}\right]\right\}(1 - e^{-g}) + \dfrac{\tau}{g}} \qquad (9.71)$$

Simplifying this expression and using the definition

$$\gamma = J/\tau \qquad (9.72)$$

(9.71) becomes

$$S = \frac{g\,e^{-g}}{g e^{-g} + \gamma ag(1 - e^{-g}) + 2ag(1 - e^{-g}) + a(2 - e^{-g})} \qquad (9.73)$$

It is sometimes convenient to express S in terms of G rather than g. Thus, using Eq. (9.65), (9.73) becomes

$$S = \frac{G\,e^{-aG}}{G e^{-aG} + \gamma aG(1 - e^{-aG}) + 2aG(1 - e^{-aG}) + (2 - e^{-aG})} \qquad (9.74)$$

It is relatively straightforward to derive a similar throughput-offered traffic relationship for slotted nonpersistent CSMA/CD. In fact, the analysis closely parallels that for slotted nonpersistent CSMA presented in Section 9.4. As in the earlier analyses of CSMA and of nonpersistent CSMA/CD, throughput is given by (9.56) in terms of $\bar{U}$, $\bar{B}$, and $\bar{I}$. The length of a successful transmission period, $\bar{U}$, is expressed in terms of P_s by (9.69). The length of the busy period, $\bar{B}$, is also expressed in terms of P_s, but $\bar{C}$ is also required, as is seen from Eq. (9.57).

The probability of a successful transmission, P_s, is derived in Section 9.4 for slotted nonpersistent CSMA, and the result carries over to slotted nonpersistent CSMA/CD. Thus, from (9.45)

$$P_s = \frac{a G e^{-aG}}{1 - e^{-aG}} = \frac{g e^{-g}}{1 - e^{-g}} \qquad (9.75)$$

Now consider the average length of the contention period with reference to Fig. 9.29, which shows such a period for slotted CSMA/CD. As the figure indicates, for slotted operation, packets are only transmitted at the beginning of a slot. Further examination of the figure shows that the contention period has a constant length $(2\tau + J)$, where, of course, τ is the slot time as well as the end-to-end propagation delay. For slotted operation, the jamming time, J, is an integer number of slots. Since the contention period is of constant length, it follows that

$$\bar{C} = 2\tau + J \qquad (9.76)$$

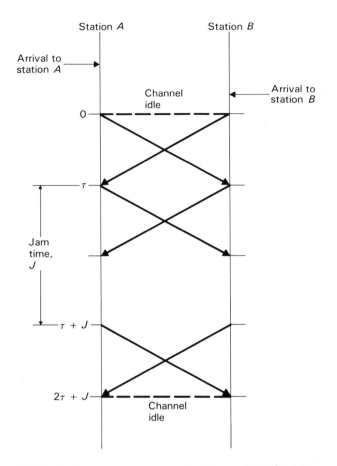

Figure 9.29   A Contention Interval for Slotted CSMA/CD

Equations (9.75) and (9.76), along with (9.57), completely determine $\bar{B}$. Since $\bar{U} = P_s P$, it is determined by (9.75). The remaining quantity, $\bar{I}$, required to express throughput is given by (9.52) since the length of the idle period does not depend on whether or not the CSMA protocol has collision detection. The result of (9.52) is restated as

$$\bar{I} = \frac{a P e^{-aG}}{1 - e^{-aG}} = \frac{a P e^{-g}}{1 - e^{-g}} \tag{9.77}$$

It is now possible to collect the results for $\bar{I}$, $\bar{U}$, and $\bar{B}$ and use them in Eq. (9.56) to obtain

$$S = \frac{ge^{-g}}{ge^{-g} + a\gamma (1 - e^{-g} - ge^{-g}) + a (2 - e^{-g} - ge^{-g})} \tag{9.78}$$

If it were desirable to do so, (9.78) could be expressed in terms of G rather than g, as is done to obtain (9.74) from (9.73).

It follows that the slotted nonpersistent CSMA/CD result gives slotted nonpersistent CSMA as a special case. The essential difference between CSMA/CD and CSMA, as previously pointed out, lies in the fact that collision detection potentially reduces the time a station must continue transmitting a packet that has suffered a collision. For slotted CSMA, this time is the full packet period, P. Figure 9.29 shows that the corresponding time for slotted CSMA/CD is $(\tau + J)$.

For the special case that

$$P = \tau + J \tag{9.79}$$

operation of CSMA/CD reduces to that of CSMA. Thus, making the identification of (9.79) causes γ to become

$$\gamma = \frac{J}{\tau} = \frac{P - \tau}{\tau} = \frac{P}{\tau} - 1 = \frac{1}{a} - 1 \tag{9.80}$$

Introducing $(1/a - 1)$ for γ in (9.78) then yields

$$S = \frac{g e^{-g}}{1 - e^{-g} + a} \tag{9.81}$$

which is identical to (9.53) if g is replaced by aG.

Note that the result for nonpersistent CSMA/CD does not reduce to the result for nonpersistent CSMA. This is because the length of the contention period for CSMA/CD depends on the time of arrival of the *first* colliding packet, while that for CSMA depends on the *last* colliding packet. For slotted operation, of course, all colliding packets are transmitted at the beginning of a slot so that the results do not depend on the times of arrival of the packets within the slot.

A throughput-offered traffic analysis has also been carried out by O'Reilly [7] for slotted 1-persistent CSMA/CD, using essentially the same assumptions as used in the preceding discussion. The details of the analysis are beyond the scope of the present treatment. The closed-form result, although rather complicated, is

$$S = L g e^{-(\gamma+2)g}[\gamma + 2 - (\gamma + 1)e^{-g}]/W \tag{9.82}$$

where

$$\begin{aligned} W = &(L + 1)g e^{-(\gamma+2)g} [\gamma + 2 - (\gamma + 1) e^{-g}] \\ &+ (\gamma + 2) [1 - (L + 1) g e^{-(L+1)g} - e^{-g} + Lg e^{-(L+2)g}] \\ &+ e^{-(\gamma + 2)g} - (L - \gamma - 1)g e^{-(L+\gamma+3)g} \end{aligned} \tag{9.83}$$

and

$$L = P/\tau = 1/a \tag{9.84}$$

In the special case of $\gamma = P/\tau - 1$, previously established as making slotted

CSMA equivalent to slotted CSMA/CD, (9.82) reduces to (9.55), the *S–G* expression for slotted 1-persistent CSMA.

9.5.3 Performance Studies for CSMA/CD

The results derived in the previous section make it possible to compare the throughput versus offered traffic behavior of the several types of CSMA/CD protocols and to determine the sensitivity of throughput to the network parameters. A comparison of the behavior of the several types of protocols is made first.

Figure 9.30 plots throughput, *S*, versus offered traffic, *G*, for nonpersistent, slotted nonpersistent, and 1-persistent CSMA/CD. Normalized jamming time, γ, is unity in all cases, and curves are shown for normalized propagation time, *a*, taking values of 0.001, 0.01, and 0.1.

Note from the curves:
1. Nonpersistent CSMA/CD, both slotted and unslotted, give for small *a* greater maximum throughput than 1-persistent CSMA/CD; and
2. Slotting the time axis tends to increase throughput at higher values of *G*, but has negligible effect for small values of this parameter.

It can be recalled that CSMA shares the behavior of both these points with CSMA/CD.

Turning now to the sensitivity of throughput to jamming time, consider Fig. 9.31, which shows maximum throughput, S_{max}, versus normalized jamming time, γ, for three values of normalized propagation delay, namely, $a = 0.01$, 0.05, and 0.1.

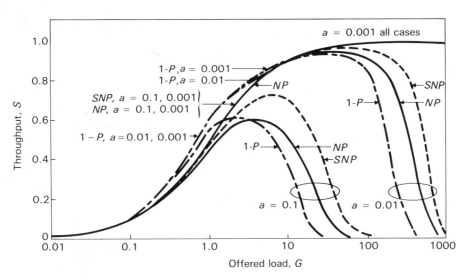

Figure 9.30 **Throughput versus Offered Traffic for Nonpersistent (*NP*), Slotted Nonpersistent (*SNP*), and Slotted 1-persistent (1-*P*) CSMA/CD ($a = 0.001, 0.01,$ and $0.1; \gamma = 1$)**

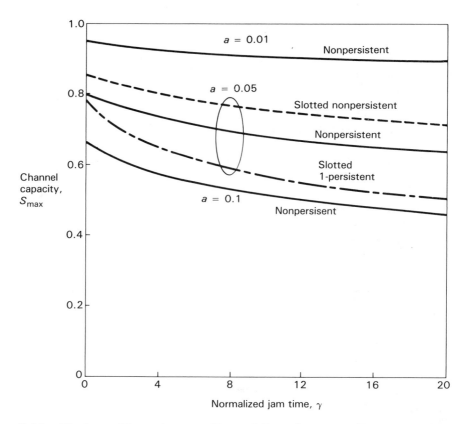

Figure 9.31 **Maximum Throughput or Channel Capacity versus Normalized Jam Time for Nonpersistent CSMA/CD (a = 0.01, 0.05, 0.1), Slotted Nonpersistent CSMA/CD (a = 0.05), and Slotted 1-persistent CSMA/CD (a = 0.05)**

The figure substantiates the intuitive conclusion that minimizing jamming time maximizes throughput. Of course, the curves, which assume ideal behavior, do not assess the utility of jamming in ensuring that stations back off when they should.

The effect of propagation delay on throughput is shown in Fig. 9.32 by plots of maximum throughput, S_{max}, versus normalized propagation delay, a, for normalized jamming time equal to unity. Curves are plotted for nonpersistent CSMA/CD, slotted nonpersistent CSMA/CD, and slotted 1-persistent CSMA/CD. Note that increasing the parameter a decreases throughput in all three cases, with the least effect felt by slotted nonpersistent CSMA/CD. The decrease of throughput with normalized propagation delay is consistent with intuition since longer propagation delays cause the contention periods to be longer and more numerous—the former because collision detection occurs later, and the latter because carrier sensing is based on less current information.

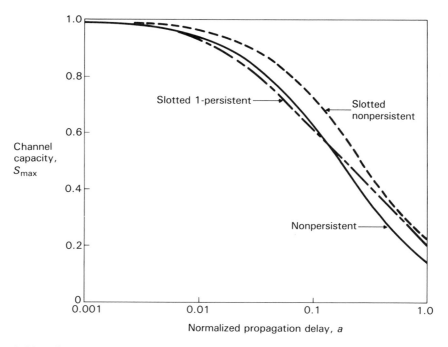

Figure 9.32 S_{max} **versus Normalized Propagation Time for Nonpersistent, Slotted Nonpersistent, and 1-persistent CSMA/CD (with $\gamma = 1$)**

Analytical studies of delay for CSMA/CD are even less tractable than for CSMA. Results have been found for only the one case of slotted nonpersistent CSMA/CD. For this protocol, Tobagi and Hunt [8] use an embedded Markov chain approach to obtain a numerical solution for the delay–throughput performance. Although the details of this work are beyond the scope of the present treatment, the results are presented in Fig. 9.33. Curves are provided for a 50-station network with $\gamma = 1$, $a = 0.01$, and several values of β, the mean backoff time. The Tobagi–Hunt analysis assumes that backoff times are chosen from an exponential distribution of fixed mean β slots. The family of curves also includes an optimal delay curve obtained by adjusting the mean backoff to give the minimum average delay for each fixed value of S.

As in the case of CSMA, the results worked out in Section 9.3 for delay versus throughput for slotted ALOHA give a general idea of the behavior for CSMA/CD. When the protocols are compared, it is evident that the slotted CSMA/CD algorithms can be regarded as refinements of slotted ALOHA. Each refinement, namely, carrier sense, collision detection, jamming, and so forth, affects the delay–throughput relationship and complicates the analysis. However, the underlying approach is the same, and the final curves retain the same general shape, as can be verified by comparing Fig. 9.10 with Fig. 9.33.

In common with all other random access procedures, the infinite population CSMA/CD network is essentially unstable. Fortunately, finite population networks, which are of course the practical case, can always be made stable by

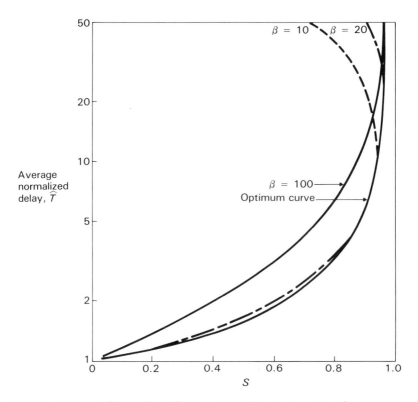

Figure 9.33 Average Normalized Delay versus Throughput for Slotted Nonpersistent CSMA/CD—$a = 0.01$; $\gamma = 2$; β, Mean Backoff Time, is 10, 20, and 100 (From Tobagi and Hunt [8])

increasing the mean backoff time to a sufficiently large value. The stability arguments for slotted ALOHA carry over to similar results for CSMA/CD.

Next, the throughput-offered load performance of CSMA/CD protocols are compared to those of CSMA and ALOHA. The results point to the advantages of CSMA/CD for local area networks. Figure 9.34 gives the S–G curves for a number of the random access schemes studied in this chapter, all for $a = 0.01$, and with $\gamma = 1$ for the CD protocols. The figure shows the improvement in maximum throughput achieved by CSMA/CD over all other schemes. The fact that CSMA/CD protocols maintain a throughput relatively high and close to the maximum over a large range of offered load suggests that CSMA/CD is probably more stable than other random access protocols.

The improvement of CSMA/CD over CSMA is to a large extent dependent on the normalized propagation delay, a. For small values of a, CSMA/CD is clearly superior to CSMA. However, as a approaches 1, the differences between the protocols tend to diminish. This is shown in Fig. 9.35, in which the maximum throughput is shown as a function of a for the complete range of random access protocols.

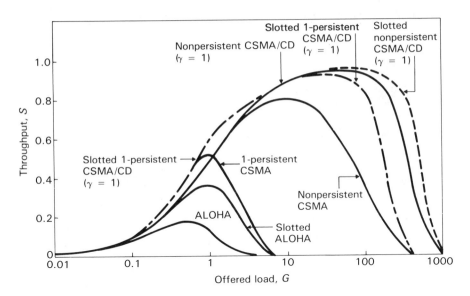

Figure 9.34 *S* **versus** *G* **for All Protocols Studied: Nonpersistent, Slotted Nonpersistent, and Slotted 1-persistent CSMA/CD; 1-persistent, and Nonpersistent CSMA; Slotted ALOHA and ALOHA (with** $a = 0.01$**)**

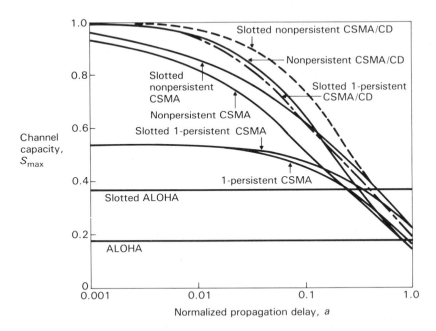

Figure 9.35 **Comparison of Maximum Throughput versus Normalized Propagation Time for ALOHA, CSMA, and CSMA/CD Protocols**

Section 9.5 **Protocols that Use Carrier Sensing with Collision Detection** **337**

If the definition of a, given as

$$a = \tau/P = \tau R/\overline{X}$$

is recalled, the conditions for a to be small, and hence for CSMA/CD to exhibit behavior superior to CSMA, can be stated in terms of more basic network properties. Although the actual value of a is determined by the relative values of the three variables listed, small values of a are obtained when: the bus is relatively short, so that τ is small; the channel bit rate is not too high; and the packet length is relatively long.

In conclusion, it is possible to make some delay–throughput comparisons between CSMA/CD and other random access protocols. Figure 9.36 shows the optimized average normalized delay versus throughput for slotted ALOHA, slotted nonpersistent CSMA, and slotted nonpersistent CSMA/CD for $a = 0.01$ and $\gamma = 1$ (CSMA/CD). The number of stations is 50 for CSMA and CSMA/CD, whereas slotted ALOHA assumes an infinite number of users. (Figure 9.36 is essentially a composite of Figs. 9.23 and 9.33.) All three

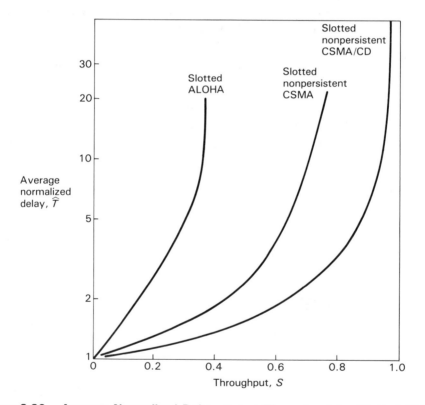

Figure 9.36 **Average Normalized Delay versus Throughput for Slotted ALOHA, Slotted Nonpersistent CSMA, and CSMA/CD for $a = 0.01$ (From simulation results by Kleinrock and Tobagi [5], and numerical solution by Tobagi and Hunt [8])**

protocols give minimal, almost equivalent, delay for very small S; CSMA/CD, however, is clearly much superior for larger throughputs.

9.6 Summary

This chapter deals with random access networks, which are characterized by the absence of a channel-controlled access mechanism. This is in contrast to other types of networks that have a mechanism for controlling when stations can transmit. The chapter discusses several different protocols of increasing complexity, beginning with the ALOHA protocol first discussed in Chapter 6. For the ALOHA method, the stations have no interaction and transmit whenever there is a ready packet.

A second method discussed is slotted ALOHA, for which stations interact only to the extent of maintaining slot synchronization. This method provides a substantial increase in the maximum possible throughput. Slotted ALOHA is not typically used for local area networks, but it has many aspects of behavior that are representative of more sophisticated methods. Apart from the even simpler ALOHA method, slotted ALOHA is the only method to which a tractable analysis can be applied under realistic conditions. It is thus analyzed rather thoroughly to obtain throughput versus offered load and average delay versus offered load. The results serve as a guide to corresponding behavior for other methods more commonly used on local area networks.

The chapter discusses two other classes of access methods that can provide further increases in maximum throughput. These methods are carrier-sense multiple access (CSMA) and carrier-sense multiple access with collision detection (CSMA/CD). Both classes of methods can be further classified as nonpersistent and p-persistent, and slotted and nonslotted.

Carrier-sense methods, as the name implies, require hardware at each station that listens to the channel and determines that the channel is free before the station is allowed to transmit. Adding this feature increases the maximum throughput for any of the subcategories.

The last category, CSMA/CD, adds still another hardware feature to CSMA, namely the ability for a station to listen to the channel while it is still transmitting. This feature makes it possible to abort a packet as soon as the station detects the presence of an interfering transmission, instead of having to wait until the end of a complete packet transmission to determine that a collision has occurred, as is the case for CSMA without collision detection.

The improvement in maximum throughput that is possible for CSMA or CSMA/CD depends on the size of the normalized propagation delay over the channel (i.e., the ratio of propagation time to packet transmission time). Small normalized delays, which are typical for local area networks, allow significant improvements in maximum throughput. Generally speaking, CSMA/CD performs better than CSMA does.

The chapter presents equations for throughput versus offered traffic under simplifying assumptions for all cases considered; most equations are derived in the text. An analysis of average delay versus throughput is given only for slotted ALOHA. For other methods, for which the calculations are not tractable, simulation results are presented.

Appendix: Determination of the Average Number of Retransmissions for Slotted ALOHA

Equation (9.15) expresses the average number of retransmissions, H, in terms of the probabilities q_n and q_t. The purpose of this appendix is to derive Eqs. (9.18) and (9.19), which relate q_t and q_n to the basic network parameters S, G, and K.

As a first step in the derivation, refer to Fig. A.1 and consider the conditions under which a successful transmission can take place in the current slot, labeled slot C. The packet successfully transmitted in slot C can be either a newly arrived packet or a retransmitted packet. The probabilities q_n and q_t are the probabilities of a successful transmission in slot C, given respectively that the transmitted packet is newly arrived or that it is a retransmission.

For the packet successfully transmitted in slot C to be a retransmitted packet, a collision from an earlier slot must have been rescheduled for the current slot. Thus, the collision must have taken place in one of only K earlier slots such that the current slot is $(r + k)$ slots after the collision, where k is an integer in the range $0 \leq k \leq K - 1$. (Recall that after a collision, a packet is retransmitted after a delay of $(r + k)$ slots, where k is chosen at random from $0, 1, 2, \ldots, K - 1$.)

For the retransmission to be successful, three events must occur:

1. No other packets that collided in slot A should be retransmitted in slot C;
2. No new packets should be generated in slot C; and
3. No packets that collided in one of the $(K - 1)$ slots, other than A, should be rescheduled for slot C.

It is assumed that the three events listed are independent, so that the probability of their intersection is the product of their individual probabilities.

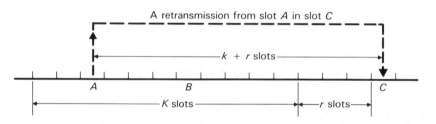

A retransmission from slot A in slot C

$k + r$ slots

A B C

K slots r slots

Figure A.1   **Retransmission of a Packet in Slot *C* from a Collision in Slot *A***

The probability of event 1, that no other packets that collide in slot A are retransmitted in slot C, is denoted q_c; it is evaluated in Eq. (9.A.7). The probability of no new packets being generated in slot C, event 2, can be computed from the assumed Poisson arrival process as e^{-S}.

Finally, consider the probability of event 3. Denote the probability of no retransmission from a collision in a specific slot, other than A, taking place in slot C as q_o. Since there are $(K - 1)$ slots, other than A, in which collisions can occur that could cause retransmissions in slot C, and since the collisions are independent, the probability of event 3 is q_o^{K-1}.

The probability of the intersection of the events 1, 2, and 3 can now be expressed, using the previous definitions and results, as

$$q_t = q_c\, e^{-S}\, q_o^{K-1} \tag{9.A.1}$$

Before evaluating q_c and q_o, the probability, q_n, of a successful transmission for a newly arrived packet, is expressed in terms of these quantities. As in the previous case, a successful transmission requires the simultaneous occurrence of several events that are assumed to be statistically independent:

1. No other new arrivals are generated in the current slot, C; and
2. No retransmissions occur in slot C from collisions in any earlier slots.

The probabilities of events 1 and 2 are determined in the same manner as for the first case to obtain e^{-S} and q_o^K, respectively. The result for q_n is then given by

$$q_n = e^{-S}\, q_o^K \tag{9.A.2}$$

It is now necessary to determine q_o and q_c in terms of S, G, and K. Consider q_c, which is the (conditional) probability of the event, "one or more packets is transmitted in slot A (in addition to the one successfully retransmitted in slot C) *and* none of these additional packets is retransmitted in slot C," conditioned, of course, on a collision in slot A. Let X be this event without any conditions on what happened in slot A. Let $q(j)$ denote the probability of the unconditioned event just defined, but with exactly j additional packets transmitted in slot A. The probability of the unconditioned event is then $\sum_{j=1}^{\infty} q(j)$.

The probability of exactly j arrivals in slot A, either new or retransmitted, is determined from the formula for a Poisson arrival process as

$$\frac{G^j e^{-G}}{j!}$$

The probability of not retransmitting a particular collided packet in slot C is the probability of not choosing the one value of the backoff integer (denoted k in earlier discussions), which results in retransmission in slot C. This probability is $(1 - 1/K)$. Assuming all events are independent, $q(j)$ can then be expressed as

$$q(j) = \frac{G^j e^{-G}}{j!}\, (1 - 1/K)^j \tag{9.A.3}$$

To complete the calculation of q_c, recall that the definition of the conditional probability of event X given Y is the probability of X *and* Y divided by the probability of Y. In the present application, $\Sigma_{j=1}^{\infty} q(j)$ is the probability of X *and* Y, where X is as defined, and Y is the event that a collision occurs in slot A, or that one or more additional packets is generated in slot A. The probability of at least one other packet being generated in slot A is determined from the Poisson arrival distribution as $(1 - e^{-G})$. Finally, q_c is given by

$$q_c = \sum_{j=1}^{\infty} q(j)/(1 - e^{-G}) \tag{9.A.4}$$

Substituting (9.A.3) into (9.A.4) gives

$$q_c = \sum_{j=1}^{\infty} \frac{G^j e^{-G}}{j!} \frac{(1 - 1/K)^j}{1 - e^{-G}} \tag{9.A.5}$$

The series in (9.A.5) can be evaluated by using the series for e^X, namely

$$e^X = \sum_{i=0}^{\infty} X^i/i! \tag{9.A.6}$$

Thus, using (9.A.6) with appropriate manipulations to begin the series at 1 rather than 0, and after an algebraic step, (9.A.5) becomes

$$q_c = \frac{e^{-G/K} - e^{-G}}{1 - e^{-G}} \tag{9.A.7}$$

As a check, note that q_c approaches 1 as K approaches infinity. This says, in effect, that no additional colliding packets from slot A are retransmitted in slot C. This is intuitively reasonable since the probability, $1/K$, of choosing any single number of backoff slots, including the choice that retransmits in slot C, approaches 0 as K approaches infinity.

As a final step, consider q_0, the probability of the event that no retransmissions from collisions in a slot other than slot A (for example, slot B), appear in slot C. This event can occur in three mutually exclusive ways:

1. No transmission at all occurs in slot B;
2. A successful transmission occurs in slot B, and therefore no retransmission is needed; and
3. Two or more transmissions take place in slot B, but none is retransmitted in slot C.

The probability of the first event is determined from the Poisson arrival process as e^{-G}. The probability of a successful transmission in a slot is given by the Poisson process as Ge^{-G}.

Examination of the last event shows that it is just the union of events, determined previously to have a probability $q(j)$, from $j = 2$ to ∞. The probability of event 3 is thus $\Sigma_{j=2}^{\infty} q(j)$.

Since q_0 is the probability of the union of the three mutually exclusive events 1, 2, and 3, it can be expressed as

$$q_0 = e^{-G} + Ge^{-G} + \sum_{j=2}^{\infty} q(j) \tag{9.A.8}$$

Substituting for $q(j)$ in (9.A.8) from (9.A.3), and carrying out some simplification, gives

$$q_0 = e^{-G/K} + \frac{G}{K} e^{-G} \tag{9.A.9}$$

As another check, q_0 also approaches 1 as K approaches infinity. This makes intuitive sense for the same reason as discussed for q_c. It can also be shown that q_0^K approaches e^{S-G} as K approaches infinity. This indicates that the probability of no retransmissions in a slot approaches e^{S-G} as the number of potential retransmission slots becomes infinitely large.

Final expressions for q_t and q_n are now obtained by substituting for q_c and q_0 in (9.A.1) and (9.A.2). The results, which are given in the text as Eqs. (9.18) and (9.19), are

$$q_t = \left[\frac{e^{-G/K} - e^{-G}}{1 - e^{-G}} \right] \left[e^{-G/K} + \frac{G}{K} e^{-G} \right]^{K-1} e^{-S} \tag{9.A.10}$$

$$q_n = \left[e^{-G/K} + \frac{G}{K} e^{-G} \right]^{K} e^{-S} \tag{9.A.11}$$

References

[1] S. S. Lam. "Packet Switching in a Multi-Access Broadcast Channel with Application to Satellite Communications in a Computer Network." Ph.D. diss. Computer Science Dept., University of California, Los Angeles, March 1974.

[2] L. Kleinrock. *Queueing Systems*. Vol. 2, *Computer Applications*. New York: Wiley–Interscience, 1976.

[3] L. Kleinrock and S. S. Lam. "Packet Switching in a Multiaccess Broadcast Channel: Performance Evaluation." *IEEE Trans. on Communications* COM-23 (April 1975): 410–423.

[4] S. S. Lam and L. Kleinrock. "Packet Switching in a Multiaccess Broadcast Channel: Dynamic Control Procedures." *IEEE Trans. on Communications* COM-23 (September 1975): 891–904.

[5] L. Kleinrock and F. A. Tobagi. "Packet Switching in Radio Channels: Part I—Carrier Sense Multiple Access Modes and Their Throughput–Delay Characteristics." *IEEE Trans. on Communications* COM-23, no. 12 (December 1975): 1400–1416.

[6] F. A. Tobagi and L. Kleinrock. "Packet Switching in Radio Channels: Part IV—Stability Considerations and Dynamic Control in Carrier Sense Multiple Access." *IEEE Trans. on Communications* COM-25, no. 10 (October 1977): 1103–1119.

[7] P. J. P. O'Reilly. "A New Technique for Performance Studies of CSMA/CD Local Networks." Ph.D. diss., School of Electrical Engineering, Georgia Institute of Technology, June 1983.

[8] F. A. Tobagi and V. B. Hunt. "Performance Analysis of Carrier Sense Multiple Access with Collision Detection. *Computer Networks* 4 (1980): 245–259.

[9] E. Parzen. *Modern Probability Theory and Its Applications.* New York: John Wiley and Sons, 1960.

Problems and Exercises

1. Slotted ALOHA is to be used on a 9800 bps channel. Packets are 1000 bits long. There are only two users on the channel, and in any slot interval, user 1 transmits with probability p_1 and user 2 with probability p_2. However, if user 1 has not transmitted in the previous $K - 1$ slots, the probability is 1 that this user transmits in the next slot, slot K. The same applies to user 2. Find the throughput of user 1 as a function of p_1 and p_2. If $p_1 = p_2$, sketch the throughput of user 1 as a function of p_1.

2. For random access methods, a is a key parameter because for small a, sophisticated methods (e.g., CSMA/CD) can have a large throughput.
   (a) Explain in words why a large a causes poor performance for CSMA/CD.
   (b) List the parameters on which a depends and indicate the size (i.e., large or small) that causes a to be small.

3. A channel used for random access has an end-to-end propagation delay of τ seconds. Station A is at one end of the channel, and stations B and C are at the other end, essentially at the same place. The following time diagram shows the arrival times of packets to each station, t_A, t_B, and t_C, and the transmission of the packet from A. (The packets are assumed to be available for transmission immediately on arrival, but of course transmission is controlled by the access algorithms.)
   (a) Complete the diagrams for ALOHA, CSMA, and CSMA/CD by showing the transmission times from stations B and C as controlled by the algorithms.

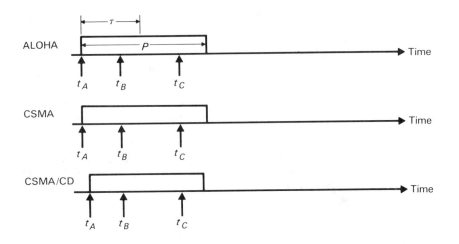

(b) In each case, determine an expression for the time at which station A observes the channel to be free again after the transmission.

4. A slotted ALOHA protocol selects a backoff integer from the set of numbers 0 to (and including) 39. After completing a transmission, a station must wait two slot times to determine if a transmission is successful.
   (a) Find the normalized time required on the average for each retransmission, i.e., the time from beginning to transmit a packet until the station determines its fate.
   (b) Use the data in Table 9.3 to plot a family of normalized transfer delay curves showing T versus S with a as a parameter. Let a take on the values 0.01, 0.1, and 1.

5. For the probability distribution function shown in Fig. 9.17 and defined by Eq. (9.33), show that the mean is given by Eq. (9.34).

6. Assume that $S = Ge^{-G}$ is a valid relation between S and G for slotted ALOHA.
   (a) Determine an expression for average packet delay for successfully transmitted packets in terms of G and the following variables:
       P—packet transmission time; and
       τ—one-way propagation delay for the channel.
       The backoff algorithm selects k at random from the equally likely integers $0, 1, 2, \ldots, K$ and sets the backoff at $k\tau$.
   (b) Determine the delay in slots, or packet times, for the following parameter values:
       Channel bit rate = 1 Mbps;
       Average packet length = 1000 bits;
       $\tau = 0.25 \times 10^{-3}$ sec;
       $S = 0.3$; and
       $K = 15$.

7. (a) Use Fig. 9.35 to determine a range of normalized propagation delays for which all CSMA/CD protocols have a channel capacity greater than any of the other algorithms shown in the figure.
   (b) What maximum channel bit rates can be used for 1 km and 100 km bus lengths and packet lengths of 1000 bits if the CSMA/CD protocols are to have the largest capacity?

8. A group of personal computers uses a pure ALOHA access scheme to communicate over a bus network. All packets are 30 bytes long and the channel bit rate is 100 kbps. If each computer generates 10 packets/minute on the average, how many computers will the system support? How do the results change if the packets are 60 bytes long? What if 50 packets are generated per minute by each user?

9. Repeat problem 8 for a slotted ALOHA access scheme.

10. The transmissions of two stations on a CSMA/CD network collide. Assuming that the backoff algorithm is untruncated binary exponential with negligible propagation delay between the colliding stations, find:
    (a) The probability that the retransmissions collide again on the first transmission attempt;
    (b) The (unconditional) probability that the retransmission will collide on the second retransmission attempt, and thus on the nth attempt;
    (c) The probability that exactly n retransmissions are necessary before the contention is resolved; and

(d) An expression for the expected number of retransmission attempts using the results of (c).

11. Repeat problem 10 for the Ethernet backoff algorithm. (With the Ethernet backoff algorithm: retransmission attempts 1–10 are as previously described; for attempts 12–16, the maximum backoff remains at $2^{10} - 1$; and the packet is discarded [i.e., the algorithm ceases] after 16 attempts.) What is the probability that the contention is not resolved and the packet is discarded?

12. A CSMA/CD network has M stations, each of which has a continuous supply of packets (i.e., each station always has a packet queued). Assume that in each time interval, T, of length twice the end-to-end propagation delay, the probability of *any* station initiating a transmission is q.
   (a) Calculate the probability, Q, of some station initiating a successful transmission in the time interval T. What value of q maximizes this probability? Evaluate Q for this value of q.
   (b) Compute the average number of time intervals before some station successfully acquires the channel. Express this time, the average contention time, in terms of q, M, and T.
   (c) Assume that P is the transmission time of a (successful) packet. Derive an expression for the average throughput, S, in terms of P, T, q, and M. (Neglect propagation delays, interframe times, and so forth.) Show that S is maximized with respect to q by the same value of q as maximized Q. Find an expression for the maximum throughput. What is this throughput as the number of stations becomes infinitely large?
   (d) For a channel bit rate of 3 Mbps, packets of length 1024 bits, and propagation delays of 8 μsec, calculate the maximum throughput when $M = 4$, 64, and 256. What limit does the throughput approach as the number of stations becomes very large?

CHAPTER **10**

*P*rotocols and Network Architecture

10.1 Introduction

The emphasis in this text is on performance analysis of local area networks. Accordingly, it is assumed that a structured network is available for study so that interest can be focused on those parts of the network that are the major determinants of its performance in transmitting packets across the network.

Performance analysis, in this somewhat limited sense, is obviously not the only component of network design. Furthermore, the issues considered in earlier chapters are not the only ones that contribute to network performance in the broader sense of providing services to users coupled to the network. The purpose of this chapter is to introduce the reader to some of the broader issues in the design of networks that are necessary to provide higher-level functionality than just the transport of packets.

In contrast to the analysis approach taken so far, an overall design approach begins with a consideration of network architecture, which is the structure that determines how the various logical and physical components of a network are interconnected.

To minimize design complexity, modern networks tend to use a *layered architecture* in which each layer in the hierarchy is a logical entity that performs certain functions. The services performed by the highest network layer are for the network users directly. Each layer provides services for the next layer above it and shields the details of how the services are carried out from this higher layer. In this hierarchical structure are performed all the intermediate tasks and functions required for the provision of desired user-to-user services over the network.

When users located at different network nodes communicate, the corresponding layers at each node also communicate. A well-defined set of rules called a *protocol* is necessary for each level to carry out its conversation in an orderly, structured manner. These protocols establish what can be regarded as logical communication paths between communicating entities, which are called "peer processes."

Protocols are organized in a hierarchical fashion to correspond to the network layers, as illustrated in Fig. 10.1. The protocols control conversations across a single layer, and all but the lowest layer communicate over logical, or virtual, communication paths. The lowest-layer protocol is the only one to control data flow over a physical connecting channel. Information flow from one level to another is through an interface, and such an interface must be

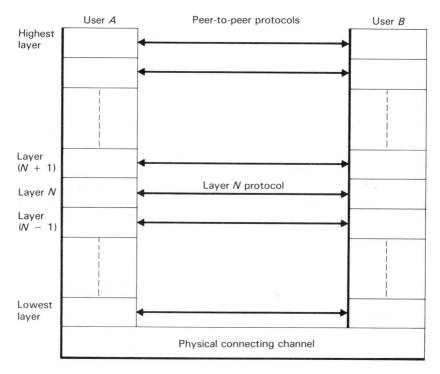

Figure 10.1   A Layered Network Architecture with Layers and Associated Protocols Indicated

present between each pair of adjacent layers. The purpose of the interface is to interpret formats and other protocol features from one protocol layer to another. The relationship between protocols and layers adjacent to each other is shown in Fig. 10.2.

The number of layers, the name of each layer, and the function of each layer differs from network to network. The two extreme layers are usually the application (or user–user) and physical layers. The application layer, as its name implies, deals with the user's specific application—for example, access of legal files, or graphic output on computer aided design. This layer is always the highest level. The physical layer, on the other hand, is always the bottom layer; it deals with the transmission of physical time signals between the two nodes. As indicated in Fig. 10.1, the physical layer includes the physical transmission channel and provides an electrical, as well as a logical, connection between the communicating processes.

In designing a network architecture, a number of general guidelines must be followed. Protocols at lower levels should be transparent to higher-level protocols in the sense that the performance of the lower level services should not require any attention from the higher levels. Each layer should also perform a well-defined function, and layer boundaries should be chosen to minimize the amount of interfacing required between adjacent layers. Advantages of a layered approach include flexibility to adapt lower level protocols without affecting higher-level ones and the ability to isolate well-defined functions.

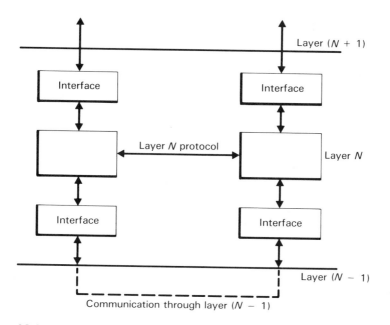

Figure 10.2   Relationship Between Neighboring Layers in a Network Architecture

Important existing network architectures are IBM's System Network Architecture (SNA), Digital Equipment's Distributed Network Architecture, and the architecture associated with the U.S. Department of Defense's ARPANET.

The remaining sections of this chapter develop network architecture in more detail. Sections 10.2 and 10.3 discuss two reference standards for such architectures: the International Standards Organization (ISO) reference model and the Institute of Electrical and Electronic Engineers 802 (IEEE 802) standard. Section 10.4 then gives a description of bit-oriented data-link protocols. Several typical network architectures are discussed in Section 10.5, and the chapter is concluded with comments on *internetworking,* the problem of coupling together several local networks.

A good general reference on the design of networks that use a layered architecture is the book by Tanenbaum [1]. Stallings, [2], in his book on local networks, discusses details of protocols specifically for this class of networks.

10.2 The ISO Reference Model

In an effort to standardize network architectures and protocols, the ISO has developed a reference model for use in comparing different architectures and in constructing new networks. This model is called the Reference Model of Open Systems Interconnection (OSI). *System* in this context refers to anything from a simple terminal to a complicated network. The term *open* is used to show that the model is concerned with the transfer of information between *interconnected* systems and is not concerned with the inner operation of the systems themselves.

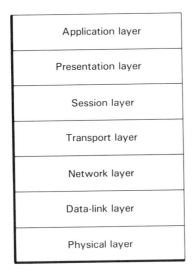

| Application layer |
| Presentation layer |
| Session layer |
| Transport layer |
| Network layer |
| Data-link layer |
| Physical layer |

Figure 10.3   Layers of the ISO Reference Model

As shown in Fig. 10.3, the ISO reference model has seven layers. The functions of each of these layers and the services provided are discussed in the next subsection. All seven layers may or may not be used at any given network node for any given user–user interaction. Normally all seven layers are used at the originating and terminating nodes of a connection, whereas only three layers are used at any intermediate nodes that serve only to transport packets to their destination nodes.

For example, if hosts *A* and *B* are interconnected through nodes 1 and 2 as shown in Fig. 10.4, a message from *A* to *B* is handled in nodes 1 and 2 by only three layers: the physical, data-link, and network layers. The protocols associated with the layers used at source and destination hosts are called *end-to-end protocols;* those used to connect each host to the first network node in a communication path are called *network access protocols;* and those used for communication between contiguous nodes on the path through the network are termed *internal network protocols.* Identification of the different classes of protocols is made in Fig. 10.5 using a diagram that also shows the ISO seven-level hierarchy.

10.2.1 The Seven ISO Layers

In this subsection, the seven layers of the ISO reference model, shown in Figs. 10.3 and 10.5, are described from the bottom up. The functions incorporated in each layer and the services provided to the layer above are emphasized. The ISO Reference Model is described in much greater detail in Tanenbaum [1].

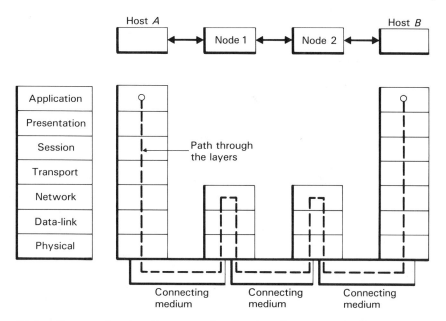

Figure 10.4 Communication Between Application Processes in Hosts *A* and *B* Through Two Network Nodes

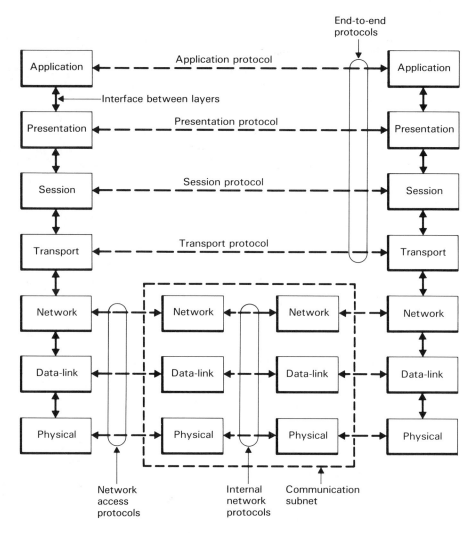

Figure 10.5   Protocols for the ISO Reference Model

The *physical layer* is concerned with the transmission of each bit in a bit stream over a direct physical connection. Interest is focused on all electrical, mechanical, and functional characteristics needed to transmit the bit stream properly. Design specifications encompass all the physical features of the signals, such as amplitude, period, frequency spectrum (i.e., baseband or broadband), and modulating scheme. The physical features of connections, such as number of connector pins, and so forth, are also considered, as are such additional aspects as the mode of operating the physical connection (i.e., full or half duplex).

When viewed from above in the hierarchy, the physical layer provides bit synchronization and for the establishment, maintenance, and release of the physical connection that transmits the bit stream between two communicating nodes. Note that the bits in the bit stream are not grouped by this layer, and some may be in error.

The layer above the physical layer is the *data-link layer,* which provides for character and message (frame) synchronization, and ensures the reliable transmission of data blocks or frames between physically connected nodes. It is the function of this layer to detect and if necessary correct errors that occur in the raw bit stream maintained by the physical layer. To accomplish this, the data-link layer must create and recognize the boundaries of frames and use redundant bits in these frames to detect errors. Frames that are in error must be retransmitted, and the data-link layer software must make provision for such retransmissions by generating acknowledgments and managing all other necessary details.

The data-link layer, supported by the physical layer below it, provides an apparently error-free link between physically connected nodes for use by the next higher layer, the network layer.

The *network layer* software provides the services required to set up and maintain the flow of messages between users coupled to the network. The data unit dealt with by this layer is the packet, and one function of software at the network level is to ensure that such packets are directed toward their designated destinations. Since communicating users are not necessarily connected by a direct physical link, this layer is responsible for routing and switching. The network layer not only controls the operation of the communication subnet, as noted in Fig. 10.5, but also determines the nature of the interfaces between the hosts and their neighboring nodes.

The type of service provided to the transport layer by the network layer is usually specified as either virtual-circuit or datagram service. The differences between these services are explained in the next subsection. Another issue that arises with respect to the flow of packets over the network is that of congestion. Network efficiency is reduced if too many packets are directed over one route, and the network layer software often provides congestion and flow control. Congestion and flow control are also discussed in more detail in the next subsection.

The *transport layer* is the next in order above the network layer. From the point of view of this layer, all services, such as routing, switching, and possibly congestion control, that are necessary for end-to-end users to exchange packets are provided by lower layers. A basic function of the transport layer is to subdivide messages passed down from the session layer into smaller units (namely, packets), if this is necessary, and to ensure that the smaller units are properly transmitted to the intended destination.

In progressing to higher and higher layers in the ISO hierarchy, the emphasis shifts from functions implemented by hardware and software at the network nodes to provide for proper bit flow and packet flow, to services associated with application processes running in host or user devices. The transport layer is the first of the higher layers to reflect this change in emphasis because its function is to provide transparent transfer of data between application programs. It is a true end-to-end layer. Software in this layer is designed to make this data transfer between application programs as network-independent as possible.

The transport layer can also set up and maintain a specified type of service as efficiently as possible using the resources of the network. Examples of such services are: process-to-process message delivery with proper ordering of messages; the broadcast of messages to multiple destinations; and isolated message delivery without guarantee of order. The first of the three services listed is connection oriented. If the network layer has provided a virtual-circuit service, then the transport layer is relatively simple; if, however, the network layer supports only datagrams, then the transport layer is more complex.

Following the transport layer is the *session layer*. A *session* is a term used for a dialog carried out over a connection between application processes that run in user devices. Thus, as its name implies, the session layer sets up and maintains a connection between application processes and, in fulfilling this function, serves as the user's interface to the network. The session software not only establishes the appropriate connection, but may need to check for user authenticity, provide billing, and decide on the type of communication—full duplex or half duplex.

Above the session layer is the *presentation layer,* which is assigned the task of providing as many general functions as possible for simplifying communication between end users. Examples of services provided by the presentation layer are code conversion, text compression, and the use of standard layouts for printers or terminals. In general, this layer is used to make communication between end users as straightforward and as device-independent as possible.

The *application layer* is the highest of the seven identified in the ISO model. The composition and functions of this layer are almost totally application-dependent. Thus the software at this level would be expected to contain the specific application programs with provisions for managing the resources required.

10.2.2 Types of Service and Congestion Control

Most of the functions provided by the various layers in the ISO model are adequately described in the concise overview presented in the preceding subsection. However, two functions normally provided by the network layer of the ISO model require further elaboration. These functions are the type of service and congestion control.

The type of service refers to the details of handling packets by layers below and including the network layer. The two most important methods of this sort are called *datagram* and *virtual circuit* in the ISO literature. (As noted in Section 10.3, the IEEE 802 standards use a different terminology.)

Datagram service is the more basic of the two just named. In providing such a service, the network and lower layers couple the sender and receiver by merely transferring packets in a completely independent manner over the virtual connection. Datagram service can be likened to the postal service: packets are delivered to a destination address, which must be specified in the packet, but such delivery constitutes all that is required. No end-to-end error control or acknowledgments are provided, and datagrams are passed to the user host in the order in which they arrive. If these latter functions are required, they must be provided in a layer higher than the network layer.

As can be seen from the preceding description, datagram service is fairly primitive. Virtual-circuit service is at the other extreme; it provides all the functions previously noted as absent from the datagram service. Thus the virtual-circuit service not only delivers each packet to its destination, it also provides all proper sequencing of packets, error control, flow control, and acknowledgments on an end-to-end basis. Virtual circuits require an initial call-setup procedure that sets up a series of logical connections. Note that such connections, unlike comparable circuit-switched connections, do not require a permanent allocation of resources. The call-setup procedure is followed by a data transfer phase and finally by a disconnect procedure.

Datagram service seems to be a common choice for use in local networks, although such service is not currently popular for public networks. For public networks, a third type of service termed *fast select* has been proposed for transaction-oriented applications, which are essentially single-packet messages. Fast select is a type of virtual-circuit service that has a relatively short call-setup time and is intended to function for a single message and its acknowledgment. It is expected that fast select will supplant datagram service in many public packet-switched networks.

Congestion and the related but separate issue of flow control also require elaboration. Congestion occurs at a node in a computer network when the resources of the node are stretched to capacity. This happens when the total input traffic rate exceeds the output rate so that all available buffers become full. As a consequence of buffer overflow, packets have to be dropped, and there is the likelihood that the whole network will become deadlocked, with no packets getting through.

Congestion and its control is a localized issue, whereas flow control applies to end-to-end control of packets between a source-destination pair. Flow control attempts to ensure that packets do not arrive at the destination node faster than the receiving device can handle them. The simplest flow-control procedures are applied with the error-control mechanisms, for example, with the automatic repeat request (ARQ) schemes discussed in Chapter 2. Variable window schemes have also been developed for incorporation into data-link protocols to limit the number of unacknowledged packets in the data stream at any given time. A standard and frequently used data-link protocol called High-level Data-link Control (HDLC) uses such a variable window scheme.

10.3 IEEE 802 Standards for Local Area Networks

Standards for local area networks are currently being formulated by the IEEE through the IEEE 802 Standards Committee. The ISO has agreed to process these standards for adoption as international standards as they are finalized by the IEEE 802 Committee.

The IEEE 802 standards are divided into six parts; the relationship between the six members of the IEEE 802 family is indicated in Fig. 10.6. The standards specify the physical and data-link layers of the ISO reference model with a single logical link protocol and four types of media access technologies. The component parts of the 802 standard are:

IEEE Standard 802.2, a common logical link-control protocol;
IEEE Standard 802.3, a bus that uses CSMA/CD as the access method;
IEEE Standard 802.4, a bus that uses token passing as the access method;
IEEE Standard 802.5, a ring that uses token passing as the access method; and
IEEE Standard 802.6, a metropolitan area network.

Finally, IEEE Standard 802.1 is a companion document that describes the relationship between the various parts of the standard and their relationship with the ISO reference model and with higher-layer protocols. This document also discusses internetworking and network management issues.

Although the IEEE 802 standards are currently incomplete and in draft form, they give a clear picture of what is likely to be the accepted architecture for local network access protocols. The IEEE local area reference model is shown in comparison to the ISO model in Fig. 10.7.

As suggested in Fig. 10.7, the physical layer in the IEEE local network standard encompasses essentially the same features for transmitting and receiving bits as does the ISO model. An exception is that the media access model of the IEEE 802 standard includes media access protocol features such

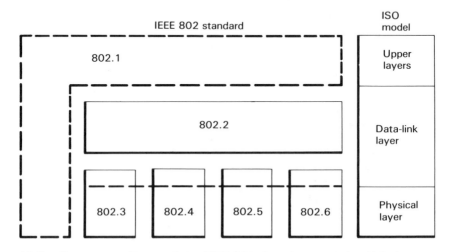

Figure 10.6   Component Parts of the IEEE 802 Standard and the ISO Reference Model

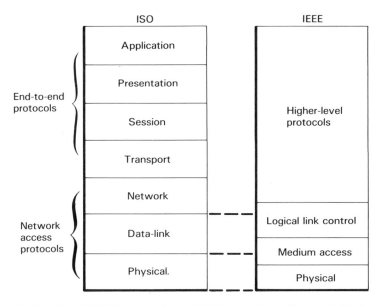

Figure 10.7   The ISO Model and the IEEE Local Area Network Reference Models Compared

as the backoff algorithm for CSMA/CD, whereas such features remain in the physical layer for the ISO model.

As indicated in Fig. 10.7, the functions of the ISO data-link layer are essentially carried out by the logical link control (LLC) and part of the media access control (MAC) of the IEEE 802 standard. The MAC layer provides for use of a random access or token procedure for controlling access to the channel. (See standards 802.3 through 802.5 at the beginning of this section.) In addition to the basic procedures, the MAC layer also includes addressing of data frames and frame-check sequences.

The LLC layer in the 802 standard is above the MAC layer and essentially provides a basic data-link protocol with at least two kinds of service:

- *Unacknowledged connectionless* service, which is similar to datagram service with no guarantee of frame delivery; and
- *Connection-oriented* service, which is similar to virtual-circuit service and provides acknowledgments of data units, flow control, sequencing, and error recovery.

A third type of service, *acknowledged connectionless* service, is being considered for approval by the committee. The LLC protocol also permits multiplexing of up to 128 distinct logical links for each station. Whereas the unacknowledged connectionless service permits point-to-point, multipoint, and broadcast connections, the other services support only point-to-point connections. Note that whereas the principal function of the LLC layer is analogous to the data-link layer of the ISO model, the LLC layer also provides some of the functions assigned to the network layer of that model.

For the ISO model, the network access layers have been identified as the physical, data-link, and network layers. A level that corresponds to the network layer is not identified in the IEEE 802 standard for the reason that functions such as routing and switching are not required in local networks, which typically share a common channel. As previously noted, a number of network layer functions is performed by the LLC layer. With such exceptions, however, the network layer either is not used for the local network or is accomplished outside of the layers that are defined.

In reviewing the layered structure for local networks, note that the IEEE 802 standard layers—physical, media access control (MAC), and logical link control (LLC)—encompass essentially all that is needed for network access. As discussed for the ISO model, the group of layers for network access provide all the necessary features and functions required to provide basic datagram or virtual-circuit services, although actual delivery of these services is a function of the transport level in the ISO model. Most additional services, provided by levels higher than the network access levels, are no longer in the area of basic packet communication, but fall into application-specific tasks or services.

After this review of the IEEE 802 standard for a layered structure of basic packet communication over a local network, it is clear that from a network-design point of view, all three protocol layers—the physical, media access, and logical link control—must be considered in the design. Although the emphasis in this text is not on network design, consideration of the content of earlier chapters shows that elements of the physical layer are treated in Chapter 2, and that media access control is the major topic dealt with in Chapters 6–9. Proper functioning of both of these layers depends on both hardware and software.

A complete local network design must also include the logical link control level. This level provides a basic data-link protocol and either connectionless or connection-type service, functions provided principally in software. Thus, to complete the treatment of all layers in the basic local area network structure, the logical link control-level protocol is discussed in the next subsection.

10.4 Data-link Protocols

This subsection introduces the central features of data-link protocols through discussion of a basic protocol of this type. It then continues with a subsection that outlines the features required of a logical link control (LLC) protocol for a local network.

10.4.1 Basic Data-link Protocols

For a data link to function, there must be communication facilities with appropriate transmitters and receivers at each communicating node. Since the nodes normally are separated by some distance, processes at these nodes are coordinated by exchange of control information. Further, as noted in Chapter 2, it is necessary to provide for error detection and recovery. The major function of the data-link protocol is to manage communication between nodes in a network, providing both process coordination and error control.

Process coordination has a number of aspects that include synchronization of bits, frames, and also higher-order entities. As noted in Chapter 2, the bit stream can be managed either synchronously or asynchronously. Synchronous operation is the more efficient of the two types, and it is commonly used in modern networks. Bit synchronization, however, is not normally a function of the data-link protocol, so this feature is assumed without further discussion.

There are two classes of protocols that use synchronous bit streams: character oriented and bit oriented. Character-oriented protocols, the older of the two types, use dedicated characters to delineate frames. Use of such characters renders the protocol nontransparent from the point of view of higher levels, which is a serious disadvantage. Bit-oriented protocols, on the other hand, use a sequence of bits, rather than characters, to mark the beginning and ending of frames. As is discussed later, the bit sequence can be rendered transparent to higher levels, and for this reason, bit-oriented protocols are now the common choice.

For bit-oriented protocols, the beginning and ending of each frame is often marked by a unique bit sequence, for example, 01111110, which is often called a flag. Such flags are prevented from occurring in the body of a frame by a process called *bit stuffing*. For the example given, whenever transmitting hardware encounters five consecutive 1's after the first flag that marks the beginning of a frame, it automatically inserts a 0 as the next bit. The receiver hardware automatically removes every 0 after five consecutive 1's. The process of bit stuffing thus maintains the flags as unique identifiers of the beginnings and endings of frames.

For bit-oriented protocols, the body of the frame contains four fields for addresses, control information, data, and an error-detecting checksum. Frames themselves can be divided into three types: information types that carry data, supervisory types, such as acknowledgments, and unnumbered types that are used for initialization and other control purposes.

Insight into the operation of a data-link protocol can be gained by examining an elementary "stop-and-wait" protocol for one-way transmission of messages. (Although messages go only one way, the channel must be half duplex to allow for transmitting acknowledgments.) Figure 10.8 gives a flow diagram for such a protocol.

The protocol makes use of information and supervisory-type frames. The information type contains the address of the destination stations in the address field, a sequence number in the control field, messages to be transmitted in the data field, and, of course, the checksum.

The supervisory-type frame, when used for acknowledgments, contains the address of the sending station, an indication that the frame is an acknowledg-

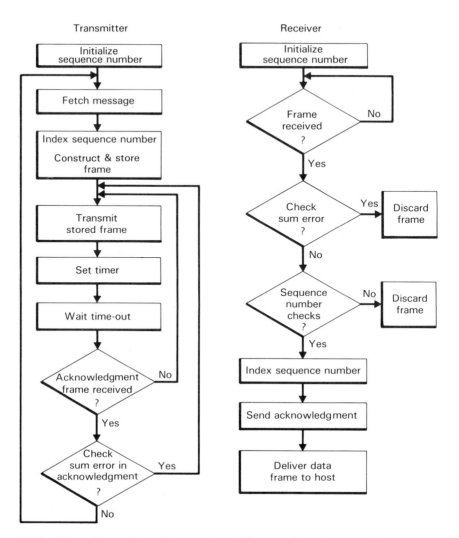

Transmitter

Receiver

Figure 10.8   Flow Charts for a Stop-and-wait Protocol for One-way Transmission of Messages

ment frame in the control field, nothing in the data field, and again the checksum.

Now consider the operation of the transmitting station as shown in the flow chart of Fig. 10.8. Prior to transmitting a set of messages, the sequence number is initialized both at the transmitter and at the receiver. A message is fetched from the host at the transmitter, and a frame is constructed that contains the message and an appropriate sequence number. The frame is transmitted, and a timer is set for a time-out period somewhat longer than the time required for the destination to receive the frame and return an acknowledgment.

At the end of the time-out period, one of three events has occurred:

1. No return frame is received;
2. A return frame is received with errors; or
3. A return frame is received with no errors.

The last of these events is proof that the receiver has received the transmitted frame correctly. The transmitter can then change the sequence number and proceed to transmit the next frame. If either event 1 or 2 occurs, the original frame must be retransmitted since neither of these events guarantees that it was correctly received. When retransmitting a frame, the sequence number is not changed from the original transmission.

The receiver operation shown involves checking the original message frame for errors and for a proper sequence number. If no errors are detected, and the sequence number is correct, then an acknowledgment frame is returned, and the data from the received frame is delivered to the host of the receiving station. If either an error is detected or the sequence number is incorrect, the frame is rejected and the receiver awaits the next frame.

Practical data-link protocols have more features than the protocol just described, but the basic operating principles are the same. Some characteristics of practical logical link control protocols are given in the next subsection.

10.4.2 Logical Link Control Protocols

If a local network is organized with the structure of the IEEE 802 model, the logical link control protocol must perform most of the functions of a normal data-link protocol, plus a few features included in the network layer of the ISO model, because this layer is not present in the IEEE model.

Normal functions of a data-link protocol considered necessary for a local network include:

- Addressing of frames;
- Transmission of information in frames;
- Sequence numbering of frames; and
- Error control by retransmission of incorrectly received frames.

End-to-end flow control at the LLC level is required for some access protocols (MAC-layer protocols in IEEE 802 notation) and not for others. For example, the slotted ring access protocol inherently provides flow control since the number of minipackets on the ring is limited. On the other hand, such a self-limiting feature is not present for random access protocols.

In the IEEE 802 standard, the LLC layer provides either connection- or connectionless-type service. As previously noted, these services correspond to datagram and virtual-circuit service and require protocol features not normally present at the data-link level in the ISO model. The more important additional features are source and destination addresses for datagram service, and provisions for frames to be delivered correctly and in order for virtual-circuit service.

A provision that allows multiple users at each station to be multiplexed and a provision for broadcast-type messages from one station to all others on the network are also desirable features.

Most of the features required for a local network logical link control protocol are specified in the two most important standards: ADCCP (Advanced Data Communication Control Procedures) developed by the American National Standards Institute (ANSI), and HDLC (High-level Data-link Control) developed by the Comité Consultatif Internationale de Télégraphique et Téléphonique (CCITT). The two standards are almost identical; they differ only in some specialized options. Various companies have developed their own specialized protocols with minor modifications from these standards: SDLC, by IBM, is such an example. The LLC protocol in the IEEE 802 draft standard is modeled after one mode of the HDLC standard.

In the remainder of this section, the frame structure and the procedural elements of the so-called balanced asynchronous class of HDLC procedures are surveyed. The general HDLC procedures specify three modes of operation from which the choice of balanced asynchronous mode has been made for the LLC protocol. This mode is intended for point-to-point connections where both stations can initiate transmissions.

The frame structure is shown in Fig. 10.9. Note that there are beginning and ending flags, protected by bit stuffing. In general, these flags enclose four fields for address, control, information, and the frame-check sequence. Each of these fields is described in this section. If information is to be transmitted, all four fields of Fig. 10.9 are occupied. On the other hand, if only control sequences are to be transmitted, the information field is empty.

The address field in a normal mode can identify 256 addresses and can be extended to identify as many as desired. An "all-ones" address is specified as a broadcast transmission to all stations. When a command frame is sent, the address of the station to receive the frame is used. When a response frame is sent, the address of the transmitting station is used.

An 8-bit control field is used to classify the function and purpose of each frame into three different formats: information transfers (I frame), supervisory (S frame), and unnumbered (U frame). The control field format is shown in Fig. 10.10. The I frame is denoted by 0 in the first bit position, whereas the

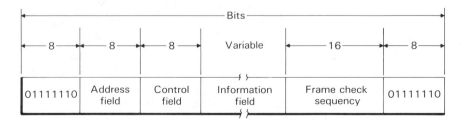

Figure 10.9   HDLC Standard Data-link Frame Format

0		N(S)		P/F		N(R)	
1	0	S	S	P/F		N(R)	
1	1	M	M	P/F	M	M	M

Eight bits

Information frame (I):0
Supervisory frame (S):10
Unnumbered frame (U):11
S bits = Supervising functions
M bits = Commands/responses
N(S) = Number of send frame
N(R) = Number of receive frame
P/F = Poll/final bit

Figure 10.10   Control Field Format for the HDLC Standard Data-link Protocol

S and U frames are denoted by 10 and 11, respectively, in the first two bit positions. The notation I, S, or U frames is used in the following discussion.

An I frame has a transmitted frame number $N(S)$ and received frame number $N(R)$. An S frame has only a received frame number $N(R)$. Whereas $N(S)$ denotes the sequence number of the frame being transmitted, $N(R)$ denotes the sequence number of the *next* frame expected.

The P/F (poll/final) bit provides a means to solicit a response from a destination station at the earliest opportunity. The bit is considered to be a P bit if the frame is a command, and an F bit if the frame is a response. The response to a P bit set to 1 in a transmitted frame is an F bit, also set to 1 in the next appropriate frame from the destination station. Transmission of a second P bit is prohibited until the earlier one receives a response. The P/F bit is used for several purposes, including a checkpoint for tracking which frames have been transmitted and received. The S and M bit positions in the control field provide specified supervisory and control functions.

The information field can contain an unrestricted amount of data. Finally, the last element in the frame is the frame-check sequence, which is a 16-bit cyclical redundancy check that uses the CCITT generator polynomial $X^{16} + X^{12} + X^5 + 1$.

Now that the frame structure has been described, the elements of the HDLC protocol procedure are considered. Each frame, whether I, S, or U, contains either a command or a response. The HDLC standard defines a substantial number of command/responses appropriate to the three operating modes for the data-link procedure. Several command/responses are used to set up and terminate one of the three operating modes.

As pointed out, the asynchronous balanced mode is the choice for LLC protocols. Thus, only those command/responses appropriate to the basic operation of this mode are described. The basic command/response possibilities are:

I *Command/Response*	U *Commands*
Information (I)	Set Asynchronous Balanced Mode (SABM)
S *Commands/Responses*	Set Asynchronous Balanced Mode Extended (SABME)
Receive Ready (RR)	Disconnect (DISC)
Receive Not Ready (RNR)	U *Responses*
Reject (REJ)	
Selective Reject (SREJ)	Unnumbered Acknowledgment (UA)
	Frame Reject (FRMR)

Each of these command/responses is discussed briefly in turn. The I command/response is an I frame used to transmit sequentially numbered information fields. The RR command/response is used to indicate readiness to receive I frames. The RNR command/response is used to indicate a busy condition. The REJ command/response is used to request retransmission of all I frames, starting from a designated point in the numbering cycle. The SREJ command/response requests retransmission of a single specified I frame. All five command/responses that use I or S frames (I, RR, RNR, REJ, SREJ) can carry acknowledgments of frames received from the other station. This "piggybacking" of acknowledgments in I or S frames adds to transmission efficiency.

The SABM and SABME commands, which use U frames, establish the asynchronous balanced mode of operation. When one is accepted and acknowledged, the receiving station resets its information-sequencing variable, $N(S)$, and its $N(R)$ variable to 0. The SABM command determines operation with a sequence of 8 different values $(0, 1, \ldots, 7)$ for $N(S)$, whereas SABME allows for a sequence of 128 different values. The control field format of Fig. 10.10 must be enlarged to 16 bits for this case. The DISC command logically terminates an operating mode.

The UA response is used to acknowledge control information such as initializing, resetting, and so forth. It uses a U frame. The FRMR response also uses a U frame to indicate that a frame received was in error in a manner not recoverable by retransmitting the same frame.

A typical dialog for two stations A and B in an error-free environment is now described, using the notation (frame type, address, command/response, $N(S)$, $N(R)$, P/F) to describe the transmitted frames. If $N(S)$ or $N(R)$ are not applicable, they are replaced by a minus sign $(-)$.

Station A could initiate the dialog by transmitting the frame (U, B, SABM, $-$, $-$, 1). Station B acknowledges with the frame (U, A, UA, $-$, $-$, 1), which indicates that the message was received. Station B is in the information-transmitting state after receipt of the frame from A, and station A moves into this state upon receipt of the acknowledgment. The P-bit is set to 1 by station A to ensure a prompt acknowledgment of its command.

Stations A and B can share the channel by exchanging messages. Assume, for example, that over the period of the dialog, A has 15 messages to transmit to B, and that B has 5 messages to transmit to A. The details depend to some extent on when the messages are sent and received. In any case, station A sends I frames addressed to B, numbering its messages by setting $N(S)$ to 0, 1, 2, ..., 7, 0, 1, ..., 6. The value of $N(R)$, the number of the next message expected, starts from 0 and is indexed by 1 after receipt of each message from B. No more than 7 messages can be outstanding without acknowledgment; the P/F bit is left at its 0 value for the information exchange. In passing, note that this is an example of a sliding window ARQ scheme.

Station B transmits its own messages when it has use of the channel, acknowledging messages from station A at the same time. The arrival and transmission times for messages could, for example, result in the following sequence of frames from station B: $(I, A, I, 0, 0, 0)$; $(I, A, I, 1, 0, 0)$; $(I, A, I, 2, 1, 0)$; $(I, A, I, 3, 2, 0)$; $(I, A, I, 4, 2, 0)$.

According to the assumption stated, station B runs out of messages to transmit after it has transmitted five. Thus, to acknowledge the remaining messages from station A, it must use S frames, such as RR. These are response-type frames, and thus the remaining sequence from station B could be: $(S, B, RR, -, 3, 0)$; $(S, B, RR, -, 4, 0)$; $(S, B, RR, -, 5, 0) \ldots (S, B, RR, -, 6, 0)$.

After station A has transmitted all its messages and has had them acknowledged, it can signal to break the connection by sending $(U, B, DISC, -, -, 1)$. Station B can acknowledge with $(U, B, UA, -, -, 1)$, and the dialog is over.

Now consider an elementary example of the error-recovery properties of the HDLC procedure. Assume that a transmission error occurs in transmitting message 4 from station A to station B. If this occurs, station B recognizes the sequence numbers 0, 1, 2, 3, 5, 6, and notes the absence of number 4 after timing out. One way to recover from this error is for B to send $(S, B, SREJ, -, 4, 0)$. This asks A to retransmit frame 4 only. Alternatively, B could send $(S, B, REJ, -, 4, 0)$; in this case A must retransmit frame 4 and all succeeding frames. Finally, B could send a message with the P bit set to 1 and with $N(R) = 4$, indicating that this is the next message to be expected. The P bit set to 1 causes a checkpoint to take place at station A, which notes that only messages 0, 1, 2, and 3 have been acknowledged, even though messages 0, 1, ..., 6 have been transmitted. Thus station A retransmits frame 4 with an F bit, followed by frames 5 and 6, and the error is corrected.

For the 802 protocols, addressing for both source and destination stations is included in the MAC layer; however, addressing for logical locations within a station (up to 128 maximum) is included in the LLC protocol. The LLC frame format, which is shown in Fig. 10.11, includes fields for destination and source access points (DSAP and SSAP), control, and data. The least significant bit (i.e., the first bit transmitted) of the DSAP byte indicates whether the address is a single or multipoint address. The least significant bit of the SSAP byte indicates whether the frame is a command or response frame. The control byte

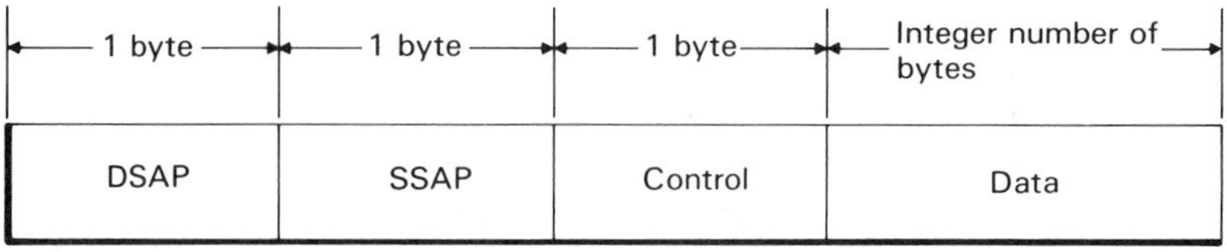

← 1 byte →	← 1 byte →	← 1 byte →	Integer number of bytes
DSAP	SSAP	Control	Data

DSAP = Destination service access point
SSAP = Source service access point

Figure 10.11   IEEE 802 LLC Frame Format

is essentially the same as the HDLC standard for the balanced asynchronous mode, as shown in Fig. 10.10.

The account of data-link protocols in this subsection does not cover all the innumerable details. On the contrary, it covers only the basic ideas of what is possible. More detail can be found in the paper by Carlson [3], the books by Tanenbaum [1] and Stallings [2], or in the standard publications for ISO [4] and IEEE 802 [5].

10.5 Local Network Architectures

Section 10.3 reviews the IEEE 802 standards for local networks. As noted in that section, these standards are still in draft form, and even when completed, will represent the opinion of only one group, although clearly a significant one. Currently, the IEEE 802 standards address only the bottom three layers of a multilayer network architecture.

In this section, the architectures of three existing local networks are briefly reviewed after several general comments. The existing architectures illustrate what can be done and, not surprisingly, point out that a number of approaches are possible.

It has been noted that local networks have different requirements from the wide area networks that motivated the ISO standards. One major difference is the absence of a need for switching and routing. Since these are not required, many of the functions performed by the network layer of the ISO model are not needed. On the other hand, most local networks share a common channel, so there is a clear necessity for media access control.

10.5.1   Intel Local Network Architecture

The basic Intel architecture (see Ryan et al. [6]) is tailored to use Ethernet as the physical link layer. The interrelation of the six defined layers is shown in Fig. 10.12. Note that the physical and data-link layers are in direct correspondence with the ISO model. The network layer of the ISO model is omitted, but the transport and session layers of the Intel model also fall in the same order as

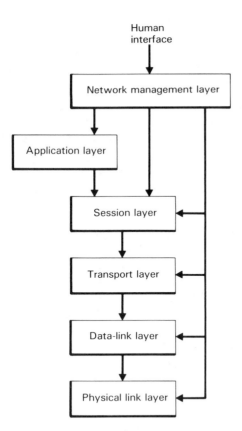

Figure 10.12   Intel Local Network Architecture (From Ryan et al. [6])

the ISO model. A presentation layer is not present, but an application layer roughly corresponding to that of the ISO model is. The Intel model has a network management layer that is higher than the application layer and coupled to all the lower layers.

PHYSICAL LAYER: This layer provides an electrical connection for transferring bits. The Intel network uses a coaxial cable as a passive broadcast medium with no central control for the connecting channel.

DATA-LINK LAYER: This layer uses CSMA/CD to provide "best-effort" packet delivery. As discussed in Chapter 9, CSMA/CD allows multiple access to the channel; however, with this access method there is a probability that packets will be lost or will be received out of order.

TRANSPORT LAYER: The transport layer sets up virtual circuits, which can be managed dynamically by the communicating processes. Such virtual circuits provide reliable, full duplex, process-to-process message delivery, and have both error control and flow control.

SESSION LAYER: The session layer interfaces between specific host operating systems and the network, providing, among other functions, a mapping of process names.

APPLICATION LAYER: This layer contains application-specific programs.

NETWORK MANAGEMENT LAYER: The network management layer provides for monitoring and control of the complete network. As Fig. 10.12 shows, network management programs have special interfaces into all lower levels to carry out their task.

The functions of the physical and data-link layers are performed in the basic architecture by the Ethernet intelligent controller, regarded as a subsystem of the overall network. The concept of a subsystem performing the functions of the two lowest levels is used by Intel to provide for an extended architecture that uses a network layer to couple multiple application processes to multiple lower-level subsystems. The lower-level subsystems can be Ethernet controllers, or subsystems that use HDLC or SDLC at the data-link level, and telephone lines or dedicated serial buses for the physical connection. The application processes couple to the network layer through appropriate session and transport layers tailored to each application process.

The format of the frame used at the data-link level with Ethernet is shown in Fig. 10.13(a). The data field includes the user data and headers from the application and transport layers, as shown in Fig. 10.13(b).

Addressing in Intel's network is hierarchical, with an identification number for each network, each node, and each process. The network-ID, which

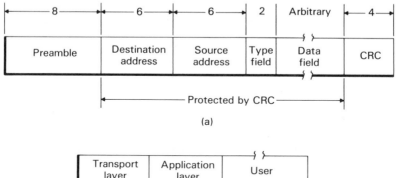

(a)

(b)

Figure 10.13   Intel Local Network Frame Format, with Field Lengths in Bytes (From Ryan et al. [6])

(a) Data-link frame format

(b) Data field format

Chapter 10 Protocols and Network Architecture

identifies each network in an internetwork environment, is not used with a single local network. The node identifier is called a host-ID and is unique for all installed hosts. Each node, or host, is allowed multiple processes, each of which is identified by a port-ID. Ports are unique within a node, and the combination of a host-ID and a port-ID, called a socket, provides the complete address of a process. Virtual circuits can be set up and maintained between sockets.

10.5.2 Local Network Architecture for a Token Ring

The architecture for a single-token-type ring network, which may be implemented by IBM, is described in separate papers by Andrews and Schultz [7] and by Dixon, Strole, and Markov [8]. The architecture, which is described only for the first two levels, is shown in Fig. 10.14. The diagram shown is the architecture of one ring station attached to the ring or transmission medium. Each ring station can support one or more data-link control (DLC) stations, which are devices or processes located at the ring station. Each DLC station has its own layered structure of data-link and higher-layer protocols. Data

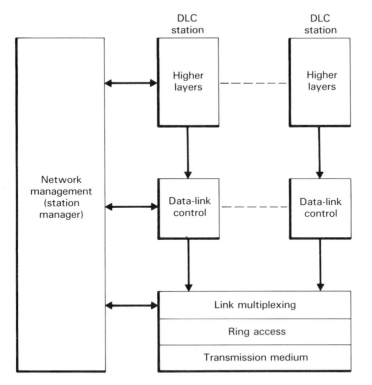

Figure 10.14   **Architecture for a Token-ring Network (From Andrews and Schultz [7]) (Figure is for one ring station connected to the ring, with several DLC stations connected to the ring station)**

flow from the DLC stations is multiplexed at the physical layer for access to the ring through the ring-station interface.

One feature of the architecture shown is the establishment of essentially independent links between DLC stations. For any such link, the levels above data-link control for each DLC station are largely independent of the physical communication network. This feature is an advantage that, when compared to other approaches, is potentially offset by loss of efficiency and duplication of functions.

The functions of the elements of the architecture shown in Fig. 10.14 are now briefly reviewed starting with the data-link control.

DATA-LINK CONTROL: The data-link control sequences the frames transmitted between two nodes and provides for error recovery. Distinct DLC software must appear at each end of a logical connection between DLC stations.

LINK MULTIPLEX: This component of the physical layer multiplexes traffic from the DLC stations onto the ring through the ring-station interface. It maintains the identification of the DLC stations, routes data from the ring to the appropriate DLC stations, and passes frame-error indications to the data-link control layer for error recovery. If only one DLC station is present at a ring station, no multiplex is required.

STATION MANAGER: The station manager provides such network management services as fault location, statistics gathering, and maintaining and updating DLC station addresses.

RING ACCESS: The ring access layer provides single-token ring access in the manner described in Chapter 8. The following services are included: address recognition, token generation, error logging, frame buffering, time-out control, and frame management. One ring station monitors the token to provide for recovery if normal token operation fails.

TRANSMISSION MEDIUM: The lowest level in the hierarchy is concerned with maintaining the electrical signals on the ring and generating timing information.

The frame structures for use with the architecture of Fig. 10.14 is shown in Fig. 10.15. (The observant reader will note that this structure is used in Fig. 8.4 as an example of a ring packet format.) Note in Fig. 10.15 that the frame is defined with starting and ending delimiters that correspond to the 8-bit flags used with HDLC frames. In the present case, the delimiters are waveforms in the general format of the differential Manchester encoding scheme, discussed in Chapter 2. These signals violate the required polarity transitions at the midpoint of the bit period, and are suitable delimiters because they cannot be confused with data bits. Recall that bit stuffing is required when the HDLC frame is used to avoid the possibility of having the flag duplicated by a run of data.

Several features of the frame structure of Fig. 10.15 are discussed in Chapter 8. An additional point of interest with respect to the network

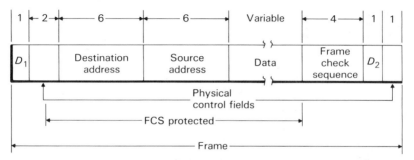

D_1 and D_2, starting and ending delimiters (code violations)

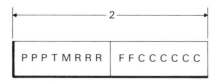

Starting physical control field

PPP = Priority mode
T = Token
M = Monitor count
RRR = Priority reservation
FF = Frame format
CCCCC = Control indicators

Figure 10.15   Frame Structure for a Ring Architecture, Showing Field Lengths in Bytes (From Andrews and Schultz [7])

architecture is that each DLC station has a unique address that is determined as follows. The source address in each frame is the address of the ring station that generates the frame; the destination address identifies the ring station that is to copy the frame. Each DLC station at a particular ring station is identified with a leading identifier in the data field of the frame.

The starting control field, which contains the token, is discussed in Chapter 8. Further examination of this field and other parts of the frame sheds little additional light on the network architecture.

10.5.3   Sytek Inc. LocalNet Architecture

The LocalNet provides an example of the architecture for a broadband local area network (see Ennis and Filice [9]). The network uses CSMA/CD at the media access level and, in that sense, is comparable to the Intel architecture discussed in Subsection 10.5.1. Because of its use of broadband channels, the LocalNet architecture differs from that of Intel in significant respects.

Moreover, provisions for coupling between a number of broadband channels and several different cable systems are well developed in the architecture. Although these provisions are not referred to as such, they illustrate an implementation of internetworking, a subject discussed in the next section.

A layout of typical LocalNet hardware is shown in Fig. 10.16. The principal hardware devices include the broadband cable, the packet communication units (PCUs), the bridges and the links.

The PCUs give users' devices access to the broadband cable through radio frequency (RF) modems that can be tuned to one of many channels frequency-division multiplexed on the cable. The PCUs on a single channel

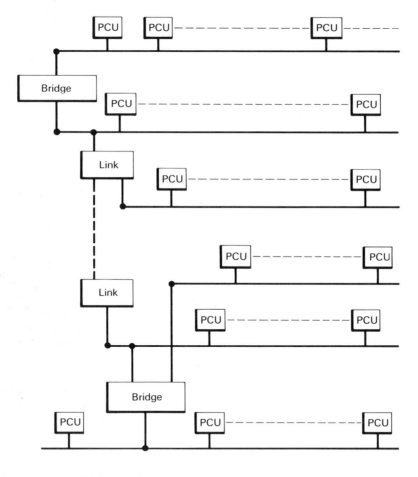

——————— Broadband channel
— — — —Point-to-point connection
PCU = Packet communication unit

Figure 10.16   A Typical LocalNet Installation (From Ennis and Filice [9])

share the channel, using a CSMA/CD access protocol. The bridge units serve as packet switches between different channels on a single cable, whereas the link units serve as packet switches between different cable systems.

The LocalNet architecture is designed to have a protocol structure that corresponds to most layers in the ISO structure. The specific protocols and the corresponding ISO layers are:

ISO Layer	*LocalNet Protocol*
Session	Session Management Protocol (SMP)
Transport	Reliable Stream Protocol (RSP)
Network	Packet Transfer Protocol (PTP)
Data Link	Link Access Protocol (LAP)

The LocalNet features, other than specific protocols, that correspond to the remaining ISO layers are: physical layer—broadband channels; presentation layer—services supported include asynchronous terminals and stream transfer services; and application—user-specific protocols.

LINK ACCESS PROTOCOLS: These protocols manage access to the cable for a particular channel, add framing to the data stream, and detect transmission errors. The access protocol is CSMA/CD. Framing and error detection are carried out with standard HDLC techniques. All parts of the HDLC protocol are not used, however, since error recovery is not a function of the link access level.

PACKET TRANSFER PROTOCOL: The PTP protocol is responsible for routing, which would be unnecessary if only one channel of one cable were used. This protocol represents one aspect of internetworking because it manages routing over bridges and links between different channels. The PTP provides an unacknowledged datagram service that delivers each packet independently and provides no guarantee of delivery or proper ordering.

RELIABLE STREAM PROTOCOL: The RSP at the transport level provides a virtual connection service between any pair of PCUs. This service provides error recovery, using acknowledgments and retransmissions on an end-to-end basis, properly sequenced packets, and sliding window flow control.

SESSION MANAGEMENT PROTOCOL: This protocol provides extended addressing, which permits the definition of ports located at the PCUs, and directed communication, termed a user session, between these ports. The SMP also provides a type of priority service.

Figure 10.17 shows the LocalNet packet structure as an encapsulation of the headers and other information generated by each protocol. Several comments on the fields in the packet are in order.

Each PCU is assigned a unit ID that uniquely identifies the node within the entire LocalNet installation. When the PCU is assigned to a particular

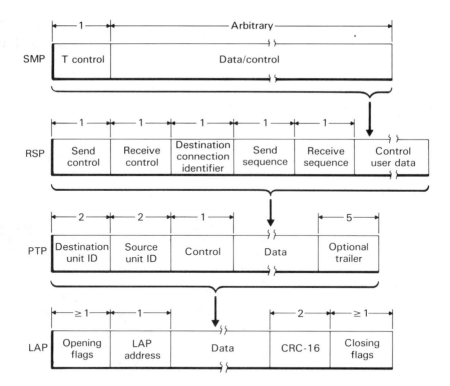

Figure 10.17   LocalNet Packet Structure (From Ennis and Filice [9]) (Field lengths in bytes)

channel, it is also assigned a LAP address that uniquely identifies it on the given channel. (LAP addresses can be duplicated, however, on different channels.) A final part of a complete address is a port ID assigned at the SMP level to identify specific user devices.

Note in the packet format of Fig. 10.17 that the LAP address field is part of the LAP header information, whereas the source and destination unit IDs are a part of the PTP header. The port ID for source and destination should appear in the data/control portion of the SMP part of the frame.

The RSP portion of the packet contains, among other things, a receive control field that communicates flow control information. It also contains send and receive sequence numbers. In addition to the unit ID numbers, the PTP part of the packet contains a control field that indicates to which higher-level protocol the packets' data field belongs.

As a final comment on LocalNet, the transfers across the bridges and links, unlike the transfers over channels, are carried out on a noncontention basis. The bridges and links are, in fact, packet switches that experience the routing and flow control problems normal for such devices. LocalNet has particular algorithms and protocols for carrying out these functions, but they are considered to be beyond the scope of this text.

10.6 Internetworking

A user on a local network is often required to be able to communicate with a user on another local network or perhaps on a long-haul network. This introduces the problem of internetworking, the interconnection of either similar or different types of networks. Typical internetworking configurations are shown in Fig. 10.18(a), a situation that involves the interconnection of local area networks within the same building complex or campus, and Fig. 10.18(b), the interconnection of two or more LANs located in different cities through a long-haul packet-switched network. (In fact, the LANs may be interconnected through any number of intermediate networks.)

As can be observed from the figure, networks are interconnected through gateways. The function of these gateway nodes is to convert packets from one protocol to another and to keep track of the addresses of users. The role of a gateway is somewhat analogous to the role of an interpreter, translating, for example, Swahili to Japanese. In some cases, it is possible to convert the protocol of one network (Net 1) to that of the other network (Net 2) directly. This one-to-one approach is only possible for networks that have essentially the same semantics.

In general, it is necessary to first convert the protocol of Net 1 to a standard internet protocol, and then to convert this internet protocol to that of Net 2. In the language analogy, it can be likened to translating Swahili first to a

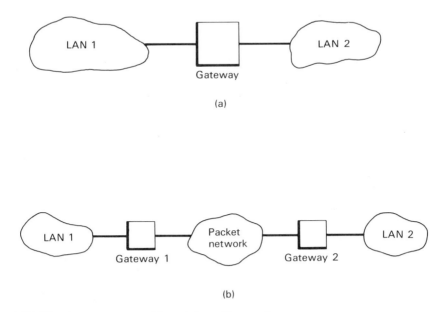

(a)

(b)

Figure 10.18   Interconnected Local Area Networks
(a) Directly connected
(b) Connected through a packet-switched network

standard international language such as English and then to Japanese. To carry out the protocol conversion, it is necessary to have an internet protocol. If the gateway is bilateral, in the sense that Net 1 has access to Net 2 and vice versa, then four protocol conversions are required in the gateway interface, two for traffic from Net 1 to Net 2, and two for traffic in the opposite direction.

Not all protocol levels are affected by internetworking. Gateways are usually not affected by the highest protocol layers or by the physical layers, which are unique to specific networks. In addition to protocol conversion, protocol issues that concern gateways are flow control, error control, addressing, and routing as well as the service offered to the transport layer—datagrams or virtual-circuit service. Gateways, of course, require sufficient buffer space to manage bit-rate mismatch and protocol conversion.

The issue of ownership of a gateway often arises when the networks involved have different owners. Two solutions are possible: the full gateway, as shown in Fig. 10.19, can be owned by both organizations, or each organization can own a half-gateway, with a communication link connecting the two halves.

The type of service offered to the transport layer by the network layer (i.e., datagram or virtual-circuit service) has a major effect not only on intranetwork design but also on internetwork design. Datagram service is simpler to

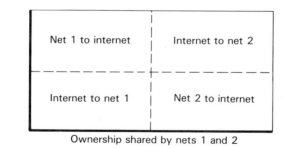

Ownership shared by nets 1 and 2

(a)

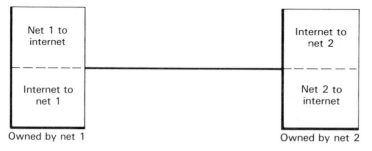

(b)

Figure 10.19   Two Ways to Implement Gateways

(a) A full gateway

(b) Two half gateways

provide, and many local networks are adequately served by such a service. For datagram-based LANs directly interconnected as in Fig. 10.18(a), datagram mappings by a gateway are very straightforward. On the other hand, when LANs are interconnected through a packet-switched network (often a public network such as Telenet), it is usually necessary to use virtual-circuit service for entering and exiting gateways. In these cases, the ISO recommendation X.75 for internetworking is used. Recommendation X.75 is based on the idea of building up an internetworking connection by concatenating a series of intranetwork virtual circuits.

When two networks with identical architectures are connected, there is clearly no need for protocol conversion. The term *bridge* is used for interconnection units of this type. Due to the restrictions generally placed on the bus length of CSMA/CD networks, for example, bridges are often required to interconnect two Ethernet-type local networks. Bridges in applications such as these are usually simple forms of packet switches.

This section is concluded with a mention of an internetwork architecture developed by Xerox (see Boggs et al. [10]), which is based on a standard internetwork datagram known as a Pup. This architecture, also known as Pup,

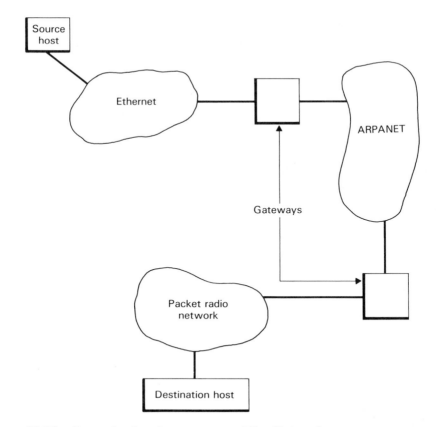

Figure 10.20   Example of an Interconnected Pup Network

can integrate a number of different types of networks into the architecture. Gateways, which interconnect the networks, process the Pups by:

1. Stripping off the overhead of the network that passes the Pup into the gateway;
2. Routing the Pup to the next network on its path to its ultimate destination; and
3. Encapsulating the Pup in the overhead of the next network to be traversed.

The architecture does not guarantee reliable delivery of datagrams, although, of course, the end processes are free to build higher-level protocols that provide whatever level of reliability is required.

An example of a Pup network, which interconnects ARPANET, a packet radio network, and an Ethernet, is shown in Fig. 10.20. In this network, the source host generates a basic Pup internet datagram and then encapsulates it in the protocol overhead of the Ethernet, which is the first network to be traversed. On exiting the Ethernet, overhead is stripped off in the gateway, and the datagram is routed toward the next network—the ARPANET. Encapsulation for ARPANET takes place before the gateway is left and the datagram is finally passed from the gateway into the ARPANET. The process continues until the Pup is transmitted through the packet radio network to the destination host.

10.7 Summary

The primary emphasis in the book prior to this chapter has been on local area network performance, with attention to those issues that pertain to transmitting packets across the network. This chapter introduces some of the broader issues in network design, with a concise discussion of protocols and network architecture.

Protocols for all the functions of a network are conveniently classified into layers. The International Standards Organization (ISO) has defined a reference model with seven layers for general networks; these are defined and discussed in the early part of the chapter.

The Institute of Electrical and Electronics Engineers (IEEE), through its IEEE 802 Committee, has introduced another standard layer structure specifically for local area networks. This structure, which is discussed in detail, has as its three lowest levels the physical layer, the medium access layer, and the logical link control layer.

It is pointed out that most of the network structure that affects performance, in the sense discussed in the majority of the book, is classified as being in the physical and media access layers. This material is complemented in the present chapter with a discussion of some aspects of logical link control protocols. This material, along with the information on physical and media access protocols in the major chapters of the book, covers all three network protocol layers classified by the IEEE 802 Committee.

This chapter also contains a section that summarizes several commercial local area network architectures. An introduction to some of the problems of connecting two or more local area networks is given in a final section on internetworking.

References

[1] A. S. Tanenbaum. *Computer Networks*. Englewood Cliffs: Prentice–Hall, 1981.

[2] W. Stallings. *Local Networks: An Introduction*. New York: Macmillan Publishing Co., 1984.

[3] D. E. Carlson. "Bit-Oriented Data Link Control Procedures." *IEEE Transactions on Communications* COM-28 (April 1980):455–467.

[4] ISO-3309. "HDLC, Frame Structure."
ISO-6256. "HDLC, Balanced Classes of Procedure."

[5] *IEEE Standard 802.2—Logical Link Control Specification,* Draft D. Silver Springs, Md: IEEE Computer Society, Dec 1982.

[6] R. Ryan, G. D. Marshall, R. Beach, and S. R. Kerman. "Intel Local Network Architecture." *IEEE Micro* (November 1981):26–41.

[7] D. W. Andrews and G. D. Schultz. "A Token-Ring Architecture for Local-Area Networks—An Update." *Proceedings of COMPCON* (Fall 1982):615–624.

[8] R. C. Dixon, N. C. Strole, and J. D. Markov. "A Token-Ring Network for Local Data." *IBM Systems Journal* 22, nos. 1/2 (1983):47–62.

[9] G. Ennis and P. Filice. "Overview of a Broad-Band Local Area Network Architecture." *IEEE Journal on Selected Areas in Communications* SAC-1 (November 1983):832–841.

[10] D. R. Boggs, J. F. Shoch, E. A. Taft, and R. M. Metcalfe. "Pup: An Internetwork Architecture." *IEEE Transactions on Communications* COM-28 (April 1980):612–623.

Problems and Exercises

1. A datagram service, as defined by the ISO standards, is available on a given network. Describe how this service can be used with additional functions to achieve a virtual-circuit-type service. Be specific about the additional required functions.

2. Consider a bus-type network with the structure shown in Fig. 9.2, using a CSMA/CD access protocol.
   (a) List the features required by the medium access and logical link control protocol layers as defined by the IEEE 802 Committee. Indicate which of these is implicitly provided by the CSMA/CD access protocol as defined in Chapter 9.
   (b) Indicate how each feature not provided by CSMA/CD would be provided.

3. In Subsection 10.4.2, the asynchronous balanced mode for the HDLC protocol standard is described and illustrated by an error-free dialog between two stations A

and *B*. For this example, sketch a timing diagram, such as in Fig. 9.25, to indicate the frame exchanges. Use similar diagrams to show how the protocol recovers from the error to message 4 (*A* to *B*) for the three error-recovery schemes discussed.

4. Develop a flow chart for a link-control protocol for two-way transmission over a channel that does not introduce errors, but can lose packets. Use positive acknowledgments sent in separate acknowledgment packets.

5. Refer to the token-ring architecture discussed in Subsection 10.5.2. A network that uses this architecture is constructed with two ring stations, each serving two DLC stations, for a total of four DLC stations.
   (a) Show the complete network in an expanded diagram of the type shown in Fig. 10.14.
   (b) Give a complete description of a data packet originating at DLC station number 1 and addressed to DLC station number 4.

IEEE 802 Bus Networks

11.1 Introduction

Two standards for the physical and medium access control layers of bus networks are specified by the IEEE 802 standards: Ethernet for CSMA/CD baseband buses, and token passing for single and multichannel buses. Neither of these access methods has been treated in its entirety in earlier chapters of the text. The CSMA/CD access method has been treated with a model that does not include the backoff algorithm, and token-passing buses have not been considered at all.

The objectives of this chapter are to give the IEEE 802 standards for bus networks and to determine approximate analytic expressions for their performance. In the case of Ethernet, the approach is to determine the range of accuracy of the CSMA/CD result of Chapter 9. In the case of the token bus, a result from hub polling is adapted to provide an adequate approximation. The performance of the two bus access methods as determined from the analytic expressions are compared in the final section of the chapter.

11.2 Ethernet

One of the first commercially available local area network products was *Ethernet*. This term, which has been used in a somewhat ambiguous fashion in the nontechnical literature, has a specific meaning in conjunction with the

Ethernet Specification produced by several manufacturing companies and endorsed by preliminary IEEE standards. Some background on Ethernet and its evaluation is presented by way of introduction to the standard.

The Ethernet Specification encompasses the data-link and physical layers of the ISO model, and the medium access and physical layers of the IEEE 802 model for random access networks. The original Ethernet was an experimental network developed by Xerox in the early seventies. The network, as described in [1], linked over 100 workstations on a 1 km coaxial cable bus with a bit rate of 2.94 Mbps. The Ethernet design has since been updated by Xerox, Intel, and Digital Equipment Corporation, and an *Ethernet Specification* has evolved. This specification is not only a multicompany standard, but is also the basis of the IEEE local area network standard for baseband buses that use CSMA/CD as the access method.

At this point it should be emphasized that there is no such thing as a commercial Ethernet. Instead, the Ethernet/IEEE Standard has been used to provide the data-link and physical layer specifications for a number of commercial networks, such as Net/One (an Ungermann-Bass product). Higher-level issues in the development of a network architecture, such as end-to-end error control and virtual-circuit/datagram service, still have to be resolved for each network that uses the Ethernet Specification.

11.2.1 The Ethernet Specification

The current Ethernet design, in brief, specifies a bus of maximum length 2.5 km, connected in segments of 500 meters with a data rate of 10 Mbps, and with up to 1024 connected stations. The CSMA/CD access procedure can, in theory, use any broadcast multiaccess channel, including radio, twisted-pair, coaxial cable, or fiber optic. However, Ethernet is designed specifically for baseband transmissions over coaxial cable. Figure 11.1 illustrates a typical Ethernet implementation. There are four major components to an Ethernet: the station, the controller, the transmission system, and the controller-to-system interface.

The station is typically a computer or a cluster of terminals. Individual terminals are not usually connected directly to an Ethernet.

The controller is the set of functions and algorithms needed to manage access to the network. These include encoding and decoding, serial-to-parallel conversion, address recognition, signaling conventions, packetization, CSMA/CD channel management, error detection, and buffering. The controller functions are usually implemented in a combination of hardware, software, and microcode, depending on the nature of the station. Many Ethernet controllers have been implemented on a single chip, using recent advances in VLSI.

The transmission system includes all components necessary for a communication path between the controllers. This includes the transmission medium itself, transceivers, and any repeaters necessary to extend the range of the medium. For coaxial cable, the medium includes the cable as well as all

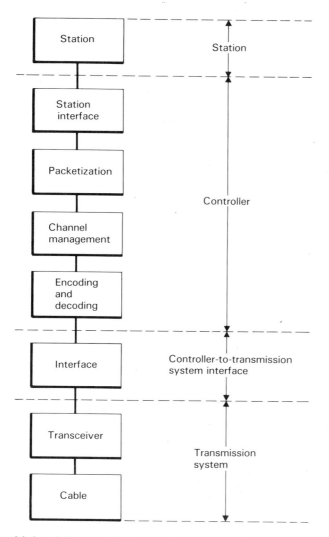

Figure 11.1   A General Ethernet Implementation for One Node

essential hardware: connectors, terminators, and taps. Terminators prevent signal reflections back along the bus by matching the characteristic impedance of the cable. Transceivers transmit and receive signals on the cable and also carry out the functions of carrier sensing and collision detection, which are respectively the detection of signals on the cable before beginning a transmission, and the detection, while transmitting, of multiple signals on the cable. Repeaters, which consist of two transceivers (one for each direction) are generally used to connect Ethernet segments. Such repeaters must be transparent to cable signals in order not to interfere with carrier sensing and collision detection.

Finally, the controller-to-transmission system interface is typically a short cable that connects the transceiver to the controller. This interface provides a path for signals going to and from the cable. These signals provide information on carrier sensing, collision detection, and so forth.

An explanation of how Ethernet evolved from the original prototype to the specification is given in Shoch et al. [2]. This paper also gives the rationale behind many of the parametric choices made in the system design. In addition, greater detail on the specification itself is provided.

The CSMA/CD access method as implemented in Ethernet has the following characteristics:

- The interpacket spacing (i.e., the minimum time between consecutive transmissions from a single station) is 9.6 μs;
- The backoff algorithm is the truncated binary exponential described in Section 9.5.1, with 51.2 μsec as the basic unit of backoff, or *slot time* in the Ethernet terminology;
- If the original attempt fails, the backoff time before the nth retransmission attempt is an integer number of slot times determined as follows: for values of n from 1 through 10, the backoff time is set at r slots, where r is chosen at random from the set $\{0, 1, 2, \ldots, 2^n - 1\}$. For the 11th through the 15th retransmission attempts, the upper limit of the set of values for r is fixed at $2^{10} - 1 = 1023$. After a total of 16 attempts, the Ethernet algorithm reports an error, and a higher-level protocol must then decide whether to discard the packet or to continue the attempt to access the network.
- When a collision is detected by a station, it aborts its transmission and sends a jam signal. The IEEE 802 recommendation for the jam length is 4 bytes of arbitrary data.

The frame format of an Ethernet packet is shown in Fig. 11.2. The first field is a 7-byte preamble followed by a start-frame delimiter. The preamble, which is long enough to ensure receiver synchronization, consists of alternating 1's and 0's; the delimiter is similar except that it ends with two consecutive 1's.

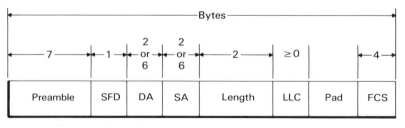

SFD = Starting frame delimiter
DA = Destination address
SA = Source address
LLC = Information field supplied by LLC layer
FCS = Frame check sequence

Figure 11.2   Frame Format for Ethernet/IEEE 802 Standard

Both the source and destination address fields may be either 2 or 6 bytes long. The length field that follows is 2 bytes long and indicates the number of information bytes supplied by the LLC layer for the data field. If the value is less than the minimum required for proper operation of the protocol, padding bits are appended to the end of the data field. The pad, if required, is also an integer number of bytes. The 802 standard recommends that the length of the data field be between 46 and 1500 bytes.

The last part of the frame is a 32-bit cyclic redundancy check sequence constructed with the standard polynomial of degree 32 discussed in Chapter 2: $X^{32} + X^{20} + X^{23} + X^{22} + X^{16} + X^{12} + X^{11} + X^{10} + X^8 + X^7 + X^5 + X^4 + X^2 + X + 1$. The frame-check sequence covers all the information in the frame except for the preamble and the starting field delimiter.

At the physical level, Ethernet uses Manchester encoding on the baseband coaxial cable. The transitions in the center of each bit period are used for carrier sensing. Collision detection can be implemented in a number of ways by, for example, monitoring the voltage level on the bus, which increases if transmissions overlap.

11.2.2 Performance Studies for Ethernet

Ethernet uses a CSMA/CD medium access protocol that is analyzed in Chapter 9. The analytic model, however, is of necessity restricted; for example, it assumes an infinite number of stations and does not account for a specific backoff strategy. It is difficult to extend this or any other analytic model to represent a practical CSMA/CD network completely. Thus the thrust of the performance study for Ethernet is to present measured and simulation results; the results of simulation studies give an accurate picture of Ethernet performance, and they can be used to determine the range of accuracy of the model for CSMA/CD developed in Chapter 9.

Results of Measurement and Simulation

Shoch and Hupp [3] have reported on measurements made with a prototype Ethernet that uses a channel bit rate of 2.94 Mbps and a span of 550 meters. This span gives an end-to-end propagation delay of 2.4 μsec. Traffic for loading the network was produced by generating packets at constant intervals from each station.

Figure 11.3 shows throughput versus load data obtained from 1 to 15 stations with parameters adjusted so that each station produced 10% of full load. (For example, in the figure, the point for 50% loading was obtained with five stations; that for 100% was obtained with 10 stations, etc.) The packet lengths were constant and set at 64, 128, and 512 bytes, under conditions that made no distinction between overhead and data. Note that the curves in Fig. 11.3 show very high channel utilization or throughput at high loads, a result consistent with the long packets that were used.

It is worth noting in passing that the arrival pattern for station traffic in the Shoch and Hupp study was artificial in that it is different from actual

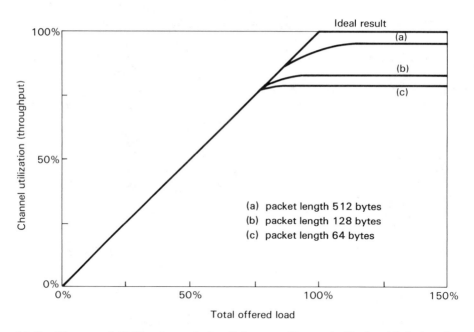

Figure 11.3   Measured Utilization of the Ethernet Network Under High Load (From Shoch and Hupp [3])

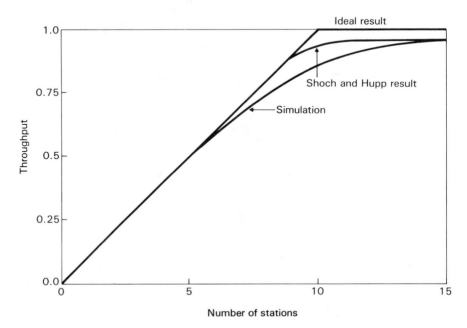

Figure 11.4   Throughput versus Number of Stations for the Ethernet Network with Packet Length of 512 Bytes

operational traffic and also different from the Poisson arrival statistics assumed throughout the text and in most analytic work.

A number of simulation studies of Ethernet have been made, including several with the parameter values used by Shoch and Hupp. Figure 11.4 shows the measured results of Shoch and Hupp in comparison to the results of one such simulation study (see O'Reilly [7]) that used a Poisson arrival pattern for input traffic and fixed length packets. The difference in throughput that can be observed under medium load conditions is largely accounted for by the difference in traffic arrival statistics. Hughes and Li [8] and Nutt and Bayer [9] report discrete-event simulation studies of Ethernet under conditions comparable to those of O'Reilly [7], and the results are consistent with the simulation curve in Fig. 11.4.

The simulation study of Ethernet protocols reported in O'Reilly [7] was extended to investigate several issues. One such issue involved the question of the effect on throughput of the number of stations that produce a particular value of load. For example, is there a significant difference in the throughput produced by, for example, 100 stations, each providing 1% load, and 10 stations, each providing 10% load? Results of the study show that there can be a significant difference for short packets, large loads, and a relatively small number of stations, typically less than 20. On the other hand, for long packets the differences are in general relatively minor.

Another issue investigated in O'Reilly [7] concerns the throughput of the Ethernet protocol over a wide range of loads. This issue is treated in the next section, along with the results of analytic studies.

Analytic Results

Having presented measured and simulated results for Ethernet, it is of interest to determine the utility of the analytic model of Chapter 9 for CSMA/CD-type access protocols. It has been pointed out throughout the text that the analytic models are developed with the most tractable assumptions possible. Thus close agreement between theoretical and measured or simulated behavior cannot be expected over the full range of parameter values. On the other hand, for the analytic work to have any utility at all, it must predict behavior over some range of parameter values with reasonable accuracy. An assessment of the accuracy of the mathematical models of Chapter 9 is possible using the measured and simulated results for Ethernet from the previous subsection. The analytic work, along with the comparison to data obtained through measurement and simulation, also sheds further light on Ethernet performance.

Performance results for CSMA/CD networks derived in Chapter 9 have two significant assumptions. First, the number of stations accessing the cable is assumed to be infinite. Second, no distinction is made between newly arrived and retransmitted packets, so specific backoff algorithms are not included in the analysis. The detailed analysis of the slotted ALOHA algorithm, in Subsection 9.3.2, shows by analogy that the approximate analysis used is, in some sense, equivalent to assuming that the backoff time for packets approaches infinity.

The analytic results produced on the basis of these assumptions must now be cast in a form suitable for comparison to the measured and simulated results for the physical network, which has a finite number of stations and uses a specific backoff algorithm that adapts to network congestion.

The analytic result for slotted 1-persistent CSMA/CD given in Eq. (9.82) is considered to be the best approximation to the throughput-offered load curves measured for the prototype Ethernet. Reference to the subsection in which the analytic result is discussed shows that offered load in (9.82) is expressed by the parameter g, which is the total offered channel traffic per slot, newly arrived plus retransmitted. A slot in this case has a length equal to the end-to-end propagation delay. This offered load parameter for the *infinite* population model must be related to offered traffic in the physical network. In the physical network, offered traffic consists of newly arrived packets to a *finite* number of stations.

The issue of the number of stations can be resolved first by recalling the simulation results cited in the last subsection. These results show that for relatively long packets, the number of stations is not critical, and hence comparing results of the analytic model, which assumes an infinite number of stations, to a physical network with a finite number of stations is reasonable for long packet lengths.

To put the experimental Ethernet curves and the S–g curves of Eq. (9.82) on the same graph, a correspondence between offered load, as given by g, and offered load for Ethernet can be made with the following reasoning. The traffic parameter $G = g/a$ is the average number of packets offered for transmission per packet transmission time. Full load occurs when there is one packet offered per packet transmission time on the average. Thus $G = 1$, or $g = a$, is taken as full load in the analytic result and, as should be the case, this loading accounts for both newly arrived and retransmitted packets.

The load as defined for the experimental Ethernet in contrast to that for the analytic model, measures only newly arrived packets; retransmitted packets are not included. If a small load is considered, however, retransmitted traffic is small and can be neglected. Thus the scales of the analytic and experimental Ethernet curves can be aligned so that the $G = 0.1$ point in the analytic model corresponds to a 10% load or one station for Ethernet. Other values for small load are made to correspond in a similar manner, and this fixes the relative positions of the two curves.

Aligning the Ethernet and analytic curves results in Fig. 11.5, for which other parameter values are:

Cable bit rate—2.94 Mbps;
Network span—550 meters;
End-to-end propagation delay—2.4 μsec;
Packet length—128 bytes;
Jam time—0; and
Load per station—10% (experimental network).

The parameter a can be determined to be 0.00689.

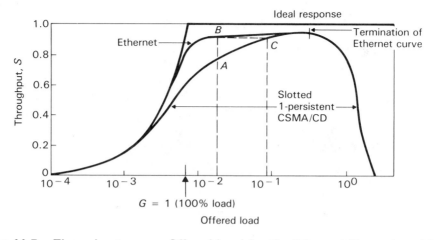

Figure 11.5 **Throughput versus Offered Load for the Ethernet Network and for the Analytic Model with $a = 0.00689$**

Before considering Fig. 11.5, note that the offered load axes of the two curves correspond with small error only for values of load for which retransmissions are a small part of total traffic. A precise upper limit to g for close correspondence is difficult to establish, but a reasonable range should extend to at least $g = a$ ($G = 1$). Furthermore, the simulated and measured Ethernet curves (shown in Fig. 11.4) fall close together in Fig. 11.5, which incidentally uses a log scale for offered traffic. Differences between these curves are much less than the difference observed between the analytic and Ethernet curves.

A study of the curves of Fig. 11.5 shows that for medium values of throughput, the throughput for Ethernet is always greater than that for the analytic result. At small values, however, the two curves coincide, and they also have the same maximum value.

The fact that the Ethernet throughput is larger than the analytic result over a range of loads is accounted for by the fact that the Ethernet adaptive backoff algorithm is more effective than that assumed for the analytic model and also by the fact that the analytic model does not accurately handle retransmissions.

The improvement in throughput due to the adaptive Ethernet retransmission strategy can be quantified to some extent. For example, consider throughput at the point $g = 2a = 0.014$, which corresponds to a 20-station load on Ethernet. At this load, Ethernet throughput is 0.91 (point B), whereas the analytic result is 0.76 (point A).

If the offered traffic in the solution to Eq. (9.82) must account for all the throughput at point B for Ethernet, then the analytic curve must be observed at point C, for which $g = 0.076$. This value of g is interpreted as the total traffic load (new plus retransmitted) necessary to give the throughput value observed for Ethernet. The actual load at point A for the analytic curve is only 0.014, as previously noted. Thus the added throughput made possible by the

Ethernet backoff algorithm can be estimated as the difference between 0.076 and 0.014 (i.e., 0.062 packets/slot).

Using the Ethernet simulation model, it was possible to separate the new and retransmitted traffic, and measure the retransmitted traffic that corresponds to a 20-station load. The result was extremely close to 0.062 packets/slot, giving some evidence that the throughput for the analytic result was essentially due to newly arrived packets, and that retransmitted packets had little effect at $g = 2a$.

It has been shown in O'Reilly [7], that when $\gamma = 1$ in Eq. (9.82) for slotted 1-persistent CSMA/CD, the maximum throughput (sometimes called the channel capacity) is given by $1/(1 + 7.34a)$ if a is less than approximately 0.03. With $a = 0.00689$, the maximum throughput is 0.952, very close to the maximum attained by the Ethernet simulation.

Concluding Comments on Performance of Ethernet

The preceding discussion brings out several points. First, it shows that the analytic model of Chapter 9 is sufficiently accurate at large values of load to give a good approximation for the maximum throughput or channel capacity of an Ethernet implementation. Furthermore, properly interpreted results seem to be good for small and large values of load, even in networks with a finite number of stations. For medium values of load, for example, one-half to twice full load, results from the analytic model are low because they do not accurately account for retransmissions or the differences between backoff algorithms.

It can be concluded from the overall study of the Ethernet protocol that it is almost optimum for a 1-persistent CSMA/CD network for the following reasons:

1. The maximum throughput is obtained;
2. This throughput is maintained over a wide range of load; and
3. The ideal response curve is tracked closely for small loads.

When distinction is made between overhead and actual user data in the content of a message, the actual channel utilization or throughput can be found by multiplying S by $L_d/(L_0 + L_d)$, where L_d and L_0 represent the amount of data and overhead (in bits) respectively. For an Ethernet packet, the total overhead, as observed in the previous discussion, is 18 or 26 bytes. For an accurate comparison of the performance of Ethernet to local networks with other access methods, this overhead factor should be taken into account.

11.3 Token Bus

In this section, the IEEE 802 token bus standard is given, and a result from hub polling in Chapter 7 is used to obtain an approximate analytic model for its performance. The 802 standard was written to include both single-channel and broadband implementations. The single standard covers both implementations, so that relatively little change is required in the medium or the interfacing units for the two types.

The basic principles of operation for the token bus are largely the same as for the token ring. Although the token bus, as its name implies, has a bus rather than a ring topology, the stations are logically organized into a ring. For example, in the token bus shown in Fig. 11.6, the stations can be organized so that the token is passed in the sequence: station *A* to *B* to *C* to *D* to *E* and back to *A*, as shown in the figure.

There are several ways in which token buses differ from token rings. Stations on a token bus are passive rather than active, and thus there is no station latency or delay. The fact that stations are passive has a positive implication for reliability and a negative implication with respect to regeneration of signals. Since token passing is essentially a broadcast protocol, it is possible for stations on a logical token ring to receive messages while they are not cleared to transmit, i.e., not members of the logical ring. Further differences, with implications for performance modeling, are pointed out in Subsection 11.3.2.

11.3.1 IEEE 802 Draft Standards for Token Buses

Under steady-state conditions, operation of a token bus consists of alternating data transfer and token transfer phases. When a station finishes transmitting its data, or when its access time limit is reached (whichever happens first), it sends a control token frame to the next station in the logical ring. During its access time, the token holder may transmit one or more frames and may poll other stations and receive responses. Control in a token bus is, however, completely distributed, and when a station has used its allocated access time, it must relinquish control of the token.

Whereas operation of a token bus generally consists of the transmission of data frames and token frames, at periodic intervals the bus goes through a

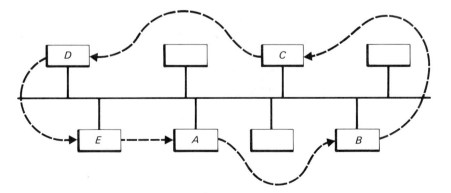

Figure 11.6   A Logical Ring Operating on a Physical Bus

contention process in which stations that up to that time were not participating in the logical ring have the opportunity to join the ring. This contention process is controlled with *response windows*. In general, the greater the number of stations trying to join the ring, the wider the window. However, the response resolution algorithm has a finite length, and thus a deterministic upper bound exists on delays caused by the contention process. Although the arbitration process is rather complicated, all stations that want to enter the logical ring are given a position in the logical sequence. Details of the arbitration process are discussed in the Draft IEEE Standard [10].

In addition to the ability to join the ring, any station can also remove itself from the ring by splicing together the access times of its predecessor and successor stations. This is done at the time the token is received: the predecessor station is informed of the successor station's address and it is asked that this address be its revised next-station address.

Each station is assigned a maximum token holding time, which ensures that no station hogs the ring and that the access time is always finite. Access to the bus can also be prioritized by providing up to four different classes of service. This is accomplished by placing token rotation timers at each station for each class of service with priority less than the highest priority. The objective of the priority system is to allocate network resources to the higher priority frames first, and to send lower priority frames when these resources are free. The preset token rotation timers allocate network resources by assigning amounts of network time to each class of service. The highest priority class of data is transmitted first and, after its time is up, lower priority classes are served in a systematic manner provided time is available. Details of the allocation method are given in the Draft Standard [10].

The basic frame format as specified at the MAC (Medium Access Control) level is shown in Fig. 11.7. The first pattern to be transmitted in each frame is

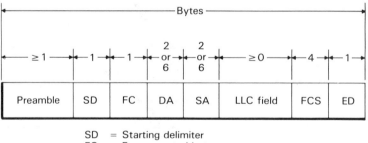

SD = Starting delimiter
FC = Frame control byte
DA = Destination address
SA = Source address
LCC = Information field supplied by LCC layer
FCS = Frame check sequence
ED = Ending delimiter

Figure 11.7   Frame Format for the IEEE 802 Token Bus

a preamble at least 1 byte long. The preamble transmission time, which must be at least 2 μs, is followed by a 1-byte start delimiter and a frame control byte that specifies the type of frame being transmitted. Two important types of frames are the data message frame, for which the control byte reads 01PPP000 (the P's give the priority of the frames), and the control token frame, for which the control byte reads 00001000. Other frame control bytes are possible—all of these are used for network control and are not passed to higher layers. These frame control bytes take care of procedures such as contention between stations that want to enter the ring, and logical ring initialization procedures for sorting out positions in the logical sequence after loss of a token.

Note that each frame contains both a source and a destination address. The destination address can be 2 or 6 bytes; the same is true for the source address. When the frame is a control token frame, the destination address is the address of the next station to receive the token. Following the addresses is the data message supplied by the LLC layer; this space is empty for a control token frame. A frame check sequence (FCS), which uses the same standard generator polynomial of degree 32 as is used in Ethernet, occupies the 4 bytes next to the last position in the frame. The frame is concluded with a delimiter.

The complete formats for a control token frame and a data frame are shown in Fig. 11.8. Note that 12 bytes is both the minimum length for a token frame and the least amount of overhead in a data frame.

The IEEE 802.4 Standard for token bus local area networks gives essentially three choices at the physical level. All are transparent to the MAC layer. The options are the following.

1. *Single-channel phase-continuous FSK (frequency shift keying).* This method has a data rate of 1 Mbps in a baseband channel using modulation frequencies of 6.25 and 3.75 MHz. The bit stream is precoded with differential Manchester encoding.
2. *Single-channel phase-coherent FSK.* The data rate for this choice can be 5 or 10 Mbps, again in a baseband channel. The baseband bit stream is directly encoded—with a 5 Mbps data rate, the FSK modulation frequencies are 5 and 10 MHz, whereas for a data rate of 10 Mbps, the corresponding frequencies are 10 and 20 MHz.
3. *A broadband directional bus with an active headend repeater.* The bus may be single cable or dual cable. The data rates possible are 1 Mbps, 5 Mbps, and 10 Mbps. The modulation scheme is multilevel duobinary AM/PSK. Three amplitude levels are possible; the third level is reserved for nondata symbols such as appear in delimiters. The channel bandwidths for the 1, 5, and 10 Mbps data rates are respectively 1.2, 6, and 12 MHz. The standard also recommends channel assignments for the different data rates—two in each case, one for the upstream channel and one for the downstream channel.

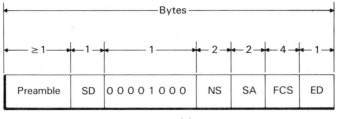

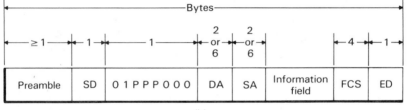

SD = Starting delimiter
NS = Next station address
SA = Source address
DA = Destination address
FCS = Frame check sequence
ED = Ending delimiter

Figure 11.8   Frame Formats for the IEEE 802 Token Bus:
   (a) Control token frame
   (b) Data frame

11.3.2   Performance Studies for the Token Bus

Before the performance analysis is considered, note several significant operational differences between token rings and token buses:

1. For ring networks, an interface delay exists and the signal is regenerated at each station. As previously noted, this delay does not exist on a bus because the signal is transmitted from end to end on the cable without interruption or regeneration in the same manner as for a random access bus.

2. Propagation delays are usually short on a physically connected ring because the token is typically passed from a station to its nearest neighbor. On the other hand, for a token bus the token can be passed over longer distances (e.g., from one end of the bus to another) to satisfy the logical

sequence of stations specified. As a consequence, propagation delays are generally longer for the token bus than for the token ring.

3. The time to transfer between stations, or walk time, for a token ring is given by Eq. (8.6) as the sum of a station latency and a propagation delay. For the token bus, the access method is essentially hub polling, so walk time is the time to transfer the token, plus the propagation delay, between successive stations in the logical ring.

An expression for the average transfer delay of a token ring can be derived as a special case of hub polling. The following parameters are specified:

- X_t—The control token frame length in bits;
- $\overline{X}$—The average length of a data frame, including overhead (with second moment $\overline{X^2}$);
- R—The channel bit rate in bits/second;
- M—The number of active stations on the bus; and
- τ—The end-to-end propagation delay in seconds.

Assuming Poisson arrivals to each station with average arrival rate λ, and assuming exhaustive service at each station (and thus no upper bound on a station's wait for the token), Eq. (7.13) can be used to give the average waiting time for packets at a station, or average access time, as

$$W = \frac{Mw(1 - S/M)}{2(1 - S)} + \frac{S\,\overline{X^2}}{2\overline{X}R\,(1 - S)} \tag{11.1}$$

where the throughput S is given by

$$S = M\lambda\overline{X}/R \tag{11.2}$$

The walk time, w, depends on the average propagation delay between stations. This delay is determined with the assumption that transfer between any two stations on the bus is equally likely. The solution to this problem in probability is well known, assuming that the number of stations is relatively large, and gives approximately one-third the length of the bus as the average spacing between randomly chosen stations, or an average time delay of $\tau/3$ seconds.

Using this average delay of $\tau/3$ seconds, the walk time can be expressed as

$$w = X_t/R + \tau/3 \tag{11.3}$$

The average transfer delay, T, can be obtained with (11.1) by adding average propagation and packet transfer times to yield

$$T = \frac{\overline{X}}{R} + \frac{\tau}{3} + \frac{Mw(1 - S/M)}{2(1 - S)} + \frac{S\,\overline{X^2}}{2\overline{X}R(1 - S)} \tag{11.4}$$

For fixed length packets, $\overline{X^2} = (\overline{X})^2$ and thus (11.4), after substitution of (11.3), becomes

$$T = \frac{\overline{X}}{R} + \frac{\tau}{3} + \frac{M\,X_t(1 - S/M)}{2R(1 - S)} + \frac{\tau(M - S)}{6(1 - S)} + \frac{S\,\overline{X}}{2R(1 - S)} \tag{11.5}$$

or, after simplification,

$$T = \frac{\overline{X}}{R} \frac{2 - S}{2(1 - S)} + \frac{M\,X_t(1 - S/M)}{2R(1 - S)} + \frac{(M + 2 - 3S)\tau}{6(1 - S)} \qquad (11.6)$$

For exponentially distributed packet lengths, $\overline{X^2} = 2(\overline{X})^2$, and the corresponding average transfer delay is given by

$$T = \frac{\overline{X}}{R(1 - S)} + \frac{M\,X_t(1 - S/M)}{2R(1 - S)} + \frac{(M + 2 - 3S)\tau}{6(1 - S)} \qquad (11.7)$$

Curves that show T versus S can be plotted from either (11.6) or (11.7). Specific results, however, depend on the choice of the parameters $M, X_t, \tau, \overline{X}$, and R. Some general plots for similar equations are given in Chapter 7, whereas a curve based on (11.6), determined for a specific choice of parameter values, is given in the next subsection.

The model developed for the token bus assumes that the number of active stations (i.e., stations on the logical ring) is constant and that no stations are either added to or deleted from the ring. A model that would account for stations being added or deleted is beyond the scope of the analytic tools developed in this text.

For an arbitrary distribution of packet lengths, (11.3) and (11.4), with S set to 0, give the average minimum delay as

$$T = \frac{\overline{X}}{R} + \frac{M\,X_t}{2R} + \frac{\tau(2 + M)}{6} \qquad (11.8)$$

As mentioned previously, the model assumes that service at each station is exhaustive (i.e., when a station obtains the token, it does not release it until all messages queued in its buffer have been transmitted). The IEEE 802 standard, however, allows the network manager to impose a maximum token holding time for each station. Assuming that each station has the same holding time, T_h, the maximum throughput becomes

$$S_{\max} = \frac{T_h}{T_h + T_t + \tau/3} \qquad (11.9)$$

where T_t is the average time to transfer the token (i.e., X_t/R), and $\tau/3$ is the average propagation delay between adjacent stations on the logical ring. For example, with $\tau = 5\,\mu\text{sec}$ (a 1 km bus), a token frame of length 12 bytes, and a bit rate of 10 Mbps, the maximum throughput is

$$S_{\max} = \frac{T_h}{T_h + 9.6\,\mu\text{sec} + 1.7\,\mu\text{sec}} = \frac{T_h}{T_h + 11.3\,\mu\text{sec}} \qquad (11.10)$$

For token holding times of 100 μsec, 1 ms, and 10 ms, the maximum throughput is respectively 0.898, 0.989, and 0.999. With exhaustive service, $S_{\max}$ is obviously 1. Clearly the maximum bus utilization is independent of data frame length and is marginally dependent on bus length.

Although no attempt was made to develop a detailed model that includes a contention phase for stations to access the logical ring, it can be stated that the minimum possible average delay would be greater if this phase of operation were included in the model. Furthermore, inclusion of the contention phase would be another factor to cause the maximum throughput to be less than 1.

11.4 Comparison of Bus Access Methods

This section compares the two bus access methods—those used for Ethernet and for the token bus. A general comparison based on S_{max} is made first, followed by a choice of more specific parameters that make possible more detailed comparisons. Since it is essentially the access methods that are being compared, they are simply referred to as CSMA/CD and token passing.

Channel utilization is a primary factor in comparisons of any two access methods, and maximum channel utilization is an important special case of this parameter. Maximum channel utilization is measured most directly in terms of maximum throughput, which is the maximum average steady-state data rate for a network divided by the bit rate of the channel.

For token buses, channel utilizations close to 1 can be obtained in practice if exhaustive service at each station is used and if no stations are allowed to enter or leave the logical ring. With CSMA/CD, the maximum utilization depends critically on the relationship between packet length, the data rate, and the length of the bus. As previously mentioned, the maximum utilization, S_{max}, for a slotted 1-persistent CSMA/CD access protocol is given by

$$S_{max} = 1/(1 + 7.34a) \tag{11.11}$$

where a (less than 0.03) is given by

$$a = \tau R / \overline{X} \tag{11.12}$$

Thus, as either the channel bit rate R or the end-to-end propagation delay τ increases, a increases, and as a consequence, S_{max} decreases. On the other hand, as packets become longer, a decreases and S_{max} increases towards 1. Figure 11.9 shows the relationship between S_{max} and a for both CSMA/CD and token passing. This figure shows maximum throughput for token passing with exhaustive service and with maximum holding times of 200 μsec and 1 ms. For the latter two cases, it is necessary to specify other network parameters, and these are: channel bit rate—10 Mbps; end-to-end propagation delay—15 μsec (3 km); and data message frame length—50 bytes. The token frame length is 12 bytes. The curves, plotted with the use of (11.9) and (11.11), show the minimal effect of propagation delay on throughput.

The maximum effective channel data rate, R^*, is given by

$$R^* = R \cdot S_{max} \tag{11.13}$$

Hence, R^* increases linearly with R for the token bus (with exhaustive service), whereas for CSMA/CD, R^* increases monotonically with R, as

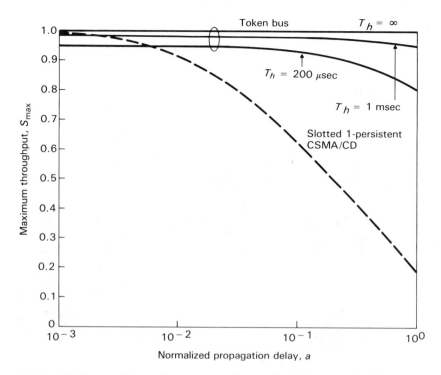

Figure 11.9 Maximum Throughput versus Normalized Propagation Delay

shown in Fig. 11.10 for different values of $\overline{X}/\tau$. The curves of Figs. 11.9 and 11.10 do not account for the overhead per packet. To account for this overhead, it is necessary to multiply $S_{\max}$ (or R^*) by the ratio of the information, or LLC, field length to the total packet length for each value of a (or R).

An obvious conclusion of this preceding study is that token passing in general makes much more efficient use of the channel bandwidth than does CSMA/CD. Under most operating conditions, the IEEE 802 token bus can provide a maximum utilization close to 1. With a data rate of 10 Mbps and maximum bus length of 2.5 km, the maximum utilization for the IEEE 802 CSMA/CD protocol is a function of the packet length; for minimum length packets (64 bytes long), a is 0.234, giving a maximum utilization of only 0.46. For maximum length packets (1518 bytes long), a is 0.010, giving a maximum utilization of 0.93. The reference by Stuck [6] can be consulted for a somewhat similar throughput study done for the IEEE 802 Committee.

Delay–throughput comparisons between any two access methods are very sensitive to network parameters. Even in comparing two bus schemes that have the same bus length, the same data rate, and the same information field length, other parameters can have a significant effect. The following example is illustrative of such a comparison.

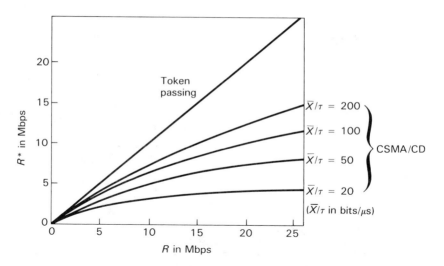

Figure 11.10 Maximum Achievable Channel Bit Rate, R^*, versus Nominal Channel Bit Rate, R, for Token Passing and CSMA/CD on Bus Networks

Example

Token passing and CSMA/CD are to be compared for use with a bus of length 1 km (and thus a propagation delay of approximately 5 μs). Let the data rate for both schemes be 1 Mbps and the LLC field length be 107 bytes, with 40 active stations on each bus. The IEEE 802 standard gives a token frame length of 12 bytes and an overhead per data frame of 12 bytes. For CSMA/CD, the overhead per data frame is 18 bytes.

TOKEN BUS: Equation (11.6) can be used to give an approximate expression for the average delay in terms of the channel utilization or throughput, S. With $\overline{X} = (12 + 107)$ bytes $= 952$ bits, $X_t = 96$ bits, $R = 1$ Mbps, $M = 40$ and $\tau = 5$ μsec, (11.5) gives the average delay in μseconds as

$$T = 952 + \frac{5}{3} + \frac{1920(1 - S/40)}{1 - S} + \frac{5(40 - S)}{6(1 - S)} + \frac{476\,S}{2(1 - S)}$$

which simplifies to

$$T = 2907 \left[\frac{1 - 0.181\,S}{1 - S} \right] \mu sec$$

The relationship between T and S is plotted in Fig. 11.11.

This result shows that the average minimum transfer delay is 2.907 ms, and, from the first two numbers in the first expression for T, that the average packet transmission time plus average propagation delay is 0.954 ms. The access delay is obtained as $2.907 - 0.954 = 1.953$ ms.

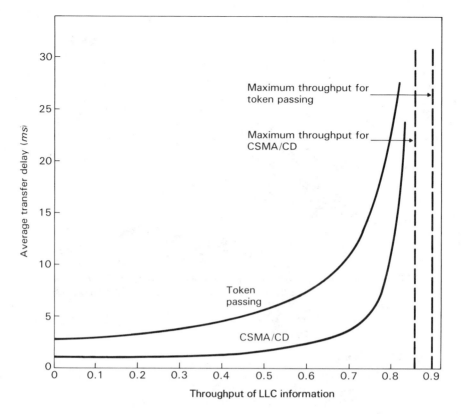

Figure 11.11 **Delay–Throughput Comparison for Two Bus Access Schemes Used in Illustrative Example in Text**

For a channel utilization of S, the throughput of LLC data, S^*, is given by

$$S^* = \frac{107}{(107 + 12)} S = 0.90 S$$

Thus the maximum normalized data throughput is 0.9.

CSMA/CD: Simulation results taken from O'Reilly [7] are used in this case. The minimum average delay is simply

$$T_{min} = \overline{X}/R + \tau/3 = 1002 \ \mu s$$

The theoretical maximum throughput is given by

$$S_{max} = 1/(1 + 7.34a)$$

since the normalized propagation delay, $a = 5/1000 = 0.005$. Thus S_{max} is 0.965.

As in the case of token passing, the overhead must be accounted for by using the ratio of data bits to total bits in a packet as a factor to multiply S. Thus

$$S^* = \frac{107}{125} S = 0.86\,S$$

and the theoretical maximum information throughput is 0.83. The simulation model includes only the lowest two layers of the Ethernet protocol, so packets that experience 16 failed transmission attempts are discarded completely. Thus the evaluation of average delays at high loads does not include these discarded packets that might be retransmitted with higher-level protocols.

Figure 11.11 shows that for this particular network and these parameter values, the Ethernet gives for most loads a much better delay–throughput characteristic than does token passing. General features to note are that CSMA/CD gives smaller delays at low loads, whereas token passing provides greater maximum throughput of information. The point at which the two curves intersect depends greatly on parameter values.

11.5 Summary

This chapter discusses two bus networks that are defined as standards by the IEEE 802 Committee.

The Ethernet standard uses CSMA/CD, which is covered in Chapter 9, as an access protocol. The material in the present chapter gives the IEEE 802 standard specifications and uses measured and simulated data for a network constructed to meet many of the standard specifications to determine the range of accuracy of the analytic model of Chapter 9. Results show that the model gives good results for small and large values of network load.

Standards are also given for a token bus, a type of network not discussed earlier in the text. An approximate model for the performance of the token bus network is developed with polling equations from Chapter 7.

This chapter concludes with an example in which the performance of the random access and token passing schemes are compared.

References

[1] Digital Equipment Corp., Intel, Xerox. "The Ethernet: A Local Area Network: Data Link Layer and Physical Layer Specifications." Version 1.0. September 1980.

[2] J. F. Shoch, Y. K. Dalal, D. D. Redall, and R. C. Crane. "Evolution of the Ethernet Local Computer Network." *Computer* 15, no. 8 (August 1982):10–27.

[3] J. F. Shoch and J. A. Hupp. "Measured Performance of an Ethernet Local Network." *Communications of the ACM* 23, no. 12 (December 1980):711–721.

[4] R. M. Metcalfe and D. R. Boggs. "Ethernet: Distributed Packet Switching for

Local Computer Networks." *Communications of the ACM* 19, no. 7 (July 1976):395–404.

[5] *IEEE Standard 802.3—CSMA/CD Access Method and Physical Layer Specifications,* Draft D. Silver Springs, MD: IEEE Computer Society, December 1982.

[6] B. W. Stuck. "Calculating the Maximum Mean Data Rate in Local Area Networks." *Computer* 16, no. 5 (May 1983):72–76.

[7] P. J. P. O'Reilly. "A New Technique for Performance Studies of CSMA/CD Local Networks." Ph.D. diss., Georgia Institute of Technology, May 1983.

[8] H. D. Hughes and L. Li. "A Simulation Model of Ethernet." Technical Report TR 82-008. Dept. of Computer Science, Michigan State University, 1982.

[9] G. J. Nutt and D. L. Bayer. "Performance of CSMA/CD Networks under Combined Voice and Data Loads." *IEEE Transactions on Communications* COM-30, no. 1 (January 1982):6–11.

[10] *IEEE Standard 802.4—Token Passing Bus Access Method and Physical Layer Specifications,* Draft D. Silver Springs, MD: IEEE Computer Society, December 1982.

*I*ndex

ADDISON-WESLEY ♠ THE SIGN
AND CO   EERING
OF EXCE   ECTRIC
ADDISON   SIGN
AND COMPUTER ENGINEERING
OF EXCELLENCE IN ELECTRIC
ADDISON-WESLEY ♠ THE SIGN
AND COMPUTER ENGINEERING
OF EXCELLENCE IN ELECTRIC
ADDISON-WESLEY ♠ THE SIGN
AND COMPUTER ENGINEERING
OF EXCELLENCE IN ELECTRIC
ADDISON-WESLEY ♠ THE SIGN
AND COMPUTER ENGINEERING
OF EXCELLENCE IN ELECTRIC
ADDISON-WESLEY ♠ THE SIGN
AND COMPUTER ENGINEERING
OF EXCELLENCE IN ELECTRIC
ADDISON-WESLEY ♠ THE SIGN
AND COMPUTER ENGINEERING
OF EXCELLENCE IN ELECTRIC
ADDISON-WESLEY ♠ THE SIGN
AND COMPUTER ENGINEERING
OF EXCELLENCE IN ELECTRIC